The Rise and Fall of the
German Air Force
1933-1945

the national archives

First edition published in 2001
Paperback edition published in 2008 by
The National Archives
Kew, Richmond
Surrey, TW9 4DU
United Kingdom

www.nationalarchives.gov.uk

The National Archives brings together the Public Record Office, Historical Manuscripts
Commission, Office of Public Sector Information and Her Majesty's Stationery Office.

A catalogue card for this book is available from the British Library.

ISBN 978 1 905615 30 8

Front cover: *above* German Heinkel He IIIs in action. Brought into service in 1937, around 6,000
were built, but they did not compete well with Hurricanes and Spitfires in the Battle of Britain.
Photograph courtesy of the Imperial War Museum, London (MH6547); *below* Hermann Goering,
Commander-in-Chief of the Luftwaffe. Photograph courtesy of the Imperial War Museum,
London (MH6041).

Cover design by Ken Wilson | point 918
Printed in Singapore by KHL Printing Co

PUBLISHER'S NOTE

This publication reproduces *The Rise and Fall of the German Air Force 1933–1945*, first issued in
1948 by the Air Ministry. The original document is preserved in the file AIR 41/10 which can be
consulted at the National Archives, Kew. A new index has been compiled for this edition.

RESTRICTED

AIR MINISTRY PAMPHLET No. 248

THE RISE AND FALL

OF THE

German Air Force

(1933 to 1945)

ISSUED BY THE AIR MINISTRY (A.C.A.S.[I])

1948

Foreword

by the Assistant Chief of Air Staff (Intelligence)
Air Vice-Marshal Sir T. W. ELMHIRST, K.B.E., C.B., A.F.C.

THIS VOLUME is our first attempt to relate the operational history of the German Air Force during the war of 1939 to 1945. It recounts in some detail the progress of the principal campaigns, and traces the problems encountered, both in the field and in the direction of the air war at the higher staff levels. It must be left to the historians to make an extensive study, but this book, written at the command of the Air Council, is designed to provide in the interim for the needs of Staff Colleges and for the information of all concerned. The short time which has elapsed since the events described took place makes it impossible for the account to be anything but imperfect, but it has been written by men and women who themselves conducted the intelligence attack against the German Air Force during the war years, and, insofar as rapid demobilisation has permitted, it constitutes the best contribution Air Intelligence can make to cover the period until authoritative and comprehensive histories are available.

So far as it goes, therefore, the present work may be regarded as a reasonably accurate historical record, presented in a form which, by avoiding technicalities as far as possible, should be acceptable to most readers. It is, throughout, based on reliable German documents and statistics, either captured during the war or subsequently recovered from the scattered archives of the Luftwaffe. While the course of the first eighteen months of German air operations may be generally known, the launching of the Norwegian and French campaigns and the Battle of Britain as seen from the German side will make fresh reading. The account of the part played by the German Air Force in events on the Russian front, and the details of its operations in the Mediterranean, are also largely new, and the story of the struggle against Allied day and night bombing offensives in 1943 and 1944 is likely to be of considerable interest. The final vicissitudes of the Luftwaffe, the losing battle of the German Air Staff against the obstinacy of Hitler and the incompetence of Goering, and the failure of the German Supreme Command to appreciate the consequences of their declining air supremacy, reveal only too clearly the errors and lack of foresight of those directing the Nazi war to enslave Europe, defeat Britain and dominate the World.

Nevertheless, every effort has been made to approach the subject from an objective and unbiased viewpoint, and full credit has been given to the undeniable successes of the German Air Force. Many German shortcomings are revealed, the principal probably being the lack of an objective policy directed by experts in air warfare, able to express their views and translate them into action untrammelled by the dictates of political intrigue and unhampered by the whims of incompetent and vacillating superiors. It must be remembered, however, that, in spite of these weaknesses, those directing the German Air Force were faced throughout the war with an undeniable restriction of resources of every kind. In short, Hitler bit off more than he could chew, and the Germans had insufficient resources to provide an adequate air arm to support the operations to which they consequently became committed;

iii

the importance of this miscalculation is eloquently described in General Koller's epilogue to this book. Nevertheless, although hopelessly outnumbered and fighting a losing battle from 1943 onwards, the Luftwaffe remained a substantial force to be reckoned with in all military calculations up to the closing stages of the war. It is doubtful if a greater realisation of the importance of air power, as we came to understand it, would have done more than prolong the war, but the German Air Force would certainly have given a still better account of itself if those controlling its destiny had not underestimated the threat of Allied air power. If they had realised the vital necessity for air supremacy, if they had not been so complacent after the first flush of their successes, and had not made their final effort in the technical field too late, the story might have been different.

Every aspect of the work and organisation of the German Air Force during this time is already covered in existing reports and captured documents. Certain of them may be written up and issued in a form which can be read in conjunction with this book.

In studying this history, the reader will find many situations where decisions were taken at a high level of command and which can only be puzzling if the background of those decisions is not fully appreciated. The character of Hitler and Goering and the cumbersome machinery of the Supreme Command were ever-present factors in Air Force policy and action. A short study of the workings of the Supreme Command has been prepared, and appears in the Appendix to this book.

1947

Air Vice-Marshal.

iv

Contents

Chapter 4. The First Failure of German Air Power : the Battle of Britain and the Battle of the Atlantic

Chapter 5. Hitler's " Continental Policy " : the Invasion of the Balkans and the Capture of Crete, accompanied by the Establishment of the German Air Force in Italy

Chapter 6. The German Air Force in the Mediterranean Campaigns of 1941 and 1942

PART IV—DECLINE AND FALL OF THE GERMAN AIR FORCE (1944–1945)

PART V—CONCLUSIONS

List of Plates

List of Plates—*continued.*

List of Plates—*continued.*

xiii

List of Maps and Diagrams

Goering and Hitler

Prologue

" *I have done my best, in the past few years, to make our Luftwaffe the largest and most powerful in the world. The creation of the Greater German Reich has been made possible largely by the strength and constant readiness of the Air Force. Born of the spirit of the German airmen in the first World War, inspired by faith in our Fuehrer and Commander-in-Chief— thus stands the German Air Force today, ready to carry out every command of the Fuehrer with lightning speed and undreamed-of might.* "

Reichsmarschall

(August 1939)

PART ONE
Pre-War Policy and Preparations (1919–1939)

CHAPTER 1

THE RECONSTITUTION OF THE GERMAN AIR FORCE

CHAPTER 2

THE GERMAN AIR FORCE ON THE EVE OF THE EUROPEAN WAR

THE RECONSTITUTION OF THE GERMAN AIR FORCE

From the Armistice to the End of the German Republic (1919-33)

The Versailles Treaty

1. The Treaty of Versailles, signed in June 1919, contained Air Clauses which were intended to end military aviation in Germany and to preclude a resurrection of the German Flying Corps of the war of 1914-18. Under the supervision of an Allied Control Commission, Germany was obliged, in 1920, to demobilise the whole of her Flying Corps and to surrender all aeronautical material to the governments of the Allied and associated powers. She was further forbidden to manufacture or import aircraft, aero engines or their component parts—but only for a period of six months. At the end of the 1914-18 war Germany had possessed approximately 20,000 military aircraft, of which some 2,400 were bomber, fighter and reconnaissance aircraft in first-line operational units. In accordance with the Treaty, over 15,000 aircraft and 27,000 aero engines were surrendered ; so far the Treaty was effective.

2. Amongst the weaknesses of the Treaty of Versailles was the omission of any clause which would prohibit Germany from possessing or from manu-facturing civil aircraft. In 1922 certain limitations were, it is true, imposed on the size of civil aircraft which she was allowed to construct ; in 1924, the numbers of aircraft which could be produced and the workpeople who could be employed in their production were also circumscribed. The Paris Air Agreement of 1926, however, withdrew all these limitations, and Germany was left with complete freedom in the sphere of civil aviation. The Germans seized this opportunity and immediately began to develop and expand civil and commercial aviation, with its accompanying flying clubs, air lines, and establishments for the training of commercial air and ground crews. Under this cloak the foundations of a new air force were already being laid.

The Nucleus of a New Air Force

3. It is generally believed that Hitler and Goering were responsible for the birth of the German Air Force in the years between 1933 and 1935. This is not true ; preparations by a small body of regular officers of the old German Army and Flying Corps were being made in secret as early as 1920 (from 1920-21, and again from 1923 to 1927, Goering was in Sweden, partly as a pilot in the Swedish Air Force, and partly in hospital there under treatment as a drug addict). The fact that Germany had been permitted by the Treaty of Versailles to retain a Defence Ministry (*Reichswehr Ministerium*) gave her the opportunity to retain the nucleus of a General Staff with its traditions unimpaired.

4. The Chief of the Army Command at the Defence Ministry, General von Seeckt, may be said to be the real founder of the new German Air Force ; already in 1920 he was convinced that military aviation would some day be revived in Germany. He therefore secreted a small group of regular officers, some ex-flyers and some from the Army, in the various sections which dealt

with aviation in his Ministry. The fact that some of the officers of this small group, notably Felmy, Sperrle, Wever, Kesselring and Stumpff were destined to become outstanding commanders of the German Air Force which was presented openly to the World in 1935, points clearly to von Seeckt's foresight, and to the profound mistake on the part of the victors of the 1914-18 war in allowing this military nucleus to remain in Germany. It is interesting to note, too, that as early as 1923, von Seeckt laid down in a memorandum that a future air force must be an independent part of the Armed Forces.

The Development of Aircraft Manufacture

5. It was perhaps a natural commercial urge, aided by the lightness of the restrictions on commercial aircraft manufacture imposed by the Treaty of Versailles, that encouraged and permitted German aircraft manufacturers to begin operating and expanding once the six months standstill order of June, 1919, had expired. Early in 1920 Professor Hugo Junkers had formed an aircraft company at Dessau—later to become one of the greatest aircraft plants in Europe—and had put a new commercial aircraft on the market. In 1922, Ernst Heinkel was building an aircraft factory at Warnemuende on the Baltic coast ; by this time, too, Professor Junkers was exploring the facilities for production in Sweden and Turkey. Heinkel also set up a factory in Sweden, and Claude Dornier, the future builder of transatlantic flying boats and then the well-known Dornier bombers at Friedrichshafen, was opening in Italy and Switzerland. By 1924, Heinrich Focke and George Wulf had founded the Focke-Wulf aircraft concern at Bremen. In the next year Messerschmitt took over the Bavarian Aircraft Company and set to building fast, light sporting aircraft.

6. Thus, by the time the Paris Air Agreement of 1926 removed the remaining restrictions on the manufacture of civil aircraft (see paragraph 2), Germany already possessed an efficient aircraft industry which had kept pace with current technical developments in the rest of the World. She was also maintaining a rate of production as high as that of any other European country.

Civil Aviation

7. Two small air transport companies had been operating in Germany from 1920 onwards. In 1924 General von Seeckt made the astute move of securing the appointment of his nominee, a Captain Brandenburg[1] from the old German Flying Corps, as head of the Civil Aviation Department of the Ministry of Transport. Co-operation between this department and von Seeckt's Defence Ministry was thus assured, and thenceforward the development and control of civil aviation continued under military direction.

8. In 1926, a new State airways corporation, the Deutsche Lufthansa, was formed and enjoyed a monopoly with a large measure of Government subsidy. At this stage we see the entry of one who was destined to play an important part in the rise of the German Air Force ; Erhard Milch—later to become Field Marshal—had, since 1920, been successively employed

---

[1] Brandenburg remained in office until 1934, when he offended Goering by refusing collaboration ; he was transferred to the Department of Inland Waterways and thereafter had no hand in Air Force affairs.

with one of the small air transport companies, Lloyd Ost, and as works manager at Junkers of Dessau. It was largely as a result of Milch's efforts that the Lufthansa was formed, and he was installed as chairman of that corporation.

9. One more stage in the growth of a new German Air Force had been reached. The Lufthansa proceeded to build airfields, to exercise considerable influence in the aircraft industry, and to experiment to set up a high standard of day, night, and blind flying. The Lufthansa eventually became the best equipped and operated airline in Europe. Two years later, in 1928, however, the government subsidies were reduced by half, and the Lufthansa was seemingly entering upon a dark period. It was at this time that Milch first met Goering, by then a *Reichstag* deputy, whom he persuaded to support the cause of the Lufthansa.

Beginnings of the Secret Air Force

10. By 1926, Germany was already the most air-minded nation in Europe. The membership of its main air society, the *Deutscher Luftsportverband*, which was founded in 1920, increased gradually and by the end of the 1920's exceeded 50,000. The source of this encouragement was actually the Defence Ministry ; a means of circumventing the Treaty of Versailles was seen to be the development of gliding, and in 1920 Captain Student[1], head of the Air Technical Branch, began organising courses in glider instruction.

11. The Paris Air Agreement of 1926 had severely restricted the numbers of service personnel who were allowed to fly. General von Seeckt, however, continued to evade these restrictions, and succeeded in building up secretly a reserve of flyers. His co-operation with the Ministry of Transport provided the means of training military pilots in secret sections of the commercial flying schools which had been established under the Deutsche Lufthansa ; at the same time these schools were producing civil aircrews capable of being employed for military purposes. Again, a military flying training centre for regular officers was established in secret at Lipetz in Russia. Student and Sperrle both had a hand in the organisation of this school—as well as Wenninger, who was afterwards German Air Attaché in London. The officers attending the Lipetz courses were temporarily released from the armed forces ; German personnel records show that between 1928 and 1931 almost all the officers who later held high rank in the German Air Force passed through this School.

12. Such were the beginnings from which the Germans were to build up their new Air Force. That they were able to do so with an incredible rapidity was largely due to the energy and foresight of those few regular officers, permitted to remain as a firm nucleus by the weakness of the Treaty of Versailles. The advent of Hitler and the Nazi party in 1933 provided the political background for which these regular officers had been waiting. They were glad to throw in their lot with the Nazis and thus to achieve their ambitions.

From the Creation of the Third Reich to the Outbreak of War (1933–1939)

The Advent of Hitler

13. When, in January, 1933, Hitler took over the political leadership of Germany, the Armed Forces were subordinated to the Ministry of Defence and thus were not under his direct control. The first change came in 1934 when,

---

[1] As General he commanded the paratroops in the invasion of Holland (see Chapter 3) and Crete (Chapter 5).

with the introduction of conscription, the title of Defence Minister was changed to Minister of War and Commander-in-Chief of the Armed Forces (*Reichskriegsminister und Oberbefehlshaber der Wehrmacht*) and the post was given to General von Blomberg. At this time, too, Von Hindenburg, the Chancellor of Germany, was an old man and fast losing his faculties ; when he died in August, 1934, Hitler assumed his position as Chancellor and thus gained complete control of Germany. Henceforward, the oath of allegience to the law and people of Germany, taken by men entering the new Armed Forces, was to be made to Hitler personally. Hitler still remained in the background in military matters, however, and it was not until February, 1938, that he assumed the title and powers of Supreme Commander, and dismissed Von Blomberg. The latter was replaced by a new Chief of the Supreme Command (*Oberkommando der Wehrmacht—O.K.W.*), General Keitel, who held that position until the end of the 1939–45 war and was finally executed by the Allies at Nuremburg.

Hitler's Influence on the Development of the Air Force

14. After Hitler had assumed power over Germany, his foreign policy for the first year or so consisted mainly of allaying the fears of foreign countries at the rearmament which they knew was going on under conditions of utmost secrecy. The fast growing air force was given a free hand to develop on any lines its leaders saw fit ; following the principles laid down by Von Seeckt, it was conceived as an independent strategic force. The men governing its development at that time were also protagonists of stragetic warfare.

15. The influence of Goering in air matters may be said to have had its beginnings in 1929. In that year he told the Reichstag—to which he had been elected the previous year—that even if they did not provide the means to set up an air force at once, it must happen sooner or later. Goering had commanded a squadron in the Richthofen (Fighter) *Geschwader*[1] in the war of 1914–18 ; he had met Hitler in Munich in 1922 and then became the first leader of the Nazi Storm Troops, playing a prominent part as such in Hitler's abortive *Putsch* of 1923. When in 1933 Hitler came to power, he thus saw in Goering his perfect collaborator and a man with enough of the glory of the old Richthofen days to appeal to the popular imagination. Hitler therefore showered appointments on him, giving him four posts in the Government—amongst which was one of Special Commissioner for Aviation. In April, 1933, when the Commissariat became the Air Ministry, Goering found himself as Air Minister.

16. Meanwhile Milch, as head of the Lufthansa, had been proceeding with extreme caution ; in 1931—when he first met Hitler—he had been invited to join the Nazi Party, but had preferred to wait until the seizure of power was an accomplished fact. In 1933, therefore, he accepted the position as deputy to Goering whilst still retaining his post in the Lufthansa. At that time Goering was still mainly occupied with politics, and therefore Milch found himself virtually the head of the Air Ministry.

17. With an eye to his two parallel interests, Milch first began to expand the Lufthansa, itself also a valuable source of aircraft and trained aircrew for an air force. He extended both land and seaplane flying training schools and began an expansion of the aircraft industry, building new factories and enlarging

---

[1] Equivalent to an R.A.F. Group.

4

GENERALFELDMARSCHALL ERHARD MILCH

Born 30.3.92. Commissioned in an Artillery Regiment 1909. Served in the Flying Corps during the Great War 1914-18. From 1926 was Director of the Deutsche Lufthansa. Appointed Secretary of State for Air in February, 1933. From February, 1939, was Inspector-General of the Air Force in addition to being Secretary of State for Air. Took over the post of Director-General of Equipment—retaining his other appointments—on Udet's death in November, 1941. In June, 1944, retired from the post of Secretary of State for Air, and was appointed deputy to Speer, the Minister of Armament and War Production, and Plenipotentiary for Armament in the four-year plan. Retired from the post of Inspector-General of the Air Force in January, 1945. Captured by the Allies in May, 1945.

Goering as a squadron commander in the Richthofen Geschwader, 1917

The He.51 Fighter

The He.46 Reconnaissance-fighter

old ones. For the time being he concentrated upon increasing production of trainer aircraft and of newer existing types already in service, such as the Ju.52. At this stage the Hitler Government was still taking care not to allow his infringement of the Treaty of Versailles to be too open.

The German Air Force Takes Shape

18. In the building up of an air force, the primary task to which Milch set himself was the reorganisation of the new Air Ministry from the existing Commissariat of Aviation. The new organisation consisted of a central department and five offices, the latter dealing respectively with command matters, civil aviation and meteorology, technical matters and production, administration, and personnel, including foreign attachés, press, etc. In the first two years after the formation of the new Air Ministry its key posts were, with two exceptions, held by ex-Army officers, there being insufficient ex-Flying Corps officers available with the necessary staff experience. To overcome this deficiency, Milch proposed to devote the next 8 to 10 years to building up a corps of flying men who could assume leadership in the new arm. Over a number of years, too, he proposed to build up six bomber, six fighter and six reconnaissance Geschwader to be employed primarily as instructional nuclei for the training of still larger numbers of flying and ground personnel. Territorial commands called Air Offices (*Luftamt*), ostensibly to control civil air traffic, were set up to command these units in their respective zones.

19. This plan was worked out in 1934. It must be emphasised, however, that at this time Milch was still unaware of Hitler's plans for the future, and the need, if those plans materialised, for a rapid as opposed to a thorough development scheme. At this time, too, Milch only conferred with Goering about four times a year ; at those meetings the latter invariably demanded that Milch's long-term plans should be accomplished in a year or less, regardless of whether this was possible or not.

Aircraft Production in 1934

20. By 1933 the aircraft industry was already experimenting with military types ; in 1934 these types began to appear in production, and included the He.51 biplane fighter with two machine guns and with a top speed of 210 m.p.h., and the He.45 and He.46 reconnaissance-fighters with a top speed of 140-150 m.p.h. The main emphasis at this time, however, was upon trainer types such as the Ar.66 and FW.44. The Ju.52 was being turned out for the Lufthansa and was envisaged also as a bomber, whilst the Ju.86 and He.111 were in their early experimental stages ; the latter two were to be delivered firstly to the Lufthansa as airliners, but were in fact bomber types.

21. With the aircraft industry now tooled for producing military types in larger quantities, Milch put in hand a new production programme to commence on 1st January, 1934. In view of the needs of training, this programme contained a very large proportion of trainers, but it provided for the production of 4,021[1] aircraft up to 30th September, 1935. This programme was in fact superseded in January, 1935, but by the end of that month 2,105 aircraft— 216 short of the planned programme to that date—had been produced, showing an average rate of production over the thirteenth-month period of 160 per month.

---

[1] From records of LC (Technical) Dept. of German Air Ministry, 1934–5.

22. It is interesting at this stage to study the manner in which Milch planned to distribute the aircraft to be produced under this 1934-35 programme of 4,021 aircraft :—

Lufthansa ..	115
Units (sic)..	1,085
Training ..	2,168
Research ..	138
Airfields ..	156
A.A. Schools	5
Target towing	48
Clubs ..	33
Reichsbank	12
Hitler ..	10
Miscellaneous	80
Wastage ..	171
	4,021

It is also of interest to note the types of aircraft to be produced, the quantities of each, and the main uses to which those aircraft were to be put :—

Operational Types (Land)—

Do.11, Do.23 Bomber ..	372	
Ju.52 Bomber (supplementary) ..	450	
He.45 Reconnaissance (long range)	320	
He.46 Reconnaissance (short range)	270	
Ar.64, 65, He.51 S.E. fighters ..	251	
He.50 Dive bomber	51	
		1,714

Operational Types (Coastal)

He.60 Reconnaissance (S.E. Floatplane)	81	
Dornier Wal. Reconnaissance (long range)	21	
He.38, He.51, S.E. fighter (Floatplane)	26	
He.59 General purpose ..	21	
		149

Elementary Trainers

FW.44, Ar.69, He.72, Kl.25, Ar.66, W.34, etc. ..	1,760

Communications

Kl.31 and 32 ..	89

Miscellaneous

Including experimental series of new bombers, the He.111, Do.17 and Ju.86 ..	309
	4,021

23. In the political sphere, meanwhile, Hitler's foreign policy was beginning to assume a more aggressive form and, through Goering, he began to make demands of Milch for a readiness to meet this policy. Hitler feared that once the implications of his re-armament programme were fully understood abroad,

The Ju.86

The Do.23

Nuremberg, 1935 : The Secret German Air Force comes into the open
(Above) Fly-past over Nuremberg. (Below) A Storm Troop squadron being accepted in the Luftwaffe by Hitler and Goering

he would have to face active intervention of the Western Powers. During the first months of 1934 the aircraft production programme was mainly meeting the demand for the rapidly expanding training organisation, and the secret air force was still extremely weak as a striking force. Meanwhile Milch was busily expanding existing resources of the aircraft industry. Locomotive firms such as Henschel, rolling stock firms such as Gotha and A.T.G., and ship-building companies such as Blohm and Voss, were turned to the production of aircraft and aircraft components. The existing factories of Junkers, Dornier, Heinkel, Arado, Fieseler and Messerschmitt were granted government loans to expand their existing facilities. By January, 1935, Milch was ready with a new and more ambitious production plan. A later paragraph[1] will show how this programme was accomplished.

The German Air Force Comes into the Open

24. In March, 1935, Hitler and Goering felt sufficiently secure to proclaim to the world the foundation of the German Air Force—the *Luftwaffe*. Goering was appointed Commander-in-Chief of the new force, which became an independent part of the Armed Forces subordinated to the Chief of the Supreme Command, General Keitel. Milch, as Secretary of State for Air, was still largely in control of the new Air Force ; General Wever, a former infantry commander and head of the Command Department of the Air Ministry since 1934, was appointed as the first Chief of Air Staff. Staff posts were given by Goering largely to ex-flying officers, particularly those who had served under him in the old Richthofen Geschwader. Goering, in fact, was now beginning to pack the Air Staff with his own nominees, a move which he calculated would make his position safe and at the same time would increase his personal power.

25. The units which had been concealed in the flying clubs and as " police " units of the S.A. (Storm Troops) were now handed over to the Luftwaffe one by one at pretentious ceremonial parades, at many of which Hitler himself was present. An Air Staff College was set up, and that year, too, saw the develop-ment of the *Flak*[2] arm—now subordinated to the Luftwaffe—and the Signals Service. In its organisation the Luftwaffe was divided into four main Regional Groups (*Gruppenkommandos*), centred at Berlin, Koenigsberg, Brunswick and Munich, for the control of the flying units. For administration, supply and maintenance, airfield staffing, certain signals functions, recruiting and training, ten Air Districts (*Luftgaue*) were established.

26. At the inception of the Luftwaffe, its strength stood at 1,888 aircraft of all types, and during 1935 the new arm could muster some 20,000 officers and men. With this considerable nucleus of men and machines, and with the support of between 30 and 40 airframe and engine manufacturers, the new Luftwaffe began to organise itself upon the lines which were to continue up to and after the outbreak of war in 1939. It began to improve its aircraft and to test them in air competitions all over Europe and in large-scale air exercises over Germany. Great stress was laid on the rapid mobility of the flying units and their supporting ground staffs, and their operation at short notice from temporary landing grounds—a technique in which the Luftwaffe remained supreme until 1941, and which was to serve it so well in 1940 in the rapid German advance through Denmark, Norway, Holland, Belgium and France.

---

[1] See paragraph 29.   [2] Flak = *Fliegerabwehrkanonen* = A.A.

27. In the sphere of commercial aviation, the Lufthansa was, by 1935, rapidly extending its lines in Europe and over the Atlantic Ocean. The Near and Far East were also providing Germany with opportunities to prove her military aircraft on long overseas flights and under the whole range of climatic conditions from arctic to tropical. In 1936, 75 crossings of the South Atlantic had already been made by German Flying boats ; that total increased to 100 in 1937.

Milch Loses Power

28. Hitler's foreign policy between 1935 and 1938, constituting, as it did, a challenge to the outside World, was becoming more and more inconsistent with Milch's plans for the long-term development of the Luftwaffe. German re-armament was now no longer a secret, and the only question was one of winning the resultant armaments race against the other European powers. Goering, with his lack of understanding of technical matters, was in the habit of telling Hitler that all was well with the Air Force. When Hitler himself demanded immediate results, therefore, Goering passed the onus of responsibility on to Milch. The latter remained adamant when an earlier limit was set for the completion of this programme. Milch, however, continued to enjoy Hitler's confidence and favour—incidentally he had been transferred to the Luftwaffe as a General early in 1936—and this aroused Goering's enmity and jealousy. Milch was a brilliant organiser and an astute business man, and Goering feared him as a rival and as a contestant for the leadership of the Luftwaffe ; during 1937 and 1938, therefore, Goering gradually deprived him of his powers, including the directorship of the Technical Office of the Air Ministry. Goering now summoned others to his conferences. Amongst these was Colonel Ernst Udet, a friend of Goering's and one of the most successful fighter pilots of the 1914-18 war. Udet had been appointed to the Technical Office of the Air Ministry in 1936 ; by 1939 he was to become the Air Force Director General of Equipment, responsible for design and production of all Air Force equipment. Milch was now to remain in the background until Udet's suicide in 1941[1].

Plans for Modernisation of the Luftwaffe, 1936-1938

29. The year 1935 saw aircraft production increasing from a monthly rate of 180-200 in the first six months to an average of 300 in the latter months. The programme, as to types, remained largely similar to that of 1934, and merely increased in volume in accordance with Milch's long-term plans. During the years 1934 and 1935, however, the emphasis in advanced aircraft development throughout the world, and in Germany, had inclined more and more towards the monoplane. International contests, such as the Schneider Trophy races, were leading the way to a recognition that the military aircraft of the future would be the monoplane, and that the days of the biplane were numbered. In Germany, the chief aircraft companies had kept pace with this trend, and during the latter part of 1935 the prototypes of those aircraft which were to become so familiar in the war of 1939-45 began to appear. In March, 1936, the new Luftwaffe Research Establishment at Rechlin was conducting final trials in these types, amongst which the following are the most important :—

Fighters—	Dive Bombers—
Me.109, Me.110.	Ju.87, Hs.123.
Bombers—	**Reconnaissance—**
Ju.88, Do.17, He.111.	Hs.126, Ar.96,BV.138, He.115.

[1] See Chapter 9, paragraphs 15 and 16.

30. Early in 1936, too, the German Air Ministry was already making preliminary preparations in the aircraft industry for an expansion to large-scale production on a war basis. The now obsolescent types continued in production, but in July, 1936, a new programme of small series[1] production of the modern types was put in hand, and was due for completion in the summer and autumn of 1937. A time would obviously arrive, therefore, when—if the Luftwaffe was to be modernised throughout—the old production programmes must cease and a large-scale re-tooling of the aircraft industry must take place. There would consequently be a period late in 1937 where the rate of output would cease to expand until such a time as the industry would once more be operating to full capacity on the new types. Meanwhile, however, the Spanish Civil War had begun and, as the following paragraphs show, was to have a profound and lasting effect on the development of the German Air Force.

The Spanish Civil War

31. German intervention in the Spanish Civil war began in August, 1936, with the despatch to General Franco's forces of 20 Ju.52 bomber-transport aircraft and six He.51 escort fighters. The first operation by these aircraft was the transporting of 10,000 native troops and equipment from Spanish Morocco to Spain. By the end of that month the help to General Franco was being extended by the loan of more fighter aircraft ; some German pilots were also sent, as volunteers, to fly these aircraft. It soon became clear, however, that if General Franco were to be helped at all, he must be helped on a large scale. A small number of German aircraft could make no impression, as the He.51 was soon found to be inferior in performance to the Russian and American fighters being used by the Republican forces.

32. Eventually the decision was taken to organise a powerful force for intervention on the side of General Franco. The *Legion Condor*, as this force was called, came into being in November, 1936 ; its first commander was the then Generalmajor Sperrle who, as has already been mentioned, had been active in organising the secret flying training in Russia after 1920. His Chief of Staff was Wolfram von Richthofen, at that time Lieutenant-Colonel, and a relative of Baron Manfred von Richthofen whose " circus " had gained such fame in the war of 1914-18. Wolfram von Richthofen, like Sperrle, had risen with the secret air force under cover of the Defence Ministry from 1920 onwards. Von Richthofen eventually became Commander-in-Chief of the Condor Legion, but the Spanish War was only a beginning for him ; this book will show that he played an important part in shaping German Air Force strategy from this time up to the end of the war of 1939-45.[2]

33. Volunteers for service in Spain with the Legion Condor were called for in the Luftwaffe in Germany. Romantic stories had already been built around the fighting in Spain ; in addition the rates of pay offered were high, so that volunteers were not lacking. These men, drawn from the German Air Force, were provided with civilian papers and sailed for Spain in civilian clothes, ostensibly as " Strength Through Joy " (*Kraft durch Freude*) cruises from such ports as Hamburg. This subterfuge was resorted to for international political ends, and presented no problem, for at that time it was a common practice for the German Government to finance " Strength Through Joy " pleasure cruises

---

[1] A small, or "O" series usually comprised 10 aircraft.   [2] Photograph and career on page 67.

13

for working people. The Legion Condor had an initial complement of about 200 aircraft, including some 50 Ju.52 bombers, 40-50 fighters, mainly He.51's, and an assortment of ground-attack and short-range reconnaissance aircraft. The Legion also provided a complement of anti-aircraft, signals, airfield staffing, supply and medical units, all of which were highly mobile.

34. The first task was the strategic bombing of Spanish Mediterranean harbours to prevent the landing of supplies from abroad. The bombing had, however, to be abandoned on Franco's request for support in the land battle for Madrid at the end of November. This battle showed German air tactics in an experimental stage ; heavy artillery was lacking at the time, and air bombardment was substituted in an attempt to reduce the Republican positions. The Legion achieved little until the early summer of 1937, when it began to receive the new Me.109 fighter and He.111 and Do.17 bombers and thus soon achieved air superiority.

35. One event which was to shape the future German policy of air strategy occurred at the end of March, 1937. In an attack on the northern Republican front, He.51's, equipped as fighter-bombers, and each carrying six 10-kilogramme bombs, were employed in low-level attack on fortified positions with astonishing success. This attack marked the first close-support operations, which were to lead to Germany's lightning military successes in 1939 and 1940; the bombs were released by formations of nine aircraft from a height of 500 feet, and up to seven sorties a day were made. Subsequently three squadrons of close-support He.51's were organised, and were allotted a squadron of Me.109 escort fighters. Later in 1937 the Ju.87 and Hs.123 dive-bombers made their appearance and close-support operations began to develop on these lines as more experience was gained. These operations were the work of von Richthofen, who also developed the aspect of close co-operation with the ground forces by radio control of the airborne formations.

Influence of the Spanish War on Luftwaffe Policy

36. The Condor Legion returned from Spain at the conclusion of the civil war in March, 1939. One of the most valuable results to Germany of intervention in that war was the experience in modern warfare gained by the members of the Condor Legion. This fact was recognised by the Luftwaffe High Command at an early stage in the campaign ; the volunteer system was abolished, at least as far as officers were concerned, and only the most promising officers were sent to Spain ; as soon as they had gained experience they were replaced by others. On their return to Germany these officers were usually posted to training establishments as instructors. With aircraft, too, the German Air Force made full use of the opportunity offered for combat experience, and was able to improve equipment, eliminate unsatisfactory types and try out the new ones in battle.

37. The conclusions drawn from the Spanish war were only revolutionary where close-support operations were concerned. There had been little real strategic bombing by the Condor Legion during the campaign, operations by the bomber force being almost entirely limited to tactical support of the Army. The significance of the success which the Legion had achieved did not immediately strike the High Command, which was still imbued with the concept of the Air Force as an independent strategic force. It was left to von Richthofen to emphasise the great possibilities in the employment of an air force in direct

GENERALOBERST
ERNST UDET

Born 26.4.96. Volunteer in the Army August-October, 1914. Entered the Flying Corps June, 1915, commanded Jagdstaffeln 37 and 11 during the war. Left the service November, 1918. 1918-35 active as test, sports and aerobatic pilot. Entered the Air Force June, 1935. February, 1936, Inspector of fighters and dive bombers. June, 1936, appointed Director of the Technical Department at the German Air Ministry. February, 1939, the Technical Department became the Directorate-General of Air Force Equipment with Udet as Director-General (Generalluftzeugmeister). Committed suicide 17.11.41.

GENERALFELDMARSCHALL
HUGO SPERRLE

Born 7.2.85. Joined an Infantry Regiment in 1903. Served in the Flying Corps during the Great War, 1914-18, towards the end of which he was in command of the flying units attached to the 7th Army. In the Reichswehr, 1919-35. Transferred to the Air Force in 1935. Commanded the Condor Legion in Spain, 1936-37. Became A.O.C. Luftwaffengruppe 3rd February, 1938 (A.O.C. Luftflotte 3 and A.O.C. West from February, 1939, in which position he was joint leader with Kesselring of the Battle of Britain). He held this appointment until transferred to the reserve in August, 1944. Captured by the Allies May, 1945.

15

THE SPANISH CIVIL WAR
Von Richthofen and Franco

Ju.87 Dive Bombers of the " Condor Legion "

support of ground forces.   Richthofen had formed the far-sighted conception of creating a separate tactical air force for participation in land battles ; it was to be an adjunct to, and not a substitute for a strategic air force.   Not only did Richthofen encounter opposition to his wide plan, but it was only with the greatest difficulty that his ideas on army co-operation, which were to have such an extensive influence on air operations in the war of 1939, were accepted at all. Where Richthofen did succeed, was in convincing the High Command that by an extreme concentration of striking power the enemy could be paralysed and local supremacy could always be achieved.   Richthofen, like most of the stronger characters in the Luftwaffe, succeeded in carrying out his ideas without official sanction, and created ground attack squadrons in the Luftwaffe.   This far-seeing move was to prove Richthofen to be right ; furthermore, it was to pay handsome dividends in the victorious continental campaigns of 1940 and in the rapid German advance to the gates of Moscow in 1941.   Largely, as a result of this early turn in the course of the development of the German Air Force, its General Staff came to look upon it more as a close-support or tactical arm than a strategic weapon.   As this book will show, its excursions into strategic warfare were but few, and the same thread of tactical thought may be followed through the campaigns of the war of 1939–45.

38. The fact that operations in Spain called for tactical support rather than for strategic bombing meant that less experience was gained in the latter sphere than in Army co-operation.   Moreover, the comparatively slight opposition encountered by the bomber squadrons, particularly when the new and fast He.111 came along, inclined the High Command to the belief that they could continue to operate fast medium bombers with but light fighter protection ; indeed, the belief even grew that the fast medium bomber would be able to lay waste any country without the fighter defences even having an opportunity to interfere.   This theory only first revealed itself as a serious misconception in the Battle of Britain.

39. The anti-shipping arm had failed to show any results in Spain.   A Major Harlinghausen, who had transferred to the secret air force from the Navy in 1933, had been in command of a sea bomber-reconnaissance unit of the Condor Legion in 1937 and 1938.   He, it is true, was aware of the possibilities which lay in the development of this arm, particularly in a war against a sea power like Great Britain.   The High Command was not to be persuaded at that stage, however, being firmly convinced that war with Great Britain could be avoided.   It is interesting to note that Harlinghausen continued to work in this neglected sphere, and that it was he who eventually led the anti-shipping war against Great Britain (see Chapter 4).

40. The anti-shipping arm remained subordinated tactically to the Navy and, whilst its aircrews were well-trained ex-naval and merchant marine officers, its aircraft equipment rapidly became obsolete and was not modernised ; this equipment was thought to be adequate for the tasks which the arm was expected to undertake—mainly coastal reconnaissance.

Setting up of Technical Development Flying Unit (Lehr Division)

41. An important development of the year 1937 was the formation of a Technical Development Flying Unit, called the *Lehr Division*, at Greifswald. The Air Staff, in the first two years of its existence, had felt the need for some organisation which could experiment and could develop the lessons which

were rapidly being learned in the war in Spain and in the factories, experimental institutes, air exercises and competitions. Moreover, 1937 saw the new modern aircraft beginning to be delivered to the Luftwaffe squadrons ; in the elimination of the early mechanical troubles and in finding the best tactical use for eacn aircraft, the Lehr Division played an essential part. Special experimental units for handling each new operational aircraft type as it came into the Luftwaffe were to be formed within the Division, and throughout 1937 and 1938 the Division was gradually enlarged on these lines. It eventually comprised eight *Gruppen* (equivalent to R.A.F. Wings), of about 30 aircraft each, covering the whole range of bomber, fighter and reconnaissance types.

42. The Lehr Division acted as something more than an advanced operational training centre ; it was a post-graduate air institution which endeavoured to absorb each tactical air lesson which presented itself. When war broke out in September, 1939, however, the Division was considered to have served its purpose, and its very competent and experienced squadrons were thrown into the general battle. They retained their special title, although in fact they had become ordinary operational units of the Luftwaffe. War casualties soon robbed them of many of their most experienced pilots.

1938—A Year of Crisis in Europe

43. The year 1938 began as one of great agitation in Europe ; since 1935 Germany had already gained the Saar basin through a plebiscite and had marched into the Rhineland. Now she was to annexe Austria and occupy the Sudeten borders of Czechoslovakia, the Spanish war was to reach its climax, and the postponement of a European war was to be assured by the Munich agreement on September 29th. Hitler's political successes in the Saar and Rhineland had secured him a large number of adherents and confirmed his belief in his own infallibility ; the pace was beginning to quicken. The German Air Force was gaining in strength and deliveries of the new types to the squadrons were beginning to increase.

44. In March, 1938, the Luftwaffe played a major part in the occupation of Austria. Over 400 German aircraft, mainly He.111, Ju.52 and Ju.86 took part ; of this total, 160 were troop carriers which flew more than 2,000 fully-equipped German troops to Vienna. These operations were not carried out without hitches, but thanks to the complete co-operation of the Austrian military authorities, no serious delays occurred ; the large-scale transport of troops by air and the employment of paratroops in seizing possible strong points provided some valuable experience.

45. In the main, three advantages accrued to the Luftwaffe from the seizure of Austria. Firstly, in General Loehr, the Luftwaffe acquired a future Air Fleet commander of great value. Secondly, in the Vienna area the Germans were able to expand their production of the Me.109 fighter—by September, 1939, 200 of these fighters were being turned out annually in Austria. Lastly, new air training schools were set up, and strategic bases were obtained for the later attacks on Poland ; in addition, the Austrian Air Force provided a small number of skilled pilots, who were thrown into the general pool of the Luftwaffe.

46. The Munich agreement of September, 1938, gave the Sudeten areas of Czechoslovakia to Nazi Germany. By this agreement Europe secured a breathing space which it knew could only be a postponement of a major

European war. The Luftwaffe itself was no less relieved at this postponement; it was in fact, in the middle of a period of transition and was not yet ready for a major war. Full production of the newest types had not yet been reached, but another year or more could see substantial progress towards that programme of re-equipment which had been instituted in the spring and summer of 1936.

The Luftwaffe at the Time of the Munich Agreement

47. An opportune period for a review of the strength of the Luftwaffe is that of August and September, 1938, at the time of the negotiations for the Munich agreement. The German Propaganda Ministry had been busily and successfully sowing a belief in the world that the German Air Force was so mighty as to be capable of crushing any country it pleased by massed bombing. Fantastic figures of the Luftwaffe's strength were carefully supplied to the presses of one country and were then duly repeated around the world as sensational news. The occupation of Austria and the Sudetenland had provided token demonstrations of the Luftwaffe's strength, and the fear of the Luftwaffe began to grow throughout Europe.

48. In the sphere of aircraft production in Germany, the industry had already been pressed to increase its output—in June an order for a 10-hour day in the plants was circulated—but in the latter half of the year production did not increase beyond the monthly figure of 450-500 of the end of 1937, owing to the large-scale re-tooling of the industry during the year. By 1939, the effects of re-tooling began to be overcome, and output rose to 700 monthly, but was not to exceed 800 after outbreak of war and up to 1940. (See Chapter 2, paragraph 11).

49. By August, 1938, first-line strength of the Luftwaffe had increased to some 2,900 from a figure of 2,000-2,500 in 1937. This expansion was taking place whilst the squadrons were being re-equipped with the new types, the old being progressively withdrawn and either relegated to the flying training schools or sold to unsuspecting foreign countries. The German Air Ministry strength returns made on 1st August, 1938, will give the best indication of actual strength at this time; these figures, reproduced below, also show that, with the preponderance of bombers, dive bombers, ground-attack and tactical reconnaissance aircraft, the Luftwaffe was developing as an instrument of attack.

Establishment, Strength and Serviceability of the Flying Units as at 1st August, 1938

AIRCRAFT

Type of Unit	Establishment	Strength	Aircraft Serviceable
Strategic Reconnaissance	228	197	136
Tactical Reconnaissance (Army)	297	285	164
Fighter	938	643	453
Bomber	1,409	1,157	582
Dive Bomber	300	207	159
Ground Attack	195	173	1
Transport	117	81	23
Coastal and Naval	230	185	151
Total	3,714	2,928	1,669

Type of Units	Establishment	Strength	Operational	
			Fully	Partially
Strategic Reconnaissance	228	NA	84	57
Tactical Reconnaissance (Army)..	297	NA	183	128
Fighter	938	NA	537	364
Bomber	1,409	NA	378	411
Dive Bomber	300	NA	80	123
Ground Attack	195	NA	89	11
Transport	117	NA	10	17
Coastal and Naval	230	NA	71	34
Total	3,714	NA	1,432	1,145

Prelude to War

50. In March, 1939, German troops crossed the Czech frontier and invaded the whole country. Once again they were accompanied by a full-scale demonstration, by 500 aircraft of the Luftwaffe, in which airborne troops were landed at Prague. In the operation to occupy this area 500 German aircraft took part. The Czech Air Force, unlike the Austrian Air Force, provided no senior commanders or nucleus of élite pilots ; instead, large numbers of Czech pilots were to become opponents of the Luftwaffe in the French and British Air Forces. The Germans were, however, able to take over important aircraft factories—principally the Tatra works—and, as in the case of Austria, were able to acquire a number of useful airfields to expand their training organisation. Hitler ignored the British and French protests to this act of aggression, and followed with an ultimatum to Lithuania for the cession of Memel. Thus, political unrest increased, and the vague possibility of war with England became a probability. Intelligence data on England was collated by the newly-formed Luftwaffe Intelligence Department, and in Germany exercises were being carried out simulating attacks on British harbours and shipping. Forward airfields were built in western Germany. Early in the year the Luftwaffe was reorganised on a war basis.

51. Hitler's foreign policy had decreed that Milch's long-term plans for the development of the Luftwaffe should come to nought—if allowed to proceed, these plans could have produced a formidable force by 1942—and that the short-term planners should win the day. Milch, although now in the background, did not stay silent, but became an independent and outspoken critic. Fundamentally, he was a clear thinking and practical man, and his criticisms were based on his knowledge of German resources and on observations during his travels abroad. He and Udet had paid an official visit to England in 1938 and had seen the Royal Air Force ; on their return Milch had made a report to Hitler in which he warned him against Ribbentrop, the German ambassador in London, who was damaging relations between the two countries. In the summer of 1939, the question of Danzig and the Polish corridor was looming as the next European problem, and Milch gave a warning that England would go to war on this question, and that it would be folly for Germany, with her rearmament programmes not yet completed, to provoke such a war.

CHAPTER 2

THE GERMAN AIR FORCE ON THE EVE OF THE EUROPEAN WAR

Strength, Equipment,[1] Production and Manpower

First and Second-Line Strength and Reserves

1. In August, 1939, on the eve of the European War, the German Air Force was in a more favourable position for waging war than at the same time in 1938. The year's grace which the Munich agreement had allowed had permitted a great measure of expansion, although production was still too low to permit of prolonged fighting in actual war. Hitler's policy of the short victorious campaign, so successful in the series of bloodless victories achieved so far, could, however, permit of a recovery in strength after the autumn campaign then being planned against Poland. This policy, too, was actually a strong factor in imposing the period of stalemate during the winter of 1939, commonly known as the " Phoney War " period.

2. Thus, at the end of August, Luftwaffe strength stood at 3,750[2] as against 2,928[3] a year previously ; of this figure 1,270 were twin-engined bombers, mostly He.111 and Do.17, but with a few of the new Ju.88, which had gone into production earlier in the year. Behind this first-line strength there was but a small reserve, varying between 10 per cent. and 25 per cent. of first-line strength, according to the individual types. Behind this strength and its reserve was the training organisation, with 2,500 to 3,000 trainer aircraft, as well as some 500 operational types of aircraft used for operational training.

Aircraft Equipment

The Bomber Force

3. German aircraft equipment at this time was superior to that of any possible European opponent, although that superiority became less and less marked as the war went on. In the twin-engined bomber category the Germans had two main types in the squadrons, the He.111 and the Do.17 ; at the outbreak of the war the latter was not only one of the chief German twin-engined bombers but was also the main general reconnaissance type in use. Before the war was a year old, however, it was being superseded, both as bomber and reconnaissance aircraft, by the Ju.88. The Ju.88 was the high-performance bomber of the Luftwaffe at this time, but it was not until the summer of 1940 that the Germans were able to operate it in more than very small numbers. In the autumn of 1939 the bomber force also still included about 100 Ju.86K twin-engined bombers. This type had an inferior performance, its two Jumo Diesel engines giving only 600 h.p., a top speed of less than 200 miles an hour with a cruising speed of about 175 miles an hour and a maximum range of only 1,000 miles with a maximum load of a ton. Such an aircraft, so obviously inferior to the Heinkel, Dornier and Junkers 88 bombers, was bound to be discarded, and after a brief operational employment in the Polish campaign it was relegated to training and transport work ; later, in 1942, it was revived in small numbers, as the Ju.86P, a special high-altitude bomber-reconnaissance aircraft.

---

[1] For Fuel, see Chapter 15.
[2] Table 2 on page 209 sets out fully the aircraft types and categories comprising this total.
[3] See Chapter 1, paragraph 49.

4. German bombs, compared with R.A.F. standards, were slightly inferior in their ballistics, being designed rather for easy production. The following were standard in the Luftwaffe : a 10 Kg. anti-personnel bomb, a 50 Kg. bomb of two kinds—general purpose and armour-piercing, a 250 and 500 Kg. bomb—each in both the above categories, a 1 Kg. incendiary, a 2 Kg. incendiary. The bomb-fusing system was all-electric, and, compared with the British percussion-type pistols, was decidedly superior, having a higher safety factor and requiring a more simple ground organisation for fusing of the bombs. The Germans also had gas bombs ready for use, in which there were two main classes, the " Green Cross " gas bomb, which produced irritation of the eyes and breathing organs, and the " Yellow Cross " which was of a mustard variety. There is no evidence of any special pre-war training in the Luftwaffe in the use of gas.

5. Armament of German bombers consisted of machine guns, both free and fixed, of 7·9 mm. calibre ; both types were simple and compact and relatively free from stoppages. A free gun magazine held 75 rounds of ammunition which could be put in easily with a single move ; its maximum rate of fire was 1,200 rounds per min. The fixed machine guns used a continuous belt. The Germans also had a 20 mm. cannon—the Swiss Oerlikon—but except for one or two fitted to Ju.86's, this weapon was at this period installed almost entirely in the Me.109 single-seat fighter.

6. Up to the eve of the war the Germans did not use power-driven turrets on their bombers, and free guns were mounted for the most part in open cockpits with a scarff ring, or in enclosed machine-gun positions in which the gunners were protected behind panel screens through which the guns protruded. Armour plating was in the experimental stage and not in general use. Self-sealing tanks, however, were standard.

The Dive-Bomber Force
7. The whole of the dive-bomber force was now equipped with the Ju.87 Stuka[1]. Even then the Ju.87 was classified as a short-range moderate performance aircraft in which its virtues were not in its speed, range or bomb load, but in the accuracy of bombing achieved by its special design. Like other German bombers it was lightly protected by two machine guns, but was not armoured.

Single-Engined Fighters
8. By now the single-engined fighter squadrons had been re-equipped with the Me.109. There is no doubt that in 1939 the Me.109 was superior to any Allied fighter aircraft except the Spitfire which, however, was then only available to the R.A.F. in small numbers.

Twin-Engined Fighters
9. All German twin-engined fighter squadrons were equipped with the new Me.110. In 1939, the Me.110 was probably the best twin-engined fighter in Europe, superior to its opposite number in the R.A.F., the Blenheim fighter. Against good single-engined fighter opposition, however, it lacked speed and manœuvrability for combat purposes.

Reconnaissance
10. For short-range reconnaissance and work with the Army, the Luftwaffe employed the Hs.126. This two-seater high-wing monoplane was similar in appearance and performance to the British Westland Lysander. The Naval

---

[1] Stuka is a contraction of *Sturzkampf*, meaning Dive Bombing.

The Ju.88 Bomber

The Do.17 Bomber

The He.111 Bomber

The Me.109 Fighter   The sub-type illustrated above is the Me.109F, which appeared after the Battle of Britain.

25

The Me.110 Fighter   The sub-type illustrated is a later development which appeared late in 1942.

equivalents to the Hs.126, used for short-range coastal and fleet reconnaissance were the He.60 and He.114. They played little part in the War, however, and were quickly replaced by the faster low-wing monoplane, the Arado 196.

Significance of Pre-war Equipment

11. This brief glance at German Air Force equipment on the eve of the war illustrates the thesis that the Luftwaffe was designed mainly as an instrument of army support. The absence of special aircraft for long-range strategic bombing, and the failure to develop radar[1] and ground control of fighters for defensive purposes, further illustrate the well established view that the Luftwaffe was intended as an instrument of close and intensive support of land forces, and that the air defence of the Third Reich was as yet a secondary consideration for the German Air Staff.

The Failure to Expand Aircraft Production[2]

12. In the year preceding outbreak of War, aircraft production had failed to expand, and by the Autumn of 1939 the position was only just beginning to improve towards the figure of 700 aircraft a month. There were several reasons for this failure to expand in the vital 1938-39 period. In the first instance there was no increase in the number of workers in the aircraft industry during that period ; moreover, the supply of skilled workers already presented a serious problem. The relative stagnation of the industry between 1919 and 1933 had resulted in an unduly high proportion of employees in the 1935-38 period being young men of the lower age groups required for military service—a problem which was not absent in other countries, such as Great Britain in 1940. Afterwards this problem was surmounted to some extent by the employment of more women and foreign workers. Indeed later on, 70 per cent. of workers in the German aircraft industry were women compared with some 50 per cent. at the outbreak of the European war. A further reason already elaborated in Chapter I, was the fact that many of the operational aircraft of the 1935-37 period had become obsolescent. The firm of Junkers had to re-tool when both the Ju.52 and Ju.86 bombers became obsolescent and were replaced by Ju.88. Dornier had to abandon the twin-engined Dornier 23 bomber during this period and turn over to the Do.17 twin-engined bomber of entirely different design. Moreover, many of the Dornier flying boats produced during the 1938-39 period, in particular the three-engined Do.24 and the four-engined Do.26 never became operational in Luftwaffe squadrons except in isolated cases. The firm of Heinkel had to abandon the He.45 and He.70 as well as the He.112 single-engined fighter ; in the floatplane category the He.59, He.60 and He.114 were rapidly becoming obsolescent and being replaced by the He.115. The Messerschmitt firm alone suffered relatively few setbacks, but even here the Me.109 in the 1936-39 period underwent considerable modifications in armament and engine, and had to have its undercarriage strengthened.

13. The reorientation of the year or so before the war, as well as the difficulty in providing increased numbers of skilled workers, were thus the main reason for the failure of the German aircraft industry to expand. It should be added that aircraft repair organisation was on a very small scale in the pre-war period. Hitler's policy of the short victorious campaign was largely responsible for this

---

[1] Radar was already under development in Germany, and as such had reached an advanced stage, but its tactical employment was as yet neglected.

[2] See also Chapter 1, paragraphs 20–23, 29–30 and 49 and Chapter 9, paragraphs 16–24.

failing ; losses of one campaign could be replaced during the period of preparation for the next. On the other hand, the concentration upon production during the years 1938 and 1939 had presented no opportunity for the preparation of a massive repair organisation, even if it had been thought of. Repair facilities on airfields were well organised and efficient, but there was no thorough workshop and factory organisation capable of sustaining a steady output of repaired aircraft equivalent to half of the new output, a proportion which might have been expected.

14. By the general standards of the war, German aircraft production on its outbreak was on only a modest scale. It remained on the scale of around 800 aircraft a month throughout the first year or so of the war. It was not until after the Battle of Britain, and when the German checks and disasters in Russia began to pile up, that the High Command was goaded into operating a plan for substantially increased aircraft production. It was this failure, too, which led to the suicide of Udet in 1941 and to the recall of Milch. The almost incredible optimism which prevailed in Air Staff circles is typical of the Nazi indifference to Germany's mounting air problems during the war.

Manpower

15. At the outbreak of war in September, 1939, the Luftwaffe had a strength of about $1\frac{1}{2}$ million men. Nearly two-thirds of these consisted of anti-aircraft personnel, the remainder forming the flying and ground units. Of the 500-600,000 men in these two latter categories, about 5 per cent. were Air Ministry and headquarters staffs, between 10 per cent. and 15 per cent. aircrew, about 15 per cent. in airfield servicing units, between 15 per cent. and 20 per cent. with signals, between 10 per cent. and 15 per cent. were engaged on airfield construction work and general Air Force labour projects, 15 per cent. were engaged on the maintenance and supply services and between 10 per cent. and 15 per cent. were personnel under training.

16. In the pre-war period Goering had done everything possible to make the German Air Force the élite arm of the *Wehrmacht*[1]. Candidates generally volunteered at the age of 17 for periods varying between 2 and 12 years, according to the branch in which they were destined to serve. In addition to the normal special inducements of service life in peacetime—free clothing, a good standard of food, regular pay, and the general incentive of playing a part in Germany's " resurrection ", Goering created special encouragements in order to ensure the recruitment of specially selected men. One of these was that special labour certificates were issued to ex-members of the Luftwaffe, and a Government loan was made available for setting them up in civil life after expiry of their term of service. Until a member of the Luftwaffe could find employment he was paid by the German Government for several months. In addition, when German Air Force personnel had finished their active service days, Goering saw to it that there was a host of special posts for them in the Lufthansa, the Weather Service and in the non-flying services of the Luftwaffe itself. It is therefore not surprising that the German Air Force attracted the very cream of German youth to its ranks.

Training

17. German Air Force training had, by 1939, reached a degree of quality not exceeded in any other European air force. The foundation of the civilian National Socialist Flying Corps in 1937 had done little to make any real

---

[1] Armed forces.

The Hs.126 Army co-operation reconnaissance aircraft

The He.115 Reconnaissance, Bomber or Torpedo aircraft

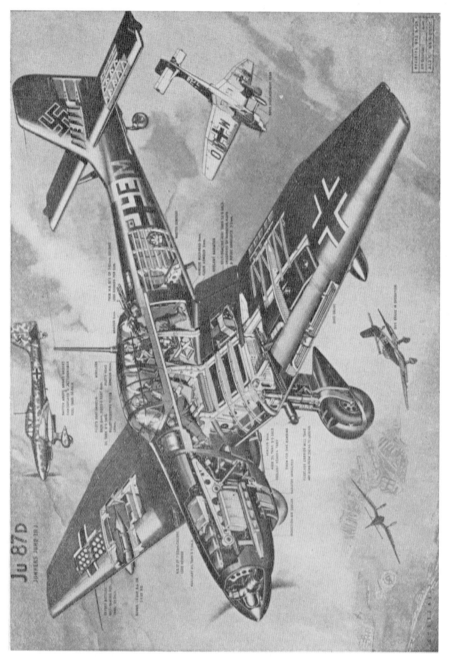

The Ju.87 Dive Bomber. The sub-type illustrated here was a later development of the earlier Ju.87 series employed in the Spanish war and the Battle of Britain.

contribution towards the creation of German pre-war Air Force pilots, but Goering, by placing all flying training on a military basis from 1936 onwards, and by creating a special training inspectorate at the Air Ministry, had done much to centralise control and to ensure a high standard in all flying training schools.

Initial Training

18. Recruits, including officer candidates, were sent on joining the Air Force to a *Flieger Ausbildungs Regiment* or Recruit Depôt. This corresponded roughly to the Royal Air Force I.T.W. (Initial Training Wing) stage. A recruit would spend about 6 to 12 months learning little else but military discipline and physical culture ; the air aspect was only introduced in lectures on the elementary principles of wireless and in map reading. All entrants, both for flying and ground duties, passed through this course which later, and under pressure of war, had to be reduced in duration to 2 to 3 months.

Flying Training

19. On the passing-out from the Recruit Depôt, two months were spent by the recruit at a pool known as the *Fluganwaerterkompanie*. Here the recruit awaited his flying training posting and spent up to two months studying general aeronautical subjects. Flying training began at an Elementary Flying Training School (the Luftwaffe called it an A/B School) where the pupil was given from 100 to 150 hours' flying, of which about 5 hours were dual and about 25 hours comprised circuits and bumps, take offs, simple banking turns and attempts at three-point landings in light Focke-Wulf, Klemm or Buecker biplanes. In the second stage of the Elementary Flying Training course, the candidate pilot was being closely watched, for he was now about to be awarded his pilot's certificate and wings[1]. His instructors were deciding if he would be more suitable as a bomber or fighter pilot, or perhaps as an observer or reconnaissance pilot. Thereafter flying training depended on the nature of the specialisation.

20. Prospective bomber and reconnaissance pilots were drafted to " C " Schools, where they trained on twin-engined aircraft. The course lasted from 3 to 6 months and included about 60 hours' flying ; night flying, as well as a certain amount of blind and cross-country flying were also features of this stage of training. The training aircraft included obsolescent operational types and current service aircraft. On leaving the " C " School, bomber and reconnaissance pilots would be sent to a six weeks' course at a specialised Blind Flying School, where a further 50 to 60 hours' flying would be done, including work with the Link ground trainer. The next stage was at the bomber or reconnaissance specialist school. This course, lasting about three months, was devoted to combined crew training of pilot, wireless operator and observer in operational aircraft of the latest design. The general training at these specialised bomber and reconnaissance schools was on similar lines to that of the " C " Schools, though the night and cross-country flights were of longer duration and undertaken in all types of weather. After completion of the course, bomber and reconnaissance crews were usually posted to an operational unit, having passed through a total training of between 18 months to 2 years with approximately 250 hours of flying.

---

[1] The " wings " took the form of an oval metal badge embodying an eagle, and worn on the left pocket. (See Goering's photograph in the Prologue to this book.)

21. The prospective fighter pilot, on being awarded his pilot's certificate and badge, passed on to a Fighter School and took a three months' course in elementary fighter types which eventually led to training on the operational Me.109 or twin-engined Me.110. He might be given some 50 hours' flying, in either of the latter, so that before being posted to an operational squadron he would have done a total of some 200 hours' flying.

22. Dive-bomber training at a specialised Dive-Bomber School lasted about four months. The pupil would make about 15 flights of dive-bombing practice with an instructor, and would then dive-bomb solo. As the strain on pilots was considerable, the maximum number of solo dives permitted in a day was about 15. The normal training height of dive was from 12,000 ft. to the bomb release and pull-out at 3,000 ft. The main purpose of the course was to achieve dive-bombing accuracy ; tactics and navigation were only of secondary importance.

Observer Training

23. One of the most interesting aspects of pre-war Air Force training was that of observers. In a German bomber the observer was to be the captain of the aircraft ; thus he had to be the most experienced crew member, and capable of taking over the duties of other members of the crew in an emergency. His training, therefore, was both comprehensive and varied. He was trained as a pilot up to the " C " standard, i.e., had done some 150 hours' flying as a pilot. He then went to an Observer School, where he began an intensive course in navigation and night flying, lasting from nine months to a year. In addition to navigation instruction, observers were also expected to train in radio, gunnery and bomb-aiming, as well as to pass through a blind flying school. Soon after outbreak of war the rule of the observer being the captain of the aircraft was dropped, and observer training deteriorated progressively from 1942 onwards. Finally, observers were only receiving 4-6 months' training.

Wartime Modifications in Training

24. This general scheme of Luftwaffe flying training was only in force in the pre-war period ; once the war began, one modification took place after another. For instance, in 1940, operational Training Schools (*Ergaenzungsgruppen*) and Reserve Training Units (*Ergaenzungstaffeln* and *Gruppen*) were established to give pilots further training after completing the course at the specialised bomber or fighter school. Here the pilot would receive training on the type of aircraft in which he was to specialise, and would learn tactical methods peculiar to the employment of the individual aircraft he was to fly and of the unit to which he was to be posted. In addition, of course, the war brought in many *ad hoc* training courses. For instance, before the war, there were no night fighter training schools, and in the early stages of night flighting, the specialised final training of the pilots was outside the basic Luftwaffe training scheme. Again, special anti-shipping training courses for operational units were constantly being run at airfields on the Baltic coast, while in the squadrons themselves training flights, particularly with new crew members, were a constant feature.

Parachute Training

25. Pre-war parachute training in the Luftwaffe was in three stages. The first consisted of a disciplinary course similar to the normal infantryman's army training. The next stage was at the Parachute Training School proper

and lasted two months. The final stage was an attachment to a parachute unit, the training lasting six months. Before proceeding to the unit the German parachutist would have made some six jumps from about 400 ft., and in the final jump would be one of a parachute descent in company strength from about 10 aircraft. There were about five Parachute Schools in Germany prior to the outbreak of war, each capable of training over 1,000 parachutists. The limitation was in the setting up of air transport units to train with the paratroop units. At the outbreak of war, although there were some 500 transport aircraft which theoretically might have been used for paratroop operations, only about 200 were permanently available in regular units of the Luftwaffe. The remaining aircraft, which were brought in when large-scale paratroop or transport operations were undertaken, had to be borrowed from advanced twin-engined pilot training schools when the occasion arose.

Output of Aircrew in 1939

26. On the eve of the outbreak of war the Luftwaffe training scheme was turning out between 10,000 and 15,000 pilots a year, a number in excess of the current requirements of the German Air Force. This output was achieved by between 75 and 100 flying training schools, of which 40 to 50 covered the elementary A and B courses and the rest were specialist schools—fighter, dive-bomber, signals armament instructor, photographic, observer, blind flying, etc. The creation of operational training and reserve training units in 1940 is explained partly by the desire to re-absorb some of the surplus Luftwaffe pilots graduating from specialist schools.

Breakdown of Training in 1942

27. By 1942, in spite of the territorial expansion of Luftwaffe training all over Europe, the training organisation, efficient and well organised at the outbreak of war, was beginning to crack. As a result of heavy casualties sustained by the German armed forces in the summer of 1941 and the winter of 1941-42, German manpower was reaching a point where either industry or the armed forces could only be reinforced at the expense of the other. In 1939, the German manpower and flying training organisations were efficiently groomed to fight short successful campaigns ; they were not groomed for reverses such as the Battle of Britain, or the wastage resulting from protracted and sustained operations in Europe caused by the rising tide of Allied air supremacy.

Organisation of the German Air Force[1]
Reorganisation of Command in 1939

28. By February, 1939, the increased size of the Luftwaffe, and also of the area over which it was disposed, necessitated a large-scale reorganisation to bring the machinery of command into line with this expansion. Thus, early in that month radical changes were made, both in the High Command and in the organisation of the commands in the field. Firstly, the offices of Secretary of State for Air and Inspector-General of the Luftwaffe were combined under the latter title and remained under Milch. Kesselring had replaced Wever,

---

[1] In this history, the German terms denoting the various types of operational commands, flying units, etc., will be employed. Table 1 will be a useful source of reference if the reader is to refresh his mind from time to time as to terminology. The present part of this chapter is an explanation of that table, and should be studied before a reading of the history is attempted.

the first Chief of Air Staff on the latter's death in an accident in 1936. Kesselring, however, was a forceful character and potentially troublesome to Goering, and in 1937 was replaced by Stumpff. The latter was now superseded by Jeschonnek, a young officer of forceful character who had previously been in command of the *Lehr Geschwader* at Greifswald, and therefore had acquired a lively appreciation of the potentialities of Luftwaffe aircraft equipment ; he was a strong protagonist of the fast medium bomber.

29. The operational flying units of the Air Force were now subordinated to three newly-created operational Commands known as Air Fleets (*Luftflotten*), commanded respectively by Generals Kesselring, Felmy and Sperrle. Luftflotte 1 had its headquarters in Berlin and covered northern and eastern Germany, Luftflotte 2, with headquarters at Brunswick, covered north-west Germany, and Luftflotte 3—which with Luftflotte 2 was to form the attacking force in the Battle of Britain—had its headquarters at Munich, and covered south-west Germany. There was, in addition, a separate Air Command in East Prussia. A month later, in March, 1939, a fourth Luftflotte covering south-east Germany, Austria and the Czech territory was established at Vienna and was placed under the Command of General Loehr who, it will be remembered, came over from the Austrian Air Force after the annexation of Austria. It will be noted that these Luftflotten, the operational Commands and future striking forces of the German Air Force, were organised on a territorial basis[1] and not, as with the Royal Air Force, functionally. Each Air Fleet contained self-contained and balanced striking forces, composed of bomber, fighter, ground attack, reconnaissance and other units.

The Air Ministry

30. The German Air Ministry at the outbreak of war was divided into roughtly 15 main departments or directorates. There was in the first instance an Operational Staff (*Fuehrungsstab*) which had sub-departments for navigation, weather, technical matters, propaganda, publicity, politics, security, etc. This Staff made the operational decisions and issued Air Ministry operational orders. Quite separate from the Operational Staff was a General Staff divided into five or six main departments which dealt with the formation of new squadrons and new ground organisations. One whole department dealt with tactics. Another main department dealt with supplies, maintenance and transport, a further main department dealt with intelligence. Yet another administered the allocation of aircraft, motor transport and anti-aircraft guns, and at the same time investigated aircraft casualties and allocation of aircrews ; there were also Directorates of Signals, Equipment, Postings, Training, etc. A Central Office existed to deal with questions of Air Ministry establishments, while its sub-departments dealt with the press, legal matters and such miscellaneous subjects as the printing services and the Air Attaché branch. An Administrative Department covered pay, claims and finance, buildings and accommodation, rations and clothing. There was also a main department for air communications which covered air control, the meteorological service and the German Air Force security service. Finally, there was a group of about 15 Inspectorates, each of which covered a special subject such as A.R.P., the medical services, education, navigation, parachute and airborne forces, naval co-operation, motor transport, signals, etc. There were also special

---

[1] See Map 1.

GENERALOBERST HANS JESCHONNEK

Born 9.4.99. Entered an Infantry Regiment in 1914. Transferred to the Flying Corps August, 1917, pilot with Jagdstaffel 40. Belonged to a Cavalry Regiment after the war and served in the Reichswehr Ministry. Transferred to the Air Force in September, 1933, as Staff Officer to the Secretary of State for Air, Oberst Milch. Appointed head of the operations staff of the General Staff April, 1937. Chief of the General Staff of the Air Force from February, 1939, to August, 1943, when he committed suicide.

The Return from Spain : Ceremonial parade of the Condor Legion before Hitler in Berlin. Richthofen may be seen on the right, and the bulky form of Sperrle on the left centre.

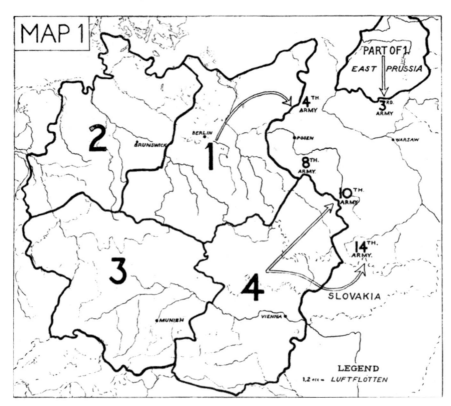

OPERATIONAL AREAS OF COMMANDS
OUTBREAK OF WAR, ATTACK ON POLAND (SEPTEMBER, *1939*)

*This map shows the home areas of the Luftflotten at the beginning of the War,
in September, 1939.*

*The original Luftflotte areas were those of Luftflotten 1, 2 and 3, with headquarters
at Berlin, Brunswick and Munich respectively. The fourth, with headquarters at
Vienna, was added in March, 1939, after Austria and Czechoslovakia had been
annexed. The district of Silesia, previously under Luftflotte 1, was then incorporated
in the new Luftflotte 4.*

*This map also shows the position of the Fliegerdivisions (later known as Flieger-
korps) in Luftflotten 1 and 4 at the opening of the Polish campaign in September,
1939. One of the Fliegerdivisions under Luftflotte 1 (based N.E. Berlin) supported
the 4th Army attacking in a South-easterly direction. Another Fliegerdivision
(based in East Prussia) supported the 3rd Army attacking Southwards. Luftflotte 4
supported the 8th, 10th. and 14th Armies attacking in an Easterly and North-
easterly direction, the main strategy involving a huge pincer intended to enclose
the Polish military forces in the Posen area. There were subsidiary pincers such as
those which dealt with S.W. Poland, tactics which were facilitated by the use of
Czechoslovakia and Silesia as starting-points. (The approximate positions of the
German Armies are shown on this Map.)*

Inspectorates for army co-operation, and for bombers, dive bombers and reconnaissance aircraft; fighter aircraft had a separate Inspectorate to themselves. The function of these Inspectorates was to exercise some control for the Air Ministry over Luftwaffe units in the field. They were to be a link between operational theatres and the Air Ministry. In addition much of their work was concerned with training, and for this purpose they were subordinated to the Directorate of Training.

31. It will be seen from the above that the organisation of the German Air Ministry in the pre-war period was fairly normal. In wartime the number of Inspectorates was increased and the Air Ministry itself was dispersed, but it continued to exercise major control over German Air Force commands in the field.

Composition of the Air Fleet[1]

The Fliegerkorps, Division and Luftgau

32. Within each Air Fleet the administrative work was undertaken by a *Luftgau* (Air District). Whilst the Luftgau organisation was responsible for all administrative matters, the parallel organisation for operational purposes was the Air Division (*Fliegerdivision*)—later renamed Air Corps (*Fliegerkorps*). Before the war there were approximately 10 Luftgau headquarters in Germany, and seven Air Divisions, one of which was a parachute Division. Each Air Fleet would normally consist of two to three Luftgau Commands and might have one or two Air Divisions as its striking force. On paper, the organisation of the Air Division and the Luftgau look similar to that of the Air Fleet; each organisation had an operations department, an adjutant's department, a legal department, an administrative department, a signals department and a quartermaster's department, all with many sub-sections. There was, however, a clear-cut division of responsibility in that the Luftflotte issued the orders and directed, the Luftgau undertook the supply and maintenance organisation, and the Air Division constituted the striking force and carried out the operations. This clear-cut division between the flying side of the Air Force and the administrative and supply side is perhaps best exemplified in the case of German Air Force Airfield Commands.

Airfield Commands

33. When a flying unit was in occupation of a German Air Force airfield, the unit commander took precedence over all other officers at the airfield for as long as the flying unit was based there. At the same time there was a permanent airfield command with a staff supplied by the administrative side of the Air Force through the local Luftgau organisation. When a unit left the airfield, the C.O. of the station once again became the senior responsible officer. In each Luftgau there was a number of Airfield Regional Commands (*Flughafenbereich Kommandanturen*), the number varying between two and twelve according to the size and importance of the area. These Airfield Regional Commands, known as Controlling Stations (*Leithorste*), were located at the most important airfields. The Controlling Stations had to make a regular return to the Luftgau on serviceability of airfields and requests for supplies on behalf of all the airfields in their area, and also to see that supplies and

---

[1] See Table 1.

other maintenance services provided by the Luftgau were distributed to the right quarter. An Airfield Regional Command would normally comprise about five main airfields and up to a dozen secondary type airfields called *Einsatzhaefen*.

34. At the beginning of the war, Germany possessed some 250 main and some 150 secondary airfields. The main airfields, at this time measuring some 1,200 yards square, were occupied by the flying units, flying training schools and experimental establishments. The secondary landing grounds were of similar dimensions, but it should be noted that they were not local satellites to the main airfields. They were sited throughout the country, intended for use during manœuvres or in operational necessity. They had at this time few, if any, facilities. There were no hangars and no quarters beyond a few huts occupied by the small staff employed on the maintenance of the landing ground. None of the main German airfields were equipped with paved runways at the beginning of the war, although in 1939 a start was made on paved runway construction at a few major airfields in North-West Germany.

35. In order to prepare the secondary airfields for quick occupation by flying units, it was obviously necessary to instal airfield staffs at short notice. Therefore, each Luftgau had to be prepared to detach enough personnel from its permanent air force stations to man the proportion of these reserve operational airfields within the Luftgau boundaries. This rapid movement, by transport aircraft and motorised columns, was practised during pre-war manœuvres, when the airfields were temporarily occupied by flying units. In this way the Luftwaffe was able to switch operational units from one part of Germany to another at almost a few hours' notice, with the knowledge that airfields would be staffed and ready to receive them. This airfield system within Germany was extended to the occupied territories in the course of the war.

The Flying Units

36. The basic flying unit was the *Gruppe*, which consisted of about 30 aircraft. Every type of flying unit in the German Air Force was organised on the basis of the Gruppe. There was a sub-division into the *Staffel*[1] which had a normal strength of about 9 or 10 aircraft ; each Gruppe therefore contained three Staffeln. Individual Staffeln might be based at separate airfields—or at seaplane bases in the case of sea reconnaissance or patrol aircraft—but in the case of bomber, dive bomber and fighter units, it was normal to base a whole Gruppe of about 30 aircraft at one airfield. Bomber and fighter units were also organised into individual *Geschwader*[2] which normally comprised three Gruppen, that is, a strength of about 90 aircraft. In the pre-war conception the three Gruppen of bombers or fighters were to be based at adjacent airfields, but in war, Gruppen were often detached from their parent Geschwader, and quite often smaller detachments of aircraft were operated from individual airfields in order to meet some local requirement.

37. The Staffel had a commander known as the *Staffelkapitaen*. Selected officers of the Staffel, usually pilots, were also expected to supervise the technical, signals and navigation branches as spare time work. The Staffel would use the M.T. of its parent Gruppe and sometimes had a mobile repair shop of its own for light repairs. The numbers of aircrew in the Staffel naturally varied according to crew strength of aircraft. The ground personnel of a Staffel

---

[1] Equivalent to the R.A.F. Squadron.

[2] Equivalent to the R.A.F. Group.

TABLE 1

OPERATIONAL CHAIN OF COMMAND IN THE GERMAN AIR FORCE

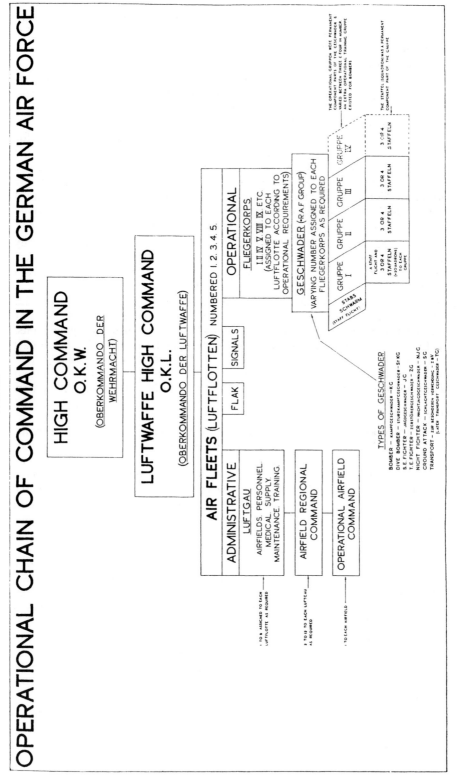

HIGH COMMAND O.K.W.

(OBERKOMMANDO DER WEHRMACHT)

LUFTWAFFE HIGH COMMAND O.K.L.

(OBERKOMMANDO DER LUFTWAFFE)

AIR FLEETS (LUFTFLOTTEN) NUMBERED 1. 2. 3. 4. 5.

ADMINISTRATIVE

LUFTGAU

AIRFIELDS. PERSONNEL. MEDICAL. SUPPLY. MAINTENANCE. TRAINING.

AIRFIELD REGIONAL COMMAND

OPERATIONAL AIRFIELD COMMAND

FLAK

SIGNALS

OPERATIONAL

FLIEGERKORPS

I II IV V VIII IX ETC
(ASSIGNED TO EACH LUFTFLOTTE ACCORDING TO OPERATIONAL REQUIREMENTS)

GESCHWADER (R.A.F GROUP)

VARYING NUMBER ASSIGNED TO EACH FLIEGERKORPS AS REQUIRED

STABS SCHWARM
(STAFF FLIGHT)

GRUPPE I

GRUPPE II

GRUPPE III

GRUPPE IV

A STAFF FLIGHT AND 3 OR 4 STAFFELN (=SQUADRONS) TO EACH GRUPPE

3 OR 4 STAFFELN

3 OR 4 STAFFELN

3. OR 4 STAFFELN

THE OPERATIONAL GRUPPEN WERE PERMANENT COMPONENT PARTS OF THE GESCHWADER & VARIED BETWEEN THREE & FOUR IN NUMBER. AN EXTRA OPERATIONAL TRAINING GRUPPE EXISTED FOR BOMBERS

THE STAFFEL (SQUADRON) WAS A PERMANENT COMPONENT PART OF THE GRUPPE

TYPES OF GESCHWADER

BOMBER — KAMPFGESCHWADER — KG
DIVE BOMBER — STURZKAMPFGESCHWADER — St.KG
S.E. FIGHTER — JAGDGESCHWADER — JG
T.E. FIGHTER — ZERSTÖRERGESCHWADER — ZG
NIGHT FIGHTER — NACHTJAGDGESCHWADER — NJG
GROUND ATTACK — SCHLACHTGESCHWADER — SG
TRANSPORT — ZUR BESONDERN VERWENDUNG — ZbV
(LATER TRANSPORT GESCHWADER — TG)

1 TO 4 ASSIGNED TO EACH LUFTFLOTTE AS REQUIRED

2 TO 12 TO EACH LUFTGAU AS REQUIRED

1 TO EACH AIRFIELD

comprised about 150 in the case of a single-engined fighter unit, and about 80 for a twin-engined fighter unit. The twin-engined Staffel had a smaller ground staff because much of their servicing and administration was done for them by the permanent airfield staffs.

38. The Gruppe normally had a total of about 500 ground personnel in the case of single-engined fighters and about 300 in the case of twin-engined types. The Gruppe had a commanding officer, an adjutant, an operations officer who might be responsible for navigation and signals, a technical officer and a medical officer. In contrast to R.A.F. policy there was no whole-time intelligence officer appointed at Staffel or Gruppe levels. Even though the Gruppen and Staffeln of a fighter or bomber Geschwader might be separated, the headquarters staff of the Geschwader remained as a separate headquarters and consisted of a commanding officer, adjutant, operations officer, organisation officer, intelligence officer, navigation officer, technical officer, signals officer, photographic officer and meteorological officer. The Geschwader Staff (*Stab*) also had a few operational-type aircraft of its own which flew when circumstances demanded, often on reconnaissance work.

Strength of the Air Fleet

39. While the size of Staffeln, Gruppen and Geschwader was fairly constant at the outbreak of the war, the strength of the Luftflotten and Fliegerdivisionen varied enormously. With a first-line strength of about 4,000, the average strength of a 1939-40 German Air Fleet would be 1,000 aircraft. When the war against Poland was under preparation, operational units from the western Luftflotten (Numbers 2 and 3) were naturally transferred to the eastern Air Fleets (Luftflotten 1 and 4) which were to undertake the attack on Poland. During the various periods of the war, the strength of an Air Fleet varied between a minimum of 200 to 300 aircraft and a maximum of some 1,250 aircraft.

40. The Air Division (Fliegerdivision) within an Air Fleet, which would consist of all types of flying units—bomber, dive bomber, fighter and reconnaissance—had a minimum of about 200 to 300 aircraft and a maximum of about 700 to 750 aircraft. The size of the Air Division (later renamed Fliegerkorps (Air Corps)) and of the Air Fleet was always dependent on the overall strategy of the German Air Force, tempered by the exigencies of the local situation.

Signals

41. No small part of the success of the German Air Force in the early campaigns of the war was due to the high degree of organisation of the Signals Service, which formed an integral part of the Air Force. The Signals undertook the following duties : the transmission of all orders and communications, if possible both by landline (telephone and teleprinter) and by wireless telegraphy and telephony ; the establishment and supervision of all navigational aids, such as W/T, D/F and radio and visual beacons ; defensive work against air attack through the Observer Corps ; the interception of enemy signals traffic ; the control of German air traffic ; the German Air Safety Service and certain rescue services.

42. The C.-in-C. of the German Air Force had at his disposal a command network through which he could communicate with all the different authorities of the Air Force. Each operational command, including the Air Fleets, Air

Corps and Air Divisions and the non-flying Luftgau organisations, had their own signals units. The signals units were divided into regiments and sub-divided again into companies, each company dealing with a specialist aspect. Each company in turn had a number of platoons, which were again sub-divided into detachments. The typical regiment might comprise nine companies, of which the first might consist of telephone and teleprinter operators, the second W/T operators, whilst the third might specialise in army co-operation work. Other companies of the regiment would specialise in telephone construction, aircraft reporting, aircraft safety service or radio interception. Some regiments had attached to them signals aircraft, generally Ju.52's, which in campaigns or invasions landed on forward airfields and acted as advanced radio or D/F stations. Like the rest of the Air Force ground organisation, the signals regiments were organised for mobile warfare. Those attached to the operational commands had the duty of laying out communications networks as soon as newly-occupied territory was taken over, as well as the erection and supervision of radio and visual beacons, etc. In addition to the above framework, each major group of airfields had its own signals company for organising communications in its area. Each major formation of 100 fighters or bombers also had its own signals company and each group of 30 operational aircraft had a signals platoon.

43. The command network was linked to the C.-in-C. of the Army and the C.-in-C. of the Navy and each operational command had signals links with the anti-aircraft artillery, supply depôts, major airfields and, of course, the flying formations. For air defence, there were special signals networks, linking with civil defence and first aid centres ; a large proportion of these networks grew out of the existing German Post Office service.

44. Taken as a whole, the Luftwaffe signals organisation on the eve of the European war was very competent to deal with most aspects of modern air warfare. There were perhaps two major weaknesses. The first was the failure at this stage to develop radar either for defensive or offensive purposes and the second was the rather primitive nature of the Air Force ground control of fighter formations.

German Air Policy—The Rôle of the Luftwaffe in War

The German Lead in Experience

45. Before the reader is taken to the opening campaign of the second World War, it is opportune to examine the policy of the German Air Force at the time of the final stages of preparation in the summer of 1939. Between 1935 and that year the Luftwaffe had grown up to adulthood, its organisation and equipment had now been regularised, and its resources were ready to back Hitler's political moves. The time was ripe for its employment in a European war provided that a series of quick *Blitzkrieg*[1] successes could be achieved. The Luftwaffe staff had had more practical experience of modern flying than any other air force, and in the employment of aircraft on a large scale in its widespread commercial air lines, in the war in Spain, in manoeuvres and in the annexation of Austria and Czechoslovakia, it had learnt something of the

---

[1] A term meaning " Lightning War " which was much used by Hitler and Goering in public speeches, and as part of the German propaganda campaign to produce a fear of the Luftwaffe. The word was adopted in England in 1940 as " Blitz ".

limitations imposed by weather and terrain, and of the many difficulties which could crop up in the production and employment of large numbers of modern aircraft.

Air Staff College Lectures

46. Perhaps the most comprehensive and authoritative ideas of the rôle the Luftwaffe was intended to play in war can be obtained from the lectures delivered by the German Air Force to its staff college at Gatow during this period. The ideas and principles expressed in these lectures certainly formed the basis of the policy of German air operations in the first year of the War, although inevitably air policy had to be constantly revised. The German Air Force as a whole, although constitutionally an independent arm of the armed forces, was obviously not expected to conduct an independent war. It was intended to operate tactically in support of both the Army and the Navy, as well as conducting, at certain stages, strategic warfare of its own in defence of German cities and industries or in the attack on enemy industry, shipping and communications. It should be stressed straight away that the German conception of strategic warfare was different from that of the Western Allies. Whereas the Allies often thought of strategic attack in the form of long-term as well as long-range bombing, strategic bombing was for the Luftwaffe a short-term and often short-range affair. The German Air Force thought in terms of air *Blitzkrieg* and their strategic attack on the enemy Air Force or enemy industrial centres was intended to be the immediate prelude to an army follow-up. The Allied bombing of Sicily, Sardinia and Italy which preceded the invasion of Sicily in July, 1943, corresponds roughly to the German conception of strategic attack.

The Influence of Douhet (Doctrine of Attack)

47. The keynote of German air policy was the theory of attack, in which the influence of Douhet is apparent. This insistance on attack occurs time and time again in Luftwaffe staff lectures. Nor was it mere theory, for about 40 per cent. of the Luftwaffe at the outbreak of war consisted of bomber and dive-bomber units, whereas only 25 to 30 per cent. were fighter units, and even some of these—the twin-engined—were thought of partly as fighter-bombers to give tactical support to the Army. The defence of Germany by fighter aircraft was a secondary consideration and no night fighter units had been formed ; the major burden of the permanent home defences was in the hands of the anti-aircraft units. An initial assault by the Luftwaffe was to be directed against the enemy air force, including its supporting aircraft and aero-engine factories and ground installations, in order to gain air superiority from the outset. Surprise was to be the essence of these opening operations. The next stage in the Luftwaffe attack policy was in some sense strategic in concept. Vital enemy centres, now uncovered through their depleted air defences, were to be assailed with maximum bombing forces. Production centres, food supplies, ports, railway and traffic centres, military recruiting centres, government and administrative centres, are cited as examples for the second phase of air attack. The bombing of Rotterdam in May, 1940, and of Belgrade come into this category and were, therefore, part of normal Luftwaffe strategic bomber policy.

48. Thus, the Luftwaffe, in applying tactical bombing power in co-operation with the Army, supported it whole-heartedly, and as a matter of deliberate policy was prepared to throw in its long-range bomber force for strategic

operations intended to aid the Army in its decisive engagements. The conception of co-operation with the Army was generous as it was efficient in details of aircraft recognition and wireless signals in the field. There was promptness in bombing, and accuracy, intensiveness and effectiveness in the execution of operations.

The Night Bomber

49. A further point in Luftwaffe pre-war bomber policy was that both day and night attacks were part of Luftwaffe planning. Until the summer of 1940, practically no night bombing operations were undertaken, though one or two were carried out in the Spanish war, but both in training, staff planning and general strategical conception, the night bomber was to play an important part right from the beginning. At the Staff College, tactics in night bombing operations formed the subject of lectures, and although the Luftwaffe realised that such operations did not promise the quick success of day operations, their value was undoubtedly realised in 1939.

The Dive Bomber

50. In view of the almost legendary reputation of the Ju.87 dive bomber in the first year or so of the War, it is important to attempt to clarify its position in the Luftwaffe concept of air warfare. The German Air Staff itself in 1938–39 was divided on the subject of dive bombing and the employment of the Ju.87, but the majority opinion was that it should be used in both strategic air warfare and in co-operation with the Army. The dive bomber, said the German Air Force Staff, was intended to destroy vital objectives in the heart of enemy industrial centres as well as bridges, ammunition, fuel and food dumps ; with the Spanish experience as an example, it was also appreciated that dive-bombing attacks would affect the morale of front-line troops. Tactically, it was to co-operate with the Army, both in supporting its advance and in holding up the advance of the enemy. In short, the employment of the dive bomber was in German Air Staff opinion not to be very different from that of the long-range bomber. In some phases of the Polish and French campaigns it was used much more for softening up the enemy generally and for attacking communications of vital rear areas, than for directly supporting the Army in the battle area.

51. The fact is that at the outbreak of War the German Air Staff was not yet clear as to which types of bomber were suitable for close-support work. In actual practice the Luftwaffe concentrated all the striking power available to co-operate with the Army, the aircraft consisting of dive-bomber types together with any ground-attack fighters and high-level bombers which could be made available. The overriding German theory of employing maximum forces at the decisive point of the battle, took precedence over any local theory of the tactical employment of this or that aircraft type.

Naval Air Policy

52. An interesting aspect of the pre-war German theory of naval co-operation was the planned use of dive bombers in co-operation with the Navy for the destruction of enemy shipping. The offensive equipment of the aircraft carrier *Graf Zeppelin* launched at Kiel in 1938, was intended to be the Ju.87, but the limited range of this aircraft, which in practice had a radius of action of less

than 100 miles, was soon recognised. In the Norwegian campaign of April-May, 1940, experimental extra tanks were fitted to the land-based Ju.87's, and in some of the early versions of the longer range Ju.88 twin-engined bomber, dive-bombing brakes were specially installed. In the end, the Luftwaffe failed to produce a dive bomber of extra range, and the overwhelming bulk of bombing attacks on enemy shipping were made by normal twin-engined bombers in low-level or high-level attacks.

53. The employment of torpedo carrying aircraft was naturally part of Luftwaffe pre-war air plans, but in spite of the obvious importance of this air arm to them, they were incredibly backward in developing torpedo bombing. German air theory believed in combined attacks by bombers and torpedo bombers, and they theoretically divided their He.115 squadrons into bomber and torpedo flights, believing that twin attack carried out simultaneously would promise the greatest measure of success. But once again deficient equipment made German air theory rather empty. The He.59 and He.115 floatplanes, intended at this juncture to carry out the first combined torpedo and bomber attacks, never carried out a single combined operation. Under war conditions, Luftwaffe torpedo bomber theories had to be completely recast[1].

54. It was in the rôle of reconnaissance and patrol, conceived at the time of the Spanish War, that the Luftwaffe succeeded best in its support of German naval operations. Even here it was not the pre-war Naval Air Arm with short-range floatplanes and longer range flying boats which produced the most successful war-time reconnaissance results, but rather the land-based reconnaissance aircraft supported in offshore patrols by local fighter units. As for shipborne reconnaissance, German cruisers and battleships, when they did put to sea, were quite adequately served by their Arado and Heinkel floatplanes[2].

55. In summary, 1935-39 German naval air theory conceived of a separate Naval Air Arm equipped with floatplanes, flying boats and naval fighter squadrons undertaking the responsibility of co-operating offensively and defensively with the Navy. The arbitrament of war proved that the pre-war judgment of the German Air Staff was unsound. By 1940, the Naval Air Arm was being partially re-equipped with land-based types and was becoming gradually absorbed into the main stream of Luftwaffe units. Neither Goering, Milch nor Udet paid the pre-war attention to naval air warfare which the subject deserved. The failure to complete the aircraft carrier *Graf Zeppelin* in the War is symbolic of the rather lethargic attitude of the German Air Staff to naval co-operation in the 1935-39 period. When the full implications of the Battle of the Atlantic were realised in 1941, energetic measures, it is true, were taken, and intensive anti-shipping training was carried out, crack German land-based bomber squadrons being set aside for almost unique employment in attacks on shipping. As will be seen in Chapter IV, specially created anti-shipping operational commands were but belated attempts to repair the mistakes of the pre-war period ; as the two-front and then three-front war made increasing demands on the bomber units, and as the cream of the bomber crews were lost on operations, German hopes of building up the anti-shipping arm were bound to recede.

---

[1] See Chapter 4, paragraphs 75–79.

[2] Illustration on page 98.

The Fighter Force

56. German conception of the employment of fighter aircraft was not in a very developed stage on the eve of war. The majority of the fighter force was intended for employment over the battle area, the wide plan allowing for the allocation of some 25 fighter Staffeln for the defence of the Ruhr and Western Germany, i.e., less than a third of the total fighter strength. In support of ground operations, one of the main functions of the single-engined fighter units was to prevent or hinder activities by enemy reconnaissance aircraft. In addition, single-engined fighter units were intended to protect and escort bomber and dive-bomber formations operating against enemy ground targets.

57. From 1938 onwards the Luftwaffe had developed the Me.110 twin-engined fighter ; called the " heavy " or " destroyer " fighter (*Zerstoerer*). The rôle of this fighter was theoretically to be the pursuit of enemy formations operating over the Reich or returning over their own territory. In point of fact many squadrons of these aircraft were employed as fighter-bombers in the early war campaigns. The twin-engined fighter was something new in German pre-war concepts, and in the Staff College lectures its experimental nature was constantly emphasised.

58. Single- and twin-engined fighter squadrons were allotted to coastal air defence as part of their co-operation with the German Navy. In actual practice, however, no permanent allocation of such fighter units was possible. In the early months of the war, when fighter units were readily available, the German Fleet at Kiel and Wilhelmshaven had adequate air protection, but when fighter units were later required for the defence of the Reich and for tactical work over the battle areas, the Fleet had to be left occasionally with little or no fighter cover. This applied particularly to the German Fleet anchorage in Norway after 1940. Not only did the German pre-war plan for fighter defence for the Navy fail to materialise, but the 25 squadrons earmarked for the defence of the Ruhr were soon borrowed in 1940 for other fighter duties, in particular for the coastal defence of the huge new European coastline stretching from Trondheim to Bordeaux. *Blitzkrieg* brought the exciting fruits of dazzling and easy victories, but it also brought new areas of fighter patrol and prevented the German Air Force from implementing many of its pre-war theories about the orthodox employment of its limited fighter forces.

59. In the defence of the industrial areas of Germany both single and twin-engined fighters were to be employed in close co-operation with the anti-aircraft defences, which were relied upon as the main defence against air attack. It should be pointed out that Germany's pre-war anti-aicraft units were an élite body of men and members of the Luftwaffe, and that they were probably more effective in hindering enemy air operations and shooting down or damaging enemy bombers, fighters and reconnaissance aircraft than any other anti-aircraft organisation in Europe. Germany was organised into fighter patrol areas which overlapped so that raiding bomber formations could be fought continuously. The German view was that attacks were to be made with maximum forces on the main bomber forces ; attacks with partial fighter forces were to be reserved for straggling bombers only. The Germans had not developed fighter control on any scale at the outbreak of war, let alone an early warning radar system. They had an efficient aircraft reporting system, to which both anti-aircraft and fighter units were linked, and which was capable of informing them fully on the current air situation. The failure to use ground

45

control interception was not due to lack of radio equipment, but to the German pre-war view that the fighter pilot should be allowed to operate on his own initiative. After the experience of the Battle of Britain, and when Germany herself was threatened with large-scale daylight air assault in 1942, this view of the ground control of fighter aircraft was modified, and an elaborate system of control of large fighter formations was evolved.

60. In general, Luftwaffe conception of the employment of fighters was orthodox, but there was considerable conflict of view in the German Air Staff as to the best method of their employment. There were some who thought that greater stress should be laid on the strategic use of fighters for defence of Germany. Others held the view that the Luftwaffe should have made more use of its fighters as fighter-bombers for tactical support of the Army. There were also the protagonists of the night fighter, which was hardly in the experimental stage in the pre-war Luftwaffe. Eventually the circumstances of war canalised these different conceptions and compelled the Luftwaffe to be employed according to the ever-changing demands of the war situation.

Reconnaissance
61. Great stress was naturally laid on reconnaissance work in pre-war plans. Some of the Luftwaffe's leading Generals even went so far as to say that the military powers which had the most comprehensive reconnaissance would win a war. When one remembers that about 20 per cent. of Luftwaffe pre-war operational squadrons were equipped with reconnaissance and patrol types of aircraft, it will be realised that the German Air Ministry gave practical backing to its reconnaissance doctrines. The most important task was reconnaissance observation of the enemy air force, the complement to the Luftwaffe view that the first task of the bomber and fighter force was to gain air superiority by weakening the enemy air force.

62. The long-range strategic reconnaissance units were relied upon to obtain early indication of enemy plans and thus to provide a basis for German strategic decisions. The short-range tactical reconnaissance units were to watch over the employment and deployment of enemy land forces up to the point where contact was made between the two sides.

63. Realising that the depth of reconnaissance penetration would depend on imponderable factors such as the weather and the state of enemy defences, the Luftwaffe had no planned radius of action for its aircraft. It also expected its aircraft to undertake both day and night reconnaissance.

64. It was postulated that whenever a situation demanded, bomber missions were to be given to the reconnaissance units. In German pre-war air theory, special reconnaissance squadrons were to be organised to follow enemy bomber units to their home bases so that immediate attacks could be carried out on the airfields. These special reconnaissance aircraft were called *Klebeflugzeuge*[1] and they were kept in readiness in each operational area to carry out quick reconnaissance for the follow-up bombing attacks on airfields. In the practice of war, the theory of the *Klebeflugzeuge*, like many other Luftwaffe theories, came to nothing.

65. In the short-range tactical reconnaissance units, emphasis was laid on co-operation with mechanised ground forces, on undertaking artillery spotting and on photographic and visual reconnaissance of enemy movement. A

---

[1] Literally "adhesive aircraft," because they were to stick to the enemy bomber formations.

The Ju.52 Transport

German Four-engined Aircraft
(Above) The FW.200 (Condor).   (Below) The Ju.90

(83331)

squadron of army co-operation reconnaissance aircraft was placed under the orders of each armoured Corps and armoured Division, and in addition every Corps of the German Army was also to have its own reconnaissance squadron comprising about 10 aircraft. In the early battles, this allocation of tactical reconnaissance aircraft to Army formations was in fact made, but from 1941 onwards the tactical reconnaissance units failed to keep pace with the expanding Germany Army, and later on, in 1942, they reverted to Luftwaffe command and were put to Army co-operation work as and when they were available. Some of the squadrons originally working under Army Commands were sometimes diverted to other duties such as sea reconnaissance and costal patrol.

Mobility : The Use of Transport Aircraft

66. The Luftwaffe, believing that mobility was the very essence of concentrating striking forces at the right time and at the right place, naturally made the maximum use of transport aircraft. At the outbreak of war every squadron had one or two transport aircraft on its strength ; these were for routine movements of equipment and personnel. When a big operational move was taking place, however, hundreds of Ju.52's were immediately made available so that bombs, fuel, ammunition, ground staffs, aircraft spares and airfield equipment could be moved quickly from one airfield to another. Moreover, the Ju.52 could act as a mobile wireless station, thus helping to ensure the rapid establishment of advanced base communications.

67. It was the development of airborne troops in the Luftwaffe which stimulated the creation of a German Air Transport Command. The first unit, of some 40 to 50 Ju.52's, was formed in 1938. From that time onwards the German Air Transport Command expanded hand in hand with the airborne troop and parachute units and in 1939 had reached a total strength of some 250 aircraft. However, in the case of large-scale operations the needs of the 7th Air Division (the Airborne Troop Command) had from the very beginning to be met by drawing upon transport-type aircraft from advanced training schools. This created many administrative difficulties which were fairly easily smoothed over in the early war operations. But once the Luftwaffe felt the strain of prolonged air operations from 1941 onwards the hiatus between the two sources of transport aircraft broadened, and reorganisation of the German Air Transport Command was necessary.

The Heavy Bomber

68. The most striking omission in Luftwaffe pre-war plans was the four-engined bomber. The Dornier, Junkers, Heinkel and Focke-Wulf firms each produced a good four-engined aircraft in the pre-war period, but only the Ju.90 and the F.W.200 went into serious production, and then only in small numbers, for they were used exclusively as Lufthansa transport aircraft in the 1935-39 period. High-ranking German Air Force Officers interrogated after the war, have considered that it was the personal prejudice of Ernst Udet which was the main reason for the German failure to develop the four-engined bomber. It is certainly true that Udet was enamoured of the twin-engined medium bomber, and thought that the four-engined bomber would be too slow and vulnerable for modern air operations. An equally important factor, however, was Germany's need to equip the largest possible air force in the quickest possible time. Already the Luftwaffe had had to undergo wholesale re-equipment in the 1937-39 period which had meant the re-tooling of the aircraft industry and

a slowing down of aircraft production. If the Luftwaffe had indulged in a programme of four-engined bomber production, a further slowing down of the industry would have been entailed ; indeed, in engines alone the extra demands would have overloaded the industry, to say nothing of increased fuel requirements. Moreover, the Luftwaffe was designed at this juncture to operate mainly in support of land battles, and four-engined bombers would not have been well suited to this purpose.

Conclusion

69. It is difficult to summarise the intended rôle of the Luftwaffe on the eve of the second World War. Ideas on air power, both in Germany and elsewhere, were at this time in an experimental stage, and Germany was as advanced in this sphere as any other country. The Luftwaffe's main rôle was to annihilate enemy air power and then to give the army maximum support. Had the campaigns from the Battle of Britain onwards gone according to plan and a series of short, sharp victories had been achieved—as indeed they were in Poland, Norway, the Low Countries and France—the theories of the German Air Force Staff would have been sound enough. But, in the event, the war was prolonged and Allied air opposition compelled the Luftwaffe in the very first year of war to modify its pre-war conceptions. Four-engined bombers were needed for the long Atlantic Ocean anti-shipping patrols, and night fighters were required to defend Germany against the growing weight of Royal Air Force bombing. In general, it may be said that after the first year or so of war it was only in the field of tactical support of the Army, in which it remained supreme until 1941, that the Luftwaffe adhered to its pre-war theories.

PART TWO

The German Air Force on the Offensive (1939–1942)

CHAPTER 3

THE FIRST FLUSH OF TACTICAL SUCCESS : FROM WARSAW TO THE FALL OF FRANCE

The Battle of Poland (1st-28th September, 1939)

War—Goering's Order of the Day

1. Early in August, 1939, Goering issued an Order of the Day to the Luftwaffe which echoed the enormous German confidence in their Air Force, and was a measure of the tremendous fear amongst European nations of the possible consequences of any attempt at resistance to its strength—a fear increased threefold by German propaganda in press and radio. This order may well be contrasted with the final words of the German Chief of Air Staff in 1945, quoted in the epilogue to this book. Goering's order of August, 1939, appears as the prologue to this book.

September, 1939—Vindication of German Theory

2. The Polish campaign, begun on 1st September, 1939, and completed by September 28th was, from the German Air Force point of view, the supreme test of all the theories of air warfare on which the Air Force had been built up ; in its overwhelming success it was viewed as the complete justification of all the hopes and principles which had been enumerated consistently by the German Air Staff and tested experimentally in Spain. The principles laid down for the employment of the Luftwaffe were simple and direct. First and foremost was the concentration of all available effort on one specific task ; only when the one task was completed was there to be any diversion of effort towards the next. It was the theory of the *Blitzkrieg*[1] ; the elimination, stage by stage, of each and every obstacle which might frustrate the freedom of movement of the ground forces. It was an art of war which attributed to the Air Force almost every possibility except that of occupation of enemy territory. It was ideal for the type of continental warfare which the German High Command had planned. It was inadequate and impossible of realisation as soon as Germany's enemies ceased to allow themselves to be tackled singly and when warfare became something more than a series of isolated campaigns where German air supremacy was unchallenged.

3. Luftflotten 1 and 4, commanded by General Kesselring and General Loehr respectively, occupied the eastern areas of Germany and the annexed territories of Austria and Czechoslovakia, and it was to these two Luftflotten that the task of supporting the campaign in Poland fell. Luftflotte 1 was assigned to the support of the 3rd and 4th Armies in Prussia, Luftflotte 4 to the 8th, 10th and 14th Armies in the Wartheland, Silesia and Slovakia, respectively (see MAP 1). In Command of the operational Divisions subordinated to these two Luftflotten were Generals Wimmert and Grauert to the North and Generals Loerzer and Richthofen to the South. In all between

---

[1] Lightning war.

C*

1,550-1,600 aircraft were available for employment against the Poles, whose Air Force numbered no more than 400 to 500 first-line aircraft. The destruction of these aircraft, together with the dislocation of the whole air force organisation was the first objective of the Luftwaffe, for only after the establishment of complete air superiority could the German Air Force provide the unfettered concentration of effort in support of the ground troops which was its aim.

The Course of Operations

4. After widespread reconnaissance of all the principal Polish airfields early in the morning of September 1st, the whole of the German striking force of Do.17's, He.111's, Ju.87's accompanied by both single- and twin-engined fighters was turned, with complete surprise, to the destruction of the Polish Air Force before it could take part in the campaign that was now launched. On the first day widespread destruction was caused at the airfields of Kattowitz, Cracow, Lwow, Radom, Lublin, Wilna, Lida Grodno, Warsaw and many others. So complete was the surprise delivered that at many airfields, including even the important airfield of Radom, not even A.A. fire was encountered. That proportion of the Polish fighter force which was successful in getting into the air to meet the attacking forces was effectively warded off by the escorting Me.109's and Me.110's ; the Do.17 bombers and Ju.87 dive bombers were then able to deliver both low- and high-level attacks with little opposition. By the end of the first day large numbers of Polish aircraft were already destroyed on the ground and the greatest and most important part of the ground organisation was very seriously damaged. On the second day, Luftwaffe operations were renewed from early morning, with the most important airfields as well as a large number of fresh ones again as the objective. Such success was gained that by the end of this day superiority was complete : such Polish aircraft as remained intact had dispersed to small isolated landing grounds with no communications and hence no possibility of co-ordinated operations.

5. On September 3rd, whilst the Polish Air Force, and more particularly the Polish aircraft industry, still remained the first objective, some diversion of effort was possible. The first impetus of the advance of the ground forces had left many strong points and nests of resistance in the rear and it was to the reduction of these that a diversion of air effort was now directed. From September 3rd onwards the German Air Force turned its full weight to its second task—full co-operation with the Army for the destruction of the Polish Army.

6. This co-operation took the form of direct support in the bombing and strafing of strong points, artillery batteries and concentrations whenever the Poles sought to make a stand, all with the object of furthering the freedom of movement of the Army. Indirect support was also given by the bombing of depots, dumps, barracks, and factories in order to dislocate the supply organisation. Rear lines of communication—railways, stations, bridges and road junctions were also heavily attacked, with the object of preventing the bringing up of fresh forces to the battle areas. Further close co-ordination between the Army and the Air Force was shown in the use of transport aircraft for the bringing up of supplies for the armoured divisions operating far forward of the infantry. No time was lost in moving operational units forward into captured airfields, and the efficiency and flexibility of the servicing and communications organisations were clearly demonstrated.

A German photograph of the bombing of Warsaw airfield. Compare this scale of bombing with that of the Anglo-American bomber forces in 1945, shown in the picture of Rheine airfield on page 337.

A Ju.87 Dive Bomber in Action
(From the German film " Stukas ")

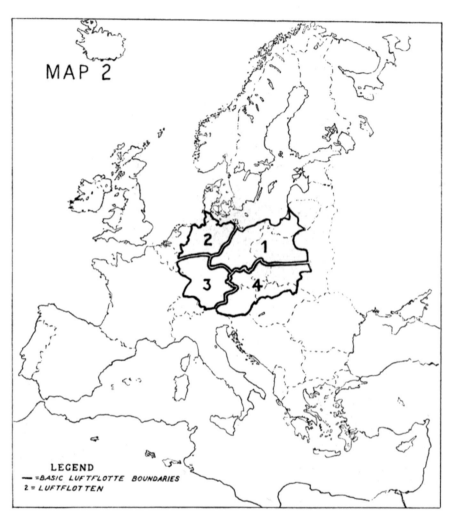

MAP 2

LEGEND
— =BASIC LUFTFLOTTE BOUNDARIES
2 = LUFTFLOTTEN

OPERATIONAL AREAS OF COMMANDS
END OF BATTLE OF POLAND (OCTOBER, *1939*)

This map shows the home areas of the Luftflotten as at October, 1939, at the end of the Polish campaign and covers the period sometimes described as that of the " phoney " war. Both Luftflotte 1 and Luftflotte 4 have their home areas enlarged eastwards into Poland—as far East as the German occupation of Poland went at that time. The home Luftgaus (administrative areas within the Luftflotten) were enlarged, and a new one established, so as to cover the newly-occupied territory (compare Map 1).

7. By September 17th, the end of the campaign was in sight, with the fall of Warsaw imminent and the Polish Army no longer a co-ordinated force. On this day withdrawals of German units for the West began, so complete was the German victory. Throughout the next week continuous attempts were made to convince the Commander of Warsaw that resistance was futile, but these attempts proving of no avail, preparations were made for a large-scale air attack on the city. Thus, on September 25th, continuous air attacks were made all day supported by the guns of the Army and of the Flak brigades, and the assault of the city was launched. With the capitulation of Warsaw on September 27th the campaign came to an end.

8. The outstanding success of the campaign was the successful use of the Ju.87 dive bomber. With little or no opposition to hamper them the units equipped with this aircraft were able to exploit the accuracy of bomb aiming inherent in the steep dive, as well as the demoralising effect on personnel exposed to dive-bombing attacks. It was noticeable that in the early phases of the campaign, attacks by all types of aircraft were directed consistently against military targets. Later, the confusion and chaos created among the civilian population, which in turn caused deterioration in military organisation during the course of attacks on military targets situated in thickly-populated areas, did not go unobserved and was, in fact, exploited.

9. The success of the campaign was overwhelming. The contribution of the Luftwaffe to this success was undeniably great, and credence was given to the wildest claims concerning the potentialities of the Air Force. In writing of this campaign, General Loehr, the A.O.C. of Luftflotte 4, stated : '' The Air Force was to operate for the first time in world history as an independent arm. Thereby it was to open up new aspects of a strategy which in its principles had remained unaltered throughout the course of history.'' Later, Kesselring, reflecting on the Polish Campaign, wrote in similar terms : '' Beyond all other military arms, the Luftwaffe, by virtue of its mobility in space, accomplished tasks which in former wars had been inconceivable. . . . The Polish campaign was the touchstone of the potentialities of the German Air Force and an apprenticeship of special significance. In this campaign the Luftwaffe learned many lessons . . . and prepared itself for a second, more strenuous and decisive clash of arms.''

The Norwegian Campaign (9th April-9th June, 1940)

An Invasion : Conception and Plans[1]

10. After the victorious autumn campaign in Poland, the units which had taken part were withdrawn to their bases in Germany and the German Air Force settled down to a winter of rest, refitting and expansion in preparation for the spring campaign in the West in which Holland, Belgium and France were to be subdued and Great Britain invaded. During the winter of 1939-40 operational activity was held at the lowest possible level ; the few fighter units on the western front facing the Maginot Line were forbidden to seek combat, whilst activity against the British Isles was confined to armed reconnaissance of ports and naval bases, with occasional bombing attacks on naval units. Thus, Europe settled down to the winter which came to be known as the '' Phoney War '' during which, however, the Luftwaffe planning staffs were far from idle.

---

[1] See Appendix, paragraph 13.

11. In the projected campaign for the spring of 1940 the German armies were to drive westwards through France, and it was therefore necessary for the Germans to secure their flank in Denmark and Norway against any possible diversion by the enemy. At the same time it was necessary to gain a vital strategic advantage for naval and air warfare against the United Kingdom, an advantage which had been lacking in the 1914-18 war. The basing of strong air formations in Norway and later in western France would materially assist the blockade of Britain by combined sea and air power. The occupation of Norway in particular as a prerequisite to the main campaign was accordingly an essential first step. Its geographical situation, separated from Denmark by the waters of the Skagerrak, and with its main towns only connected by narrow mountain valleys, made the use of large armoured land forces on the Polish scale impossible. With the Polish experience, Denmark could be quickly overcome in this manner, but then the Norwegians would be given an opportunity to mount resistance and call in British help, which might upset the timetable of the whole main campaign in France.

12. The method chosen by the Germans was that of a simultaneous attack on both Denmark and Norway in which surprise would play a large part in securing the main ports and airfields before any outside help could arrive. Once the period of surprise had passed, the problem of the reinforcement and supply of the forces already landed would become acute, since enemy mining of the approaches to the ports and of the Skagerrak could be expected, as well as bombing attacks on the main points already secured. The Germans therefore planned an airborne operation as part of the surprise attack, using paratroops for the swift occupation of vital points, followed by an airborne reinforcement and supply operation, and constituting an entirely new departure in air warfare.

13. By its nature the invasion operation demanded the extremely close integration of Army, Navy and Air forces ; the air aspect of command was placed in the hands of General Geisler, Commander of Fliegerkorps X, formed in the early months of 1940 from Fliegerdivision 10 which had existed since the beginning of the war for the purpose of anti-shipping operations. For the control of the large numbers of transport aircraft to be employed, a special staff known as *Transportchef Land* was created to operate under the control of Fliegerkorps X.

14. By March, 1940, the German plans for the campaign had taken shape, and on the 20th of that month an order outlining final plans for the invasion— known as " Operation Weser "—was issued by Fliegerkorps X to the forces concerned. The plan provided for the surprise landing at dawn of combat troops of the Army from warships and other vessels in the harbours of Oslo, Arendal, Kristiansand, Egersund, Stavanger, Bergen, Trondheim and Narvik. At exactly the same time, the occupation of Denmark was to be accomplished by a surprise march in of German troops with simultaneous landings from the sea at Copenhagen and the Danish Islands. The part to be played by the operational units of the Luftwaffe at this stage was to support the march into Denmark and the landings in Norway by demonstrations of its strength, only taking action where resistance might occur. The air demonstrations were to be undertaken by small forces of bomber and fighter aircraft. Before the war German propaganda had been busy frightening European countries with greatly exaggerated accounts of the power of the German Air Force, and during the winter following the campaign in Poland the Propaganda Ministry was not idle

in exploiting the same theme. These air demonstrations planned for Denmark and Norway could therefore be counted upon as having a not inconsiderable effect in forcing the peaceful submission of the governments of those countries through sheet fright.

15. The air transport forces were to play their part in the invasion by carrying paratroops and airborne infantry to certain specified vital points in Denmark and Norway to link up with the advance of the land forces in Denmark and with the troops landed at the ports in Norway. Two hours after the crossing of the Danish frontier paratroops were to be dropped at the airfields of Aalborg West and East under cover of fighter escort, to be followed up by the landing of airborne infantry and then supplies. In Norway two similar drops were to be made, one at Oslo/Fornebu airfield and the other at Stavanger/Sola, and were timed to take place 3½ hours after the seaborne landings. Each and all of the ports were then to be reinforced and supplied from the air as soon as in German hands. It was planned that the airfield at Trondheim/Vaernes should be taken by the forces landed from the sea, and made ready for the transport aircraft and for subsequent occupation by operational units of the German Air Force.

16. There was some element of risk in the opening stages of the airborne invasion of the two points in Norway, firstly from the small Norwegian air force based largely at Oslo, and secondly from aircraft of the R.A.F. It was, however, arranged to take the Norwegian air force by surprise on the ground in attacks by twin-engined fighter units, and it was further reckoned that, provided the secrecy of the operation could be maintained until the time of its launching, the R.A.F. could not appear on the scene before midday. By that time it was considered that German defensive fighter forces as well as some light Flak units could at least already be established on the airfields at Stavanger and Oslo.

Available Forces

17. The forces which the Luftwaffe initially allocated for the Norwegian campaign totalled some 1,000 aircraft, evenly divided between operational and transport units. For reasons of range the main striking force comprised long-range bomber units, only relatively weak elements of dive bombers and twin-engined fighters being employed for close support work. The rôle of the long-range bombers was to afford air support when and if necessary at the more distant landing points such as Trondheim, Bergen and Narvik, and at the same time to be in readiness to attack British naval forces attempting to approach the Norwegian coast ; they were also available to provide additional reconnaissance of the North Sea and naval bases in Northern England and Scotland. Thus, the main task of the German Air Force was to be protection against any British landing attempts and the means of maintenance of supplies and reinforcements to the German troops already landed. The forces at the disposal of Fliegerkorps X for the opening of the invasion were as follows :—

L.R. Bombers	..	..	..	..	..	290
Dive Bombers	..	..	..	..	..	40
S.E. Fighters	..	..	..	..	..	30
T.E. Fighters	..	..	..	..	..	70
L.R. Reconnaissance	..	..	..	..	..	40
Coastal	..	..	..	..	..	30
Total	..	..	..	..	..	500
Transport Aircraft (Ju.52, Ju.90)		..	..	..	500

59

18. Of the transport forces employed, the fully trained units of the Luftwaffe, counting a strength of 160 Ju.52s, were to be employed for the more difficult task of dropping the paratroops on Aalborg, Oslo and Stavanger. The remainder of the transport force, with a strength of some 340 aircraft, had been drawn early in April mainly from the twin-engined pilot schools, and was to be used for the secondary task of landing airborne infantry, light Flak units and supplies after the paratroops had secured their objectives, and then of maintaining supplies and reinforcements during the ensuing campaign. This task was to mark the first operational employment of transport aircraft carrying airborne combat forces to the most forward areas of battle and, with the large number of aircraft employed, demonstrated no mean achievement in organisation.

Invasion of Denmark and Norway

19. On April 7th, two days before the date fixed for the invasion, air reconnaissance was made of British naval bases and of the North Sea to ensure that the secrecy of the impending operations had been maintained. On the following day the transport units loaded the airborne troops and supplies and moved into airfields in the Schleswig area.

20. Soon after 0500 hours on the morning of April 9th, the invasion opened according to plan with the crossing of the Danish frontier by land forces and with seaborne landings on the Danish Islands and in the Norwegian ports. Following upon these movements the air transport operation began 1½ hours later with paratroop drops at Aalborg East and West airfields, followed 20 min. later by landings of airborne infantry by transport aircraft. These two airfields fell to the German forces with ease, as did the whole of Jutland and Copenhagen itself. Demonstrations by bomber and fighter units combined with the massed fly-past of the transport aircraft bound for Norway had the desired effect, and Denmark fell on the first day.

21. Meanwhile in Norway, the seaborne landings at the ports had been followed 3½ hours later by twin-engined fighter attacks on Stavanger/Sola and Oslo/Fornebu airfields. The small Norwegian air force had been taken by surprise and annihilated on the ground. The paratroop operations which immediately followed at those two airfields went off smoothly but for a small mishap at Oslo where some of the airborne infantry were landed on the airfield before the parachutists had been dropped. By midday ground operations in the Oslo area had been extended ; the airfield at Oslo/Kjeller with its supplies, including some 60 tons of aircraft fuel, had been taken and the first German transport aircraft began to land troops and supplies. The two airfields were then used as forward bases for the twin-engined fighters and Stukas supporting ground operations and providing protection against British air opposition.

22. The airfield of Stavanger/Sola likewise fell to the airborne troops, and some 180 aircraft, including bombers, twin-engined fighters and dive bombers, together with transport aircraft carrying light Flak units, supplies and ground staff, landed on the first day. The airfield at Trondheim/Vaernes did not fall until the second day, having been held for a time by the Norwegians, but on the first day an improvised landing strip was made in the snow near Trondheim itself and transport aircraft were able to fly in with their loads. By the second day the small airfield at Kristiansand was also secured by the forces landed from the sea, and was immediately occupied by some 20-25 single-engined fighters.

A German Paratrooper

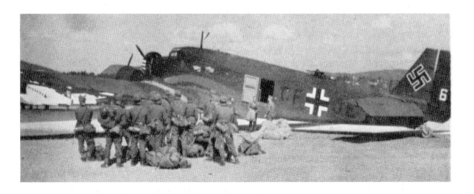

Loading Troops in the Ju.52

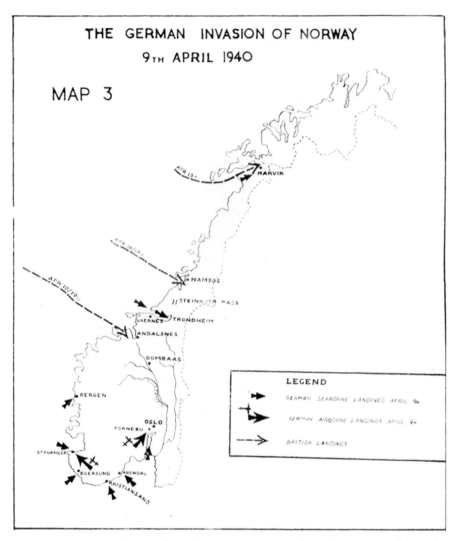

THE GERMAN INVASION OF NORWAY
9TH APRIL 1940

MAP 3

LEGEND

GERMAN SEABORNE LANDINGS APRIL 9th

GERMAN AIRBORNE LANDINGS APRIL 9th

BRITISH LANDINGS

Simultaneous landings at dawn of seaborne forces at the main ports were followed 3½ hours later by paratroop operations to capture the airfields of Oslo/Fornebu and Stavanger/Sola. Those airfields were then to be secured by landings of airborne infantry, who would make the grounds serviceable for operational use by the Luftwaffe.

23. Map 3 gives a picture of the German sea and airborne invasion of Norway which, thanks to the tactical surprise achieved, may be said to have been a success on the first day.

The Campaign

24. A continuous daylight effort by German reconnaissance aircraft maintained a watch on the coastal areas of Norway as well as on the North Sea, so that interference by British naval units could be held at a minimum. Such reconnaissance had established that British transports were heading in the direction of Norway for the landings which took place on April 15th at Narvik and between the 16th and 19th at Namsos and at Andalsnes. From this time the main effort of the operational units at the disposal of Fliegerkorps X was turned to the bombing of British landing points and of the sea transports and their naval escort. Considerable heavy bomber and Stuka forces were thrown into attacks on shipping, whilst sorties by bombers, Stukas and heavy fighters against British and Norwegian ground forces, their supply points and communications, were maintained at a high level. Attempts by the British to establish landing grounds for fighters on frozen lakes were detected by air reconnaissance and the surfaces made useless by bombing.

25. By the time the British landings took place, the bases which had been won by the Germans had already been secured and extended ; the area around Oslo had been completely overcome and land communications between Oslo, Kristiansand and Stavanger had been achieved. Further North, Trondheim and the Swedish frontier had been joined by the German forces, so that the remaining difficulties for the Germans lay in the Gudbrandsdal from Dombaas to Andalsnes, between the Steinkjer Pass and Namsos, and at Narvik, where the British forces which landed on the 15th had taken the town, thus presenting the Germans with the one serious setback in their programme.

26. From the latter part of April onwards it was necessary for the Germans to increase their operational air strength in Norway[1], and fresh bomber, fighter and Stuka units were therefore thrown in, some of the bomber units operating from the German mainland. At the peak of the Norwegian campaign early in May, German operational air forces had been increased to the following strengths :—

L.R. Bombers	360
Dive Bombers	50
S.E. Fighters	50
T.E. Fighters	70
L.R. Reconnaissance	60
Coastal	120
Total	710

Note.—Four F.W., 200 Condors were employed for both armed reconnaissance and supply work.

27. Once the phase of invasion had passed, the German Air Force settled down to its four main tasks, firstly supply and reinforcement, secondly reconnaissance of coastal areas and the North Sea with attacks on British supply shipping and naval forces, thirdly support of the ground forces operating in the Norwegian valleys, and fourthly the protection by fighters and Flak

---

[1] See paragraph 30 for the reasons for this increase.

of the areas already won. After the first ten days of the campaign the air transport forces were progressively reduced, being withdrawn to Germany to refit in anticipation of the next phase of the campaign in the West which opened with the invasion of Holland on May 10th. The air transport arm had still, however, a heavy task to perform in the supply and reinforcement of Narvik which, but for this source of supply, would have been completely cut off from German support.

28. Administratively, the German Air Force had, during April, been organising the areas of Norway already firmly under control. An advance staff of Fliegerkorps X had already moved to Oslo, and signals and supply networks had been established. Late in the month a *Luftpark* (air maintenance unit) had been founded at Oslo/Kjeller and the nucleus of a signals intelligence service had been established at Oslo, Stavanger and Trondheim. On or about the 15th of that month the new Luftflotte 5, which was to take over the air command of the whole of Norway, was formed at Hamburg and on the 24th this staff began to be transported by air to Oslo ; Gerneraloberst Stumpff arrived at the end of the month to take over this post, which he held until his return to Germany in January, 1944, to assume command of Luftflotte Reich.

29. Early in May the British and French forces which had been fighting in Norway were re-embarked from Andalsnes and Namsos and resistance was left to the isolated Norwegian units fighting in the mountains. That the British were able to withdraw in spite of German air superiority was largely due to the fact that the Luftwaffe did not operate during darkness and that their bombing of shipping in face of anti-aircraft defence was not effective. Thus, by the time the battle of France was due to begin on May 10th, Norway was practically in German hands, although Narvik still remained a serious problem.

30. On May 5th Hitler himself, in an order to Luftflotte 5, emphasised the importance of the air support of the German troops at Narvik ; to that end the air transport effort was therefore stepped up, whilst bomber operations against the remaining British forces were considerably increased[1]. On June 10th Narvik was re-occupied by the Germans, thanks mainly to paratroop and re-supply operations by the German Air Force ; on the same day hostilities in Norway were ordered to cease and the campaign concluded.

31. The special significance of this campaign lay in the fact that the Air Force proved to be a decisive factor in its success. The rapid occupation of Oslo and Stavanger on the first day was only made possible by parachutists and airborne troops, whilst the Air Force intervened effectively in the ground fighting, particularly in the valleys between Oslo and Trondheim and Oslo and Bergen. In affording the first test under operational conditions of the airborne forces and the air transport organisation, the Norwegian campaign had proved an invaluable preliminary test for their subsequent employment against Holland and Belgium ; furthermore, the campaign had demonstrated the supreme value of airborne operations as an element of surprise, under the favourable conditions of German air superiority at the time, by spreading confusion among their opponents and facilitating the seizing of the initiative. The extent to which air transport could assist in reinforcing isolated fighting groups and subsequently maintaining them by air was also to furnish useful data which could be applied to future campaigns.

---

[1] See paragraph 26.

The Battle of France (10th May to 25th June, 1940)

Plan of Campaign

32. The German plans for the spring campaign of 1940 aimed at the conquest of France and Britain and the conclusion of the war on their western frontiers. The first objective of the German armies in their projected drive westwards through France was the destruction of the British and French armies to the north of the Aisne and Somme. This objective was to be achieved by breaking through the frontier fortifications in the Ardennes between Namur and Montmédy and making a wide sweep towards the Channel coast at the mouth of the Somme. In contrast to the small encircling movements of the Polish campaign, a big armoured spearhead was to be thrust forward on a narrow front and with great rapidity.

33. This move had a certain element of risk, but with powerful and direct air support by the most concentrated air forces yet employed in warfare, a form of moving artillery barrage could prepare the way with a degree of surprise that could not be achieved by artillery. As long as the resultant confusion of the enemy forces could be maintained and no pause allowed for recovery, the thrust could succeed. This plan for massive air support was indeed the practical application of the principles learned in Spain and improved in Poland, and was due in no small measure to the energy and foresight of Generalmajor von Richthofen, A.O.C. of Fliegerkorps VIII, whose dive-bombers had achieved a high reputation in the Polish campaign.

34. Before this opening phase of the main western campaign could be set in motion, the German armies had to secure their northern flank in Holland, as in the case of Denmark and Norway, to prevent the British from using Dutch territory as a threat to the success and timing of the main operation. As with Norway, therefore, the rapid occupation of Holland had equally to be achieved by surprise before the Dutch had time to organise their defences and call in British help.

35. It was expected that the first serious resistance by the Dutch would be made behind the rivers Maas and Yssel ; once these obstacles had been breached the Dutch could hold the area north of Rotterdam—" Fortress Holland "— and would possibly maintain contact with Belgium. In the case of Belgium the fortified areas depended upon the line of the Meuse and Albert Canal and hinged on Fort Eben Emael. For the taking of these obstacles, the Germans conceived a plan similar to, but far exceeding the scale of, the paratroop and airborne operations of Denmark and Norway. In this plan the main bridges and roads were to be secured by paratroops and held for the passage of armoured forces, the airfield of Waalhaven outside Rotterdam was to be made ready for the landing of airborne forces, and general confusion was to be spread by the dropping of sabotage units. Fort Eben Emael was to be captured by glider-borne troops, and bridges over the Albert Canal were to be held. A paratroop division was also to be dropped on The Hague to capture the Dutch Royal family, the Government and Army Command.

36. In the campaign for the invasion of France the part to be played by the German Air Force was, firstly, to clear the way for airborne operations by a concentrated and co-ordinated attack on the airfields occupied by the Allied air forces, secondly, to undertake the transport of the airborne forces and

thirdly, to support the German armies in the operations to secure Holland and Belgium and in the projected armoured thrusts to the Channel coast and across the Marne and Seine to central France.

Air Organisation and Forces Employed

37. Map 4 shows the disposition of the German Air Force and armies at the time of the opening of the western campaign. Air operations were in the hands of Luftflotten 2 and 3, to which all air forces taking part were subordinated. Luftflotte 2, under Generaloberst Kesselring, was allotted the northern area of the front and was to work with Army Group B (von Bock) ; under Kesselring's command were Fliegerkorps IV and I, placed geographically in that order from North to South, as well as Fliegerdivision 9 in charge of sea mining units. Luftflotte 3, under Generaloberst Sperrle, covered operations by Army Group A (von Rundstedt) in the centre, and Army Group C facing the Maginot Line in the South. Subordinated to Sperrle were, from North to South, Fliegerkorps VIII, II, and V.

38. Air transport of the paratroop and airborne infantry divisions was in the hands of a special staff known as Fliegerfuehrer z.b.V.[1] This staff, originally part of Generaloberst Student's 7th Fliegerdivision (paratroops) had been divorced from the latter in 1939 and had existed as Fliegerfuehrer 220 until its reorganisation in January, 1940 ; General Putzier was in command and was subordinate to Luftflotte 2.

39. Thus, the air forces ranged for the opening of the heaviest commitment in airborne and army support operations which the Luftwaffe had as yet undertaken were ready to strike. As it became obvious early in May that the conclusion of the Norwegian campaign was only a matter of time, all but a few operational and transport units were withdrawn from the control of Luftflotte 5 in that area and transferred to Luftflotten 2 and 3.

40. The maximum forces employed by the German Air Force in the campaign amounted to some 3,530 operational aircraft out of a total first-line strength of 4,500 at that time, together with some 475 transport aircraft, and 45 gliders for operations in Holland. The categories of aircraft operating were approximately as follows :—

L.R. Bombers	1,300
Dive Bombers	380
S.E. Fighters	860
T.E. Fighters	350
Long-range Reconnaissance	300
Short-range Reconnaissance (Army Co-operation)	340
Total	3,530
Transport Aircraft	475
Gliders	45

Opening Phase : Invasion of Holland

41. At first light on May 10th, German heavy bombers opened a co-ordinated attack on Dutch and Belgian airfields, as well as on bases of the British and French Air Forces in France ; at the same time rail communications and the

---

[1] Fliegerfuehrer = Air Command.
z.b.V. : zur besonderen Verwendung = for special purposes.

66

GENERALFELDMARSCHALL WOLFRAM FREIHERR VON RICHTHOFEN

Born 10.10.95. Entered a Hussar Regiment as an ensign 1913. Transferred to the Flying Corps September, 1917 and served in JGI (Richthofen[1] Geschwader). Left the Flying Corps in 1920, studied engineering and re-entered the Reichswehr 1923. Transferred to the Air Force in 1933, employed in the Air Ministry. Commanded the expeditionary force to Spain in November, 1936, becoming Chief of Staff of the Condor Legion January, 1937, and O.C. the Condor Legion, November, 1938. Commanded Fliegerkorps VIII during the Polish, Flanders, Balkan and Russian campaigns. During this period he built up his reputation as the foremost exponent of intensive close-support operations. In July, 1942, Richthofen became A.O.C.-in-C. Luftflotte 4 and A.O.C. South-East in succession to Loehr. Appointed A.O.C.-in-C. Luftflotte 2 (Mediterranean area) in June, 1943. Sick and transferred to the reserve November, 1944. Died 12.7.45 of a tumour on the brain.

[1] His cousin, Baron Manfred, was the Commander who gave the *Geschwader* its name.

Warsaw

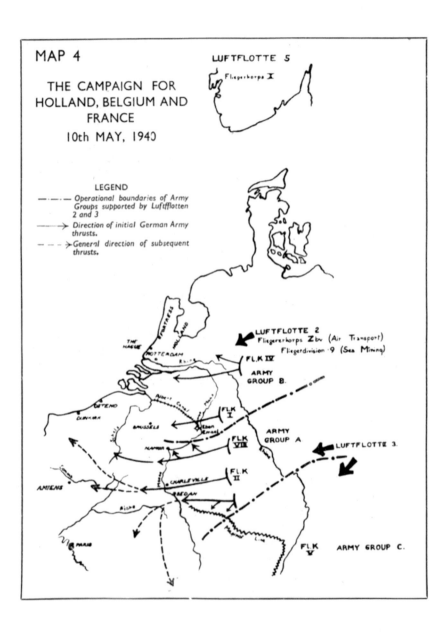

MAP 4

THE CAMPAIGN FOR HOLLAND, BELGIUM AND FRANCE
10th MAY, 1940

LUFTFLOTTE 5

Fliegerkorps X

LEGEND

—·—·— Operational boundaries of Army Groups supported by Luftflotten 2 and 3

————➤ Direction of initial German Army thrusts.

— — —➤ General direction of subsequent thrusts.

LUFTFLOTTE 2
Fliegerkorps Zbv (Air Transport)
Fliegerdivision ·9 (Sea Mining)

FLK IV

ARMY GROUP B.

FLK I

FLK VII

ARMY GROUP A

LUFTFLOTTE 3.

FLK II

FLK V   ARMY GROUP C.

THE HAGUE
ROTTERDAM
FORTRESS HOLLAND
Rhine
OSTEND
DUNKIRK
BRUSSELS
Albert Canal
Eben Emael
NAMUR
CHARLEVILLE
SEDAN
AMIENS
Aisne
PARIS

French Air Force bases at Metz, Nancy, Romilly, Dijon and Lyon were heavily bombed. At least the Dutch and Belgian Air Forces were rendered impotent by destruction of their aircraft and facilities, although the Germans left the landing areas on some of the airfields clear for their own eventual use. This bombing lasted for an hour and in Holland was immediately followed by transport aircraft with strong twin-engined fighter escort. The airborne operations for the capture of Holland had begun.

42. At The Hague the three main airfields were taken and German transport aircraft landed after obstructions had been removed from the landing areas ; the operation to capture the Dutch Royal Family and Government nevertheless failed. In the Rotterdam area the important Moerdijk bridge was captured and held intact, whilst some 1,200 airborne troops were landed at Waalhaven airfield before midday. Airborne infantry were also brought into Rotterdam by transport floatplanes.

43. In the Albert Canal area and at Fort Eben Emael the operation went according to plan. At the latter point 70 paratroops in seven gliders landed at dawn within the outer walls of the fortress complex. The paratroops broke up into small groups and, armed with explosive charges and grenades began to force their way into the inner workings of this modern fortress. The defenders were taken by surprise, and the paratroops thereby had the initial advantage. A small dive-bomber attack was meanwhile directed on the nearby village of Eben Emael, where the presence of Belgian reserve troops was suspected. This small company of paratroops was to be reinforced by others dropped at Maastricht, but the expected help was late in arriving, although both groups established radio communication. Inside the fort the lights had failed and on the following morning, as the paratroop reinforcements arrived, the demoralised Belgian crew surrendered. Thus, one of the most important forts of the Belgian defence line fell with only five casualties to the paratroops. Elsewhere throughout Holland confusion was successfully spread by the paratroops. The airborne operation had succeeded, and the main bridges and roads, which were held for the advancing German armies, opened up the way into Holland and Belgium.

44. The German air transport force had suffered heavy losses in the opening stages of the operation. After five days, its task completed, its regular units were held for the second phase of the support of the German advance into Holland, Belgium and France, whilst the remainder were returned to the training schools whence they had been drawn in the previous month.

45. During the occupation of Holland the German Air Force had complete control of the battle areas and at this stage supported the army by attacks on points of resistance, troop concentrations and communications. In Holland, as in Denmark, the obvious power of the Luftwaffe, backed by the carefully planned effort of the German Propaganda Ministry during the previous years, had the desired result ; a particularly savage bombing attack on the centre of the city of Rotterdam had its immediate effect and on May 15th the Dutch Army capitulated after five days' fighting.

Second Phase : The Thrust to The Channel

46. In Belgium the German armies had meanwhile been pressing forward, and in the Ardennes had been feeling the way for their main armoured thrust. Day and night air reconnaissance was maintained on an enormous scale, so

that the German High Command had a continuous picture of enemy positions, movements and weaknesses. This reconnaissance, undertaken by long-range and tactical units, ranged from the front-line areas to the Channel and Atlantic coasts of France, the North Sea and eastern and south-eastern England. Sifting of these reconnaissance reports, many of which overlapped, gave the Germans an accurate view of the Allied dispositions, and on May 13th their main armoured spearhead struck from Charleville and Sedan across the Meuse towards the West.

47. At this stage a strong effort by the Luftwaffe was thrown in to the tactical support of the advancing armoured forces. The long-range bomber force, with strong escorts of twin- or single-engined fighters, was engaged in attacking bases, troop concentrations, railway marshalling yards and movements by the Allied armies by rail and road. In a renewed attempt to destroy the British and French Air Forces, airfields and bases in France were subjected to continual bombing. Attacks on airfields were usually made at low level to achieve surprise, twin-engined fighters leading with cannon and machine-gun fire and the bombers following closely behind with bombs fused for a delay of a few seconds. Ports on the Channel coasts and in eastern and south-eastern England, as well as shipping passing from England to the continent were, as part of essential Allied communications, attacked with bombs and sea mines. German air reconnaissance, helped by the good weather, continued on a large scale, and contributed in no small measure to the possession and retention of the initiative by the German Air Forces and Armies.

48. The strong dive-bomber force of Fliegerkorps VIII, also with powerful fighter escort, was continually called in to prepare the way for the armoured units. As soon as air reconnaissance or ground combat reports established that any points of resistance were holding up, or where likely to hold up the advance, an extreme concentration of air striking power, with up to nine sorties a day for each aircraft, paralysed the British and French armies to a degree that was a revelation even to the German themselves. Thus, the legend of the dive bomber grew, and the *Blitzkrieg* became a reality.

49. By May 18th, the main German armoured spearhead had reached the upper Somme, and by the 20th had formed a bridgehead lower down the river between Abbeville and Amiens. Dive-bomber and bomber forces were called in to support the extension of the bridgehead by direct attack and by bombing of rail communications in the area between Rheims and Paris as well as Allied airfields.

50. The rapid advance of the German armies had meanwhile confronted the German Air Force and Army Commands with the problem of maintaining ever-lengthening lines of supply. The short-range S.E. fighters, dive bombers and reconnaissance aircraft were moving their bases forward almost daily. The regular German Air Force transport force successfully maintained essential supplies in accordance with its well practised pre-war theories[1]—although fighter units were often short of fuel—and evacuated wounded to the rear areas.

51. On the front of little less than 200 miles the German armies thrust towards the Channel, with the main striking power of the Luftwaffe concentrated between these narrow confines. The S.E. and T.E. fighters,

---

[1] The method of moving airfield staffs forward rapidly has been discussed in Chapter 2 paragraphs 66–7.

Luftwaffe Bombs in France

Luftwaffe Bombs in France

when not engaged in escort of bombing operations, were occupied in ground attack or in sweeps to engage Allied aircraft ; at this time some 550 S.E. fighters were operating in Belgium and northern France. By May 24th, the spearhead had passed Arras, had taken Boulogne and had reached Calais ; the German Army Group in the North was also closing in on Ghent. The main British Army had been separated from the French, and a large part of the task of the Luftwaffe was now to prevent their fighting back to rejoin.

52. When, on May 30th, the British Army began to evacuate Dunkirk, the main effort of the German Air Force was again turned, in the manner typical of German tactics of that time, to the one object of attempting to prevent the evacuation. Bombers and dive bombers with their attendant fighters were thrown in to the fullest extent to which lack of local airfields allowed, but met the R.A.F. fighter forces in strength. The German fighter forces frequently found themselves engaged in combat with Spitfires and Hurricanes so that they missed their rendezvous for escort of their bomber forces ; the latter suffered considerably in consequence as also did the dive bombers, and German Air Force losses over Dunkirk were heavy. For the first time the Luftwaffe had met an opponent of equal fighting capabilities, and failed to prevent the evacuation of Dunkirk, which was completed by June 4th.

Final Phase : Defeat of the French Forces

53. After the British evacuation of Dunkirk the German Air Force, largely freed from its commitments in northern France and still working in close collaboration with the Army, turned its attention to another single objective, the support of the armies striking towards Paris. Only at one period in the whole of the western campaign, during the first four days of June, had the bomber force been used strategically. In that period one attack on the French aircraft industry in the Paris area was made, and another on fuel depôts at Marseilles. Direct support of the German armies again made its demands, however, and was indeed justified by the high speed of the advance ; by June 9th, Guderian's armoured forces waiting at Sedan had begun their thrust which within twelve days extended on a narrow front as far as Dijon and the Saône. This thrust also received full Air Force support in the now well-tried manner, with the accompanying bombing of communications and airfields connected with the area of operations.

54. After the German occupation of Paris on June 14th, the German Air Force also turned its attention to the Atlantic and western Channel ports, whence the remaining British forces were being evacuated. In eastern France the French Air Force was rendered helpless and the Maginot Line had been turned from the rear ; in the West the German armies reached the Atlantic coast and Spanish frontier, and by June 25th the campaign had been won. The German Air Force was then withdrawn to rest and refit for the next and expected final phase of the war in the West, the invasion of the British Isles.

Air Doctrine After the Battle of France

55. The successful campaigns in Poland, Norway and France, rather than crystallising German conceptions of the use of air power, led to increased and deeper controversy. Hitler and Goering only saw themselves as the victorious gods of their own invention, the *Blitzkrieg* ; they regarded their Generals and General Staff merely as lay helpers in a war that was already won. Nothing

further was done to expand the German Air Force or to improve its equipment and training, and there was a widespread inclination to relax and enjoy the fruits of a victory as good as won.

56. The bomber force had been used solely as a tactical air arm, with the single exception of four days' strategic employment in France. This use of the bomber arm, although extremely effective in its support of the army, led to confusions and misconceptions as to the employment of the bomber which lasted throughout the War. The Stuka (dive bomber) had emerged from the campaigns with its legendary reputation, a reputation that had a disastrous influence on the subsequent development of the German close support arm and persisted until 1943. The fighter force knew that it had met its equals in the Spitfire and Hurricane, but the general belief that its own aircraft were slightly superior was allowed to remain and was encouraged.

57. The campaigns had proved that an air force with superiority and in possession of the initiative could give powerful and decisive support to rapid armoured thrusts by preparing the way with concentrated bombing, and by sealing the flanks of the armoured forces to enemy interference. The effectiveness of the airborne operation, also with the prerequisite of air superiority, had also been proved. Both lessons were to serve well in the campaigns in Crete and in Russia in 1941. As yet, however, the German Air Force had only had a foretaste of effective fighter opposition, but in the flush of victory Goering had not recognised its implications.

THE FIRST FAILURE OF GERMAN AIR POWER: THE BATTLE OF BRITAIN AND THE BATTLE OF THE ATLANTIC

The Battle of Britain (August-September, 1940)

German Conceptions of Invasion

1. The conclusion of the campaign in the Netherlands and France on June 25th left the German General Staff with the task of preparing and executing an invasion of Great Britain within the three months of good weather to be expected before autumn gales would make the undertaking impossible. The necessary regrouping of the armies and air forces and the collection of suitable vessels precluded the possibility of any immediate exploitation of the rapid victory just achieved.

2. It is perhaps not surprising, in view of the successes of the German armed forces from the Polish campaign onwards, that the General Staff retained a purely continental conception of an invasion across the Channel. The now well-tried formula of annihilation of the enemy air force, followed by the rapid advance of the German armies with powerful and direct air support, was held also to apply to Great Britain. There was, in the German conception, only one difference, that the R.A.F., being the most powerful single air force yet encountered, would necessarily require for its destruction some time longer than the 12 to 48 hours previously allotted to other air forces.

3. Deliberations by the German Combined Staffs produced a directive from Field Marshal Keitel on July 12th to the effect that the German lack of command of the sea could be substituted by supremacy in the air. The directive recognised that in an invasion of Great Britain no strategic surprise was possible, but the landings must take the form of a powerful river crossing with the air force acting as artillery. The first condition before such a crossing could take place was the defeat of the R.A.F. so that the essential prerequisite of German air supremacy would be assured. Thus, the German High Command, in regarding the whole undertaking in the same light as a large-scale crossing of a river such as the Meuse, allotted to the Air Force its normal preliminary task and, as before, planning of this task was left in Air Force hands[2].

Disposition of Luftwaffe Forces

4. The regrouping of the German Air Force in preparation for the expected final stage of the western campaign showed few changes as compared with the Battle of France. Luftflotten 2 and 3 merely extended their areas into France and took over existing airfields; their common boundary on the Channel coast at the mouth of the Seine was extended northwards through the centre of England so that each was allotted its own sphere of operations (see Map 5). The subordinated Fliegerkorps remained as before, with the exception that II and IV were exchanged between the two Luftflotten, largely because Fliegerkorps IV disposed of the main units specialising in anti-shipping

---

[1] The German figures of strengths, etc., in this chapter are taken from German Air Staff Historical Section (8th Abteilung) records.

[2] See Appendix, paragraph 6, where Supreme Command methods of planning are outlined.

operations and could be better employed in the Western Approaches, St. George's Channel and Irish Sea areas. These two Luftflotten were thus given the task of delivering the main attack on England, whilst forces of Luftflotte 5 in Norway were to be brought in to create a diversion of British defensive forces to the North-East coast of England.

5. Another development was the grouping of the single- and twin-engined fighters of the Fliegerkorps in Luftflotten 2 and 3 under tactical fighter commands—known as Jagdfuehrer or Jafues—which, within the framework of the main operations by the Luftflotten, retained a measure of independence in the planning of fighter escorts and sweeps. These Jafues could be compared with R.A.F. Fighter Groups in their functions, but at this stage they suffered from the disadvantage, which was to prove to be the undoing of the whole German fighter effort, that they had at that time no method of plotting of enemy air forces or of controlling their own aircraft once airborne. Although, therefore, they performed the functions of operational commands, the operations themselves had to be flown blind, and without further direction from the ground. The two Jafues in question, Jafue 2 under Luftflotte 2 and Jafue 3 under Luftflotte 3, controlled respectively 460 single- and 90 twin-engined fighters, and 300 single- and 130 twin-engined fighters.

6. At the end of the campaign in France many of the units of the German Air Force had been withdrawn to Germany to rest and refit, particularly fighters, dive bombers (Stukas) and short-range reconnaissance (Army Co-operation), the latter having suffered heavy losses. Meanwhile Luftflotten 2 and 3 disposed of small forces of bombers to continue the day and night attrition against the supply of Great Britain by sea. During July, the air forces were gradually disposed at airfields between Hamburg and Brest, and by the 17th of that month, when the order for full readiness was given, the striking force had been built up to its intended strength. The actual strength of the forces controlled by Luftflotten 2 and 3 for the assault on southern England and the Midlands comprised :—

L.R. Bombers	1,200[1]
Dive Bombers	280
S.E. Fighters	760
T.E. Fighters	220
Long-range Reconnaissance	50[2]
Short-range Reconnaissance (Army Co-operation) ..	90
	2,600

7. The additional forces based in Norway and under control of Luftflotte 5 cannot be said to have taken part in the Battle of Britain, at least in its early stages, but they did play a diversionary part valuable to the Germans in forcing the R.A.F. to retain fighter defences in the North. The striking forces available in Norway, as distinguished from those held for purely defensive purposes, were :—

L.R. Bombers	130
T.E. Fighters	30
Long-range Reconnaissance	30
	190

---

[1] Serviceability on 20th July stood at 69% of this figure
[2] 90 of the L.R. Bombers were also available for bomber-reconnaissance operations against coastal areas and shipping.

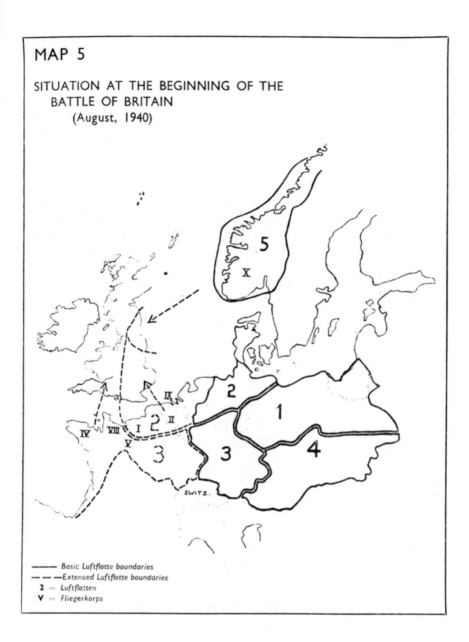

MAP 5

SITUATION AT THE BEGINNING OF THE
    BATTLE OF BRITAIN
        (August, 1940)

————— Basic Luftflotte boundaries
— — —Extended Luftflotte boundaries
  2 = Luftflotten
  V = Fliegerkorps

Schmid (right) the Chief of German Air Intelligence, with Hitler, Goering and Mussolini

The two Commanders of the Battle of Britain and the " Blitz ", Sperrle (left) of Luftflotte 3 and Kesselring, of Luftflotte 2.

The Luftwaffe Plan

8. Within the wider Combined Staff plans for the invasion, the task of the German Air Force was twofold: in the middle of July orders by the Air Force Operations Staff to the Luftflotten made clear their two main aims as follows :—

  (a) To eliminate the R.A.F., both as a fighting force and in its ground organisation.

  (b) To strangle the supply of Great Britain by attacking its ports and shipping.

The elimination of the R.A.F. was to be accomplished in two stages. In the first place the fighter defences located to the South of a line between London and Gloucester were to be beaten down, and secondly, the German offensive was to be extended by stages northwards until R.A.F. bases throughout England were covered by daylight attacks. Meanwhile, as part of the same plan, a day and night bombing offensive was to be directed against the British aircraft industry.

9. The elimination of the R.A.F. and the British aircraft industry was to begin early in August, and the day for its launching was given the somewhat dramatic code-name of *Adler Tag* (Eagle Day). It was considered by the Germans that the first phase, the destruction of R.A.F. Fighter Command in the South, would take four days and the whole task of eliminating the R.A.F. four weeks, after which the invasion itself, with Luftwaffe support of the *Blitzkrieg* type and with negligible opposition from the now beaten R.A.F., was to be aimed in its greatest strength at the coast between the Isle of Wight and Dover. On August 6th Goering called a conference of the Luftflotte chiefs at Karinhall, as a result of which Adler Tag was provisionally fixed for August 10th, given favourable weather. The invasion itself could therefore take place at some time in the first two weeks of September.

The Opening Phases : Testing of Fighter Command

10. From June 25th, until the middle of July air attacks on England had been confined to scattered night raids and minelaying sorties—sometimes by as few as two aircraft on one target—directed mainly against the ports and centres of the aircraft industry. After July 17th, however, when the German Air Forces had been ordered to be at full readiness, activity immediately began to increase and for the ensuing four weeks worked up to a crescendo which marked the launching of the full-scale offensive on *Adler Tag*. Fliegerkorps VIII, whose Stukas had distinguished themselves as the moving artillery barrage for the advancing armoured columns in France, was now given the task of closing the western Channel to all British shipping by day, whilst the heavy bombers were to make shipping movements and port activity impossible by day and night and aircraft were to lay mines in the shipping channels. Thus, in the last fortnight of July and the early days of August shipping and ports in St. George's Channel, the English Channel and on the East coast were attacked on a mounting scale, whilst small numbers of aircraft continued with night attacks on the aircraft and associated industries.

11. From this time onwards the German bomber forces began to show themselves in greater strength over the Channel, Straits of Dover and South-East, coast areas of England during daylight. Their activities were still, however, mainly confined to the ports and shipping and occasionally to coastal airfields.

79

It was at this stage that the Luftwaffe began to test the qualities of the R.A.F. fighter force and to embark on the process of wearing it down. Large German fighter formations were sent inland over England with the sole object of seeking combat. At first the response from the R.A.F. was satisfactory ; formations of Spitfires and Hurricanes came up to fight, but were at a serious disadvantage in that they were obliged to climb to combat height and thus were vulnerable from above. The close formation fighting tactics which they adopted at this stage also put them at a disadvantage, but the R.A.F. soon saw its error and its modified loose formations met with more success.

12. The small formations of 8 to 12 bombers with escort of 9 to 30 fighters which attacked shipping and ports in the area of South-East England during this period were also largely designed to draw the R.A.F. fighters into combat ; the larger formations were still being aimed mainly at shipping and ports—for instance, on August 8th two waves, respectively of 57 and 82 Ju.87's with fighter escort, attacked convoys off the Isle of Wight and on August 11th, 38 Ju.88's attacked the port installations at Portland, whilst another heavy attack was directed against Dover. With the smaller formations, the duties of the escorts were to protect the bombers, whilst other fighters were detailed to inflict losses on R.A.F. fighters which attacked, and thus to weaken Fighter Command for the final test of strength.

13. German losses at this stage were bearable, but the Luftwaffe was meeting with increasing difficulties. It was clear that the R.A.F. was still an effective fighting force and that it was not suffering sufficiently heavy casualties in the actions on the coastal fringe ; it therefore became necessary for the German bomber formations to penetrate further inland so that their escorting fighters would be able to engage Fighter Command decisively. This deeper German penetration allowed more time to the defending fighters to climb to combat altitude, and so to fight on more equal terms. It was only at this stage that the Germans realised that the R.A.F. fighters were controlled from the ground by a new procedure, for they intercepted R/T orders directing the fighters to the German formations with great accuracy.

14. A German intelligence appreciation of Fighter Command's control system, circulated on August 7th to the operational commands, is worth quoting in full as an indication of the conceptions which led the Germans to mount large-scale penetrations in the belief that what they regarded as a rigid territorial control system could be swamped by mass attack :—

" As the British fighters are controlled from the ground by R/T their forces are tied to their respective ground stations and are thereby restricted in mobility, even taking into consideration the probability that the ground stations are partly mobile. Consequently, the assembly of strong fighter forces at determined points and at short notice is not to be expected. A massed German attack on a target area can therefore count on the same conditions of light fighter opposition as in attacks on widely scattered targets. It can, indeed, be assumed that considerable confusion in the defensive networks will be unavoidable during mass attacks, and that the effectiveness of the defences may thereby be reduced."

In point of fact, R.A.F. Fighter Command's control system was sufficiently flexible for the maximum number of fighter formations to be simultaneously and separately controlled within a zone of operations.

15. German intelligence was fairly well informed of the order of battle and ground organisation of Fighter Command, and it is evident from the above quotation that they now knew the early warning radar system was connected with fighter control. The Luftwaffe had, however, neglected this aspect of the defence of Great Britain in their pursuit of the *Blitzkrieg*, and Goering was in no mood to listen to any possibility of a serious opposition to the Luftwaffe. The German fighter commanders who met daily at their Jafue headquarters to discuss and plan operations began to see their difficulties, however, and to realise that their 980 single- and twin-engined fighters (Me.109 and Me.110) were insufficient to gain a decisive superiority over the 675 fighters which German intelligence estimated were at the disposal of the R.A.F.[1] and which could be used so economically with the aid of their efficient control.

16. As the preliminary stage drew to its close the German fighter forces found themselves seriously split. The Me.110 twin-engined fighter was proving a failure as an escort fighter, being too vulnerable to the more manoeuvrable Spitfire and Hurricane. The fighter forces found themselves obliged to provide escorts roughly three times as great as the bombers which they were protecting, and in addition more fighters had to be held back to meet returning bomber formations, so persistent were the R.A.F. fighters in chasing the bombers to the French coast.

Adler Tag—The Battle Begins

17. Up to August 9th, it had been foreseen by the German Air Force Operations Staff that the launching of the full air assault on the R.A.F. would begin on the 10th, but meteorological reports caused the date to be deferred until the 13th. Even on the day itself Goering postponed the start until the afternoon. It was then that large-scale bombing attacks began to be directed against such R.A.F. airfields in the South of England as were part of, or were likely to be used as part of, the defensive organisation of Fighter Command. The German scale of effort on August 13th by the aircraft of Luftflotten 2 and 3 was 485 bomber sorties and 1,000 by fighters. The bomber forces of Luftflotte 5 were brought into operation on August 15th, the third day, with diversionary attacks in the Newcastle area. On that day, and in the succeeding week the scale of attack on airfields of all types in southern England was of the heaviest and great air battles were continuously fought over southern England. Meanwhile, the day and night attacks on ports and shipping continued, whilst special targets of the aircraft industry were singled out for bombing.

18. The short-range reconnaissance aircraft, which had been used with such success in France, could not be employed over England owing to the fighter opposition, and the long-range reconnaissance units were unable for the same reason to produce a picture comparable with that which had kept the German High Command so well informed in previous campaigns. Nevertheless, reconnaissance showed the landing areas and installations of many of the airfields vital to Fighter Command to be heavily damaged. In spite of this physical damage, however, the R.A.F. was still able to offer considerable and effective opposition, and by the 19th of the month, when bad weather forced a five-day break in operations, the Luftwaffe seemed to be no nearer to forcing a decision.

---

[1] R.A.F. operational strength in S.E. fighters on July 15th amounted to 603.

81

19. In this phase of the battle German losses of both fighters and bombers had increased[1], but rapid replacements of both aircraft and crews allowed of a holding of the rate of serviceability to a level which still permitted large-scale operations. On August 17th, serviceability of the single-engined fighter units engaged, both in aircraft and pilots, stood at 85 per cent. of strength as against 95 per cent. on July 15th ; comparable figures for the long-range bombers, however, remained at approximately 70 per cent. throughout the period.

20. On August 20th, the German Air Force Operations Staff issued a further order to the forces engaged to continue the fight against the R.A.F. with ceaseless attacks which would force the British fighter formations into combat and thus reduce their strength ; special attention was still to be paid to the ground organisation, as well as to the aircraft and aluminium industries and rolling mills. When, on August 23rd the weather improved, the attack was once more opened on the R.A.F. ground installations. Reconnaissance had shown that the main forces of Fighter Command had been withdrawn to the area surrounding London, and the main strength of the German attack was shifted accordingly.

21. It was now that the bombers began to suffer more heavily. both in losses and in damaged aircraft. Their own armament was not sufficient even to discourage fighter attack, and the Me.109 single-engined fighters themselves were troubled firstly by limited endurance, which would not permit more than a short period of combat en route or over target areas, and secondly by the rapidly improving fighter tactics of the R.A.F. The Me.110 twin-engined fighter had seemed to the Germans to be ideal for long-range escort purposes, but the R.A.F. fighters usually forced these escorts into defensive circles long before the bombers had reached the targets ; it soon became necessary for the Me.109's to protect the Me.110's as well as the bombers. The twin-engined fighter units nevertheless continued to make fantastic claims of their victories—which in the prevailing *Blitzkrieg* spirit were believed—and the Me.110, which should have been withdrawn at this stage, was allowed to continue operating. The Ju.87 dive bomber, too, had proved a costly failure in the attacks on Dover, on Channel shipping and on airfields nearer the South coast. On August 19th, Fliegerkorps VIII, which possessed 220 of the total of 280[2] Ju.87's engaged was withdrawn from the Cherbourg area and put under the control of Luftflotte 2 in the Pas de Calais area. This move, besides pointing to the realisation by the Germans that the dive bomber had been a failure in attacks on shipping, was in effect a new disposal of forces in preparation for the invasion itself. The dive bombers were now placed in a tactical position for army support in the coming invasion operations in a similar manner to other continental campaigns.

22. At the end of August the R.A.F. was still inflicting damaging losses[3] on the German attacking forces and consequently little progress was being made in the Luftwaffe programme—already far behind schedule in its first aim of destroying Fighter Command within four days, and little nearer to its second aim of achieving mastery of the air by mid-September. A German Air Force Staff

---

[1] German Air Staff records give total losses sustained from August 8th–19th inclusive as 246 fighters and 298 bombers.

[2] The Germans had an establishment strength of 456 Ju.87 dive bombers at this time, but owing to losses in the Flanders and French campaign, they could only muster a total of 280.

[3] Between August 23rd and 31st, German losses were 197 fighters and 139 bombers.

Bombing up

Heinkel Bombers

Distribution of Decorations.

Goering gives encouragement to aircrew of KG26 at a Belgian airfield

conference, at which Kesselring and Sperrle, as A.O.C's. of Luftflotten 2 and 3 were present, was held early in September at The Hague. The directive of August 20th to bring the British fighters to exhausting combat had been pursued, but still no decision had been obtained over the R.A.F. Doubts now began to arise as to the true strength of Fighter Command's forces. Kesselring gave his opinion that the R.A.F. was finished, but Sperrle thought it still had 1,000 aircraft at its disposal. The Chief of Intelligence had taken serviceability towards the end of August to be as low as 100 fighters, in spite of reinforcement from the Midlands and North, but considered that the rest imposed by bad weather had allowed a recovery to about 350[1]. The pilot position, the R.A.F.'s true difficulty, was not considered, in spite of the fact that intelligence had established that bomber pilots were being called in to replace losses.

Second Phase : The Bombing of London

23. The creation of the hoped-for conditions for invasion had not been, and possibly could not be, brought about by pursuing the original twofold plan. On the night of August 25th, R.A.F. bombers had attacked targets in and around Berlin. Hitler, in a speech on September 4th, seized upon this attack as an excuse for announcing his intention of a revenge bombing of London. According to the rigid pattern of previous campaigns, where the Polish and Dutch armies capitulated after the bombing of their main centres of population and the Danish Government capitulated at the threat of such bombing, it was hoped that similar tactics would paralyse the British Government to submission. Hitler's order to the Luftwaffe, dated September 2nd—two days before his speech—directed that attacks should be made on the populations and defences of the large cities, particularly London, by day and night.

24. This decision was in part an admission of failure by the Luftwaffe High Command, but at the same time Goering still hoped that the R.A.F. fighter arm might be finally exhausted and that a turn of fortune would produce a victory at the last moment. On the afternoon of September 7th, therefore, a force of 372 long-range bombers escorted by single- and twin-engined fighters attacked the thickly populated area of the docks in East London and caused large fires and considerable damage ; on this day the German fighters made 642 sorties. On that night 255 bombers followed up with an attack on the same area, still illuminated by the fires of the afternoon attack. During the succeeding days and nights forces of similar strength—although never reaching the scale of September 7th—were in operation, but extended their target area to Central London generally ; on September 9th, for example, 220 bombers and 529 fighters operated by day, and on the 15th, 123 bombers and 679 fighters by day and 233 bombers by night. (Towards the end of August, 120 of the bombers under Luftflotte 5 had been transferred from Norway and added to the strength of Luftflotte 2.)

25. Again German losses began to be serious[2], and differences of opinion arose between the bomber and fighter arms, with accusations and counter-accusations which caused the direct intervention of Goering in the dispute. The fighter arm wanted an escort system embodying loose formations built up

---

[1] Operational strength was 672 on August 23rd.

[2] Between September 7th and 15th, inclusive, German Staff documents give losses of 99 fighters and 199 bombers.

(83331)   D*

of elements of four, with top cover and a free-lance patrol at high altitude to engage the R.A.F. fighters before they could attack. The bomber arm, whose losses were causing anxiety, wanted close escort in twos and threes with a form of wider escort in close formation and the addition of top cover. In the opinion of the fighter arm such escort was too rigid and precluded any early engaging of the attacking fighters ; in addition, the bombers flew at altitudes of 21,000 to 23,000 ft. to avoid anti-aircraft fire, which height made them slow when loaded with bombs. Their low speed further increased the difficulties of the fighters, which were forced to weave continuously to maintain the required close escort. The weaving, which at intervals took the fighters away from the bombers, apart from further limiting their endurance, made the bomber crews more nervous and resulted in their demanding through Goering a still closer escort. Goering, who had allowed himself to be influenced by the bomber arm, promptly gave orders accordingly.

26. The single- and twin-engined fighters were thus bound to the bombers and could not leave until attacked, giving the R.A.F. fighters the advantage of surprise, initiative, altitude, speed, and above all, fighting spirit. The German fighter men pressed Goering to give way to their point of view ; they saw that the whole of their experience gained from the Spanish war onwards was being thrown away. Goering, however, remained adamant, and the bomber arm as well as the spirit of the fighter arm—already badly shaken by the superiority of the Spitfire—suffered accordingly.

27. As September drew to a close the Germans found that their large bomber formations were not paying a dividend comparable with their losses, and on the 27th of the month there was a new change of tactics involving the sending of small bomber forces composed of about 30 of the faster Ju.88 bombers only, and escorted by from 200 to 300 fighters. In this period German indecision was clearly demonstrated by the manner in which one form of tactics gave way to another in a groping attempt to achieve satisfactory results. The massed formation attacks had now given way to smaller and smaller bomber formations with ever greater fighter escort. Daylight bomber operations then began to give way to fighter-bombers operating singly and in small groups, penetrating as far as the London area. It had still been possible to maintain a fair rate of serviceability in the units engaged—single engined fighters had dropped by the end of September to 68 per cent., and long-range bombers to 52 per cent. in aircraft and 68 per cent. in crews—but a continual drain on strength at this steady rate from July 15th onwards could eventually lead to a serious situation.

28. Early in October the Luftwaffe was glad of the excuse of a deterioration in weather conditions to call off daylight operations ; it was Goering himself who made the decision. The Battle of Britain had been lost to the Luftwaffe, although nobody would admit the fact, but it was still hoped to wear Great Britain down to the point of capitulation by final resort to massed night attacks on its industrial cities, by making seaborne supply impossible through the destruction of the main ports, and by sea mining and shipping attacks.

Factors in the German Defeat

29. The foregoing account of the Battle of Britain throws light on the main factors which contributed to the defeat of the Luftwaffe. It is as well, however,

to enumerate those factors and to examine to what extent and to what degree each was responsible. The main factors may be summarised as follows :—

(a) A fundamental failure in German air strategy and policy, which concentrated on the doctrine of attack, and thereby led to a disproportionate weakness of the fighter arm as opposed to the strength of the bomber and dive bomber forces[1]. The armament of the German He.111, Do.17 and Ju.88 bombers which, in conjunction with their speed, had been relied upon in part to offset the deficiency of fighters, proved inadequate and led to a wasteful use of the limited strength of the fighter escort and to disastrous quarrels at a crucial point in the Battle.

(b) The consequent lack of foresight in planning the strategic use of air power in circumstances which involved the large-scale employment of big escorted formations against strong defences.

(c) A lack of appreciation by German Intelligence of the British early warning radar system and of its possibilities when employed in conjunction with control of the defensive fighter forces.

(d) German failure to take sufficient account of the fighting qualities of the Spitfire and Hurricane, which had first become evident in France and over Dunkirk. The single- and twin-engined fighter force employed in the Battle of Britain—which was thought to be ample in strength—was consequently outclassed by those very fighting qualities in combination with the British system of plotting and fighter control.

(e) A misconception of the fighting power of the Me.110 twin-engined fighter. Dependence had been put on this type for long-range escort work ; when it failed, the Me.109 single-engined fighters had not sufficient endurance (the drop-tank employed later in the war had not yet been developed), nor were they sufficiently numerous, to press the Battle on to the London area and beyond.

30. It must be fully appreciated that opinion in the Luftwaffe, and indeed of the whole of the German forces, after their rapid continental victories, ignored the mere possibility of any serious opposition to the great and victorious Luftwaffe. Goering himself was dazzled by his own self-esteem, and he and the whole of the Luftwaffe were subconsciously affected in their judgment by the outpourings of the German Propaganda Department. The German fighter men had begun to see the possibility of a tough adversary in the Spitfire and Hurricane, but the series of easy victories from Poland onwards had prejudiced their judgment in assessing the capabilities of the R.A.F. ; indeed, anybody who as much as hinted at the possibility of a fighter superior to the Me.109 incurred the risk of the serious disapproval of his superiors.

31. The attitude of Hitler and Goering themselves, rather than any lack of foresight on the part of the German Air Force General Staff, may be said to have been responsible for the launching of the offensive on Great Britain with the minimum of forethought. The probability that the employment of large forces of bombers with fighter escort over England would meet with a new set of conditions was ignored in an almost incomprehensible mood of confidence. The experience of escorted bomber operations during the

---

[1] See also Chapter 2, paragraphs 46–51.

87

campaign in France was thought to be adequate, and consequently the Battle of Britain was begun without the advantage of preliminary planning, preparation of tactics and training of aircrews. When the new conditions were encountered the inevitable result was confusion, friction, accusation and counter-accusation.

32. The existence of the British radar system had certainly been known to the Germans at some time before the war—the airship Graf Zeppelin during its peacetime cruises had been charged with obtaining data on the transmissions— but the secret of the highly developed plotting system linked with fighter control had been well kept by the British.

33. A similar set of conditions applied to the bomber force. From the Spanish Civil War onwards the Ju.88, Do.17 and He.111 had been able to outpace any existing fighter and, as the Luftwaffe had air superiority in all succeeding campaigns, it began to be accepted that the bombers could look after themselves. It was not until after the assault on Fighter Command had opened that the strength of the British defensive fighter force was realised ; by then it was too late to put heavier armament and armour into the bombers. In a flash it was found that the use of powerful fighter escorts was essential to counteract this shortcoming, but at this critical juncture the fighter force proved to lack the necessary strength, while a substantial part of it, the T.E. fighters, was more a liability than an asset. The German failure to foresee that their bomber types were not immune from fighter attack may, therefore, be said to be one of the main factors in their losing the Battle. The consequence of this inadequate armament was, that with the twin-engined fighter a failure and with the single engined fighter possessing inadequate combat range, the attempt to follow up the destruction of Fighter Command on the ground—a real threat in its early stages—failed once Fighter Command withdrew its bases beyond the effective escorted range.

34. Thus, by early October when the Luftwaffe began to throw the weight of its bombing effort into night attacks on ports and cities, its General Staff had dropped the original first objectives of destroying the fighter defences in the South and then the R.A.F. itself. The new aim was to bomb Great Britain into submission by a direct attack on its civilian population and its whole war economy. The one objective to which the High Command held throughout the Battle of Britain, and continued to hold during the subsequent night assault, was the continuous attack by small numbers of bomber and minelaying aircraft on shipping and ports.

35. In studying the German bombing and their selection of targets to be bombed, the question arises as to whether the German bomber force was used strategically or tactically. The answer is that the Germans were not clear themselves. The opening aim of the bomber forces was certainly tactical, and had it achieved success the invasion could have taken place and operations could have followed the familiar Luftwaffe pattern. As it was, with the failure to achieve the two opening objectives, German thinking became confused in the extreme. They were forced into improvisation on their original plan and the Chief of Air Staff found it impossible to draw up any clear alternative amidst the conflicting opinions and advice thrust upon Goering from all sides. The Navy demanded support in minelaying and attacks on shipping ; the original programme called for the bombing of the British aircraft industry ; other

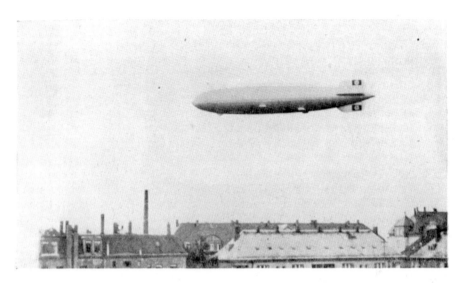

Graf Zeppelin on one of its peacetime flights

Loading a 1,000-kilogramme bomb on a He.111. Note the external bomb-rack; the He.111 could not accommodate such a large bomb internally.

The Italian BR20 Bomber

A Fiat CR42 Fighter which came to grief in Norfolk on 11th November, 1940

90

industrial experts suggested concentrating on the railways, blast furnaces and the Sheffield steel industry; the Chief of Intelligence tried to draw attention to a ponderous and academic work called the *Studie Blau* (Blue Study), which set out British industrial undertakings and essential services such as gas and sewerage and their relationship to the country's economy. Hitler, above all, wanted the destruction of cities and revenge for the R.A.F.'s bombing of Germany. Hitler had his way, but attempts were at the same time made to attack targets of a strategic and even of a tactical nature. Thus, by the time the true Battle of Britain had passed, the air war had moved by gradual stages from tactical to strategic and then to nothing but an attempt to produce a quick victory by an attack on civilian morale. When the latter bid fair to fail the Luftwaffe continued with a combination of planned strategic bombing and attacks on cities.

The " Blitz " on Great Britain (October, 1940–May, 1941)

Night Bombing of British Cities

36. In the Luftwaffe assault on Great Britain between July and November, 1940, the changes from one form of attack to another were the clearest indication of the Germans' continuous search for new expedients to replace each successive failure. The various phases of the assault cannot, however, be said to have followed one another in any clear-cut sequence. From September onwards the daylight offensive against Fighter Command continued on a gradually reducing scale, heavy bomber attacks giving way to raids by escorted fighter-bombers. During the same period the attempt to produce a quick surrender of the British Government by massed raids on London was followed by a full-scale night assault on the capital. In November, this assault in turn spread to other British cities and centres of industry, and itself alternated between pure attempts to break the nation's morale and carefully planned strategic assaults on its supply and production. These phases of the night assault, beginning with the raid on London on September 7th and dragging on through the winter to cease finally in May, 1941, came to be known in Great Britain as the *Blitz*.

37. The main reason why the Germans finally threw their heaviest effort into night bombing was that during September losses and damage to aircraft in battle were causing serviceability in the bomber force to fall at such an alarming rate that night operations, with their comparative immunity from fighter attack, were the only alternative. This resort to large-scale night bombing can only be said to have been an improvisation forced upon the German Air Force Staff, and had only been foreseen by few—much less by Goering[1]. The German objective at this stage still remained clear, however; London was to be pounded to the point where the Government would find it impossible to continue the war in face of a collapse in civilian morale.

38. For the Luftwaffe, night bombing immediately brought with it the additional problem of navigation and bomb aiming. The German bomber force, with the exception of a few specialised units, not only lacked training in night bombing, but the loss of a large proportion of its more experienced crews during the prodigal days of the Battle of Britain had, by October, seriously

---

[1] See also Chapter 2, paragraph 49.

reduced its efficiency. The Germans, however, considered that any lack of training in night navigation and bomb aiming would be more than compensated by the employment of their recently perfected radio bombing beams. These beams—a novelty in aerial warfare—had been under development at least since 1937, had been used in one form experimentally in Poland, and in another form had been employed occasionally against special targets in the United Kingdom since the fall of France. Yet another form was reaching the operational stage early in October. The beams had been devised as aids to daylight bombing in cloudy weather, and it was only the fact that they were available which gave the Germans the fortunate opportunity of continuing the assault.

39. The premature use of each of these bombing beams over England from June onwards had in turn compromised their secrecy and, once they began to be used in massed bombing attacks, British radio counter-measures—also a novelty in aerial warfare—robbed them of much of their effectiveness. Quarrels, uncertainty and improvisation again beset high quarters in the Luftwaffe and resulted in confusion in the policy of employment of the beams. Added to this, the ever-present differences of opinion as to selection of targets, produced— with a few notable exceptions such as Coventry—a lack of concentration of bombing effort, a failure to pursue advantages gained after bombing certain types of target, and a continually improvised plan of campaign. Thus, the winter assault, albeit on a massive scale, gave the British civilian populations time to recover from attacks, and the damaged industries opportunities to repair, improvise and disperse.

Strength of the Bomber Force

40. The bomber force available for the *Blitz* comprised the same units of Luftflotten 2, 3 and 5 as had been engaged in the Battle of Britain, with the addition of some 90 aircraft which had meanwhile been held in Germany. A strength of some 1,300 bombers was thus available on paper, but in actual fact, the drop in serviceability during August and September had reduced effective strength to a maximum of about 700. During the whole of the *Blitz* period the Luftwaffe was never able to recover its bomber serviceability, which remained around 50 per cent. ; the reduction in wastage of aircraft in battle was offset by an equal wastage due to bad landings at night on airfields— many in France—as yet undeveloped for night flying and for use in wet weather.

Brief Appearance of the Italian Air Force

41. The R.A.F. had meanwhile been causing Mussolini some embarrassment by its continued bombing of industrial centres in Italy, such as Turin, with bomber aircraft based in England. More as a political gesture than as a serious military effort, Mussolini despatched 40 B.R.20 bombers and 54 C.R.42 S.E. fighters to bases in the Brussels area, where they could take part in the assault on England. This force arrived early in October and, making use of German radio networks, opened early in November with a night bombing sortie by 24 bombers on the south coast of England ; again on November 11th, a force of 10 bombers escorted by some 40 fighters attempted to attack the harbour installation at Harwich. Losses to both bombers and fighters were heavy, and the next sortie by 10 bombers on a convoy off the Essex coast on November 17th had an additional heavy escort of German fighters.

42. November 23rd saw the last Italian attempt at an attack in the form of a fighter sweep over the Kentish coast ; some Italian bombers also took part in a raid on the same night. After that the Italians withdrew to their own country, and never flew against England again.

The Assault, and the Bombing Beams

43. After the massed daylight attack on the London docks on September 7th, the Luftwaffe continued to make London its main target ; on every day during the remainder of the month there were raids by bomber forces varying from 35 to 280, and on every night by 60 to 260 bombers. By the early part of October, when attacks began to be confined to hours of darkness, the Germans began to realise that the bombing beam on which they had founded their hopes—the *Knickebein*—and which they were employing over London, was being seriously upset by British radio counter-measures. Although they had yet the two other types of beam, the " *X* "—first employed in Poland—and the " *Y* ", these could not be employed as could *Knickebein* for navigating large forces of bombers to a target[1]. Furthermore, the transmitting equipment available on the western continental coasts for " *X* " and " *Y* " beams was insufficient for this purpose, and the rather more complicated training which their use entailed had only been confined to two specialist units.

44. With the realisation that the *Knickebein* system was being rendered useless for massed attacks, the Germans adopted the temporary measure of relying upon periods of bright moonlight for large-scale raiding, when the bomber forces could see their target area and could navigate independently. Such was totalitarian discipline, however, that nobody yet dared admit the failure of *Knickebein*, and during the early part of October the nightly assault continued on London by forces of bombers of an average strength of 200. On the 9th of that month, however, orders were passed to the Luftflotten to prepare for large-scale raids on London during the full-moon period in the middle of the month. The first of these raids was a heavy one by 1940 standards, and was aimed at London by 487 aircraft carrying 386 tons of H.E. bombs and some 70,000 1-kilogramme incendiary bombs ; on succeeding nights the attack was repeated by forces of 307, 150, 303 and 320 bombers. The Luftwaffe was hammering London to produce the expected surrender, but the effects of the bombing were too scattered over the great area of London to effect the expected large-scale destruction. The Germans began to realise, too, that the high-explosive bombs they were employing, by far the larger percentage of which were 50 kg. (110 lb.), were not sufficiently destructive. A resort to the use of parachute sea-mines with their powerful blasting effect somewhat compensated for this shortcoming, but their inaccuracy when released from great heights could not improve concentration of attack. The realisation of this partial failure and the fact that London civilian morale had not collapsed brought another change in policy, dictated by Goering.

The Final Plan of Strategic Bombing

45. If Great Britain could not be beaten down and invaded immediately, at least she must not be allowed to gain time for replacing the army lost in France and for increasing her war production. Goering took the decision early in November to extend the Luftwaffe effort to a long-term attrition against the

---

[1] The *Knickebein* beam was received in the bomber aircraft on the normal blind-landing radio equipment, and worked on the blind-landing (Lorenz) principle.

whole British industrial effort. The object was to destroy the main industrial centres, with their populations, so that Great Britain would be paralysed into defeat. Parallel with this new plan had come a decision to employ the " X " beams in massed attack, with the employment of KG.100, the one specialist unit capable of using this system as target-finders. Aircraft of this unit were to precede the main force and, acting on the highly accurate bomb-aiming data supplied by the beams, to light up the target areas with incendiary fires to permit visual bombing by the main force.

46. Once more the Germans were beset by quarrels in high places, with attempts by protagonists of the " X " and " Y " navigational systems to force their sole operational use. The result was that both systems were employed and, like *Knickebein*, were introduced prematurely so that their effect was largely impaired by the inevitable British radio counter-measures. The latter led to further quarrels and uncertainty which extended to the operational units and brought a general lack of confidence in the ability of the fire-raising units to find their targets accurately. The Germans had only now come to realise that the British were using the only powerful defensive weapon which they possessed at that time—the radio counter-measure. The radio high-frequency war, which was to have such a far reaching effect on Luftwaffe strategy, had begun and found the Germans unprepared.

47. From mid-October onwards the nightly attacks on London continued with average strength of 150 bombers and with the occasional employment of *Knickebein*, where reliance was placed on the surprise element. Early in November, however, the new plan for strategic bombing was launched by Goering with a new set of orders to the Luftflotten, as follows :—

1. London to remain the main target—
   (a) In daylight attacks by escorted fighter-bombers and, when there is cloud cover, by single bombers.
   (b) In night attacks by equal forces of Luftflotten 2 and 3.
2. Attack industrial areas of Coventry, Birmingham and Liverpool by small forces at night.
3. Mining of the Thames, Bristol Channel, Mersey and Manchester shipping canal by Fliegerkorps IX.
4. Destruction of the Rolls Royce aero-engine works at Hillington (Glasgow) by a Gruppe of KG.26 (using " Y " for target-finding).
5. Damaging of the enemy fighter arm by fighter sweeps.
6. Attacks, with fighter escort, on convoys in the Channel and on assemblies of shipping in the Thames.
7. Destruction of the enemy aircraft industry by special crews of Luftflotten 2 and 3.
8. Attacks on enemy night-fighter bases.
9. Preparation for attacks on Coventry, Birmingham and Wolverhampton (" X " beam).
10. Bomb loads in proposed two large-scale attacks on London—
    (a) half with heavy and heaviest bombs ;
    (b) half with incendiary bombs.

This plan shows the beginnings of the use of the " Y " beams by small numbers of aircraft against special targets, and of the " X " beams in the large-scale attacks on Coventry, Birmingham and Wolverhampton (the latter cancelled owing to British prior knowledge[1]) where the fire-raising aircraft of KG.100, at that time based at Vannes in Britanny, preceded the main forces. The attack on Coventry took place on November 14th and was undertaken by a force of 469 bombers, carrying 420 tons of H.E. bombs and large numbers of incendiaries. This raid marked the first operational use of the " X " system for pathfinding and was extremely successful. The Birmingham attack, made by over 700 aircraft, took place on the 19th and was followed during the remainder of that month and December by a succession of large-scale raids on London, Bristol, Plymouth, Liverpool, Southampton and Sheffield.

Burning of the City of London

48. The year 1940 closed with a sharp attack on London in the evening of December 29th. The raid was called off by the Germans some two hours after its commencement owing to a deterioration in weather conditions ; nevertheless, in this short attack the main part of the City area of London was destroyed by fire. It is interesting to note that, contrary to a common belief, this raid was not a premeditated attempt on the part of Goering to destroy the City of London by fire—no order to that effect appears in the German Staff documents covering that period—but was to be merely another routine night raid on London. That evening, the " X " beam was, in fact, directed on London as an aid to navigation by KG.100, the pathfinder force, but the line of the beam was actually laid in a S.E.-N.W. direction over the Charing Cross Road and Tottenham Court Road. A fresh south-west wind was blowing at the time and the pathfinders, evidently giving insufficient allowance for this wind, placed the first incendiary marker-bombs about a mile to the East and immediately to the North-West of St. Paul's Cathedral. The aircraft of the main bomber force, seeing the resultant fires, contributed their loads of H.E. and incendiary bombs without further question. Thus, was the City of London burned.

The Main Ports as the Targets of Attack

49. By December, London had ceased to be the main nightly target for attack, and the assault continued on the main ports and industrial centres, albeit with varying success owing mainly to the growing British mastery of the " X " beam and their development of elaborate decoy fire systems near main target areas. Finally, by January, general lack of confidence in the navigational and bomb-aiming systems for the leading of large-scale attacks was such that, for the next three months, German aircraft only penetrated to inland targets in force during moonlight ; instead, the main attention of the Luftwaffe was focussed on the chief ports, such as Plymouth, Bristol, Swansea, Cardiff and Hull, over which the beams could still be employed with a minimum of disturbance.

End of the Blitz : Withdrawal of Bomber Forces

50. In April, 1941, the Balkan campaign was already under way, and some of the bomber units in the West, amounting to a total of about 150, were quietly withdrawn from France and North-West Germany[2]. Other types of aircraft such as dive bombers, S.E. fighters and reconnaissance, had already been taken southwards during the winter and early spring. Fliegerkorps X

---

[1] A German photographic reconnaissance of the target area during the day preceding the attack had disclosed large movements of A.A. to the City and outskirts ; it was from this that the Germans assumed a prior knowledge of their intentions.

[2] See Map 7 on page 121.

had moved from Norway to the Mediterranean at the end of 1940 in order to reinforce the Italians in their attempt to deny the Mediterranean to British shipping. During May, 1941, when preparations for the attack on Russia were already afoot, some ground units of Luftflotte 2 and then some of the flying units were also being moved eastwards. As a cover for these moves, raids on Great Britain were accompanied by spoof radio traffic to simulate larger forces. On May 10th, a large-scale night attack was launched on London as a demonstration that if there were rumours of moves, the Luftwaffe was still facing Great Britain in strength. This raid, the heaviest of the whole of the *Blitz*, was made by 550 aircraft—a scale achieved largely by double and even treble sorties from airfields in France and Belgium—carrying 708 tons of H.E. bombs and 86,700 incendiaries, and caused tremendous damage in greater London ; three nights later the raid was repeated in similar strength.

51. At the end of May, Kesselring moved with the whole of Luftflotte 2 to the East in readiness for the attack on Russia (see Chapter 7, paragraphs 5–7). The bomber units of Fliegerkorps IV and V were also withdrawn from Luftflotte 3, leaving only a small mixed force of bomber, reconnaissance, bomber-reconnaissance and minelaying aircraft, together with S.E. fighter forces for defensive purposes in France and Holland, to continue with a holding war against Great Britain. The programme for the beating down of Great Britain had overrun its time and, although considerable damage had been wrought on her cities and industries, the time for the hoped-for collapse had passed. The Germans had had every opportunity to bring Great Britain to her knees but failed because they had no firm and continuous policy of attack. Had the Germans been prepared for radio warfare, the navigational beams, themselves an improvisation in their application to night bombing, could have achieved disastrous damage to British cities and industry. The lack of a policy at Staff level had all too frequently resulted in allowing the hard-pressed cities to recover from large-scale attacks where one more raid would have produced complete breakdown. The only solution now lay in the starving of Great Britain of food and supplies by combined air and sea attacks on her shipping, and in awaiting or forcing her surrender after the expected defeat of Russia in the autumn of 1941.

The Anti-Shipping Campaign and Battle of the Atlantic (1939-1942)

The Development of Shipping Attack[1]

52. Early in 1939 there existed in the High Command of the Armed Forces a vague conception of the possibility of combined air and fleet operations, but ideas had as yet not crystallised to the same extent as in the case of combined Army and Air Force operations with their greater background of experience from the Spanish War. The aircraft had, indeed, been considered as a means of laying minefields in the high seas, and trials had taken place, but with negative results ; minelaying was still regarded as a strictly naval affair, and as yet there were no clear conceptions of aerial minelaying in shallow coastal waters and harbours. Bombing, too, had progressed little further where shipping attack was concerned, although early in 1939 courses of training for bombing of ships

---

[1] See also Chapter 1, paragraphs 39–40 and Chapter 2, paragraphs 52–55.

were held over the North Sea ; a Ju.87 dive bomber unit was also envisaged for the new aircraft carrier *Graf Zeppelin*. In torpedo attack with seaplanes, slight progress had also been made, but development was largely handicapped by the unsuitability of the existing naval torpedo for airborne operations and the personal prejudices of Udet ; the torpedo bomber did not come into its own until 1942.

53. The German Air Force as a whole, with the exception of its fleet reconnaissance units, remained wholly untrained in navigation over the sea and therefore, by August, 1939, was in no state of preparation for anti-shipping warfare. The fleet reconnaissance units comprised a small élite Fleet Air Arm whose officers and men had been drawn almost entirely from the Navy and Merchant Service and were therefore already highly trained in sea navigation. The command of these forces was in the hands of the *General der Luftwaffe beim Oberkommando der Kriegsmarine*—abbreviated to Ob. d.M.—(Air Officer with the Naval High Command) who was responsible for equipment, training and operations—the latter, however, in cooperation with the Naval High Command. Subordinate to Ob. d.M. were the *Fuehrer der Seeluftstreit-kraefte* (A.O.C.'s Fleet Air Arm) East and West whose respective areas of responsibility corresponded to those of the equivalent naval commands. The forces at the disposal of the Fleet Air Arm at outbreak of war had an establishment of 228 aircraft, but comprised the obsolescent He.59—a twin-engined biplane with floats—for minelaying and torpedo work, the He.60 single-engined biplane-seaplane for close-range and shipborne reconnaissance, and the Do.18 twin-engined flying boat for long-range reconnaissance. Experimental formations of Ju.87 dive bombers and Me.109 S.E. fighters also existed in readiness for aircraft carriers.

54. In the late summer of 1939 the Luftwaffe General Staff became convinced of the necessity of providing modern bombers for attacking enemy naval forces which might attempt to enter German waters, as well as for the possible bombing of British warships in their own anchorages where German naval forces could not penetrate. The Fleet Air Arm could not be employed for this purpose as it possessed neither the crews trained in bombing nor the necessary aircraft, besides which the Naval High Command was prejudiced in favour of the employment of aircraft solely as the eyes of the Fleet. The only alternative then, was to train crews of the Luftwaffe bomber force in navigation over sea and in attacks on ships. The first step in this direction was taken when General Geisler (later to become A.O.C. of Fliegerkorps X) was appointed in April, 1939, as *General z.b.v.*[2] with Luftflotte 2 at Kiel and was charged with organising the Luftwaffe anti-shipping forces.

55. Two Luftwaffe bomber units, KG.26 and KG.30, equipped respectively with the He.111 and the Ju.88—the latter the most modern bomber aircraft—were chosen to undertake shipping attack. The best possible crews were selected, and after receiving the necessary training, began operations as soon as war broke out. No previous background of experience in the bombing of warships existed, and the small band of enthusiastic officer pilots engaged in these operations evolved and perfected their own methods whilst attacking warships in the North Sea and at their anchorages, mainly at Scapa Flow and the Firth

---

[1] See Chapter 3, paragraph 13.
[2] *Zur besonderen Verwendung* = for special purposes.

A He.59 Minelayer

Arado 196 Short-range Reconnaissance aircraft launched from a warship

Baumbach, one of the foremost anti-shipping pilots in the German Air Force. He took part in attacks on the British Fleet and merchant shipping in 1939, 1940 and 1941 and on the Arctic convoys in 1942. He flew a Ju.88 with the unit KG30.

The Ju.88. One of the most versatile of any aircraft in use in the war. It was used as a reconnaissance aircraft, bomber, torpedo-bomber, fighter (mainly over the Bay of Biscay) and night fighter (see also illustration on page 23).

of Forth. The extension of these activities to convoys of merchant shipping was a natural and obvious step, and the successful results achieved in convoy attack began to have their effect on the German Air Force Staff.

56. General Geisler's small command under Luftflotte 2 was elevated in status and became Fliegerdivision 10, with Major Harlinghausen as Operations Officer. The reconnaissance units of the Fleet Air Arm cooperated closely with Fliegerdivision 10 in reporting targets for attack, but still operated under the orders of the Naval High Command. As 1939 drew to a close the two bomber units, KG.26 and KG.30, were being rapidly expanded and had each reached a strength of some 40 aircraft. In February, 1940, General Geisler's Division was again upgraded to become Fliegerkorps X ; with the experience in tactics of shipping attack now accumulated, the Fliegerkorps had come to be recognised as expert in that field, and was the obvious choice for leading the Luftwaffe in the Norwegian campaign in April, 1940.

Development of Minelaying

57. Parallel with the development of shipping attack by bombing, a small nucleus of enthusiasts in the Fleet Air Arm, without any direction from above, was evolving new tactics in aerial minelaying. In August, 1939, General Coeler, the A.O.C. Fleet Air Arm West, was given operational command—under Ob. d.M.—of the whole Fleet Air Arm and took over the title of *Fuehrer der Seeluftstreitkraefte* (A.O.C. Fleet Air Arm). General Coeler immediately began agitating for permission to conduct aerial minelaying operations in British ports and coastal waters. This permission was finally granted by the Navy, and after agreement as to areas of operations, his He.59's began to lay naval mines in the Downs, Thames Estuary and off Sheerness. At this time the Navy demanded prior approval of each and every sortie, but finally General Coeler obtained permission to continue with independent operations. A firm agreement with the Navy provided for the Fleet Air Arm also to cover such shallow coastal waters as were out of reach of naval vessels ; these waters included the Clyde, Firth of Forth, Plymouth, Liverpool and Belfast.

58. The Luftwaffe High Command had as yet taken no interest in minelaying ; indeed, there was nobody but General Coeler and his staff who were competent to pronounce judgment on the subject. From September, 1939 onwards, the He.59's of the minelaying units were replaced by He.111's and Do.17's, but as operations were extended and the British defences began to develop, losses began to mount up. This brought the personal interest of Goering, who in mid-December, 1939, called General Coeler to his headquarters to give an explanation. Coeler succeeded in pointing out that if losses were heavy, successes against British shipping were correspondingly great. The result of the interview was that Goering became convinced of the efficacy of minelaying and undertook to create a special Luftwaffe command for minelaying forces ; in February, 1940, this Command was formed and named Fliegerdivision 9.

Decline of the Fleet Air Arm

59. On the formation of Fliegerdivision 9, the unit of the Fleet Air Arm which had been responsible for developing minelaying was withdrawn from the command of Ob. d.M. and the direct influence of the Navy. This move marked the beginning of a disintegration of the Fleet Air Arm, a tendency which became more pronounced between the latter part of 1940 and 1942 as one unit

atter another was seconded to the Luftwaffe proper and then absorbed. There was much disagreement between German Air Force and Navy staffs as to the functions of a Fleet Air Arm, the Navy always maintaining that these forces should be employed solely for Fleet reconnaissance. As one unit after another converted to land-based aircraft and then added bombing to its reconnaissance duties, losses were suffered with which the coastal training schools were unable to keep pace. The Luftwaffe supplied replacement crews from the bomber schools and thus obtained a lasting grip on the units. The Norwegian campaign saw an acceleration of this tendency as many of the Fleet Air Arm reconnaissance units were thrown into the common effort of shipping recon-naissance and bombing, and then seconded to the Luftwaffe never to be returned.

60. The Navy held to its Fleet Air Arm theories until the end of the war. On the other hand, however, Goering failed to employ to their full advantage the anti-shipping forces which he had built up or acquired. From the time of the fall of France and through the Battles of Britain and the Atlantic these forces were continually diverted to overland bombing duties. This misuse of forces was largely due to the weakness of Ob. b.M., who failed to form a centrally coordinated anti-shipping command from the forces which were at hand ; another no less important factor was that the two- and then three-front war which the Luftwaffe was fighting could not allow sufficient forces to be disposed in the West for simultaneous assaults on Britain and her shipping.

From the Norwegian Campaign to the Battle of Britain

61. With the opening of the Norwegian campaign, the Luftwaffe anti-shipping forces had reached a recognisable stage of development. As Fliegerkorps X was leading the Luftwaffe in the campaign, its forces were inevitably expanded by the addition of bomber, dive bomber and fighter units seconded from other Luftflotten[1]. The nucleus of specialised shipping attack units, however, still continued with their task of attacking the British Navy at its bases and the supply traffic between Great Britain and Norway. The Fleet Air Arm, meanwhile, had continued the conversion of its aircraft from the obsolete types to He.115 floatplanes and the He.111 and Do.17. The reconnaissance activities of some of its units had been extended to bomber-reconnaissance and, still experimentally, torpedo-carrying.

62. During the campaigns in the Low Countries and France the aircraft of Fliegerkorps X continued their attacks on naval and merchant shipping and improved their tactics in the bombing of coastal convoys in British waters. The large force which Fliegerkorps X had accumulated for the Battle of Norway was, however, no longer available, and for anti-shipping work the Fliegerkorps was reduced to its two original units, KG.26 and KG.30 ; the bomber and other forces were largely withdrawn to take part in the campaigns in Holland, Belgium and France. Fliegerdivision 9, on the other hand, was able to increase its minelaying forces after the fall of France by a whole Geschwader of some 100 He.111 aircraft—KG.4—which had taken part in the Norwegian and French campaigns as a bomber unit. In the period of preparation for the Battle of Britain in late June and July, 1940, planned minelaying operations were continued on an increasing scale and successes claimed for minelaying were justifiably high.

---

[1] See also Chapter 3, paragraph 17.

Vannes airfield (Britanny, France). This old French airfield was used by the original pathfinder force, KG100, in the Blitz on Great Britain. During 1941 it was modernised and enlarged, and was much used by anti-shipping units during that year. Note the dispersal, with separate hangars, each fully equipped for light repairs, and each accommodating one aircraft.

Atlantic Condors (FW.200)

MAP 6

GERMAN AIR FORCE ANTI-SHIPPING CAMPAIGN

LOCATIONS OF COMMANDS AND SPHERES OF ACTIVITY (SUMMER 1941)

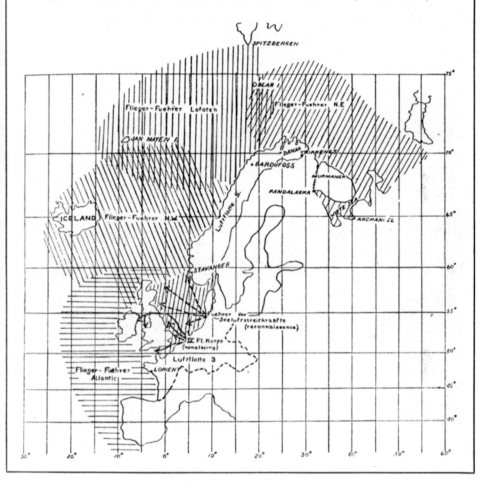

63. When the Battle of Britain opened on August 13th, shipping attack became a part of the campaign as a whole and, although at the outset the forces of Fliegerkorps X in Norway continued with their attacks on the British Fleet and convoys, the full effort of the Luftwaffe was soon thrown into the common bombing effort. The minelaying forces of Fliegerdivision 9—raised to the status of Fliegerkorps IX in October—as well as the anti-shipping units of Fliegerkorps X had to fall in with the major plan of attack. Whilst minelaying aircraft were put to bombing centres such as Birmingham, the two units from Fliegerkorps X were withdrawn from Norway and attached to Luftflotte 2 to swell the bomber forces. Conversely, other Luftwaffe forces, such as the dive bombers of Fliegerkorps VIII, were thrown in for attacking both shipping and land objectives. The whole concentration of effort at this time was on the beating down of the R.A.F. and the aircraft industry and then on bombing Great Britain into surrender. It was not until March, 1941, when the chances of a quick decision against England began to vanish, that the Luftwaffe Operations Staff turned its full attention to the supply of Great Britain from the sea.

64. A blockade of Britain had now become inevitable and a plan for shipping attack was accordingly evolved from the first time as a clear and single objective. Meanwhile, however, Fliegerkorps X had been withdrawn and moved to Sicily and attention was already turned to the Balkans, with Russia in the background, so that the forces which would be available to pursue this plan would sooner or later have to be seriously depleted.

The Battle of the Atlantic Begins

65. After the fall of France the Germans were in a position of advantage for conducting a sea blockade of Great Britain in that they were in possession of the whole coastline extending from northern Norway to the Bay of Biscay. The German Navy and Air Force made full use of this advantage in extending bases to the Atlantic Coast at the earliest opportunity and in pressing on with the construction of large modern airfields at such places as Bordeaux, Cognac, Vannes, Dinard, Rennes and Evreux in France, and Stavanger, Trondheim, Gardemoen, Bardufoss, Banak, and Kirkenes in Norway. Whilst the Battle of Britain was being fought, the Navy was busy establishing itself on the Atlantic coast and was operating U-boats against supply traffic to Great Britain passing from the Mediterranean and Atlantic through the Western Approaches and the waters to the North of Ireland. Air support was called in by the Navy for searching out convoys and shipping for subsequent attack by U-boats or surface vessels, and from early August some 15 He.115's and 6 to 8 FW.200 Condors were being employed for this purpose by Marine Gruppe West at Lorient.

66. The employment of the Condor for Atlantic reconnaissance was a novelty. During the campaign in Norway the need had been felt for a long-range transport aircraft for the supplying of Narvik, and the FW.200 Condor, a four-engined civil transport aircraft, was hurriedly supplied with defensive armament and pressed into service. Only two or three aircraft were initially available, but it was soon realised that the type might also be used as a long-range bomber to attack British forces at Narvik. A new bomber unit, K.G.40, was therefore formed and immediate steps were taken to make provision in the Condor for bomb stowage. The type was not, however, successful as a bomber, but its possibilities were developed for long-range armed reconnaissance,

mainly against shipping, where a large load of fuel and a maximum of four 250-kilogramme bombs could be carried. Thus, late in 1940, when the Navy was calling for air reconnaissance stretching far into the Atlantic, the Condor unit was at hand. By that time a new aircraft—the He.177—specially designed for shipping attack was under development ; with its four engines coupled in pairs to two propellers, its high speed and great fuel and bomb capacity, great things were expected of this type once it could be put into operations over the Atlantic. The Condor was never more than a makeshift and was to have been replaced by the He.177 in the late summer of 1941. As it was, the latter type suffered from continual mechanical and aerodynamic troubles in its development, and did not finally appear in operations until late in 1943[1]. The Condor therefore continued to be employed in Atlantic operations, although its vulnerability and low speed soon made it useless for direct attack on well-armed merchant convoys. Nevertheless, its great range for reconnaissance purposes— extending to the West of Iceland and frequently from Bordeaux to Trondheim in Norway—coupled with its striking power as a bomber, had made the Condor a serious menace to British shipping during the winter and spring of 1940-41.

67. Once the Luftwaffe General Staff had decided upon the blockade of Great Britain in collaboration with the Navy, a re-grouping of commands took place in March, 1941, whereby the whole European coastline facing Great Britain and the Atlantic was covered by anti-shipping forces. In practice this reorganisation did little more than take over existing anti-shipping forces, but their strength immediately began to increase, particularly in the area facing the Atlantic and Western approaches. In Norway, where Luftflotte 5 had assumed direct control of operations at the end of 1940, after the withdrawal of Fliegerkorps X to Sicily, two new subordinate commands were now created. These were Fliegerfuehrer Nord (later split up into Nord and Nord-Ost), and Fliegerfuehrer Lofoten ; their duties were anti-shipping operations and reconnaissance for the U-boats and other naval forces to the North of Lat. 58° N. The North Sea area from Lat. 52° to 58° N. still remained the responsibility, as far as reconnaissance was concerned, of Fuehrer der Seeluftstreitkraefte, whose Fleet Air Arm reconnaissance seaplanes were based on the West coast of Jutland. Fliegerkorps IX, based in Holland, retained the responsibility for minelaying around the British coasts. To cover the Western Approaches and Atlantic and the East Coast of England, the regrouping of March, 1941, was completed by the creation of a new command under Luftflotte 3 ; with headquarters at Lorient, this command was named *Fliegerfuehrer Atlantik*. The strategic encirclement of Great Britain and her maritime supply routes was thus complete. (See Map 6.)

Fliegerfuehrer Atlantik (Atlantic Command)

68. The main focus of U-boat and air operations during 1941 and part of 1942 lay on the convoy routes from the United States and from the South Atlantic and Gibraltar ; the greatest weight of air operations during that period therefore fell upon Fliegerfuehrer Atlantik. It was for this reason that Harlinghausen, who had taken part in the Spanish War[2] and who was one of the pioneers in 1939 of shipping attack with bombs, and chief of Staff of Fliegerkorps X during the Norwegian campaign, was chosen as A.O.C. of the

---

[1] See Chapter 13, paragraph 38, and illustration on page 304.

[2] See Chapter 1, paragraph 39.

new Command. The air forces operating under Harlinghausen had the special duty of the closest possible cooperation with the Flag Officer U-boats (*Befehlshaber der U-Boote*), also at Lorient. The aircraft, based at the new airfields then nearing completion in western France, were to provide reconnaissance reports of the positions and movements of convoys and other shipping for subsequent attack by U-boats, besides attacking shipping on their own account where opportunity presented itself. Another duty of Fleigerfuehrer Atlantik was to attack coastal shipping around the East, South and West coasts of Great Britain with bomber and torpedo aircraft.

69. Up to May, 1941, British coastal convoys, shipping and ports were under the continuous attack of the large forces at the disposal of Luftflotten 2 and 3, also at that time engaged in the bombing of Great Britain in the *Blitz*. Once those forces were withdrawn to other fronts Fliegerfuehrer Atlantik was the most important command remaining to continue offensive warfare against shipping. Fliegerkorps IX, it is true, was still in Holland, but its aircraft were engaged solely in minelaying ; the other Commands in Norway only disposed of small offensive forces and were engaged mainly in providing reconnaissance for the U-boats.

Available Forces

70. The forces set aside for anti-shipping operations from March, 1941, onwards varied considerably in strength from month to month. In March the forces of Fliegerfuehrer Atlantik had comprised 21 Condors (of which only six to eight were normally serviceable), some 24 He.115 bomber-torpedo aircraft and a mixed Ju.88 and Me.110 reconnaissance unit of 12 aircraft—a total of 44 aircraft. By April these forces had been increased to the following :—

FW.200 Condors (of which 6-8 in Norway)	21
He.111 Bombers	26
He.115 Bomber-torpedo	24
Me.110/Ju.88 Reconnaissance	12
Total	83

After only six weeks of operations the He.111's were withdrawn owing to their heavy losses. At the same time, however, the total strength was gradually being built up, mainly by the conversion of some Fleet Air Arm reconnaissance units to the Ju.88 and the creation of a new Gruppe of KG.40 to·man the new Do.217. In Norway, meanwhile, parts of the two original anti-shipping units, KG.26 and KG.30, had remained under Luftflotte 5 after the withdrawal of Fliegerkorps X. These units, with some 20 He.111's and 24 Ju.88's were operating mainly against British shipping and ports. By July, Fliegerfuehrer Atlantik's forces had reached the following strength :—

FW.200 Condors (all in France)	29
He.111 (now replaced)	31
Ju.88 Bomber-reconnaissance	45
He.115 Bomber-torpedo	18
Do.217 Bomber-reconnaissance	20
Me.110/Ju.88 Reconnaissance	12
Total	155

Operations: Atlantic Convoys

71. Had the German Air Force General Staff taken the decision to concentrate large air forces against merchant convoys in the Atlantic and Western Approaches in the autumn of 1940, the situation for the supply of Great Britain must surely have reached a more critical situation than it did. As it was, chief attention was then being paid to the bombing of cities and industries and the forces put at the disposal of the anti-shipping units in the Atlantic were meagre. At that time defensive armament on merchant ships was inadequate or non-existant, and the small numbers of Condors which attacked convoys met with some success. By June, 1941, however, when Fliegerfuehrer Atlantik had been able to build up a more effective strength, the defensive armament of merchant ships had also been developed to an extent which had began to command the respect of marauding aircraft. The Condors could no longer deliver direct attacks on merchant shipping without suffering dangerous losses, and the aircraft were consequently forced into purely armed reconnaissance. Their crews had to be content with surprise attack where cloud cover permitted unseen approach and escape from punishment.

72. Reconnaissance reports from the Condors had been demanded by the Flag Officer U-boats from the outset and a method of operation had been developed which formed a basis for anti-shipping operations for the rest of the war. Upon sighting a convoy the Condors would report position and course to the Flag Officer U-boats. Whilst the U-boats were being brought into position for an interception—a process which occupied some hours—relays of Condors, one or two at a time, continued to shadow the convoy and periodically to report its position[1]. The lust for personal fame amongst Condor crews and the initial lack of armament on merchant vessels had brought with them a tendency for the Condors to take the matter of attack into their own hands, but losses were considerable in proportion to the available forces, and I/KG.40 could barely maintain a serviceability of eight aircraft out of 25 to 30 up to June, 1941.

73. U-boat operations had so far taken place on the convoy routes within 20° W. and between Gibraltar and the North of Ireland, well within the range of the Condor. By June, 1941, however, the appearance of anti-U-boat patrol aircraft of R.A.F. Coastal Command was making U-boat operations more and more difficult. When, therefore, the C.-in-C. of the German Navy moved the sphere of U-boat operations to the mid- and western Atlantic beyond 20° W., much of the effort by the Atlantic reconnaissance aircraft of Fliegerfuehrer Atlantik became redundant. A Condor patrol which had regularly operated between Bordeaux and Stavanger was withdrawn partly for this reason and partly owing to increasing danger from R.A.F. anti-U-boat aircraft. Thereafter the only activity left to the Condor units was reconnaissance of convoys passing in and out of Gibraltar. Friction arose between the German Air Force and Navy, with accusations by Fliegerfuehrer Atlantik that the Luftwaffe was being ignored, and a resultant lack of collaboration between the two services. A frequent complaint by Fliegerfuehrer Atlantik was that the Condor forces had sighted and reported a convoy and had maintained shadowing aircraft for long periods but without any U-boat attack materialising. It would subsequently be learned that there had been no U-boats within possible striking distance, a fact which Admiral U-boats failed to communicate.

---

[1] This operation was known as " *Fuehlungshalter* ".

74. By December, 1941, one of the He.111 anti-shipping units, III/KG.40, was beginning to convert to the Condor, because by that time the conclusion had been reached that anti-shipping operations near the British coasts were too expensive in aircraft and crews. In that month, however, part of the Condor forces were withdrawn to the Mediterranean and in January further aircraft were taken on transport assignments to the Russian front, and Condor operations in the Atlantic fell to the lowest level ; they were not resumed until the summer of 1943.

Operations in British Coastal Waters

75. The campaign against shipping in British coastal waters, begun as a single objective on the inception of Fliegerfuehrer Atlantik in March, 1941, followed approximately the same course as the Condor operations in the Atlantic and Western Approaches. Conditions were favourable for the attacking aircraft before British fighter patrols and defensive armament of shipping had been developed. During that period, however, the forces of Fliegerfuehrer Atlantik had not been organised and the aircraft were not available in sufficient quantity ; nevertheless, the effect which this small number of aircraft produced was at times serious, and was out of all proportion to the size of the forces employed. It certainly obliged the British to set aside a considerable force of aircraft to act as shipping escort patrols. Once the large numbers of German aircraft did become available, the British defences had reached such a state of efficiency that, already by June, 1941, operations by the Luftwaffe were becoming difficult ; by November of that year they had become nearly impossible. The early basis of shipping attack was a method of low-level approach to the beam of a target vessel, followed by the release of bombs to hit the vessel below the waterline, whilst the aircraft passed over the vessel at mast height. This method had been evolved by Harlinghausen, and at the time when the defensive armament of shipping was non-existent it had presented little difficulty or danger and had, indeed, achieved considerable success. The method was, however, persisted in to a disastrous point where conditions had obviously been rendered impossible by the British introduction of parachute-and-cable rockets and 20-mm. cannon armament in the merchant ships.

76. By the Summer of 1941 some of the coastal anti-shipping forces of Fliegerfuehrer Atlantik were based in Holland and their He.111 aircraft were concentrating upon shipping passing along the East Coast. Another Ju.88 Gruppe of some 30 aircraft, based in Britanny, also operated in this area, at first with some success. Other Ju.88, He.111 and He.115 units operated in the Channel, Bristol Channel and Irish Sea, the latter aircraft occasionally with torpedoes. The He.111 units, which were operating whilst other units were still converting to the Ju.88, suffered heavy losses in both crews and morale ; III/KG.40 had to be withdrawn in April with only eight crews remaining out of 32. The Ju.88 and then the Do.217 appeared in operations—the latter type in August—but also suffered casualties to fighters and shipping armament, although not to the extent of the slower He.111. A restriction to dawn and dusk operations somewhat curtailed these losses, but then the main function of the anti-shipping forces, the destruction of British coastal shipping, was not being accomplished.

77. The minelaying forces were operating independently under Fliegerkorps IX in spite of continued protests by Fliegerfuehrer Atlantik that all anti-shipping operations in British coastal waters should be under his control. The original

units had, by July, been withdrawn to the Russian and other fronts and some of the He.111 units of Fliegerfuehrer Atlantik had been seconded to continue the minelaying operations. Meanwhile, another bomber unit, KG.2, was converting to the Do.217 and was appearing in minelaying operations by the late summer. Minelaying aircraft were, however, diverted to an increasing extent to bombing operations over Great Britain, for lack of other bomber aircraft in the West. This tendency became more marked towards the end of 1941 when German public opinion was demanding bombing of Great Britain in revenge for the rising scale of R.A.F. night attack on Germany. The Staff of Luftflotte 3 protested to the German Air Force Staff, the Combined Staffs, and to Goering himself against the misemployment of anti-shipping forces, and pointed out that the damage which could be done to British industry with so few aircraft was negligible. The protest was ignored.

78. In October, 1941, Generalmajor Harlinghausen, who had occasionally taken part in anti-shipping operations in order to maintain a first-hand picture of conditions, was wounded in an attack on a convoy escort vessel in the Bristol Channel. A deputy filled the post of Fliegerfuehrer Atlantik for some time, but early in 1942 Generalmajor Kessler, an officer who had only held obscure posts in the Luftwaffe, was appointed to the Command—an indication that the General Staff considered the anti-shipping campaign in this area to be of diminishing importance. As 1941 drew to a close and Russia was still unbeaten, but on the contrary was receiving enormous supplies from the outside world by the Arctic route from Iceland to the White Sea, the focus of attention moved from the supply routes of Great Britain to the Arctic convoy routes.

The Luftwaffe Adopts the Torpedo[1]

79. Since 1926, German torpedo development had been in the hands of the Navy, who had purchased the Horten naval torpedo patents from Norway in 1933 and the Whitehead Fiume patents from Italy in 1938. Development in the direction of air-launched torpedoes, in the hands of the Fleet Air Arm, was slow ; the Luftwaffe proper had as yet taken no interest. Trials early in 1939[2], when torpedoes were launched from the He.59 and He.115 floatplanes, showed 49 per cent. failure, largely due to aerodynamic difficulties of the torpedoes in launching from the aircraft and to depth control and fusing problems. From the outbreak of war up to the autumn of 1941 the Fleet Air Arm maintained two seaplane units—a total of some 24[3] aircraft—which were engaged spasmodically in torpedo operations against British shipping off the Scottish coast and against merchant shipping in the Western Approaches. Results, however, were poor and, apart from a shortage of torpedoes, showed little progress in launching practice since the 1939 trials.

80. When, in 1941, the Luftwaffe proper began to take an interest in torpedoes, its efforts were strenuously resisted by the Naval High Command. Data on development of aerial torpedo practice accumulated at the naval establishments were consistently withheld from the Technical Office of the German Air Force, and any independent development in collaboration with private firms was deliberately hindered[2]. Later in 1941 direct requests by the

---

[1] See also Chapter 2, paragraph 53.
[2] From the files of Field Marshal Milch.
[3] See paragraph 66, where actual strength is shown.

109

" The Condors could no longer deliver direct attacks on merchant shipping without suffering dangerous losses " (see para. 71). (*The incident illustrated here took place on 26th July, 1941, at 54° 00′ N., 13° 35′ W.*)

A He.111 Torpedo Bomber

Torpedo carried experimentally by a FW.190

Air Force to take over the aerial aspect of torpedo development were flatly refused by the Navy. Thus, for the first two years of the War this branch of aerial warfare had received little attention and had made little or no progress.

81. With the anti-shipping campaign against Great Britain in full swing in 1941 and with the failure of direct bombing attack on ships owing to increasing defensive armament, the Luftwaffe began to turn afresh to the torpedo as a weapon which could reduce aircraft losses by being launched at a respectful distance from ships or convoys. The Luftwaffe began exhaustive torpedo trials on its own account at the bombing school at Grossenbrode, and in the late autumn dispatched some He.111's to Athens for torpedo operations in the eastern Mediterranean. Owing to lack of torpedoes, or to their delivery without warheads, these operations were abandoned. The Luftwaffe had, however, proved that the He.111, at least, was a highly suitable aircraft for such work. Matters came to a head in December, 1941, when the subject of torpedo development was raised at a Technical Office conference[1] and reported to Goering. A direct demand was made that the Luftwaffe should take over aerial torpedo development in both Germany and Italy, that it should open experimental establishments with the inclusion of such naval staffs as had already been engaged in the aerial branch and finally, that a special Commissioner should be appointed to control Air Force torpedo development, supply, training and operations.

82. Within a month the Air Force had been granted these conditions and, with the whole field of the airborne torpedo now in its hands, pushed ahead with organisation and development with the utmost energy. Harlinghausen, the former Fliegerfuehrer Atlantik, was appointed Commissioner for Torpedoes and immediately laid plans for conversion of existing Air Force units to form a torpedo force with a strength of about 230 aircraft. Actually, this figure was never reached as the Allied invasion of North Africa and then of Italy intervened and upset the training plans.[2] With the onset of winter, the Air Force bomber school at Grossenbrode in the Baltic, where the first trials and conversion courses had taken place, was becoming unsuitable for torpedo development and training ; the whole establishment was, therefore, moved to Grosseto on the West coast of Italy, to the South of Leghorn, where winter training could proceed and a close liaison could be maintained with the Italians, who were progressing on the same lines.

83. Trials at Grosseto with all types of German aircraft confirmed that the He.111, capable of carrying two torpedoes, and the Ju.88—with a better performance as to speed—were the most suitable aircraft. The first unit to undergo conversion was I/KG.26, one of the two original anti-shipping units, and batches of crews were withdrawn from the North Norway front for the three weeks' course. By the end of April, 1942 some 12 crews of the unit were ready for operations and were based at the newly-constructed airfields of Banak and Bardufoss in northern Norway. By June the whole Gruppe, with a strength of 42 He.111's, was ready for operations and another Gruppe, III/KG.26, was undergoing the same course with the Ju.88. By July, 1942, the Luftwaffe possessed a strength of 77[3] torpedo aircraft, the He.111's in Norway and the Ju.88's at Rennes, where the latter made the first massed torpedo

---

[1] From the files of Field Marshal Milch.

[2] See Chapter 11, paragraphs 9 and 10.

[3] Exclusive of naval torpedo aircraft (see paras 75 and 80).

attack on a convoy off the Scilly Isles on August 3rd, after having been misused in a series of reprisal bombing raids on Birmingham. By September the whole of the torpedo force was being employed against the Anglo-American convoys taking supplies to the northern Russian ports. The Germans had now an effective and important weapon in the anti-shipping war ; again, had this weapon been availbale upon the formation of Fliegerfuehrer Atlantik in March, 1941— as it might well have done had the Luftwaffe High Command realised its importance earlier—the Luftwaffe must then surely have played a decisive part in the Battle of the Atlantic.

The Arctic Convoys (May to November, 1942)[1]

84. With the German failure to crush Russia before the winter of 1941-42, the British and American supplies which were being shipped to Russia by the Arctic route began to assume an even greater importance for the Germans. The Luftwaffe forces available for the interception of these convoys were based at the newly-constructed airfields on the Norwegian-Finnish border, and were normally engaged in such duties as the protection of the Petsamo nickel mines, shipping attack in the White Sea and bombing of the Russian ports and communications in the area, as well as Army support operations on the Finnish front. In February, 1942, these forces amounted to some 60 long-range bombers, 30 dive bombers, 30 single-engined fighters and some 15 floatplane torpedo-bombers of the Fleet Air Arm.

85. In March, Goering ordered these forces to operate in collaboration with the Navy whenever the Allied supply convoys to Russia should pass through the Arctic area. When such convoys were expected, their progress towards the White Sea was to be reported by long-range reconnaissance aircraft, whilst all possible striking forces were to be temporarily withdrawn from the Finnish area and placed at airfields such as Bardufoss, Banak and Kirkenes to supplement existing forces and to attack the convoys as soon as they came within range. Long-range reconnaissance was to be undertaken by the Condors of I/KG.40 operating from Trondheim and northern airfields, and was to cover the area of sea between Iceland, Jan Mayen Island, Bear Island and the North Cape. Units of the Fleet Air Arm, now largely re-equipped with the BV.138 three-engined flying boat, were to supplement the reconnaissance effort.

86. During March and April, three Allied convoys, the PQ.13 14 and 15, passed through Arctic waters into White Sea ports. As far as weather conditions allowed, the convoys were duly shadowed by reconnaissance aircraft and attacked by the small available bomber and dive bomber forces. At this time there was a continual movement of bomber units to and from Germany for refitting, and only weak forces could be brought into action. By May the first Staffel of 12 torpedo aircraft of I/KG.26 had arrived fresh from the conversion course at Grosseto, whilst some 60 Ju.88's of KG.30, the anti-shipping bomber unit, were ready in the area.

87. In the middle of May the next Allied convoy, the PQ.16, was expected to leave Iceland, and Condor and BV.138 reconnaissance aircraft were despatched to the area to maintain a watch and report progress. On May 25th, first reports of the convoy being sighted on a westerly course were received at the forward headquarters of Luftflotte 5 at Banak. The striking forces had already been disposed on the northern Norwegian airfields, and on that and succeeding days these forces, acting on information supplied by the shadowing aircraft as to

---

[1] The war diary of Luftflotte 5 has been used in fixing exact dates, available forces, etc.

composition of the convoy and placing of the escorts, attacked simultaneously with dive bombing by the Ju.88's and torpedo attack by the He.111's, supplemented by the He.115's of the Fleet Air Arm. The convoy had dispersed after the first onslaught, but the attacks continued for five days until, on May 30th, the Ju.87 dive bombers took up the fight as the ships entered the White Sea. Air reconnaissance showed that no ship had succeeded in entering a Russian port and accordingly the whole convoy was claimed as having been destroyed[1].

88. After this action the Luftwaffe forces once more retired to their duties on the Finnish front. The torpedo units, however, could not be moved owing to the difficulties of transporting their ground staffs and stocks of torpedoes, and had perforce to remain in idleness until another convoy should arrive. After the passage of PQ.16, however, new lessons were learned which were to form the basis of later tactics, when greater torpedo forces were expected to be available. It was seen that high-level dive bombing by the Ju.88's, closely integrated with the launching of torpedoes from a height of about 300 ft.—the normal height of launching—could dissipate and confuse the convoy defences. These tactics were accordingly practised, as was the actual method of torpedo attack, known as the " Golden Comb " (*Goldene Zange*), whereby the torpedo bombers would approach in a wide line abreast to launch their torpedoes simultaneously. It was planned to attack out of the twilight with the added advantage of the ships being in silhouette against the lighter sky.

89. Warnings of the next convoy, PQ.17, came early in June from espionage sources, which told of ships assembling to the South-West of Iceland. Once more the long-range reconnaissance aircraft covered the area and once more the striking forces were assembled in northern Norway ready for the action. By this time the air forces in the area of the North Cape had been considerably increased and their strength stood at the following figures :—

L.R. Bombers (Ju.88)	.. 103
Torpedo-Bombers (He.111)	.. 42
Torpedo Floatplanes (He.115) (Fleet Air Arm) ..	.. 15
Dive Bombers (Ju.87)	.. 30
L.R. Reconnaissance (FW.200 Condor)	.. 8
L.R. Reconnaissance (Ju.88)	.. 22
L.R. Reconnaissance (BV.138) (Fleet Air Arm) ..	.. 44
	264

90. On July 2nd reports from the shadowing aircraft, which at this time of year could maintain contact throughout the 24 hours of daylight, told of the composition and course of the convoy and gave warning of the positions of the protective warships. The first concentrated bomber and torpedo attacks took place on July 4th and were attended with some success. Liaison between the bomber and torpedo aircraft was, however, poor and the attack was not synchronised as had been planned. Nevertheless, the convoy scattered, as had the PQ.16, and thereafter the Luftwaffe searched for single ships and sank them one by one. As the ships entered Murmansk and the White Sea the Ju.87 dive bombers took up the attack, whilst Ju.88's attacked with bombs and circling torpedoes.[2] General Major Stumpff, the A.O.C. of Luftflotte 5, drew

---

[1] British figures give the convoy as consisting of 34 ships of which seven were lost.

[2] The circling torpedo was dropped from bombers by parachute and described wide erratic circles in the water ; a hit on a vessel was purely chance.

his own conclusions from the absence of any more ships and duly reported to Goering the destruction of the whole convoy[1] with the expenditure of 61 torpedoes and 212 tons of bombs. The part played by the U-boats and German surface vessels was of little concern to the Staff of Luftflotte 5. Complaints came from U-boat commanders of the danger to which their vessels were exposed in the bombing attacks, but there was no operational liaison beyond the passing on of the reports of the shadowing aircraft. In turn, credit for shadowing the convoys was wholly claimed by the Naval Staffs.

91. By October 13th, when the convoy PQ.18 came under attack, the torpedo forces had been increased from 57 to 92 by the addition of III/KG.26 with a strength of 35 Ju.88's. Warnings had been received of the possibility that this convoy would dispose of an aircraft carrier with single-engined fighters, which set a new and serious problem for the Luftwaffe striking forces. It was accordingly decided that the whole strength of the initial attack should be directed against the aircraft carrier ; once this vessel had been disposed of it was considered that the problem of attack for the remainder of the convoy would be solved. When, between October 13th and 19th, the convoy came under attack it was found that not only was it impossible to approach the aircraft carrier to launch an effective attack—on account of the fighters—but that a wide screen of warships made the launching of torpedoes against the inner merchant vessels an extremely hazardous undertaking. German aircraft losses were heavy and the convoy entered the White Sea with comparatively light losses[2].

92. This convoy was the last to come under heavy attack by the Luftwaffe. Once again, when the Allied invasion of North Africa took place on November 8th, the German forces were stretched to the utmost. The whole of the Ju.88 and He.111 torpedo forces were withdrawn to the Mediterranean to be based at Grosseto, Catania and Cagliari on Sardinia[3]. The remaining forces comprised the He.115 floatplanes which, owing to their low speed, had only played a minor part in attacking stragglers from the convoys ; some dive bombers, and the long-range reconnaissance force, whose sole function was now to report convoys for attack by Naval vessels and U-boats. The Luftwaffe failure in the Battle of the Atlantic and Western Approaches in 1941 was being repeated.

The Western Approaches and Biscay Area—1942

93. During the whole of 1942 activity by such forces as remained to Fliegerfuehrer Atlantik was at a low level and consisted mainly of reconnaissance, attacks on coastal shipping off the South and West coasts of England, and scattered daylight raids over England during bad weather, when fighters could not intervene. The minelaying aircraft of Fliegerkorps IX had now been given the added task of shipping attack along the East coast of England (Fuehrer der Seeluftstreitraefte was dissolved in July, 1942) and those forces also added to the daylight bombing over England. In the spring and summer of 1942 the total forces disposed against England were continually varying ; for instance, the units which had been brought from northern Norway for refitting or conversion to torpedoes were held in Holland and South Norway and such

---

[1] British figures give the convoy as consisting of 34 ships of which 23 were lost.
[2] 13 ships out of 40.
[3] See Map 10.

crews as had completed their courses were thrown in for shipping attack. Again, the airfields in France which had been left empty by the withdrawal to Russia were occupied by the Reserve Training units of the bomber Geschwader, and their crews were occasionally put into operations over England, partly as a phase of their final training and partly for the lack of other operational forces. The strength of Fliegerfuehrer Atlantik, however, stood at some 40 Ju.88's for anti-shipping operations, whilst Fliegerkorps IX disposed of some 90 Do.217's.

94. From May, 1942, onwards the Flag Officer U-boats in the Bay of Biscay began to request the help of Fleigerfuehrer Atlantik again. The duties of the aircraft were now no longer offensive, however, but consisted entirely of defensive reconnaissance for the protection of surfaced U-boats passing through the Bay to and from their home ports at Bordeaux, La Pallice, St. Nazaire, Lorient and Brest. The anti-submarine aircraft of R.A.F. Coastal Command were at this time causing some concern by their hunting of surfaced U-boats—sometimes in a damaged condition after Atlantic operations—passing in or out of the Bay. The subsequent appearance of R.A.F. twin-engined fighter patrols made German air reconnaissance more and more costly until finally, in July, a unit of Ju.88 heavy fighters was formed with a strength of nine aircraft, which rapidly expanded towards a planned establishment of 34. As 1942 drew to a close, this defensive battle over the Bay of Biscay increased in intensity, with the R.A.F. anti-submarine aircraft continually in combat with formations of Ju.88's, and the latter meeting the R.A.F. Beaufighters. During the winter of 1942-43 the Condors had again been withdrawn, this time for transport duties in the siege of Stalingrad. It was not until 1943 that the offensive was once more assumed by the German Air Force in the Biscay area. (See Chapter 13 (ii).)

Conclusions

95. The German Air Force anti-shipping campaign of 1941-42 was a failure. The German High Command had expected a conclusion of the war in the West with the Battle of Britain, but with the prolongation of that assault, followed by the improvisation of the *Blitz* and then the decision to concentrate on British supply routes, the High Command had no long-term policy. Consequently, when an advantage against British shipping could have been gained, the necessary air forces were not available ; when the forces did become available the chance of any decisive success had gone. The Luftwaffe thus played no important part in the Battle of the Atlantic, and there is no doubt that its initial weakness led the Navy to ignore Fliegerfuehrer Atlantik, with the resultant complaints by the latter of lack of liaison. Once the Air Force had embarked upon the anti-shipping campaign, it made the mistake of divided command ; there was no central anti-shipping organisation such as R.A.F. Coastal Command. Training of new aircrew for anti-shipping operations was poor— with the exception of the torpedo arm in 1942—and to this must be added the constant wastage of experienced crews by their diversion to night bombing in the *Blitz* and in the subsequent scattered attacks and reprisal raids on Great Britain. The only instance of the Luftwaffe showing itself as an effective force with an adequate planning of operations was in the Arctic area in the summer and autumn of 1942. Then, however, the effort reached its highest point too late ; the German Air Force, with its wide commitments on the European and African fronts, no longer had the power of concentration, and the continued heavy losses of torpedo-bomber crews on operations in the Mediterranean led to a steady decline in their striking power which inadequate training facilities were unable to overcome.

GENERALMAJOR
HARLINGHAUSEN

Leader of the Anti-shipping war against Britain. Born in 1902, he entered the Navy 1923, and served in torpedo boats. Transferred to the Air Force in October, 1933. Commanded the sea reconnaissance Staffel with the Condor Legion in Spain, December, 1937-38. At the outbreak of war in September, 1939, Harlinghausen became operations officer in Fliegerdivision 10, and in May, 1940, Chief of Staff of this command, renamed Fliegerkorps X, in Norway. He was appointed Fliegerfuehrer Atlantic in March, 1941; in January, 1942, Inspector of Aircraft Torpedoes and simultaneously O.C. K.G.26 (torpedo bombers); in November, 1942, Fliegerfuehrer Tunisia; acted as O.C. Fliegerkorps II in Italy, February to May, 1943. In September, 1944, Harlinghausen was appointed A.O.C. Luftgau XIV, in April, 1945, A.O.C. Air Force Command West. Captured by the Allies, June, 1945.

117

HITLER'S "CONTINENTAL POLICY": THE INVASION OF THE BALKANS AND CAPTURE OF CRETE, ACCOMPANIED BY THE ESTABLISHMENT OF THE GERMAN AIR FORCE IN ITALY

The "Continental Policy"

The Mediterranean at the end of 1940[1]

1. Before examining the part played by the Luftwaffe in preparation for the attack on Russia planned for the summer of 1941, it is necessary to study the situation in the Mediterranean as it was in the autumn of 1940—whilst the Battle of Britain was being fought. Italy had declared war on Great Britain and France on 10th June, 1940, and was concentrating troops and armour in her North African colony of Cyrenaica; Egypt was in danger of an Italian invasion. Early in September, British and Australian reinforcements began to arrive in Egypt, and on the 17th of that month the Italians struck eastward into Egypt and occupied Sidi Barrani.

2. In Europe, meanwhile, the first German objectives of the Battle of Britain had not been gained after a month's inconclusive fighting, and Hitler had already lost interest in the *Seeloewe* plan for the invasion of Great Britain. As an alternative he planned to hold Great Britain down by a sea blockade and, whilst his military forces were fully mobilised and at the peak of their efficiency, to dispose first with Russia in an overwhelming and surprise onslaught. Once Russia were beaten down, he could again turn to the conquest or the neutralisation of Great Britain as the sole remaining enemy in Europe.

3. In the onslaught on Russia which was to open in the spring of 1941, the original German plan was to leave the Mediterranean flank in the hands of the Italians, who at the end of October, 1940, began the invasion of Greece. German forces were to go no further into that country than Macedonia, whence they were to make a thrust towards Salonika. The Italian invasion of Greece was not in the plan, and actually came as a surprise to the German Supreme Command. It is true that at the time of planning the Russian campaign vague notions did exist in the mind of Hitler—and in the Supreme Command of the Armed Forces (*O.K.W.*) of a possible extension of the Macedonia-Salonika thrust towards the Persian Gulf, linked up with an Italian thrust through Egypt. Such notions, however, as yet remained in the background, and the prime objective at this stage was solely Russia, with three main German thrusts, one to the North towards Leningrad, one in the centre towards Smolensk, and another to the South aimed at the Caucasian oilfields. The further objectives would be dependant upon the situation in the Mediterranean, in Italian hands.

4. In November and December, 1940, Italian plans in the Mediterranean began to go awry. The Italian forces had become bogged down in Greece, and were actually suffering reverses at the hands of the Greeks, a situation which was further complicated by the arrival of Allied help in Greece and Crete. At the same time the Italian armoured forces which had thrust forward to Sidi Barrani had been thrown back by the British and Australians with the

---

[1] From the interrogation of General Halder, Chief of Army Staff, 1938–1942, and Generaloberst Student, G.O.C. Parachute Army.

capture of 20,000 prisoners. In January, 1941, another Italian setback occurred with the loss of Bardia and a further 30,000 prisoners. The Italians were thus faced with disaster in North Africa—a situation which promised complications for the impending campaign in Russia. Mussolini had requested help from Germany, and Hitler, convinced that he must meet these demands if only to protect Mussolini's political position at home from the consequences of military failure, agreed to give that help. This was in spite of advice from his own General Staff that such action, with the impending war against Russia, would prove a burden to the German Army's resources. With the reinforcement of the Italian armies in North Africa came the question of supply across the Mediterranean from Italy and Sicily. The British Navy and Fleet Air Arm, together with R.A.F. aircraft based on Malta, were making this supply ever more hazardous ; the crippling of three battleships, two cruisers and other naval vessels by a Fleet Air Arm bombing attack on the harbour of Taranto on 11th November, 1940, had made the situation even more acute. Similarly, British supplies were passing eastwards through the Mediterranean, and neither the Italian fleet nor the Italian Air Force could prevent them. The corollary to the German aid in North Africa, then, was the reinforcement of the Italian Air Force at the end of 1940 with elements of the Luftwaffe (see paragraph 20). The situation in Greece, too, bid fair to upset the whole German plans, and thus German forces were obliged to involve themselves in the fighting in Greece in order to dispose of opposition there in the limited time left at their disposal before the opening of the attack on Russia.

The Establishment of the Luftwaffe in the Balkans

5. The assembly of German forces for the attack on Russia was meanwhile proceeding slowly. The first necessary step was the political preparation of Russia's border states of Rumania and Bulgaria for the introduction of the German forces which were to strike the first blow. The part played by the Luftwaffe in these preparations began in September, 1940, when a German Air Force Mission was set up in Rumania, ostensibly with the object of assisting in the training of the Rumanian Air Force. By November and December, 1940, the Mission sponsored the entry of flying and ground units, thinly disguised but at the same time without publicity and with the alleged object of protecting Rumanian oilfields. During this period much was done in the surveying of Rumanian airfields, setting up of Flak defences, the construction of living accommodation and the setting up of signals, administration and supply units.

6. In Bulgaria similar developments took place. The first entry of Luftwaffe personnel, disguised as civilians, occurring in December, 1940, and continuing up to March, 1941, when Bulgaria joined the Axis ; thereafter Air Force units undisguisedly entered the country.

7. For the support of the impending military operations, air reinforcements on a major scale were planned under the general command of General der Flieger Loehr, A.O.C. of Luftflotte 4, whose headquarters was in Vienna. The actual air operations were entrusted to General von Richthofen, Commanding Fliegerkorps VIII, who had made an outstanding reputation for himself in the enterprising, successful and hard-hitting employment of his Fliegerkorps in tactical support during the Battle of France, and had taken part in attacks on shipping in the Channel and land targets in southern England during the earlier stages of the Battle of Britain[1].

---

[1] See Chapter 4, paragraphs 10 and 21.

QUICK CONCENTRATION OF FLYING UNITS IN THE BALKANS
(APRIL, 1941)

The Germans had been gradually moving flying units into Rumania (largely round Bucharest) during January, February and early March, 1941. About the middle of March most of these units, consisting of some 400 aircraft, were moved Southward into Bulgaria ready for the attack on Greece. They were based at Sofia, Plovdiv, Krumovo, Krainitzi and Belitza.

It was evident that the Germans did not anticipate that the Yugo-Slavs would do other than co-operate with them in their plans. Suddenly, there was news of the revolution at Belgrade, against the Yugo-Slav Government which had been friendly to Germany. In order to counter this danger to the Germans right flank, it was necessary for them to attack Belgrade at once.

On 26th March, therefore, orders were given for the rapid transfer of flying units from France, Germany, and the Mediterranean, amounting to nearly 600 aircraft. There were involved : 5 L.R.B. Gruppen (3 from France, 1 from N.W. Germany, and 1 from Sicily) ; 3 dive-bomber Gruppen (2 from France and 1 from Africa) ; 6 S.E.F. Gruppen (all from France) ; 1 T.E.F. Gruppe (from N.W. Germany).

Nearly all the short-range units were to occupy bases at Arad, Deta and Turnu Severin in the extreme West of Rumania, within easy distance of Belgrade. L.R.B. units were to be based on the N.W. and S.E. of Belgrade at Wiener Neustadt and at Vrba (near Sofia). [continued overleaf.

121

The attack on Greece, and on Yugo-Slavia at the same time, started on 6th April; and all, or nearly all, these units had arrived at their destinations with perhaps 75 per cent. of their aircraft and were ready to operate (with, say, two-thirds of the 75 per cent.) on the opening day.

It will be seen that the Luftwaffe was on this occasion able to move a fleet of aircraft, comparable in size to a large Fliegerkorps, distances averaging 1,000 miles from bases far apart, so that about 40 to 50 per cent. of the establishment number were able to be serviceable for operations in 10 days from the date of the order for transfer. This accomplishment was only possible, first, because the airfields at the destination were ready with assistance in M/T and ground personnel and were capable of being stocked up with fuel, ammunition, etc., from depôts within reasonable distance, and, secondly, because a large number of transport aircraft could be made available at short notice.

The two Gruppen moving from North Africa and Sicily respectively naturally had to depend more than the others on assistance at their new temporary bases, though one of them seems to have had about 150-200 men transferred in Ju.52s.

The lines on the map indicating moves of units are diagrammatic only and do not mark the actual routes followed, which were naturally not straight. The thick line indicates the move of three Gruppen together.

GENERALOBERST KURT STUDENT

Born 12.5.90. Entered a Jaeger Battalion as Ensign in 1910. Detached to a Military Flying School, 1913, transferred to the Flying Corps 1914 and commanded Jagdstaffel 9 and Jagdgruppe 3. In the Reichswehr after the war and was active in organising secret military flying training. Transferred to the Air Force in September, 1933; commanded the Technical School Jueterbog, and in August, 1935 to October, 1936, the Luftwaffe Experimental Station Rechlin. Appointed O.C. Fliegerdivision 7 and Inspector of Paratroops, September, 1938. Directed airborne attack on the Low Countries in May, 1940. December, 1940, given command of the newly-formed Fliegerkorps XI (Parachute and Airborne troops), in charge of Crete operation. Command renamed Parachute Army in March, 1944. Appointed C.-in-C. Army Group H on the Western Front in November, 1944 and G.O.C. Parachute Troops, January, 1945. Captured by the Allies, May, 1945.

8. A large-scale redisposition and deployment of forces was therefore entailed. A mixed force of over 400 aircraft, comprising long-range bombers, dive bombers, fighters and reconnaissance aircraft, had, between November, 1940, and February, 1941, been gradually established in Rumania and, immediately following Bulgaria's siding with the Axis, 120 of these were transferred to airfields in that country. Thereafter the build-up in Bulgaria steadily continued and by the time the Jugoslav revolt against Germany occurred on 27th March, 1941, the German Air Force in the Balkans was distributed as follows :—

	Rumania	Bulgaria	Total
Long-range Bombers ..	—	40	40
Dive Bombers	—	120	120
S.E. Fighters	80	40	120
T.E. Fighters	15	25	40
Long-range Reconnaissance	20	30	50
Tactical Reconnaissance ..	20	100	120
Total	135	355	490

9. Taken by surprise at the unexpected resistance of the Jugoslavs, the Germans immediately ordered large-scale reinforcements to the Balkan area. Such was the efficiency of the German Air Force ground organisation that within 10 days some 600 further aircraft, comprising long-range bombers, dive bombers and S.E. and T.E. fighters were brought up from as far afield as Africa, Sicily and France[1] and were already operational at bases as far as 1,000 miles from their original point of departure (see Map 7). Organised resistance in Jugoslavia was quickly broken, and there was little scope for the employment of this large force except for the bombing of Belgrade ; the bulk of it was quickly turned to support the German advance now moving to the aid of the Italians in Greece where, however, the course of air operations calls for little comment. These operations followed the usual pattern demonstrated with such effectiveness in the Battle of France ; at no time did the overwhelming strength of the Luftwaffe encounter more than weak opposition, and by April 27th the Germans had occupied Athens.

The Invasion of Crete

The Decision to Invade : Rapid Preparations

10. The decision to undertake an invasion of Crete was an opportunist one[2]. The German forces had achieved a rapid success in Greece, and the General Staff had actually considered no further action in the direction of Crete ; it was, of course, known that British forces were in occupation, but their strength was not really known. It was Generaloberst Student, A.O.C. of the newly-created Fliegerkorps XI (Parachute and Airborne Troops) who conceived the idea of an airborne invasion of the island, and put the scheme to Goering, pointing out at the same time that Crete would be a useful stepping stone for a further similar attack on Cyprus and eventually the Suez Canal. The latter

---

[1] See Chapter 4, paragraph 50.
[2] See also Appendix, paragraph 13(b).

123

obtained Hitler's permission with the understanding that the operation should be completed in the shortest possible space of time ; at a conference on 21st April, 1941, the decision was taken to launch the attack with parachute and airborne forces on May 16th. The whole affair was in Luftwaffe hands, and the Army General Staff was not consulted.

11. At that time Student's Fliegerkorps XI was stationed in Central Germany and this decision entailed its rapid move by road, rail and air transport to the Athens area, where it came under the command of Luftflotte 4. Great difficulties were encountered owing to the destruction of road and railway communications in Greece, and the bulk of ammunition and supplies had therefore to go by ship, causing some delay and the postponement of the operation from the original date for attack, May 16th until the 20th. During the first three weeks of May, the German Air Force in Greece was actively engaged in the laying out of airfields to accommodate the considerable forces required for the undertaking of this operation. The air forces at the disposal of Fliegerkorps VIII for the Crete operation were as follows :—

					Aircraft
Long-range Bombers	..	..	..	..	.. 280
Dive Bombers	..	..	..	..	.. 150
S.E. Fighters	..	..	..	..	.. 90
T.E. Fighters	..	..	..	..	.. 90
Reconnaissance	..	..	..	..	.. 40
					650

In addition to these operational aircraft, 530 Ju.52 transport aircraft and 100 gliders had also to be assembled in the Athens area ; although a greater number of gliders were available, the training of the unit was not considered up to the standard required for so difficult a task and there had moreover been trouble in obtaining towing rope sufficiently strong. Meanwhile, detailed reconnaissance of Crete and of the waters of the southern Aegean was actively undertaken, together with bombing attacks on the Suda Bay anchorage by Ju.88 and He.111 aircraft.

12. The final disposition of aircraft for operation " mercury " (the cover name for the attack on Crete) was as follows :—

Dive bombers and single-engined fighters were concentrated on forward airfields, all recently constructed, at Mulaoi, Melos and Scarpanto, but, owing to limited accommodation there, Corinth and Argos were also employed as base airfields.

Twin-engined fighters were based on airfields in the Athens area and at Argos and Corinth, all within a radius of 200 miles of Crete.

Long-range bombers and reconnaissance aircraft were based in the Athens area, at Salonica, in Bulgaria (Sofia and Plovdiv areas), and to a small extent in Rhodes. At least 10 all-weather airfields suitable for such aircraft were thus available within 200-250 miles of Crete.

Transport aircraft operated meanwhile from the Athens area and southern Greece, using Eleusis, Tatoi, Megara, Corinth and other airfields within convenient range.

This rapid manning of new airfields was once again due, as in the campaigns in Norway and the advance into France in 1940, to the quick movement of ground staffs by transport aircraft. The assembly of a force of such strength could not be concealed, however, and in the last few nights preceding the operation British bombers attacked the assembly areas and succeeded in causing a certain amount of disturbance. On the other hand, Fliegerkorps VIII started the " softening up " process by the systematic elimination of the weak Allied air force based on Crete.

The Attack and Invasion

13. The attack opened at 0700 hours on May 20th, in moderate visibility but with heavy ground haze, with very heavy attacks by bombers, dive bombers and fighters on the British positions at Maleme and Canea, the objectives being primarily gun positions, particularly A.A. batteries. Fighter and dive bomber escort was provided for the first airborne forces which arrived in gliders at 0800 hours, the main force being put down at Maleme and the remainder at Canea and the Akrotiri Peninsula covering Suda Bay.

14. All these objectives were to have been taken on the first day, but the attack did not go entirely according to plan and the British forces were larger and far more effective than the Germans had anticipated ; the presence of the whole 2nd New Zealand Division and a large part of the 6th Australian Division was completely unknown to the Germans. However, air support was maintained on an extremely heavy scale throughout the day and continued no less heavily thereafter. There was no hesitation on the part of the Germans to throw in ever greater forces of airborne troops. Throughout the operation the Luftwaffe had complete and practically undisputed air superiority, without which the attack might well have failed in its early stages ; however, once a strong foothold had been won at Maleme, reinforcements and supplies kept pouring in, while German air superiority, covering not only Crete but the sea approaches to the island, denied to the British forces the possibility of receiving either.

15. German casualties in the fighting for Crete were very heavy, about 4,500 parachute and glider-borne troops being killed or missing, while some 170 Ju.52's were either lost or very heavily damaged. In operational units, however, the Air Force losses were light owing to the scant opposition encountered.

16. The Crete operation was a brilliant if somewhat expensive success. The loss of this important strategic position was as great to the British as it was a gain to the Germans, who thereby were able not only to seal completely their southern flank, but also to expose the whole of the eastern Mediterranean to a strategic air threat, which, however, as events ultimately showed, never materialised to the extent which it threatened. The taking of Crete proved to be the last major airborne operation undertaken by the German Air Force.

The Rising in Iraq

17. The German timetable for the attack on Russia did not permit further exploitation of the tactical and strategical advances just won in the eastern Mediterranean. Before the Crete campaign was over, movement orders were issued for the transfer of Fliegerkorps VIII from Greece through to Poland via Germany ; by June 1st, flying units were to start entraining in southern

Rumania for re-equipment and rest at their bases in Germany, while ground elements proceeded direct to their new operational area in Poland. However, an immediate repercussion of the German victory in Crete was the rising in Iraq, under the leadership of Raschid Ali, at the instigation of German agents. Although a critical situation was thereby created for a short period, the withdrawal of the bulk of Luftwaffe flying units from Crete did not permit serious exploitation or the ability to afford much direct support to this movement. However, from bases in Greece and Crete it was possible for a small number of He.111 bomber aircraft to fly into Syria and Iraq ; they were, however, in insufficient numbers and without the necessary supplies and ground organisation to participate effectively in the rising, and the German attempt at intervention in this area came to nothing.

Development of Crete

18. During the ensuing month the Germans were mainly pre-occupied with the consolidation of their hold on Greece and the conversion of the island into a fortress. These measures involved a considerable allocation of shipping for the necessary construction work and the establishment of adequate stocks of bombs and aircraft fuel, together with the setting up of the necessary Flak defences and signals and radar installations. Having won this important strategic position in the eastern Mediterranean, the Germans were at pains not only to strengthen it to the utmost against the possibility of future assault and recapture, but even more as a base from which to intensify the assault on the communications of the British Empire in the Middle East, and from which effective air support could be given to the campaign in North Africa. At the same time the establishment of the German Air Force in strength approximately on a line stretching from Salonica through Athens to Crete and the Dodecanese, created a strategic threat to Turkey, which was to form an important consideration in the future attitude of the latter country towards participation in the war. The dispositions of the Luftwaffe in the Mediterranean theatre at the conclusion of the Balkans campaign are shown in Map 8.

Establishment of the German Air Force in Italy

20. The beginning of the first infiltration of the German Air Force into Italy took place as early as June, 1940, when, on the entry of Italy into the war against France and Britain, a liaison staff, known as *Italuft*, was set up under the command of General von Pohl. At this stage, however, the activity of this staff was confined essentially to the exchange of intelligence information ; later it represented the Luftwaffe in the Italian theatre of operations.

21. It was not until October, 1940, that the first German flying units appeared in Italy, when a transport unit was moved to Foggia in order to assist the ferrying of Italian troops and equipment to Albania, thereby contributing to the halting of the Greek offensive ; only at the end of 1940 did operational elements of the Luftwaffe begin to appear in the Mediterranean area in some strength. In order to implement that part of German strategy directed to aiding the Italians in their attempt to sever British communications in the Mediterranean, Fliegerkorps X, under the command of General der Flieger Geisler, with Oberst Harlinghausen the anti-shipping expert as Chief of Staff, arrived in Sicily from Norway[1] in January, 1941, and was thereafter to act as a valuable strengthening of the Italian Air Force.

---

[1] See Chapter 4, paragraph 50.

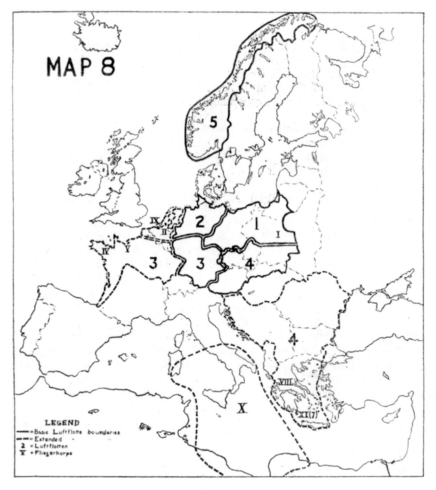

MAP 8

LEGEND
— = Base Luftflotte boundaries
— = Extended
2 = Luftflotten
Y = Fliegerkorps

OPERATIONAL AREAS OF COMMANDS
END OF BALKAN CAMPAIGN (MAY, 1941)

The area in the Central Mediterranean for which Fliegerkorps X was made responsible included South Italy, Sicily, part of Sardinia and part of North Africa. Fliegerkorps X had at this time the effective status of a Luftflotte as it operated directly under the orders of the Air Ministry.

By the middle of January, 1941, there were about 330 first-line operational aircraft based in Italy and Sicily. By March, 1941, the number was about 450, including some 200 in North Africa where a Fliegerfuehrer was established in the position, as it were, of a junior Fliegerkorps commander, owing to the detached position of the forces there. Some of the aircraft of Fliegerkorps X were used in the Balkan campaign.

Luftflotte 4, with Fliegerkorps VIII under it and also Fliegerkorps XI with Flieger-division 7 (parachute troops) at its disposal, was, owing to the position of its home area, chosen to control operations against Yugoslavia and Greece in April, 1941. Initially, operations were chiefly carried out by aircraft based in Bulgaria, Hungary and Southern Germany. Bases were established to the South as the campaign proceeded.

Luftflotte 4 is shown in this map with an extended area covering the countries overrun as a result of the Balkan campaign. The activities of the German Air Force in this area were of a varied character, including support for the Armies attacking down the West and down the East of the Balkans, as well as operations over the sea and the landing of parachute troops together with the provision of the air support necessary for such an operation.

The number of first-line operational aircraft employed in the Balkans, Greece and Crete (exclusive of transport aircraft used for dropping parachutists or for air-landing) was at first nearly 1,000 out of a total of about 4,400 first-line operational aircraft in the Luftwaffe at that time. The number was reduced in the later stages of the campaign.

22. During the spring of 1941, Fliegerkorps X thus became the Operational Command covering southern Italy, Sicily, part of Sardinia and later part of North Africa, with the effective status of a Luftflotte and operating directly under the orders of the German Air Ministry. By mid-January its forces comprised some 330 aircraft, consisting of:—

	Aircraft
Long-range Bombers	120
Dive Bombers	150
T.E. Fighters	40
Reconnaissance	20
Total	330

CHAPTER 6

THE GERMAN AIR FORCE IN THE MEDITERRANEAN CAMPAIGNS OF 1941 AND 1942

The Struggle for Air Supremacy and the Battle for Malta
(January, 1941 to April, 1942)

The First Assault on Malta (January and February, 1941)

1. The situation in the Mediterranean in the closing months of 1940, and the events which led up to the despatch of Fliegerkorps X to Sicily in January, 1941, to aid the Italians, have been made clear in Chapter 5. The main objectives of this force were threefold[1] :—

   (i) To neutralise Malta as a base for British air and naval forces and thus to secure the Axis supply route from Italy to North Africa.

   (ii) To interfere with the British Supply route to Egypt.

   (iii) To support the Axis armies in North Africa.

2. The choice of Fliegerkorps X for this duty is a clear indication of the emphasis placed by the Germans at this stage on shipping attack. It will be remembered that Fliegerkorps X led the Luftwaffe forces in the Norwegian campaign, and had respectively as its A.O.C. and Chief of Staff the two foremost anti-shipping experts of the German Air Force—Geisler and Harlinghausen (the latter left to take up the appointment of Fliegerfuehrer Atlantik in March, 1941[2]). Apart from the bombing of Malta itself, Geisler's task was to close the Sicilian straits to British shipping and to prevent the eastward passage from Gibraltar of supply convoys to Malta.

3. The first such action came on January 7th, when a British convoy of four merchant ships and escorts, amongst them the aircraft carriers '' Illustrious '' and '' Ark Royal '' and some 19 warships, was sighted off the Algerian coast near Bougie, and was attacked by strong German and Italian air forces. It is unfortunate that there are no complete German records in existence which can give a picture of the German and Italian scales of effort or losses in this action. At least 40 Ju.87 dive bombers, together with Ju.88 and He.111 bombers, took part. They could not, however, prevent part of the convoy, together with the '' Illustrious '', from reaching Malta.

4. This action was followed up by a series of concentrated day and night attacks, by bombers and dive bombers, aimed primarily at the harbour and installations of Valetta and the airfields on Malta. In these attacks it may be assumed that the total available forces[3] of long-range bombers, dive bombers and twin- and single-engined fighters was thrown in, together with somewhat smaller assistance by the Italian Air Force. At intervals of several days intensive combined dive bombing and low-level attacks by Ju.87's and Me.110 twin-engined fighters were launched against the island, whilst Ju.88 and He.111 bombers, escorted by fighters, undertook medium level bombing from 5-8,000 ft., carrying loads amongst which were bombs varying from calibres of 50 kilogrammes to 500 and 1,000 kilogrammes.

5. These attacks continued during January, February and March, 1941, but the assault, from the German viewpoint, failed to attain a sufficiently heavy

---

[1] From files of German Air Ministry Historical Section (8th Abteilung).
[2] See Chapter 4, paragraph 64.
[3] See Chapter 5, paragraph 22.

scale to achieve the primary objective of paralysing the island's defences. German air commanders have attributed this failure to the limited supplies and ground organisations as yet established in Sicily—at the end of long lines of communication—and to the magnitude of existing commitments in the Balkan and Greek campaigns, the continuance of the Blitz against England, and to a reluctance on the part of the Luftwaffe Command to undertake further major commitments in face of impending operations of the coming summer. Indeed, this first assault on Malta was rendered inconclusive firstly by the British capture of the whole of Cyrenaica in their advance to El Agheila on February 8th; this entailed a reduction of Luftwaffe strength in Sicily to bolster up the forces in North Africa. From then onwards the Luftwaffe's commitment in North Africa became prominent—although in the ensuing six months it did not amount to more than 150-200 aircraft, mainly dive bombers and fighters. By the end of March, however, developments elsewhere in the Mediterranean, described in the succeeding paragraphs, brought the German assault on Malta virtually to a standstill; from then onwards, and until the second assault on the island which began in January, 1942, this task was left in the hands of the Italians[1].

Movement of the German Air Force to the Eastern Mediterranean

6. Following upon the transfer of approximately half the total Luftwaffe operational strength from Sicily to North Africa during February, 1941, and after the capture of Crete in May, 1941, the whole air situation in the Mediterranean had to be reviewed by the Luftwaffe High Command. General Geisler maintained that the natural German supply route to North Africa was via Greece and Crete, which could, moreover, be used as a base for operations in the Eastern Mediterranean. This suggestion, however, evoked violent protests from the Italians, who said that they could not maintain their ground forces in North Africa unless the supply routes in the Mediterranean were properly protected, a task quite beyond the powers of the Italian Air Force. Geisler's opinion prevailed, however; he argued further that the failure of the Italians to provide adequate protection for their convoys had resulted in the forces of Fliegerkorps X being involved in those duties—which lay outside their own province—thereby seriously weakening their offensive powers. The German High Command upheld this view and the remaining elements of Fliegerkorps X in Sicily were thereupon transferred to the Eastern Mediterranean; immediately the sea route to North Africa became exposed to more intensive attack by the British, since the Italians alone were in no position to neutralise the use of Malta as a base for British naval vessels and anti-shipping aircraft.

German Air Force Dispositions—July, 1941

7. At the beginning of July, when the attack on Russia had just begun, the German Air Force in the Mediterranean was distributed as follows:—

	Greece, Aegean, Rhodes and Crete	Sicily	North Africa	Total
Long-range Bombers	120	—	30	150
Dive Bombers ..	50	—	40	90
S.E. Fighters ..	—	—	40	40
T.E. Fighters ..	30	—	10	40
Reconnaissance ..	40	—	30	70
Total ..	240	—	150	390

[1] See also paragraph 7.

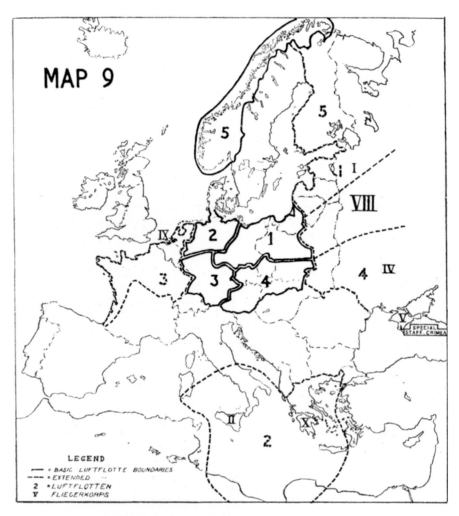

OPERATIONAL AREAS OF COMMANDS
CHANGES IN THE MEDITERRANEAN (JANUARY, *1942*)

The changes in the positions of operational Commands which had taken place by January, 1942, were due to the decision of the Germans to strengthen their air force in the Mediterranean as a result of the British advances in North Africa.

Luftflotte 2 is seen to have moved from the central sector on the Russian front to take control of the area previously under Fliegerkorps X. Luftflotte 2 took Fliegerkorps II with it from the Russian front, and Fliegerkorps X was given the more Easterly part of the Mediterranean while Fliegerkorps II had the more Westerly. The Fliegerfuehrer in North Africa who had previously been under Fliegerkorps X now came directly under Luftflotte 2. As a result of this reorganisation, Fliegerkorps X ceased to have the effective status of a Luftflotte and resumed the status of a Fliegerkorps, becoming subordinate to Luftflotte 2.

There were at this time about 560 first-line operational aircraft under Luftflotte 2 in the Mediterranean, of which 260 were based in North Africa.

GENERALFELDMARSCHALL
KESSELRING

Born 30.11.85. Entered an Artillery Regiment in 1904 and served as Brigade Adjutant and General Staff Officer during the Great War, 1914-18. First associated with the Air Force in October, 1933 when he became head of the administration office in the newly formed Air Ministry. For a year from June, 1936 he held the post of Chief of the General Staff of the Air Force. At the outbreak of war in 1939 he was in command of Luftflotte 1 in Poland. In January, 1940, he took over Luftflotte 2, which he commanded for the operations in the West and for the beginning of the Russian campaign from June to December, 1941. When Luftflotte 2 was transferred to the Mediterranean area in December, 1941, Kesselring retained command of it in addition to being C.-in-C. South until 1943 when he was replaced as A.O.C.-in-C. Luftflotte 2 by Generalfeldmarschall Richthofen. He remained C.-in-C. South, in command of all German Armed Forces in Italy, until in March, 1945, he became C.-in-C. West. Captured by the Allies in May, 1945.

All these forces were by then under the direct operational control of Fliegerkorps X, whose sphere of influence was thereby extended to cover the entire Mediterranean area, including North Africa. In North Africa, however, an *ad hoc* subordinate command known as Fliegerkorps Afrika was established and made directly responsible for operations in that theatre under Generalmajor Froehlich as A.O.C.

8. During the remainder of the summer and autumn of 1941, there was no major air development in the Mediterranean theatre. The main attention of the Luftwaffe was directed against North Africa and particularly the Suez Canal area and the Red Sea, but these activities, which involved minelaying and torpedo-bomber operations from Greece and Crete, could not be maintained on a sufficiently decisive scale. Moreover, supply difficulties in North Africa prevented the establishment of an effective Luftwaffe bomber force in that theatre. Throughout this period it became increasingly evident that German air strength in the Mediterranean was inadequate to meet the extensive commitments of such a widespread area, and the German Air Force as a whole was being thrown increasingly on the defensive for the protection of supply shipping at the expense of offensive operations.

Reinforcement of the Mediterranean (see Map 9)

9. The lack of any material progress in the Mediterranean theatre as a whole during the remainder of 1941, and particularly the increasing difficulties in maintaining an adequate flow of supplies to North Africa, let alone the possibility of any appreciable reinforcement in that area, led to a major recasting of German air strategy. This involved, despite the failure to achieve victory against Russia, the transfer of Luftflotte 2 under Generalfeldmarschall Kesselring from the central Russian front to Sicily in December, 1941, together with Fliegerkorps II under General Loerzer from the same area. As a result of this redisposition the whole of the Mediterranean theatre came under the operational command of Luftflotte 2, with Fliegerkorps II responsible for operations in the Central, and Fliegerkorps X, in the Eastern Mediterranean. At the same time an appreciable reinforcement of the Mediterranean theatre by units drawn from the Russian front and elsewhere took place, German strength in the area being almost doubled, to a total of some 650 aircraft.

10. The German intention was to dispose finally of Malta and thus to secure the Axis sea communications in the Mediterranean theatre as a whole and to North Africa in particular. This policy reflected the decision of the German High Command, having failed in its first attempt to achieve victory in Russia, to devote its utmost strength during 1942 to securing a final victory in the Mediterranean, thus giving access to the Middle East, combined with an all-out offensive in southern Russia, with the Caucasus as its objective.

The Second Assault on Malta (January to April, 1942)

11. The successful elimination of Malta was the key to the achievement of German ends in the Mediterranean. Since April, 1941, when the Germans withdrew from Sicily, British aircraft based on Malta had not only been able to cause very considerable damage to the loading and unloading ports for the supply of raw materials to Rommel's forces in North Africa by attacking the harbour installations, etc., at Naples and Tripoli, but reconnaissance aircraft had also been able to observe and follow the passage of Axis convoys to Africa,

thus enabling a considerable success to be achieved by British air and naval forces in attacking this traffic. Apart from shipping losses, all axis convoy traffic was forced to make a considerable diversion in its effort to escape detection and air attack, almost doubling the distance of the direct route from Messina to Tripoli.

12. By the end of December, 1941, German strength in Sicily had again been raised to some 200 aircraft and by the end of March, 1942, had been further increased to 425 aircraft, of which 190 were long-range bombers and 115 single-engined fighters.

13. The resumption of operations against Malta began in mid-Jaunary, 1942, on a relatively modest scale, some 65 sorties a day being flown by aircraft of all types, with a maximum of some 40-50 long-range bomber sorties. It continued at this level, amounting to little more than harassing attacks until the middle of March, when the major assault began on the 21st of that month, and was maintained throughout April on the heaviest scale yet brought to bear by the German Air Force against any single objective for so long a period. The German intention was to capture Malta by means of an airborne assault, once it was sufficiently weakened by blockade and air bombardment, and preparations with that object in view were undertaken by General Ramcke and Generaloberst Student.

14. The decision to carry out this attack was actually taken at a conference between Hitler and Mussolini in the early months of 1942. At the end of April, Student was called to Rome to take part in the preparations. It was planned that the attack—which was to take place in August—should be a combined Italo-German undertaking, with the Italian forces under the then Italian C.-in-C., General Cavallero. The scheme provided for strong German paratroop forces under Student to land first and establish a bridgehead through which further airborne forces could be brought to the island. The transport force to be made available was 500 Ju52's and He.111's and about 80 Savoia SM.82's. Student had realised that complete surprise was impossible, but to make the most of tactical surprise, he proposed to land on the south-west side of the island, which because of the nature of the terrain, appeared to be the most unlikely. During the spring, preparations for this operation were put in hand with the training of the combined forces to take part. In the summer, however, Hitler sent for Student and announced that the operation had been called off. Actually, Rommel's successes in North Africa, where between January and July he had pushed the Allied forces back from El Agheila to El Alamain, opened up such bright prospects that Malta seemed to have ceased to have any more significance.

15. Meanwhile, the Luftwaffe attacking force ranged against Malta, consisting of 190 long-range bombers and 30 Ju.87 dive bombers, had maintained an average daily effort of 130 sorties throughout April, 1942, after opening with over 300 sorties on March 21st. On April 20th, 325 bomber sorties were flown against Malta and over 200 sorties on seven other occasions during the month ; this intensity of effort was only attained by aircraft and crews carrying out up to three sorties each per day, in addition to which fighter escorts of the order of 200 aircraft per 24 hours were regularly flown to cover these attacks. Their effect was such as virtually to paralyse the defences of Malta and bring about a very critical situation on the island. As a result, its

effectiveness as a base was seriously impaired, and the Axis supply situation in Africa was thereby greatly eased ; this in turn played an important part in facilitating Rommel's subsequent advance to El Alamein.

16. Nevertheless, the Malta operations were not without their effects on the German Air Force. Some 3-400 aircraft were kept actively and heavily engaged during the greater part of the period from January to May, 1942, when they might have been conserving their resources for employment elsewhere. Moreover, wastage on an appreciable scale had to be incurred as a result of these operations, a wastage amounting to no less than 250-300 aircraft during the month of April alone, and some 500 aircraft over the whole period. Further, the heavy tonnage of bombs and aircraft fuel consumed in undertaking this assault were directly to the detriment of supplies in North Africa.

17. In the middle of May, 1942, the attack was finally called off, not only in view of the satisfactory situation in North Africa, but also because preparations had then to be put in hand for the resumption of operations in Russia, for which the aircraft engaged against Malta were required. It was becoming increasingly apparent that German commitments in all theatres of war were overtaxing the resources of the Luftwaffe and that major operations in any one theatre could only be undertaken at the expense of a weakening elsewhere. Moreover, the German failure to capture Malta was to prove a severe handicap to the conduct of the campaign in the Mediterranean during the ensuing months of 1942.

The Malta Convoys of 1942, and the Final Assault on the Island

18. The story of the Malta convoys of 1942 must be read in the light of the attack on Malta itself and Hitler's proposed invasion of the island, described in the preceding paragraphs, as well as of the land campaign taking place in Egypt. The German and Italian actions against the British supply convoys had as their prime object the holding of the siege of Malta to prevent supplies of war from reaching the island—supplies which could be used for defensive purposes as well as for offence against the Axis supply convoys passing from Italy and Sicily to North Africa. A full impression of the significance of Malta in the whole Mediterranean and North African campaign will be gained by the reader after study of the remainder of this chapter, which in turn describes operations in North Africa and the supply problems connected with those operations.

19. It must be remembered that during the summer of 1942—at the same time as the Malta convoy actions were taking place—battles of equal ferocity were being fought in the far North against the Anglo-American supply convoys to Russia (see Chapter 4, paragraphs 80-88), and that the main part of the Luftwaffe's torpedo-bomber force was then engaged in that area. The smaller Italian torpedo-bomber force, it is true, was based on Sardinia and Sicily, and played an important part in the Malta convoy operations, but had the large German force not been engaged in the Arctic area, the situation for Malta must certainly have been far more serious than it was.

20. In the early months of 1942, attempts had been made by the British to supply Malta by convoys from Alexandria. Up to the end of April, whilst the full strength of Fliegerkorps X was still available on Sicily (paragraphs 12 to 17), these convoys met with appalling air opposition ; nevertheless, some essential supplies were delivered to the island. During those first four months of 1942, if a British supply vessel did succeed in reaching Malta safely, the subsequent unloading operations were subjected to continued bombing and

were rendered extremely difficult ; indeed, unloading frequently devolved to salvage operations to recover the cargo after the ship had been sunk in harbour by bombing. In March, 1942, for instance, four supply vessels left Alexandria with a naval escort of no less than four cruisers, 18 destroyers and an anti-aircraft ship ; it must be added that the Italian Navy was still also a potent factor in such operations. After the convoy of March, the island came under the full assault of the Luftwaffe and Italian Air Force, but nevertheless a few essential supplies were still delivered, mainly by submarine.

21. The island had to wait until the middle of June—when air attack had abated—for the next attempt to supply it on a large scale. In the meantime strong reinforcements of Royal Air Force fighter aircraft had been flown off the aircraft carrier " Eagle " and the U.S.S. " Wasp " at some distance from Malta, and had arrived on the island. In the last large-scale bombing attacks on Malta on May 9th and 10th, the Luftwaffe lost heavily in bombers and fighters ; after those actions came the withdrawal of the forces of Fliegerkorps X to North Africa, for the reasons already stated in paragraph 17.

22. The operation to supply Malta in June was a double one ; a convoy of six merchant ships passing from the United Kingdom through the Straits of Gibraltar, and another of 11 merchant ships from Egypt, were to reach Malta on consecutive days. Enemy attention would thus be divided between the two convoys. In the end only two merchant ships of the Gibraltar convoy arrived, whilst the eastern convoy had to give up the attempt and turn back to Alexandria owing to the presence of major formations of the Italian fleet. The main part of the attack on the Gibraltar convoy was sustained by the Italian Air Force and a small number of Ju.87 dive bombers and Ju.88 long-range bombers of the Luftwaffe. On June 13th the convoy comprising the 6 merchant vessels with an escort of 1 battleship, 2 aircraft carriers, 3 cruisers, 17 destroyers, 1 anti-aircraft vessel and 4 minesweepers, first came under the attention of shadowing aircraft, and on the morning of the 14th, when to the North-West of Bône—at a range too great for the Malta-based fighters to interfere—the first air attacks began. The aircraft carriers, for their part, being old and of small capacity, could only maintain a force of 10 fighters in the air at a time—an inadequate number to deal with the formations of up to 40 bombers and torpedo-bombers with their escorts of up to 30 fighter aircraft. As the convoy reached the Sicilian narrows on the evening of June 14th, Malta-based fighters were able to intervene, but nevertheless the Italian and German aircraft formations took advantage of intervals between the withdrawal of one air escort owing to exhaustion of fuel endurance, and the arrival of a relief escort, to deliver several more attacks. As the convoy neared Malta on June 16th, however, even stronger Royal Air Force escorts were available, and air attacks dwindled. Out of six merchant ships, two arrived, the other four having fallen to air attack.

23. The final supply convoy to be sent to Malta under these conditions was in August, 1942, and consisted of 14 merchant ships with an escort of 3 aircraft carriers with 72 fighter aircraft—some of which were to be flown off to Malta—together with 2 battleships, 6 cruisers, an anti-aircraft ship and 24 destroyers. This convoy passed the Straits of Gibraltar on the night of August 9th to 10th, at which time there were 220 Luftwaffe aircraft based on Sicily, with the addition of 300 Italian aircraft on Sicily and a further 130 on Sardinia—a combined Axis total of 650 aircraft. On August 10th, as soon

as the Germans had established that the convoy was sailing eastwards towards Malta, they brought in a further reinforcement of 51 aircraft, of which 20 long-range bombers were drawn from Crete, 10 torpedo-bombers from the Luftwaffe torpedo-bomber school at Grosseto, 15 dive bombers resting in Sicily were hurriedly made ready, and 6 Me.110 twin-engined fighters were moved in from North Africa. From the air point of view, with a force of some 700 aircraft available to the Germans and Italians, the passage of this convoy bid fair to be a major action.

24. After a first sighting of the convoy on the afternoon of August 10th off Oran—on which information the Germans took the action of reinforcement outlined above—the ships were kept under continual observation from the air during hours of daylight. The first action came in the afternoon of that day, when some 50 German and Italian aircraft attacked—the Italians with torpedoes, and the Germans with 1,000 kilogramme armour-piercing bombs dropped from high altitude. This first attack achieved nothing, although the Germans made considerable claims. During the day and evening of August 11th, air attacks by similar formations of aircraft continued, but it was on the 12th, when the convoy came within fighter-escorted range of the Sardinian airfields, that the heavy attacks began. The first of these was by some 30 Ju.88's and escorting fighters in a position 130 miles S.S.W. of Sardinia. Dive bombing tactics were employed, but were unsuccessful. A second attack, in which German aircraft dropped parachute mines in the path of the convoy, only resulted in damage to one merchant vessel. Late in the afternoon a third attack took place in which some 40 Ju.88's and Ju.87's bombed and dive-bombed the vessels concurrently with a torpedo attack by some 20 Italian aircraft. During this action the aircraft carrier " Indomitable " was damaged for flying, and a destroyer was hit by an aircraft torpedo. A final dusk attack was launched by strong forces of dive bombers and torpedo aircraft, operating in waves of 10 ; in this two merchant vessels were sunk and two others damaged. On this day the enemy had put up a total of 180-200 sorties with the addition of fighter escorts, for which the result was one aircraft carrier, one destroyer and two merchant vessels damaged and two merchant vessels sunk by air attack. The German Air Force had contributed a greater effort than had the Italians ; this was not an uncommon happening when the German and Italian Air Forces operated together, and led to much bad feeling on the part of the Germans.

25. Between August 13th and 15th the convoy reached Malta, after having lost two more merchant vessels during the 13th and another on the 14th. The five remaining supply vessels of the original fourteen were unloaded, but on this occasion the enemy made no serious attempt to interfere ; the British fighter strength on Malta now was such as to discourage direct attacks on the island. The main enemy air effort was now directed against the naval forces returning to Gibraltar.

The Western Desert Campaigns—November, 1941, to December, 1942

The Situation in November, 1941

26. After the British Commonwealth armies had defeated the Italians in February, 1941, and had advanced to El Agheila, supply difficulties had forced a retirement on Benghazi. In March, 1941, Rommel had arrived in Tripoli

with the German *Afrika Korps,* and at the end of that month had occupied El Agheila.   During April, when commitments in Crete had further affected British strength in North Africa, Rommel had been able to advance as far as Sollum on the Egyptian frontier.   A new British offensive in November, 1941, pushed Rommel back once more to El Agheila.   The campaign from the time of that British offensive up to the end of 1942 falls into five main phases, each of which in this chapter is dealt with in turn :—

> (*a*) The British offensive from November 18th to the end of December, 1941.
>
> (*b*) The Axis counter-offensive from 19th January to 18th February, 1942.
>
> (*c*) The second Axis offensive of 26th May, 1942, leading to the fall of Tobruk and the advance to El Alamein.
>
> (*d*) The British victory at El Alamein opening on October 24th, and leading to the rout of Rommel.
>
> (*e*) The Allied landings in North Africa on November 7th and the battle for Tunis (to 31st December, 1942).

(*a*) The British Offensive from November 18th to the end of December, 1941

27. The German air strength in Africa at the beginning of the British offensive from Sollum comprised 190 aircraft, including 70 dive bombers and 50 S.E. fighters, a strength which was reinforced during the first month of the campaign by a further 100 aircraft drawn mainly from the Eastern Mediterranean and Sicily, except for 50 S.E. fighters previously employed on the Russian front.   The German strength was further supplemented by some 320 Italian aircraft—half of which were S.E. fighters.

28. Shipping difficulties in the Mediterranean, due largely to the action of British naval and air forces based on Malta, had resulted in a shortage of aircraft fuel in North Africa, while at the same time the British advances, having forced a retirement from forward airfields, only permitted a moderate scale of effort to be achieved by the German Air Force—seldom exceeding 200 sorties ; lack of ground organisation and difficulties in supply prevented a sustained effort, and on the average not more than 100 sorties a day were flown to stem the British advance back to Benghazi during the first month of operations.

29. During this campaign both the Axis air forces acquitted themselves well, despite their supply problem, although they never succeeded in gaining the initiative in the face of British air superiority.   It was only by dint of the most energetic and resourceful measures, e.g., the landing of aircraft fuel from submarines, that they were able to overcome to a large extent their difficulties and thus succeed in sustaining operations.

30. With the loss of airfields in Cyrenaica and with only the limited airfield accommodation in the Gulf of Sirte area, part of the German Air Force was obliged to return temporarily to Sicily and Crete.   The inability of the British to press their advance far beyond Benghazi, however, provided Rommel with a much-needed breathing space during which the ground organisations could be strengthened and consolidated in the Sirte area.   Supplies of all kinds were acutely short, particularly oil, fuel, bombs and rations, and, moreover, there was a shortage of M/T which further hindered the bringing up of such supplies as could be shipped through Tripoli.

Rommel (right) arrives by air in North Africa and is received by Hoffmann von Waldau, the Luftwaffe General in North Africa.

Mussolini inspects the Italian Air Force

(b) The Axis Counter-Offensive (19th January to 18th February, 1942)

31. Thanks to important convoys getting through to North Africa and the use of transport aircraft on a considerable scale, the supply position at Tripoli improved considerably, but at the same time, transport difficulties prevented anything more than a slow build-up in the forward area, and when Rommel's offensive opened from El Agheila on 19th January, 1942, both German and Italian air strengths were no greater than at the opening of the British offensive two months earlier.

32. Rommel's sudden and successful attack was remarkable in that the Axis air forces played little part in it, except during the early opening stages. Apart from the still stringent supply position in the operational area, bad weather had resulted in many of the hastily constructed airfields becoming boggy and unserviceable. However, on January 21st–22nd a considerable effort was put up by the Axis air forces, amounting to some 250 sorties on each day. But subsequently the effort fell away to about half within a few days, and the rapid advances of the German forces eastwards through Benghazi to El Gazala were carried out in the virtual absence of air support, owing to the inability of the Luftwaffe to move up its units to more advanced bases with sufficient speed.

33. The ensuing three months, during which there was little activity on the ground in Africa, was accompanied also by a lull in air operations. These were limited to no more than harassing attacks against Tobruk and the British lines of land communications with Egypt. As has been seen, however, the lull in air activity in Africa was counter-balanced during this period by the development of operations against Malta, maintained with growing intensity up to the end of April. In the eastern Mediterranean there was also a certain amount of desultory harassing activity by bomber forces based in Greece and Crete, directed mainly against the harbours of Port Said and Alexandria and British supply depôts and communications with Egypt. This force also succeeded in sinking three British destroyers on May 11th off the Cyrenaican coast.

34. The result of the offensive against Malta which began in January, 1942, soon began to show itself in North Africa, where Axis shipping convoys arrived in increasing numbers, although up to the end of April the bulk of shipping was forced to use Tripoli harbour owing to the unserviceability of Benghazi. Consequently, the long overland haul through Tripolitania to Cyrenaica, aided to some extent by coastal shipping, resulted in a slow build-up of the supply position in the forward area, and the period was one of gradual but steady consolidation of the German Air Force in Cyrenaica.

35. With the increasing use of Benghazi during May, it was possible to build up stocks of aircraft fuel in the forward area to some 3,000 tons by the 25th of that month, thus providing an ample reserve for the resumption of major air activity to support the impending German offensive. At the same time there was a slow but steady build up of German air strength in North Africa.

36. During this period, incidentally, a change of the Luftwaffe Command in North Africa had taken place. Generalmajor Froehlich, the *Fliegerfuehrer Afrika*, had been experiencing increasing difficulties in handling the ferocious and difficult Rommel, and had even taken to avoiding contact with him, to the detriment of both air and land operations. In March, 1942, he was replaced

by General Hoffmann von Waldau of the General Staff. The latter had held one of Jeschonnek's (The Chief of Luftwaffe General Staff) key positions, and by virtue of his own high position in the Luftwaffe hierarchy, was able to stand up to Rommel and to ensure not only that the machinery of Army Air Force co-operation worked efficiently, but also that operations by the forces at his disposal were not dissipated by misemployment or by not being followed up by the Army.

(c) The Second Axis Offensive and the Advance to El Alamein (May to July, 1942)

37. It has already been shown that the original German plan for obtaining mastery in the Mediterranean was for a two-round contest—the first involving the occupation of Malta and the securing of uninterrupted Axis supply from Italy to North Africa, the second involving the destruction of the British army in the Western Desert and the occupation of Egypt. The success of the latter stage was considered dependent on the first.

38. The failure to reduce Malta in round one, fought between January and April, 1942, was not, however, permitted to interfere with the prosecution of round two. The Germans probably appreciated that Malta's striking power had been appreciably weakened by its ordeal in March and April, and considered that, should the British army be destroyed and Egypt occupied, Malta would in the course of time be forced to surrender.

39. Hitler accordingly took the decision to ignore Malta (see paragraph 14) and to concentrate on a land offensive which, after breaking through the Gazala line, should ultimately reach the Nile Valley. To this end 40 dive bombers, 30 S.E. fighters and 15 T.E. fighters were transferred from Sicily to Africa, thus increasing the German air forces available for the support of the offensive to an establishment of 260 aircraft—some 70 aircraft more than were employed against the British offensive in November, 1941. The main effect of these reinforcements was to provide a considerably greater S.E. fighter force (120 aircraft as against 50) and to raise the dive bomber force to the same strength as in November. Similar increases took place in Italian Air Force strength in North Africa, and when the offensive was mounted at El Gazala on May 26th, the combined German and Italian Air Forces in the forward area amounted to some 600 aircraft.

40. German Air Force dispositions in the remainder of the Mediterranean area at this stage showed a considerable reduction following the withdrawal from Sicily of long-range bomber units on the conclusion of the assault on Malta and the transfer of close-support forces from Sicily to North Africa. The actual strength in aircraft based elsewhere in the Mediterranean was as follows :—

	Greece and Crete	Sicily	Total
Long-range Bombers	130	55	185
Bomber Reconnaissance ..	20	20	40
Dive Bombers	—	—	—
S.E. Fighters	5	30	35
T.E. Fighters	20	10	30
Coastal	35	—	35
Total	210	115	325

(83331)

F

41. Shortly before the Axis offensive began, Kesselring as A.O.C.-in-C. in the Mediterranean moved his headquarters from Taormina in Sicily to North Africa, thus emphasising the decisive importance attached to the successful outcome of the projected offensive. The immediate objective was the recapture of Tobruk, to be achieved by surprise and quick success in breaking through the Allied defensive position reaching from Gazala to Bir Hacheim. In this, however, the Germans failed to succeed and the heavy fighting which developed in the Bir Hacheim and '' Knightsbridge ''[1] areas made such demands upon the resources of the Luftwaffe that it was unable to afford more than local cover elsewhere.

42. Air operations opened with the most intensive effort yet attained by the Germans in the whole of the North African campaign, no less than 300-350 sorties per day being flown during the first week of the offensive by the African-based forces alone. Of these the dive bombers accounted for about 100, and single-engined fighters for 150-200, representing $2\frac{1}{2}$ sorties per day per serviceable aircraft. Although during the second week this very high effort was reduced by about one-third, the third week of the offensive resulted in air operations reaching a new peak of intensity, and led by the fall of Bir Hacheim on June 11th, after a stubborn resistance by the Free French forces under General Koenig, which held the enemy up for nine days. In order to bring about the capture of this strong point, the whole German dive-bomber effort with fighter escort was employed against this one target and was, moreover, supplemented by 30 to 40 long-range bomber sorties a day, in daylight, by aircraft operating from Crete. No less than 1,400 sorties were carried out by the Luftwaffe against Bir Hacheim, and this weight of air assault contributed materially to its ultimate capture.

43. Having broken through the British defences, the German advance proceeded rapidly, leading to the fall of Tobruk on June 20th—on which day the ground assault against that strong point was accompanied by a further burst of major air activity which exceeded 350 dive bomber and fighter sorties. Thereafter, the German armour advanced rapidly, but with the Air Force playing a less important part ; the latter had already suffered considerable losses in the advance, had lost a valuable nine days of effort, supplies and aircraft in reducing the Free French position at Bir Hacheim, and had frittered much of its strength in the assault on Malta between January and May (see paragraph 15). From the time Rommel's forces reached the El Alamein position early in July, the German Air Force was mainly pre-occupied, up to the end of August, in building up its supplies and in establishing the necessary ground organisation for its units on the forward operational airfields so rapidly captured in Egypt. The Luftwaffe had been unable to follow Rommel's advance—and the British retreat back to El Alamein—for this very reason, and during the British build-up behind the El Alamein position, had also been unable to interfere.

44. Considerable stocks of aircraft fuel had been accumulated in Cyrenaica for support of the offensive which opened on May 26th, but the heavy and prolonged scale of effort during the initial three weeks had resulted in a consumption far greater than had been anticipated. The first result of this was that by June 15th the prospect of an exhaustion of supplies before the end of that month had become imminent—failing the shipment of further stocks

---

[1] An area of desert, South of Bir Hacheim, named " Knightsbridge " by the British Forces.

to North Africa. Consequently, during the fourth week of the offensive—from June 16th–22nd—there was a marked decline in the German scale of air effort, a decline which reflected not only the wear and tear of operations—particularly around Knightsbridge and Bir Hacheim during the previous week—but also the need for conserving fuel supplies. The lengthening line of communications across Cyrenaica began to impose the difficulties, outlined in the above paragraph, in the movement of supplies from the ports to the forward areas.

45. The difficulty of supplying the forces in North Africa[1] led Kesselring to remark that he was nothing but a glorified quartermaster. German Navy and Army officers interrogated after the war have held that Kesselring was guilty of " criminal optimism " in promising supplies to Africa which, owing to losses in shipping and transport aircraft, never arrived ; they hold that on this score Kesselring was largely responsible for the subsequent defeat of the German forces in Africa. Kesselring's efforts were, however, energetic and continuous, and the blame must be shifted to the British naval and air efforts. In view of the fact that he had always urged the elimination of Malta as a British base, the blame for losses caused by the British Malta-based forces can hardly be laid at his door, but were rather the result of the short-sighted policy of Hitler and the Supreme Command. Rommel, and many others in North Africa merely saw that the supplies did not arrive, and relations between Kesselring and Rommel—never at any time good, since Rommel was prone to criticise the Luftwaffe, and Kesselring, when roused in this way became violent—began to deteriorate.

46. Fuel supplies were the vital factor and a continual source of anxiety. With tanker sinkings running at a high level, the greatest difficulty was experienced during the whole of July and August in building up the depleted stocks for a resumption of air operations on a scale sufficient for the further prosecution of the German offensive. It was now that the failure to eliminate Malta earlier in the year began to reveal its consequences, and the absence of any further air assault on the island during this period enabled effective use to be made of British air and naval forces against the Axis sea routes, resulting in very heavy shipping losses. In consequence, Rommel's abortive offensive lasting from August 31st to September 5th was accompanied only by a very moderate scale of air support, considerably less than the forces available were capable of achieving.

(d) The British Victory at El Alamein (24th October–5th November, 1942)

47. Having failed to make any progress with his offensive in September, Rommel was forced thereafter to hold on to his positions and endeavour to consolidate his forces in face of the growing strangulation imposed by the interference of his supply traffic. The critical situation of the German and Italian armies owing to the sinking of shipping and bad communications meant that such meagre supplies as could be got through to Africa had to be allocated to M/T fuel at the expense of aircraft fuel ; moreover, so far as the German Air Force was concerned, the maximum amount of stocks were required in the forward area of Egypt, leaving little in reserve along the supply route through Cyrenaica. Thus, although on the eve of the British offensive at

---

[1] The Air Transport and supply situation behind these activities is described in paragraphs 69 to 74, and Map 12 on page 154.

El Alamein the German operational strength in Egypt was considerable—amounting to 290 aircraft—it was impossible for administrative and logistic reasons to maintain stronger forces in Africa at that time.

48. On the opening of the British offensive on October 24th, the heavy air attacks on German airfields seriously impaired the serviceability and operational efficiency of their Air Force, already very obviously affected by the British air attacks on airfields immediately preceding the opening of the offensive. As an emergency measure 50 S.E. fighters had immediately been transferred from Sicily to the Alamein front, but no effective air opposition or support could be afforded against the weight of the British offensive and, on the collapse of the El Alamein position, German air strength fell away rapidly, due to continuous retirement and to losses on the ground. The German Air Force was therefore effectively prevented from taking any significant part in covering the German retreat, and after November 5th, when the movement back began, the scale of effort became negligible. Moreover, the bomber force in Greece and Crete could also not be effectively employed on operational duties, since its whole effort had to be diverted to the ferrying to Africa of fuel necessary to enable the German retreat to be carried out.

49. Thus, by November 15th when the Luftwaffe was still operating from airfields in the Benghazi area, its dive-bomber strength had fallen to some 30 aircraft, while no more than 90-100 fighters remained, and on the further retreat to airfields in the Gulf of Sirte, the fighter force had been reduced to no more than 60 aircraft. These remnants were moreover in no position to continue operations in the absence of any appreciable supplies or ground organisation, and in the prevailing general confusion and demoralisation of retreat. Such was the situation of the remnants of the Luftwaffe under *Fliegerfuehrer Afrika* at the moment when the Allied landing on the French North African coast suddenly materialised in Rommel's rear.

(e) The Anglo-American Landing in French North Africa, and the Battle for Tunis (to 31st December, 1942)

The First signs of the Landings.

50. The considerable increase in shipping and air activity at Gibraltar towards the end of October, 1942, caused the Germans apprehension regarding Allied intentions in the western and central Mediterranean. Partly as a result of this, but more particularly owing to the increasingly critical situation in which Rommel found himself, there was a steady German air reinforcement in the Mediterranean throughout that month, amounting between the end of September and early November to an increase of some 220 aircraft, thus bringing the total German strength in the Mediterranean to 940 aircraft.

51. When the first large convoys were detected passing through the Straits of Gibraltar, neither the German Air Force nor the High Command in the Mediterranean was able to form a satisfactory opinion as to their final destination. Possibilities foreseen were a landing in the South of France ; a passage eastwards through the Sicilian Straits, after which a portion of the convoy might be expected to branch off to supply Malta ; a landing in the Tunis area or in the rear of the North African front in the Gulf of Sirte. The true nature of the Allied undertaking, namely, a systematic occupation of the whole French North African coast, was never envisaged, and thus a complete strategical and tactical surprise was achieved. No allowance for a development fraught

144

with such serious consequences had ever entered into German calculations, and rapid and far reaching decisions, affecting particularly the air situation on the Russian front, had to be taken to meet the new situation.

52. The disposition of the German Air Force in Sicily and Sardinia on November 8th—the day on which the Allies landed in Algeria—was as follows :—

	Sicily	Sardinia	Total
Long-range Bombers	210	45	255
Bomber Reconnaissance ..	20	10	30
Dive Bombers	10	20	30
S.E. Fighters	40	30	70
T.E. Fighters	10	5	15
Total	290	110	400

In addition to these, the Italian Air Force strength in the same areas amounted to some 515 aircraft, of which 200 were long-range bombers (mainly torpedo-carrying aircraft) and 180 single-engined fighters.

Reinforcement of the Mediterranean

53. During the four weeks following the Allied landings in North Africa, strong reinforcements of Luftwaffe first-line units flowed steadily into the Mediterranean (see Map 10) and by December 12th the total for the whole theatre had reached a peak of 1,220 aircraft, of which 850 were then based in Sicily, Sardinia and Tunisia. Thus, the total reinforcement from the beginning of October to the middle of December amounted to approximately 500 aircraft, of which not less than 400 were transferred from the Russian and Arctic front and the remainder from the West. The transfer of forces from the Arctic area was particularly important in that 150 bomber and torpedo-carrying aircraft were moved from North Norway, where they had been mainly employed in operations against the northern convoy route ; that vital strategic area became therefore wholly denuded of the striking force which had played such an important part in the battle against the carriage of supplies to North Russia[1]. Moreover, for the remainder of the war this force could never again be reconstituted in the Far North on a similar scale, owing to the pressure of events in the Mediterranean and the consequent weakening of the anti-shipping force as a result thereof. The Russian front was further weakened by the transfer of a further 120 long-range bombers from the central and southern sectors ; a similar number of single-engined fighters was also moved from the same sectors to the Mediterranean. This loss of aircraft came just at a time when it was to prove a severe handicap in opposing the Russian offensive then being launched on the Don.

54. The successful establishment of Allied forces in Algeria had, of course, been immediately followed by the extension of German occupation to the whole of southern and south-western France ; while this imposed yet a further defensive commitment on the German Air Force by a widening of the perimeter, the newly-occupied territory afforded at the same time valuable new bases for the undertaking of anti-shipping operations in the western Mediterranean. The initial reaction of the German Air Force in this area was defensive, however,

---

[1] See Chapter 4, paragraph 80.

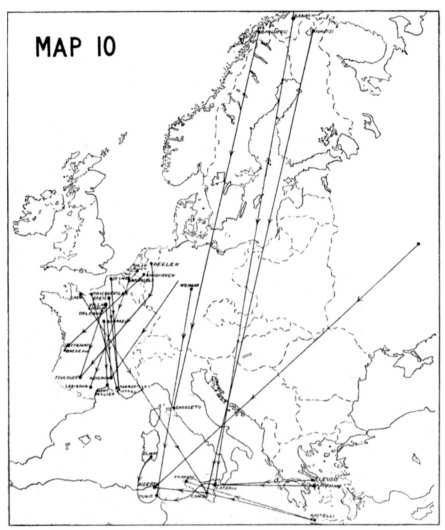

MAP 10

QUICK CONCENTRATION OF FLYING UNITS IN THE MEDITERRANEAN (NOVEMBER, *1942*)

There were, at the beginning of November, some 400 aircraft based in Sicily and Sardinia (*of which two-thirds were long-range bombers*) ; and, in Cyrenaica some 375 aircraft (*of which two-thirds were single-engined fighters, including fighter-bombers, etc.*).

It was then impossible for the Allies to prevent German reconnaissance suggesting that a considerable Allied sea-borne operation was projected. In the first instance, the Germans apparently concluded that a vast convoy was intended to reinforce the British Eighth Army in Egypt. On or about 2nd November, therefore, four Gruppen of long-range bombers (*mostly torpedo aircraft*) were ordered to move from North Norway to Catania and Comiso in Sicily and to Grosseto in Italy. These Gruppen were thought to have more scope in attacking shipping in the Mediterranean than in operating on the convoy route to Russia. This transfer took from five to nine days, though one Staffel claimed to transfer in 48 hours, and other aircraft managed the trip in three days.

Just before the landings, parts of two Gruppen (one of long-range bombers and one of twin-engined fighters for escort duties) were transferred from Greece and Crete to Sicily ; and when the Germans heard of the landings on 8th November, they ordered parts of another Gruppe of long-range bombers from Greece to Sicily and parts of a twin-engined fighter Gruppe and a long reconnaissance Staffel from Crete to Sicily.

[continued overleaf.

146

The first moves of flying units to Tunis were rapidly organised. A dive-bomber Gruppe and two single-engined fighter Gruppen (which was ferried to Sicily from Sardinia on the previous day) arrived in Tunis on 9th November. This was certainly enterprising since there can have been no more than a handful of improvised ground troops for protection. The first Company of a parachute Regiment did not arrive until the 10th or 11th November, and the ground troops were not even in moderate strength until 13th November.

By 13th November, another single-engined fighter Gruppe (which had shortly before been on the Orel front) had reached Bizerta, together with part of a short (Army) reconnaissance Staffel which had been refitting in Weimer (Germany). By 15th November a Gruppe and a further Staffel of single-engined fighters had moved from Sicily to Bizerta, and a Staffel of long-range reconnaissance aircraft moved from Sicily to Tunis.

For a short time after the landings the Germans evidently apprehended an expedition against the South coast of France or, perhaps, Corsica. Consequently, they moved such units or parts of units as could be spared from Holland, Belgium and North France (including two Reserve Training long-range bomber Gruppen and some single-engined fighter training units) to airfields in South France, which region was occupied as soon as the emergency arose.

The Germans had, in previous months, taken some interest in these airfields, but they were not ready for the reception of operational units. For this purpose it required not less than seven days' preparation. About 16th November the following transfers were made : two long-range bomber Gruppen (partly for mine-laying off Toulon) from Holland to Toulouse and Cognac ; one long-range bomber Gruppe from N. France to Istres ; two Reserve Training long-range bomber Gruppen from N. France to Toulouse and Montpellier ; one twin-engined fighter Gruppe from Holland and Belgium to Lesignan ; one single-engined fighter Gruppe from N. France to Marseilles ; 20 fighter-bomber aircraft from N. France to Istres ; two long reconnaissance Staffeln from N. France to Avignon ; two short reconnaissance Staffeln from Germany (lately on the Leningrad front) to Avignon.

Some of the long-range reconnaissance aircraft based at Bordeaux, which normally operated over the Atlantic were diverted for a few days to undertake reconnaissance over the Mediterranean.

The flying units which were moved from North Norway to Sicily and Italy (with nominally 150 aircraft) remained in the Mediterranean after the emergency ; but, with the exception of one Gruppe, all the 60 aircraft (being parts of various flying units) which were transferred from Greece and Crete on 7th and 8th November, moved back to their normal bases a few days later.

Some 100-125 aircraft were moved to Tunisia, of which over 100 were single-engined fighters and 25 dive-bombers. Nearly all these remained or were replaced ; and additional aircraft were transferred there later.

About 250 aircraft (plus a few from training units) were moved to South France on or about 16th November. Of these some 120 operational aircraft remained ; the rest (chiefly long-range bombers) returned to their normal bases as soon as the fear of a landing on the South of France was diminished.

147

its first line and training long-range bomber and minelaying units, fighters, fighter-bombers and reconnaissance aircraft being moved to airfields at Toulon, Toulouse, Montpellier, Marseilles, etc., in expectation of a further sudden Allied descent upon the coast of southern France ; the majority, however, returned to their former bases once it became clear that no new development in Allied strategy was to be expected immediately. It was not until 1943 that the bases in southern France began to be used extensively by anti-shipping bomber and torpedo-bomber forces.

55. Thus, at a single blow, the whole German air strategy was fundamentally shaken, and the inadequacy of German air strength to meet ceaseless and ever-growing commitments created a situation which no measures, however, resourceful, could adequately meet. Further, for the first time, the development of the Mediterranean campaign brought the Germans to realise the full implications of the growing strength of the Allied Air Forces, to which no effective answer could be made. The full extent of the implications of this and other developments during the winter of 1942-43 in German Air Force policy and strategy are reviewed in Chapter 9.

Establishment of the Luftwaffe in Tunisia

56. By 15th November, 1942, a new Command under Generalmajor Harlinghausen, known as *Fliegerfuehrer Tunisia*, had been set up to command the new Air Force units being rushed in to meet the Allied advance from the West. Notwithstanding the complete surprise achieved, the German reactions to the Allied landings were prompt, and by November 9th elements of dive-bomber and S.E. fighter units had already been transferred from Sardinia and Sicily to Tunis ; these moves were carried out by the use of transport aircraft and gliders for the movement of ground personnel and essential equipment. After a week Luftwaffe strength in Tunisia had already been increased to about 100 aircraft, but its resources were inadequate to enable airfields in eastern Algeria, e.g., Constantine, to be occupied at this stage.

57. During the second week a considerable expansion in the ground organisation took place, and the German occupation of airfields was extended to Gabes and Déjedeida, but supply and servicing facilities had not yet begun to function adequately and this imposed considerably restrictions on the operational efficiency of the Tunisian-based flying units at this time. There was in particular a lack of M/T and personnel for handling the supplies of bombs, ammunition and fuel, which the Germans succeeded in bringing over in adequate quantities by sea. These administrative difficulties considerably hampered operational activity during the critical early stages of the campaign, and it was not until the end of November, when the advance of the Allied ground forces threatened to cut off Tunis, that the daily average effort could be raised to 100-120 sorties. The available German air strength was, in the circumstances, unavoidably employed largely in defence for the protection of harbours and for the escort of shipping convoys and air transport formations, while the lack of good airfields also imposed a considerable handicap on the ability of the German Air Force to operate. The bad weather which accompanied this campaign and created particular difficulties for the Allied Air Forces, did not, however, have such adverse effects on the Germans, whose airfields at Bizerta and Tunis—the latter with a convenient concrete roadway nearby which served as a runway for dive bombers and fighters—remained in better condition during the heavy rains of December than did those of the Allies in Eastern Algeria.

58. An important innovation brought about by the Tunisian campaign was the introduction of the FW.190 for the first time into the Mediterranean theatre ; although strength did not exceed some 35 aircraft, it was the first indication that the Germans had begun to realise that the use of the Ju.87 dive bomber against Allied air superiority could no longer be maintained, and the FW.190's were employed to a large extent as fighters and fighter-bombers in carrying out low-level ground attacks. No attempt was made by the Germans to establish long-range bomber forces in Tunisia, partly owing to supply and maintenance problems, but mainly owing to the proximity of well-established bases for these aircraft in Sicily and Sardinia ; consequently, the aircraft operating under *Fliegerfuehrer Tunis* were exclusively of close-support and short-range reconnaissance types. Nevertheless, despite the difficulties encountered at the start, the Tunisian force by the end of 1942 was in the remarkable position of being able to maintain an equality with the numerically superior Allied air forces, owing to the even greater problems of forward supply with which the Allies were initially faced, and which could only be gradually overcome.

The Attack on Allied Sea and Supply Communications

59. As indicated above, the bulk of the Tunisian-based German air strength was committed largely to defensive operations ; it had, however, carried out a small number of low-level bombing attacks with FW.190's against advanced Allied harbours and supply installations. The main effort by the German Air Force in the central Mediterranean was directed chiefly against supply shipping and ports, in both of which the torpedo and long-range bomber forces played a considerable part both by day and night as the main hope in delaying the build-up and consolidation of the Allied forces. The important air bases in the Marseilles/Perpignon/Toulouse areas still being in process of being taken over and adapted, the bulk of the German torpedo-bombers, in company with the main long-range bomber force, were initially based mainly in Sicily, and to some extent at Grosseto, whence they used Sardinia as an advanced landing ground.

60. The German long-range bomber force in the central Mediterranean during November and December, 1942, included every possible unit with experience of anti-shipping operations which could be spared. Initially the attacks were mainly directed against shipping at Algiers and convoys at sea in that area, and were not without some success, but operations against the Algiers area and to the West thereof were severely handicapped, so far as the Sicilian-based units were concerned, owing to the extreme range and the lack of facilities in Sardinia.

61. As, during November and December, the more easterly ports of Phillipeville, Bougie and, especially, Bône, came into use by the Allies, the main long-range bomber effort was directed increasingly against these objectives, and played an important part in delaying the build-up of the Allied forces in the forward area. Every effort was made by the Germans to maintain these operations on the highest possible scale, but the consequent long period of sustained operations against increasingly effective Allied anti-aircraft and fighter defences proved a steadily growing strain upon the long-range bomber and torpedo-bomber units. Losses were heavy, both in aircraft and crews, and moreover came at a time when reserves of bomber-type aircraft were low, and when the situation on the Russian front, and particularly at Stalingrad, was imposing a further serious strain upon Luftwaffe resources.

149

THE FW. 190 FIGHTER

When this fighter first appeared, in northern France late in 1941, R.A.F. fighters were temporarily outclassed. A novel feature was the BMW.801 close-cowled radial engine with cooling fan, a departure from the liquid-cooled in-line engine found in contemporary single-engined fighters. During its operational career. the FW.190 was employed as both fighter and fighter-bomber.

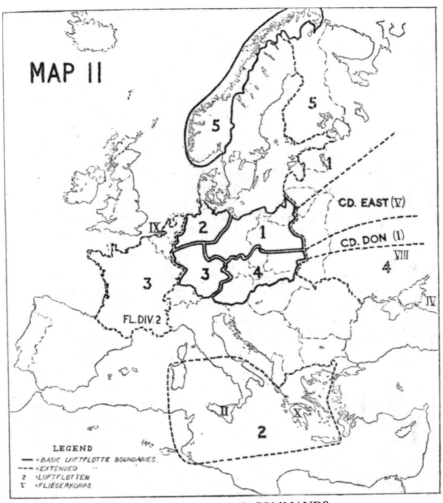

MAP II

CD. EAST (V)

CD. DON (1)

FL. DIV. 2

LEGEND
—— = BASIC LUFTFLOTTE BOUNDARIES
--- = EXTENDED ··
2 = LUFTFLOTTEN
Γ = FLIEGERKORPS

OPERATIONAL AREAS OF COMMANDS
THE GERMAN AIR FORCE IN THE MEDITERRANEAN
(DECEMBER, 1942)

In the West the extended area of Luftflotte 3 had been further extended to cover what was previously Unoccupied France. This was the German reaction to Allied landings in North Africa in November, 1942. A new operational Command (Fliegerdivision 2), which may be described as a kind of junior Fliegerkorps, was set up in the South-east of France where the Germans rapidly concentrated for a short time over 300 aircraft, mostly from second-line and training. This number was soon considerably reduced.

At the same time the Luffwaffe strengthened its position in Sardinia where a Fliegerfuehrer was established, under Luftflotte 2. The area of Luftflotte 2 is shown in the map as covering all Sardinia. It is also shown as contracted in North Africa, as a result of the Axis retreats.

By this time the Luffwaffe had a maximum of 850 first-line operational aircraft in the Mediterranean, of which about 150 were in the Eastern Mediterranean under Fliegerkorps X; and some 550 were in the Western Mediterranean under Flieger-korps II and the Fliegerfuehrer in North Africa. The numbers of aircraft on the Russian front (including North Norway) suffered some reduction in order that the forces in the Mediterranean might be reinforced.

151

62. The bomber units in the Mediterranean fell steadily below their establishment strength, few reinforcements could be provided, and the overall strength of bomber-type aircraft in the theatre could only be maintained by the transfer of further units from other operational areas, which were thus further seriously weakened. By the end of December, despite the arrival of two further bomber units in the central Mediterranean, actual strength was barely maintained at the level existing at the beginning of November. This, however, somewhat disguised the true state of affairs revealed by the fact that the average strength of bomber units in the Mediterranean had fallen to 75 per cent. of establishment, while their serviceability was little more than 50 per cent.—a repetition of the situation at the time of the Battle of Britain. Thus, the only striking force with which any attempt could be made to cripple the Allied supply and communication lines underwent a steady deterioration in efficiency, and the intensive effort of November fell off rapidly ; despite the acutely critical situation during December, only a relatively low scale of operations could be sustained by a force of nevertheless considerable numerical size.

Situation at 31st December, 1942 (see Map 11)

63. The disposition and strength of the German Air Force in the central Mediterranean area at the end of December, 1942, is given below and may be compared with the situation at the beginning of the Allied campaign given at paragraph 52 above. The figures in both cases are for actual strength, and not establishment.

	Sicily and Sardinia	*Tunisia*	*Fliegerfuehrer Africa*	*Total*
Long-range Bombers ..	240	—	—	240
Bomber Reconnaissance	35	—	10	45
Dive Bombers ..	10	20	30	60
Ground Attack ..	—	5	25	30
S.E. Fighters	50	105	85	240
T.E. Fighters	50	20	—	70
Army Co-operation ..	—	5	10	15
Total	385	155	160	700

64. It will be seen that, while there was no appreciable change in the total Luftwaffe strength in Sicily and Sardinia, the build-up of the force under Fliegerfuehrer Tunis had absorbed a further 155 close-support aircraft. This was a relatively serious additional commitment at a time when the need for these aircraft was particularly acute, having regard to the situation in Russia and to the fact that the depleted forces under Fliegerfuehrer Afrika, still covering Rommel's retreat, had called for a considerable measure of replacement aircraft to restore once again their diminished strength to a level of 160 aircraft. With a further 150 aircraft in the eastern Mediterranean, German strength in the whole theatre thus totalled 850.

65. Thus, by the end of 1942, Hitler's strategy in the Mediterranean lay in ruins with the Luftwaffe more heavily committed in all theatres than at any previous time, and not only revealing its lack of adequate resources, but even more significantly, the beginning of a decline in its fighting value.

Air Transport in the Mediterranean, 1941 to 1942

June, 1941 to January, 1942

66. The German capture of Crete, with the ensuing transfer of Fliegerkorps X from Sicily to Greece, resulted in the centre of air transport to the German forces in Africa being shifted from Italy to Athens, with Crete as the obvious transit station between Europe and Africa.

67. Following the assault on Crete, the withdrawal of the German Units from Greece in preparation for operations on the Russian front reduced German air transport resources in the Mediterranean theatre to no more than 65 aircraft ; the bulk of these had to be employed on the route from Naples/Cancello via Brindisi to Greece, since the better surface transport situation in Italy necessitated the main Air Force supply centre being set up at the Cancello air park at Naples. Italian air transport, which should have been able to supplement the limited German resources with excellent Savoia SM.82 aircraft, proved to be ill-trained and ill-equipped for blind flying, and consequently of little value in assisting the problem of supply. This situation continued up to the opening of the British offensive in North Africa on 18th November, 1941, the sole reinforcement to that date being 10 BV.222 six-engined flying boats moved to Taranto in early November.

68. The critical situation then developing on the Russian front prevented any transfer of air transport units from Russia to the Mediterranean to meet the resulting increased demands for aircraft. The Germans, however, never hesitating to become ruthless in an emergency, quickly met the new situation by withdrawing some 150 aircraft from advanced training and blind flying schools in order to form emergency transport units. This policy foreshadowed the increasing future tendency of the Luftwaffe to draw on its training resources in order to meet its overstrained air transport commitments and thereby sowed the seed which, in due course, was to lead to ever-increasing and insuperable obstacles in the provision of adequately trained flying crews for operational bomber and other units. This emergency reinforcement proved, however, to be of short duration and, with the termination of the British offensive, the newly-formed transport units had immediately to be withdrawn and diverted to the Russian front where, by this time, a first-class emergency had arisen.

April to October, 1942 (see Map 12)

69. During the lull between the German counter-attack and advance to El Gazala and the opening of Rommel's advance to Tobruk and Egypt, the main tasks of the German air transport to North Africa had been the moving of fuel, ammunition and equipment in fairly large quantities to the Luftwaffe, and the supplying of commands and operational formations. With the opening of the German offensive, however, loads were changed and troop reinforcements became a first priority.

70. At the end of June, 1942, there were, in addition to 10 BV.222's operating from Taranto, some 150 Ju.52's in the area, of which a hundred were based at Brindisi and the remainder in the Athens area ; even this strength could only be reached by taking over the special transport aircraft allocated to signals and ambulance traffic and special transport of Fliegerkorps II. Moreover, the burden on air transport was further accentuated by the interruption of surface communications across the Mediterranean by the Royal Navy and Royal Air Force, and both troops and supplies, badly needed to sustain Rommel's advance, accumulated rapidly at bases and transit stations.

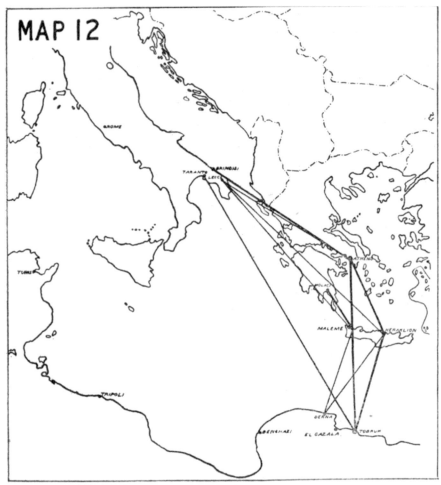

AIR TRANSPORT IN THE MEDITERRANEAN
ROMMEL IN EGYPT (JUNE-NOVEMBER, 1942)

During the campaign in North Africa the primary means of transport was by sea. When, as often happened, sea transport could not be relied upon, air transport was not merely a useful accessory, but an essential one. In fact, the Germans could not have carried on the campaign without it. The period between June, 1942 and January, 1943 is, therefore, chosen to portray in two maps the changes in the air transport routes which were necessitated as the battle moved from Egypt to Tunisia. The course of events in this period well illustrate both the potentialities and the limitations of air transport in the Luftwaffe.

The same period also illustrates the alternative preference for transport of personnel (chiefly for the Army), on the one hand, and for transport of supplies, on the other. At some stages the Germans were impelled to use air transport of personnel not only for speed but also owing to the high risk of their loss at sea. Personnel could not be replaced, whereas goods could be. But, from time to time, acute shortage of supplies, especially fuel, caused by sinkings, forced the Germans to give preference to transport of supplies at the expense of personnel.

Owing to the difficulties of railway communications through the Balkans, only a limited transport of personnel and supplies was possible by that route. The main route of supplies to the German forces in North Africa was via Italy. This fact, together with the limitation in range of the Ju.52 aircraft to 500 miles and the need for avoiding refuelling in North Africa led to the adoption, first, of the route Italy—Greece—Crete—Cyrenaica; next, Italy—Sicily—Tripoli; and, finally, Italy—Sicily—Tunisia. [continued overleaf.

The map above covers the period from the end of June, 1942 (*when Rommel reached El Alamein*) to 2nd November, 1942 (*when the British Eighth Army broke through Rommel's defences*). During this period the large majority of personnel and supplies was transported by the routes marked in heavy lines. The flights were broken in Crete so as to save refuelling at Tobruk. The number of transport aircraft available at this stage was about 200-250. There were probably 50 to 60 per cent of them serviceable on the average, but not all these would have been used except in the more urgent situations.

It is estimated that, in the three months of July, August and September, about 46,000 men (in 2,600 " lifts " of 18 men per aircraft) and 4,000 tons of supplies (in 1,900 " lifts " of 2 tons per aircraft) were transported to Africa. The maximum number of personnel carried in a single day was 1,000 ; and an average of 750 men per day was maintained over a considerable period.

Shortage of fuel for operational aircraft and for M/T. caused frequent anxiety ; but the most acute shortage of fuel was in October owing to heavy losses at sea. The Panzer Army was specially in need. The whole of the available transport aircraft, as well as some operational types such as He.111s, were employed in transport of fuel. It seems probable that the amount delivered by air to the Panzer Army during October was at least as great as, and may well have exceeded, the quantity received from the ships which escaped destruction.

During the period covered by this map, the administration of the air transport fleet in the Mediterranean was under the direction of an O.C. Air Transport at Rome, who had subordinate offices in Brindisi, Athens, Crete and Africa.

The main routes are marked in this map with heavy lines.

155

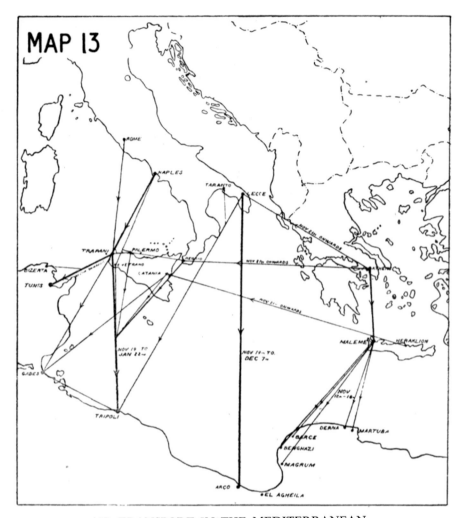

AIR TRANSPORT IN THE MEDITERRANEAN

ROMMEL'S DEFEAT AND THE OPENING OF THE TUNISIAN CAMPAIGN
(NOVEMBER 1942—JANUARY 1943)

When, in early November, 1942, Rommel was driven out of Egypt, air transport was specially valuable to him in his retreat, for often he did not know which port he could rely upon for sea transport.

Luftwaffe Air Transport in the Mediterranean had, at the same period, another exacting task to undertake. It had to play a leading part in the rapid establishment and consolidation of the Axis bridgehead in Tunisia as a counter-move to the Allied landings from 8th November onwards.

The number of transport aircraft made available for these tasks was about 350-400 in November and December, 1942. But this number fell to about 250 when the Eastern air-route could no longer be used.

Tobruk, which had been the main African terminus in the preceding months, was abandoned by the Germans on 11th November. During the ensuing week, as Rommel was retreating westwards, temporary termini were improvised at airfields in Cyrenaica (as shown in the map opposite), until the limit of range of Ju.52s from Crete was reached, namely at Magrum. [continued overleaf.

156

During the time that Rommel was in the El Agheila area a little to the East of Arco (in the latter part of November and early December), it was impossible for supplies to reach him by Ju.52s, and there was no adequate seaport nearby. He had, therefore, to rely on such supplies as could be transported from Tripoli and even from Tunisia, together with those transported from the heel of Italy in long-range aircraft such as He.111s and a few FW.200s.

At the same period, reinforcements and supplies, which had been collected in Greece for transport by the Eastern air-route and were now wanted in Tunisia, had to be flown from Athens to South Italy and Sicily to be carried to North Africa by the western air-route.

There was a considerable traffic on the route Italy—Sicily—Tripoli from mid-November until Tripoli was captured by the Allies on 23rd January.

The air transport organisation, in supplying the Axis bridgehead in Tunisia, used the route Italy—Sicily—Tunisia. Not only were Ju.52s employed, but also large powered gliders, Me.323s which carried 10 tons, that being the first occasion of their inclusion in the air transport fleet.

We have learnt from German records that, during December, 1942, and January, 1943, over 19,000 men of the German Army and Air Force and 4,500 tons of supplies and equipment were carried by air to Tunis alone. Of these amounts, 18,000 men and 3,000 tons were taken by Ju.52. The corresponding figures for Me.323 were 1,250 men and 1,475 tons. The average daily effort in aircraft was 50 " lifts " (i.e., 90 tons) by Ju.52 and 3 " lifts " (or 30 tons) by Me.323.

From the middle of November onwards, the administration of the air transport fleet was no longer under the sole command of the O.C. Air Transport, Rome. The command was divided in two, there being an O.C. Air Transport at Rome and another at Athens, each having such subordinate offices as might be necessary.

The main routes are marked in this map with heavy lines.

157

71. In the German effort to support the continuing successful advance, 100 Ju.52's were in July released from the Russian front, bringing the number of these aircraft in the Mediterranean up to 250 by the middle of the month, of which 150 now became based at Crete or the forward area in Africa ; by the end of July a further 50 Ju.52's arrived in the Athens area.

72. By that time it was possible to average between 50 and 60 daily lifts between Crete and Africa, supplemented by some 10 Italian SM.82's. Throughout July a great effort was maintained and some 16,000 men and 600 tons of freight were flown over from Europe, to be followed in early August by the transport of a further 4,000 men of Parachute Brigade Ramcke from Athens to Africa, where they were committed as ground troops to reinforce Rommel's line at El Alamein.

73. At the end of August, owing to the successful interruption of sea communications and the extended lines of supply, the Panzer Army ran short of fuel, and all available transport aircraft had then to be employed to carry this from Crete to Tobruk and thence up to the forward areas, and for this purpose a further small reinforcement of Go.242 gliders was brought into action.

74. During the three months of July, August and September, 1942, Rommel's Army was reinforced by some 46,000 men and 4,000 tons of equipment by air supply alone but, by the end of September, the intensive effort maintained had begun to show its effect, and most of the transport units were by then exhausted and the serviceability of aircraft and fitness of crews declined. Owing to losses, moreover, shortage of crews became so acute that units were reduced to borrowing from each other in order to fly such aircraft as they had serviceable. Flying conditions remained as difficult as ever owing to lack of sufficient fighter protection for the transport formations, which were constantly exposed to interception by the R.A.F. ; nor was it possible to introduce the obvious remedy of night flying, since insufficient numbers of crews trained in blind flying were available. Thus the weakening effects of the robbing of training schools of Ju.52 aircraft late in 1941 already began to show its effects. The German air transport force in the Mediterranean was therefore hardly in a position to redouble its efforts when the British Eighth Army went over to the offensive at El Alamein on 24th October, 1942.

Air Transport in the Retreat from El Alamein (see Map 13)

75. Owing to the sinking of a number of tankers by air attack immediately before the opening of the British offensive on the night of 23rd-24th October, 1942, the fuel position of the Axis ground forces became extremely acute ; further limited reinforcements of transport aircraft were made available, including some of large capacity type, the Ju.90 and Ju.290, and so critical was the situation that FW.200 long-range aircraft based at Bordeaux, and hitherto employed on anti-shipping operations over the Atlantic, had to be diverted to the Mediterranean, all aircraft being devoted exclusively to the transport of M.T. fuel. By these efforts some 250 to 275 tons a day could be brought over, sufficient barely to meet current requirements so long as the battle remained relatively static.

76. Once the German retreat began, it was solely due to the arrival of fuel supplies by air that the retiring elements of Rommel's Army succeeded in withdrawing all their forces from Cyrenaica to the El Agheila position and, but for this, it is doubtful whether any appreciable forces could have succeeded in getting much further back from El Alamein than the Egyptian frontier.

77. By November 8th, Rommel's Army had retreated so far that it was moving out of range of air supply from Crete, and after November 20th, the whole air transport service had to be re-routed from Italy and Sicily to Gabes.

Opening of the Tunisian Campaign

78. In face of the new situation brought about by the Allied landings in French North Africa, a certain number of aircraft had to be switched to fly reinforcements to Tunisia via Sicily, and a daily average of some 50-60 flights was soon established. At this juncture air transport resources were valuably reinforced by a new unit operating 20 Me.323 six-engined aircraft carrying a 10-ton load ; they were closely followed by 150 further Ju.52's, again at the expense of the Russian front, and there were now some 400 aircraft of the latter type available for operations in the Mediterranean theatre. These aircraft now operated under two air transport commands set up in early November, one of which had its headquarters in Athens and the other in Rome.

79. Severe losses now began to be inflicted on German air transport due to interception by R.A.F. fighters and attacks on airfields. Between October 25th and December 1st no less than 70 Ju.52's were destroyed in this way and still further reinforcement of German air transport strength became necessary towards the end of November, and an additional 170 Ju.52's were moved to the Mediterranean ; once again these aircraft could only be found at the expense of training, as well as the Russian front and internal air transport lines in Germany, but to a large extent the arrival of these new formations only succeeded in partially offsetting the heavy wastage which thereafter ensued.

Conclusions

80. To sum up, the Mediterranean campaign imposed an additional burden upon the German Air Transport organisation which, although it could be met by a not excessive commitment up to July, 1942, nevertheless, having regard to the heavy demands of the Russian front, not only stretched its resources to the utmost, but also made inroads on the operational training organisation. From July, 1942 onwards, however, the Mediterranean began to cause a drain on resources which grew steadily to the end of the year and was at its peak when simultaneously the demand for air transport became crucial with the impending catastrophe at Stalingrad. Nevertheless, it is not too much to say that the use of air transport over the difficult communication routes of the Mediterranean played an absolutely vital part in the conduct of German military operations in North Africa ; its intensive use had, in close succession, been sufficient to turn the scales and save Rommel from an utter and complete débâcle after the Allied victory at El Alamein, and alone enabled the Germans to snatch a slight but positive advantage and to achieve the rapid building up and consolidation of their forces in Tunisia.

*The Me.323 six-engined transport. Its useful load was 21,500 lb. and could
include lorries, tanks, A.A. guns and fuel. As an ambulance it could carry 60 men
in beds. The ten-wheeled undercarriage was designed for landings on rough ground.
The engines were Gnôme et Rhône ; its range was 445 miles.*

The BV.222 six-engined Flying Boat

CHAPTER 7

THE RUSSIAN CAMPAIGN : THE FIRST PHASE[1]
(June 1941 to December 1942)

Prelude and Preparations

Luftwaffe Opposition to Hitler's Russian Plan

1. The reasons behind Hitler's decision to attack Russia—a decision which became known to the Army and Luftwaffe Staffs soon after the fall of France in June, 1940—are beyond the scope of this history. As far as the Luftwaffe was concerned, the decision came as a surprise to most of its senior officers[2] ; they firmly believed that Hitler would have avoided a war on two fronts, and during the period in question the air attacks on Great Britain and her shipping were being increased in preparation for the all-out assault which was to precede invasion. That it was generally held to be a mistake even greater than that of involving Great Britain in war with Germany over the attack on Poland is unquestionable ; that it encountered any real opposition, however, is less certain. In so far as objections were made, they were voiced by Goering to Hitler, and as is known, Goering had never shown himself to be capable of resistance to Hitler. Both Schmid, the Chief of Air Intelligence, and Milch, are known to have opposed the plan ; the former communicated his misgivings to Jeschonnek, the Chief of Air Staff, who, as adviser to Goering, could not approach Hitler directly on such a subject but only through the C.-in-C.

2. Milch, on hearing of the decision, which to him was a catastrophic error and meant that the war was lost, went to Goering and urged him to prevent the Russian war, declaring that this was the opportunity of Goering's life to exercise an historic influence on events. Goering, who had by that time seen Hitler and had tried in vain to dissuade him from attacking Russia, basing his arguments on Hitler's denunciation in *Mein Kampf* of a war on two fronts, insisted to Milch that further representations were useless and also forbade him to make them. There is no doubt that Goering was inwardly convinced that the plan was madness. That Goering did not believe in the reason given for turning against Germany's ally by the treaty of 1939, namely that Russia herself was preparing for an aggressive war against Germany, is evidenced by his speech to commanding officers in the West when he announced Hitler's decision. In this speech he frankly said so. He had earlier tried to divert Hitler's attention from Russia by suggesting alternative employment for the German Armed Forces on the Continent not involving war with Russia ; in this case in an attack on Gibraltar through Spain. Hitler had, however, refused to be shaken in his determination to attack Russia immediately. Goering has blamed Ribbentrop for his lack of success with Hitler, but it is probable that his own lack of firmness—he himself has admitted that Hitler's decision made him " despair "—was as responsible as the Foreign Secretary's influence for Hitler's obstinate adherence to his plan.

---

[1] Reference to Map 21 will assist the reader in an appreciation of this chapter.

[2] Interrogation of Milch and Schmid, the latter Luftwaffe Chief of Intelligence at the time, and General Halder, Chief of Army Staff.

3. In fairness to Goering, it must be made clear that his conviction that Hitler's Russian project was strategically a mistake was probably offset by the fact that Hitler had many times attempted and achieved what seemed impossible. Such hopes as remained to him he pinned on the *Blitzkrieg* ; at all events, in the speech addressed to Air Force officers in the West referred to above, he gave the probable duration of the campaign as six weeks. This statement was to some extent the result of the findings of the Head of Air Intelligence, Josef Schmid, who, in his estimates of the strength of the Russian Air Force (which, according to his calculations, was numerically equal to the German but greatly inferior to the latter both technically and in experience) had not taken into consideration either the ability of the Russian Army to combat aircraft with all possible weapons, or the extent of Russia's productive capacity. Contributing factors to this miscalculation were the isolation for the last 20 years of the Soviet State, German propaganda, and the jaundiced views of Russian emigrants. On the other hand, the favourable reports of a German Industrial Commission, consisting of engineers working under Udet, which had visited factories in the Urals and on the Volga as late as the Spring of 1941, were not believed by Schmid, who suspected Udet's engineers of being the victims of Russian bluff. The reports were therefore dismissed, with Goering's approval, as untrue. Thus, Intelligence continued unchallenged until the summer of 1942 to base its appreciations of the Russian Air Force on false assumptions.

Preparations for the Campaign

4. As early as October, 1940, the " Ostbauprogramm " (Eastern Construction Programme) was already projected and from then on until the end of the year German Air Force works units and construction material were steadily moved into the newly-occupied Polish territories. Active work proceeded throughout the winter on the development of airfields and the provision of accommodation. In March, 1941, with an improvement in the weather, the development programme was accelerated ; still greater activity took place on airfield construction, and Flak units began to be set up for their defence, but it was not until April and May, 1941, that actual preparations for the reception of flying units started to be made. During those two months administrative and supply units and installations were set up, transport and supply columns were allotted, and aircraft maintenance and equipment issuing stations set up.

5. These preparations of April and May, 1941, were necessarily on a very large scale, having regard to the great size of the air force to be employed in the campaign ; all this was done unobtrusively with every security precaution, and the measures adopted proved so successful that the assault, when it came, achieved complete surprise. In particular, the move to the East of flying units was delayed until the latest possible moment in order to obviate any possible risk of detection ; these moves could, moreover, be covered to some extent by the fact that an extensive flying training organisation existed in East Prussia and occupied Poland during the winter of 1940-41, and those flying schools were secretly moved to the West and their place taken by operational units without arousing suspicion.

Transfer of the Flying Units to the East

6. It has already been shown in Chapter 5 how von Richthofen's Fliegerkorps VIII had to be moved with the greatest possible speed from Greece immediately following the conclusion of the Crete campaign at the

162

Moelders, the first German fighter Ace, and Galland's predecessor as Inspector of Fighters. Killed in 1941.

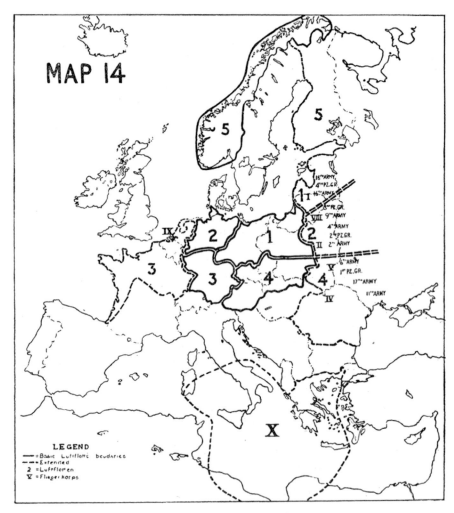

MAP 14

LEGEND
- = Basic Luftflotte boundaries
- - = Extended
2 = Luftflotten
Ⅴ = Fliegerkorps

OPERATIONAL AREAS OF COMMANDS
BEGINNING OF RUSSIAN CAMPAIGN (JUNE, 1941)

At the opening of the Russian campaign in June, 1941, Luftflotten 1, 2 and 4 were ranged on the Russian front. The home area of Luftflotte 1, as enlarged in an easterly direction after the Polish campaign in 1939, was well-placed and, doubtless, well-prepared for further extension to the East. Luftflotte 2 was introduced into the Russian front so as to reinforce it, even though this involved its being detached from its home area. Luftflotte 4, having been withdrawn from the Balkans in the previous month was given a new extended area facing East instead of South, as in the preceding campaign. As shown in the map, this sector included Rumania in the first stages of the campaign, where the G.A.F. Mission in Rumania was subordinate to it.

The sector of Luftflotte 1 looked towards Leningrad, and included the Baltic States ; that of Luftflotte 2 towards Minsk and Smolensk ; and that of Luftflotte 4 towards Kiev and the Black Sea, South of a line running East and West, through Lublin, including Southern Occupied Poland and Rumania. The length of front covered by these three Luftflotten was some 900 miles.

The primary task of Fliegerkorps in this campaign was the support of the German Armies, either directly or indirectly. The sector of Luftflotte 1 corresponded with that of Army Group North ; that of Luftflotte 2 with Army Group Centre ; and that of Luftflotte 4 with Army Group South. The approximate positions of the German Armies are shown in this Map.

As a result of the withdrawal of Luftflotte 4 from the Balkans so as to occupy the southern sector in the Russian campaign, Fliegerkorps X had its operational area extended eastwards to cover not only the central Mediterranean, but also Greece, Crete and the Aegean Islands.

end of May, 1941—a long and difficult operation across a complicated and broken line of communications—allowing less than three weeks in which to complete the move. This, however, was only one of the important moves which had to be carried out at short notice. Others involved the large-scale transfer of units on the Western Front still engaged in operations against Britain[1]. This entailed the move of Luftflotte 2 and Fliegerkorps II and V, including the bulk of their personnel and flying units and, in addition, numerous administrative, supply, signals, and other elements of the ground organisation. Advance signals and other ground units of these Commands had already begun to move by the middle of May and, by the end of the month, Luftflotte 2 had already left France. While a few small fighter and reconnaissance units had arrived in Poland between the middle and end of May, the bulk of the operational forces to be employed still remained either actively engaged on the West or refitting in Germany. As part of the measures designed to achieve surprise and to conceal what in fact was taking place, spoof W/T transmissions were maintained throughout the early part of June in order to give the impression that certain units were still operating against the British Isles. The whole of the transfer of the flying elements of the Luftwaffe to the East was, in fact, accomplished within a space of some three weeks, during which period a force of over 2,500 aircraft became established in secret along the Russian front.

Deployment of the German Air Force (see Map 14)

7. Four Luftflotten in all were engaged at the opening of the campaign against Russia ; these were disposed as follows :—

Loftflotte 1 under Generaloberst Keller, with Fliegerkorps I subordinated, was based in East Prussia for the support of Army Group North on the northern flank operating along the Baltic coast through Lithuania, Latvia and Estonia.

Luftflotte 2, under General Feldmarschall Kesselring, and controlling Fliegerkorps VIII and II, comprised the main bulk of the striking power of the Air Force for the support of Army Group Centre in its drive towards Smolensk between the Baltic States and the Pripet Marshes.

In the South *Luftflotte* 4, commanded by Generaloberst Loehr, controlled Fliegerkorps V and IV for the support of Army Group South in the area extending from the Pripet Marshes to Rumania.

In addition to these major commands a small detachment of Luftflotte 5 was also engaged in the far North of Norway.

8. The force engaged during the opening phase of the offensive comprised no less than some 2,770 aircraft out of the total Luftwaffe first-line strength of 4,300 and consisted of the following :—

Long-range Bombers	775
Dive Bombers	310
S.E. Fighters	830
T.E. Fighters	90
Long-range Reconnaissance	340
Tactical Reconnaissance	370
Coastal	55
Total	2,770

[1] See Chapter 4, paragraph 48.

Of the above, the force under Luftflotte 2 mustered not less than 1,500 aircraft, while that of Luftflotte 4 consisted of some 750 ; thus, only relatively weak forces remained for Luftflotte 1, while those of Luftflotte 5 engaged in operations in the Far North never exceeded more than 100 to 150 aircraft.

9. Such was the force deployed to undertake a lightning campaign in the East, which was to have led to the overwhelming defeat of Russia before the onset of winter. It will be noted that, massive as the air striking force was, it consisted of fewer aircraft than were, in fact, employed for the much more limited campaign in the West in 1940[1] ; the Russian front extended from the Baltic to the Black Sea over a distance of 1,000 miles and, to have afforded the requisite amount of air strength to cover such a front would by far have exceeded the total resources of the German Air Force. The grouping of the Air Force was, however, such as to afford the maximum degree of air support for the main thrusts to be made by the ground forces ; moreover, the Air Force was now at its zenith, fresh from the easy and spectacular victories in the Balkans and Crete, well-organised and experienced for battle as the result of operations in the West in 1940, and still with a strong bomber force after the winter's bombing offensive against Britain. Such a force was to be pitted against an enemy devoid of operational experience and taken by surprise ; there can be no doubt that the Germans entered upon the Russian campaign in a spirit of the highest confidence as to the outcome of the result, emboldened further by the very poor showing of the Soviet Air Force in the Finnish Campaign of 1939-40, where 900 aircraft had been lost to a handful of obsolete fighters and guns.

The First Phase of the Campaign (June to December, 1941)

The Initial Blow and the Advance

10. As in previous campaigns, an initial and heavy blow was struck at the opposing air force, and surprise attacks at the start of the offensive inflicted heavy losses on Russian aircraft on the ground. The main thrust which developed on the central sector resulted in the forces of Fliegerkorps VIII and II operating under Luftflotte 2 being heavily committed ; the dive bombers, with fighters also operating as fighter-bombers, carried out widespread and intensive attacks on Soviet airfields, communications and troop concentrations in the area between the frontier and Minsk. These operations were, moreover, further intensified by the employment of the long-range bomber force operating in direct support of the Army, necessitating low-level attacks on a large scale and operating almost exclusively by day. They were thus employed under conditions totally different from those to which they had been accustomed during the previous winter's night bombing offensive against Britain. On the Baltic flank air operations were much more limited and became mainly strategic in character, consisting primarily of the employment of long-range bombers for sea-mining around the fortress of Kronstadt near Leningrad, bombing of the White Sea canal, and anti-shipping warfare in the Baltic aiming at bottling up the Soviet fleet in the northern Baltic and the Gulf of Finland.

---

[1] Compare charts in Chapter 3 (paragraph 40) and Chapter 4 (paragraphs 6 and 7).

11. On the southern sector little initial progress was made during the first month. There was little activity from Rumania, where only slow progress could be made in crossing the River Pruth and reaching the Dniester. The main effort of Luftflotte 4 was confined to supporting the Army's assault[1] on Lemberg, Tarnopol and other frontier fortresses, north of the Carpathians.

12. The rapid advance of the German ground forces through Poland into White Russia called for the highest degree of mobility on the part of the close-support forces, and ground organisation of the German Air Force in the field proved itself fully capable of maintaining the serviceability and operational efficiency of units under these conditions. The German Air Force was in fact being employed on the now classic lines evolved by pre-war theory and confirmed with such striking success in practice in previous campaigns ; in particular it will have been noted that the tactical and long-range reconnaissance elements comprised over 700 aircraft, and the extent to which air reconnaissance was carried out was one of the outstanding features. Reconnaissance extended deep into the Russian back areas as well as covering the fighting zones, and the German headquarters were constantly able to form a clear picture, not only of Russian movements and of troop and tank concentrations, but also of the general situation on an extensive front, where the fighting was often extremely confused.

13. By the middle of July, 1941, the battle for Smolensk was already beginning and, by this time, the German advance had reached the point which made it possible to bring forward long-range bombers to carry out the first bombing attacks on Moscow on July 21st and 22nd. These operations called for the transfer of further long-range bomber reinforcements from the Western Front where, until a few days previously, they had been operating against the British Isles ; these transfers represented a further and permanent weakening of the already small German Air Forces still engaged in the West. These attacks on Moscow were to continue spasmodically for the greater part of the rest of the year but never reached any degree of intensity ; they usually amounted to 30-40 sorties and seldom exceeded 100, being in effect little more than harassing attacks.

14. By the end of July, the great width of the front on which fighting had developed had already begun to make it necessary to execute rapid changes in the subordination of flying units from one Command to another, in order to meet local tactical requirements (see Map 15). It was not, however, until the enforced halt occasioned in the central front by the failure to make progress in the assault on Smolensk that the first major redisposition of the Luftwaffe on the Russian front took place ; it was decided then to increase pressure on the northern flank through the Baltic States. For this purpose, at the beginning of August, Fliegerkorps VIII became subordinated to Luftflotte 1, the latter Command being thus reinforced to the extent of some 400 close-support aircraft. The resulting intensification of air operations on this sector contributed much to the rapid advance towards Leningrad which, by the end of the month, was seriously threatened and under direct attack by the forces of Luftflotte 1.

---

[1] One of the innovations introduced by Richthofen at this time was that of the Tank Liaison Officer (*Panzer Verbindungs Offizier*). This was an Air Force officer who accompanied the armoured columns in an A.F.V. and kept in close touch by radio with the close-support aircraft.

15. During August, while the situation remained static on the central front, the German advance also made rapid progress through the western Ukraine, where the forces of Luftflotte 4 for the first time became heavily engaged. The main effort was used in support of the Army's drive against Odessa and Nikolaiev. It was consequently impossible adequately to cover the Army and Air Force elements operating for the Kiev area, where the Russians succeeded in maintaining strong air resistance. Harassing attacks were maintained on harbours and shipping in the Black Sea ports and, as on other sectors, against communications, to hamper the withdrawal of the Russian Army.

16. Meanwhile, at the beginning of September, very considerable importance was attached to the advance southwards of strong German armoured formations from the Gomel area. This thrust threatened from the rear the Russian salient held at Kiev, and was supported by over 500 aircraft. The intensive scale of these air operations gave further proof of the German determination to employ their Air Force to the utmost in order to achieve their objective ; the ability of close-support units to follow up the advance provided a further striking instance of their success in maintaining mobility and operating at short notice from field landing grounds. At the same time operations also showed that the resources of the German Air Force on the Russian front still remained insufficient to allow strong forces to be maintained at all points ; a difficulty increasingly contended with by concentrating the main air effort in support of local operations at the expense of other sectors, thus establishing air superiority where considered most necessary.

Supplies

17. The success of German Air Force operations during the first three months of the campaign depended almost entirely on the adequate functioning of the supply organisation. The Russian " scorched earth " policy prevented the Germans from capturing any appreciable quantities of fuel, and in many instances they were forced to rely on supplies by transport aircraft. Similar conditions also affected the central sector during the first few weeks, but by a month after the beginning of the campaign the lines of communication had to some extent been reopened, and consolidation of the supply organisation in these areas already begun ; the improvement in the supply situation was probably also assisted by some slowing down of the rate of advance during the second fortnight. The Russian Air Force appears to have been too closely engaged in the battle zone to divert any of its forces against the German supply dumps and bases. The development of seaborne traffic to Riga also considerably eased the situation in the Baltic States.

18. No special difficulties seem to have been encountered on the southern front. Not only was the initial advance less rapid, but when it began, railway communications appear to have been well maintained, thus ensuring adequate supplies from Southern Poland.

Operations : October to December, 1941

19. With Leningrad effectively isolated and closely besieged, and immediately following upon the improvement on the southern front after the encirclement of Kiev, the important decision was reached by the Germans to launch a final all-out offensive against Moscow. With this object in view, far-reaching changes in the disposition of the Luftwaffe on the Russian front took place,

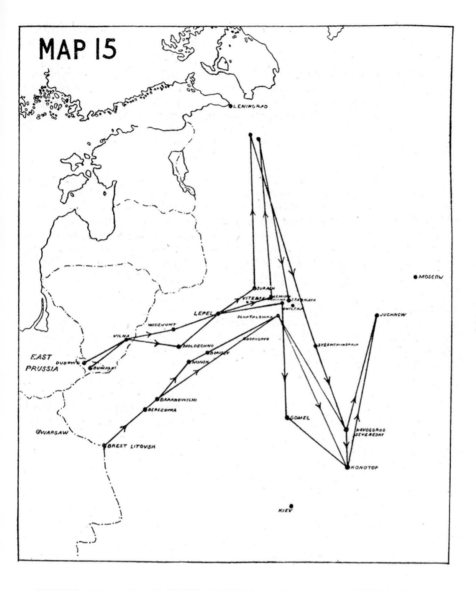

MOVES OF SHORT-RANGE FLYING UNITS ON RUSSIAN FRONT
(JUNE-OCTOBER, 1941)

The moves of five single-engined fighter and dive-bomber units on the Russian front in the first four months of the offensive against Russia provide useful illustrations of the way such units were handled by the German Air Force.

Two characteristics in the use of the selected single-engined fighter and dive-bomber units stand out during these phases of the offensive. First, the speed with which the flying units were pressed forward, close after each advance of the Army so as to give the Army the maximum support. Secondly, the manner in which the flying units were switched laterally to new sectors to support the attacks to which the High Command gave successive priority. This second characteristic is as much evidence of the inadequacy of the Luftwaffe to cover so wide a front as that in Russia as it is of mobility.

[continued overleaf.

169

Three days after the beginning of the offensive (i.e., 25th June), two dive-bomber Gruppen and three single-engined fighter Gruppen moved forward to the line Vilna–Berezovka. Four days later (29th June) they were on the line Widzjuny–Moldechno–Baronowichi, making 130-150 miles advance in the first seven days. By the end of the next seven days (5th July) they had advanced another 130 miles to the line Lepel–Dokudovo. By 21st July they had pressed on still another 100 miles to the line Surash–Demidov–Moscha–Schatalowka (i.e., a little to the West of Smolensk). Each of these moves was close on the heels of the Army. These flying units advanced their bases some 360 miles in a month.

Smolensk fell on 25th July ; and, at this stage, as already stated, the main pressure was diverted to the Leningrad front. Two of the five units were transferred there in early August (a move of some 250 miles to the North).

When, at the end of August, it was decided to concentrate all available effort on the Kiev battle, four of the five units (including one which had been on the Leningrad front) were transferred to the Konotop area (i.e., 250 miles South of Smolensk) so as to support the closing of the Northern pincer to the East of Kiev.

Finally, after the conclusion of the Kiev battle, towards the end of September, every available close support unit was based on the Moscow front. Accordingly, in early October, three at least of the units whose moves have been described were transferred to Jucknow to be incorporated in the specially formed Close Support Group which was to assist the Army in its thrust at Moscow from the South-west.

The Units selected for the purpose of this description are II and III Stuka 1, III JG.27, IV JG.51, and III JG.53.

the effect of which was to place under Kesselring, A.O.C. of Luftflotte 2 in the central sector, the strongest single concentration of air forces since the early stages of the campaign. This concentration involved the re-subordination of Fliegerkorps VIII to Luftflotte 2 together with the whole of the long-range bomber and fighter forces of Fliegerkorps I and fighter units from Luftflotte 4. As a result, the total force at the disposal of Luftflotte 2 amounted to approximately 50 per cent. of the total German Air Force strength on the Russian front and included :—

		Aircraft
Long-range Bombers	.. ..	600
Long-range Reconnaissance	.. ..	100
Dive Bombers	.. ..	120
S.E. Fighters	.. ..	400
T.E. Fighters	.. ..	100
Total ..	.. ..	1,320

The close-support forces of Luftflotte 2 were assembled in two main sectors, one extending from Smolensk South-eastwards to Roslavl, the other further South in the Konotop area, these sectors being further supported by some 400 and 200 L.R. bombers respectively.

20. The drive against Moscow opened on October 1st, and the heavy concentration of forces of all types resulted in considerable progress being made during the first few days. Within a week, however, a deterioration of the weather set in which restricted air operations. Nevertheless, it is probable that this restriction enabled serviceability to be maintained or improved, with the result that on favourable days it was possible to achieve a remarkable scale of effort, particularly by dive bomber units. In an endeavour to provide air support for a move to encircle Moscow from the North, a determined attempt was made to establish strong close-support forces at Kalinin at the apex of a salient formed by a drive North-East of Viasma. Although exposed to heavy attack by Russian ground and air forces and having to rely largely on air transport for supplies, the German Air Force succeeded in maintaining a foothold in this area for some considerable time, but it is doubtful whether they were able to exploit this manoeuvre to the full.

21. By November, airfield conditions had become exceedingly difficult, alternating between mud in which aircraft became bogged, and hard frozen surfaces which caused damage to undercarriages and tail-wheels. In contrast, the Russian Air Force, concentrated in the defence of Moscow and based on its home airfields which remained in good condition, was able to operate with success against the German Air Force and prevented formations from reaching their targets. The adverse weather conditions which continued into December appear to have had less effect generally on the Russian Air Force than on the German Air Force, which by now was being handicapped by lack of fighter support and completely failed to give adequate air support to the Army over the greater part of the Moscow front. Thus, with the approach of winter, the initiative and air superiority for the first time passed to the Russians.

22. On the southern front the German Air Force seems to have been unable to prevent the Russian Air Force from inflicting heavy casualties both by low-level and bombing attacks ; the withdrawal of close-support forces for the attack on Moscow had clearly resulted in depriving the German Air Force of air support in the South.

23. Meanwhile, an assault on the Crimea was making slow progress, and it was not until the transfer back of units from the Moscow front to provide additional air support, that the Germans succeeded in crossing the Perekop Isthmus. This check was to prove an important factor in delaying the establishment of the German Air Force at operational bases in the Crimea from which further activity in the Black Sea area could be carried out.

The Winter Campaign of 1941-1942

Winter Deployment (see Map 16)

24. With the failure of the attack on Moscow, the prospect of having to face a winter campaign in the East, and with the development of the situation in the Mediterranean, consideration had by the end of October, to be given to the general disposition of the German Air Force during the winter months. For the reinforcement of the Mediterranean it was then decided to withdraw Luftflotte 2 from the central front and, at that time, the simultaneous withdrawal of Fliegerkorps VIII was also considered. The deterioration of the military situation, however, and the crisis caused by the retreat from Moscow, seems to have resulted in a decision to retain Fliegerkorps VIII in the East and instead to withdraw Fliegerkorps II to the Mediterranean. Simultaneously, Fliegerkorps V was withdrawn from the southern flank, leaving behind a small '' Special Staff Crimea '' for the control of air operations in the peninsula.

25. Coincident with the withdrawal of operational Commands, large-scale withdrawals of flying units, badly in need of rest and re-equipment and for reinforcement in the Mediterranean, also took place, with the result that during the winter of 1941-42 German air strength on the Russian front was reduced to some 1,700 aircraft. The result of the withdrawal of the Commands outlined above was that Luftflotte 1, with Fliegerkorps I still subordinated, remained in charge of operations on the Leningrad front. On the central front Fliegerkorps VIII was left to operate alone, with no superior Luftflotte Command and, in fact, enjoying the temporary status of a Luftflotte while, in the South, Luftflotte 4 remained with Fliegerkorps IV covering the whole of the Ukrainian front with an addition of the small Operations Staff remaining in the Crimea.

Winter Conditions

26. The severity of the winter which overtook the German armed forces now deep in Russia found the Air Force, no less than the Army, ill-prepared to meet the wholly abnormal and unforeseen situation. Apart from a lack of suitable clothing and adequate accommodation, the deep snow and intense cold found the Air Force without the necessary equipment for the servicing and maintenance of aircraft and communications, conditions which resulted in the fact that the still substantial force remaining in the East could maintain only a very low proportionate scale of effort. Serviceability of units fell as low as 30 per cent., and their aircraft strength, depleted as a result of the summer and autumn campaigns, had little prospect of replacements owing to the heavy re-equipment programme for the units already withdrawn from the front. Moreover, the Russian winter offensive, both on the central front and in the South, following the loss of Rostov and the consequent threat to Kharkov and Kursk, nevertheless compelled operations to be undertaken under the most

MAP 16

LEGEND
— Basic Luftflotte Boundaries
-- Extended "
2 Luftflotten
V Fliegerkorps.

OPERATIONAL AREAS OF COMMANDS
CHANGES ON THE RUSSIAN FRONT (JANUARY, 1942)

The changes in the positions of operational Commands which had taken place by January, 1942, were due to the decision of the Germans to strengthen their air force in the Mediterranean as a result of the British advances in North Africa.

The removal of Luftflotte 2 and Fliegerkorps II from the Russian front involved readjustments there. Fliegerkorps VIII had to take over the whole of the sector which it had previously shared with Fliegerkorps II under Luftflotte 2. This sector was a very wide one to be covered by one Fliegerkorps, extending to about 400 miles, partly to the North and partly to the South of Moscow.

In view of the fact that this sector had previously been under the charge of a Luftflotte (i.e., Luftflotte 2), Fliegerkorps VIII was given the temporary status of a Luftflotte, in the sense that it operated under the direct orders of the Air Ministry.

At the end of 1941, Fliegerkorps V, which had been situated in the more northerly part of the area of Luftflotte 4 (roughly speaking, the front between Kursk and Stalino) and had been engaged in support of attacks on Kharkov, was withdrawn from operations and was a little later used, in part at least, as a " Special Staff " in connection with operations in the Crimea. Fliegerkorps IV had been engaged in the autumn in the Germans' attempts to gain access to the Crimea.

It should be noted that, by this time, Luftflotte 4's area no longer included Rumania, since the German Air Force Mission had come under the direct charge of the Air Ministry.

173

G

adverse conditions. Thus, a continued strain was imposed on crews and a steady wastage of aircraft further delayed the much needed re-equipment of units.

Effects of the First Six Months' Campaign

27. In a vain effort to reach a decisive military conclusion before the end of the year, the German Air Force had, since the beginning of the campaign, been committed ruthlessly to an unbroken period of air operations which continued even after the weather broke in mid-October and until the severe cold finally brought about an enforced suspension of activity. Little or no time was allowed for the resting of crews, and the insistent demands for air support, arising first on one sector of the front and then on another, gave little opportunity for respite. Air operations were carried on almost unbrokenly by all units engaged between June and the end of October. The intensity of effort may be gauged by the fact that during this period dive-bomber units maintained an average number of sorties per day equivalent to 75 per cent. of establishment aircraft, whilst fighters maintained about 60 per cent. and long-range bombers 40-45 per cent. on this basis. An average scale of effort for the whole period by the total force, averaging some 2,500 aircraft, worked out in excess of 1,200 sorties per day for aircraft of all types engaged on the front ; in periods of great intensity, up to 2,000 sorties a day or more were put up.

28. Despite all this effort and the constant endeavour to eliminate the Soviet Air Force by attacking it at every possible opportunity, this latter aim was never successfully accomplished, notwithstanding the fact some 20,000 Russian aircraft were claimed destroyed up to the end of October. On the contrary, it was the German Air Force itself which became seriously weakened as a result of its own immense efforts. Losses were extremely heavy, due to the enforced use of inadequately prepared and ill-equipped airfields, and especially owing to the great accuracy of Russian A.A. fire, from which both reconnaissance and long-range bomber units suffered particularly. Wastage of aircraft was such that total first-line strength, which had been steadily expanding up to the opening of the Russian campaign, underwent a decline and dropped to approximately 4,300 aircraft by the end of December, 1941. Units in consequence had, in some cases, to be merged and for the first time it became apparent that the production of aircraft was inadequate to sustain a long period of heavy air operations. Moreover, the losses of crews were excessive and could not, at short notice, be made good from the existing training organisation. In particular this affected the long-range bombing units, and sowed the seeds of their subsequent decline from their high peak of efficiency reached during the winter of 1940-41. Shortage of aircraft fuel, owing to the excessive consumption caused by operations in the East also began to be felt, due to the fact that the synthetic oil plants had not yet come into operation ; this shortage in turn was to have adverse effects on the training situation during the ensuing year, when the steady increase of output of crews became increasingly necessary.

January to June, 1942

29. The Russian winter offensive, which in the South began to threaten the important centres of Kharkov and Kursk and in the North made rapid progress towards Smolensk, enforced the employment of the German Air Force under the most adverse conditions without at the same time possessing air superiority on any sector. Whilst further withdrawals of units continued

during January, by the end of the month it was again necessary to reinforce the central front with close-support forces, a process which continued until the end of March. Thus, although a certain proportion of those forces withdrawn earlier were able to strengthen the German Air Force position in the Mediterranean, the continued Russian pressure probably prevented that position from reaching the scale actually intended.

30. During the winter months the Germans continued with the construction of airfields on a considerable scale in South Russia. The object of this was an act of foresight in order to establish not only operational bases for the resumption of the summer operations of 1942, but also to ensure adequate facilities for the maintenance of transport traffic, which was likely to develop on an increasing scale—particularly if further advances to the East were achieved, thus lengthening the already extended lines of communication.

31. The thaw period which set in in April, 1942, was accompanied by a general reduction in air activity, and the absence of any land operations on a large scale gave the Germans a further opportunity to withdraw units for re-equipment after the winter operations. At the same time the force maintained in Northern Norway became of increasing importance for operations against the convoy route to Murmansk ; in order to take advantage of the already long hours of daylight the German Air Force long-range bomber force in that area received considerable reinforcements[1].

The Summer Campaign of 1942 (June to December)
Preparations for the Campaign

32. Faced with the prospect of a further major military campaign on the Russian front, German strategy had to admit that a repetition of operations on the lines followed during the previous summer could not be expected to lead to positive results ; the length of the front in Russia forced the conclusion that it would be necessary to concentrate the maximum possible forces in one main theatre only if satisfactory results were to be achieved. The decision was therefore reached that the southern front should be the main scene of operations aiming at the overrunning of the Caucasus in order to cut off the Russian main source of oil supply, possession of which would, moreover, meet Germany's ever-growing requirements, and simultaneously to open a way to the Middle East in conjunction with the drive against Egypt to be undertaken by Rommel in the Mediterranean.

33. The first prerequisite for the launching of this plan was to cover the German southern flank by the complete occupation of the Crimea, and consequently the Russian forces were driven out of the Kerch Peninsula during April, leaving Sebastopol still stubbornly resisting. Accordingly, Fliegerkorps VIII was in May moved from the central front to the Crimea, being subordinated to Luftflotte 4. By this means a force of approximately 600 aircraft of all types was assembled on airfields in the Crimea, where they were placed at the shortest possible range for the undertaking of a major assault on Sebastopol. The place of Fliegerkorps VIII on the central front was in turn taken by Fliegerkorps V, withdrawn from the southern front early in 1942, its designation being changed to that of " Luftwaffe Command East ", with the status of a Luftflotte. (See Map 17.)

---

[1] See Chapter 4, paragraph 85.

175

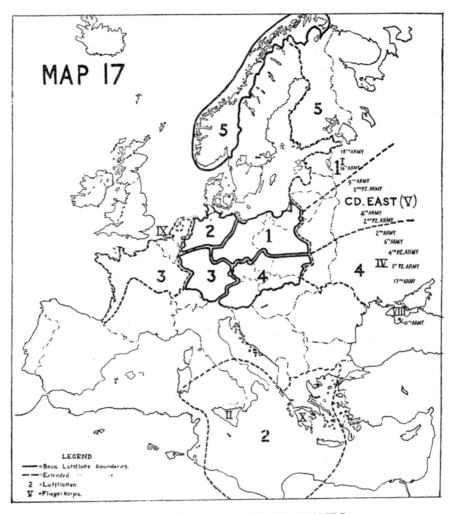

MAP 17

CD. EAST (Ⅴ)

LEGEND
——— =Basic Luftflotte boundaries.
— — — =Extended "   "
2 =Luftflotten
Ⅴ =Flieger Korps.

OPERATIONAL AREAS OF COMMANDS
SUMMER CAMPAIGN (MAY, 1942)

By this stage in the Russian campaign operations in the Crimea were regarded by the Germans as of paramount importance, as their summer offensive against the Caucasus depended on first completing the occupation of the peninsula. Kerch had just fallen; but Sebastopol was still stubbornly resisting. Accordingly, Fliegerkorps VIII, which at this period in the War was generally selected to support the most critical operations, was moved from the Moscow front to the Crimea, coming under the orders of Luftflotte 4. The support of Fliegerkorps VIII was undoubtedly a big factor in overcoming the Russian resistance in the Kerch Peninsula.

The area vacated by Fliegerkorps VIII was taken over by Fliegerkorps V, whose designation was changed to that of " G.A.F. Command East ". This Command had the status of a Luftflotte and was directly under the orders of the Air Ministry. Fliegerkorps IV had had to bear the brunt of the defence against the heavy and successful Russian attacks in South Russia during March; and, in order to reinforce it, Close Support units had to be rapidly transferred from other Fliegerkorps on the Russian front.

The approximate positions of the German armies on the Russian front are shown on this Map.

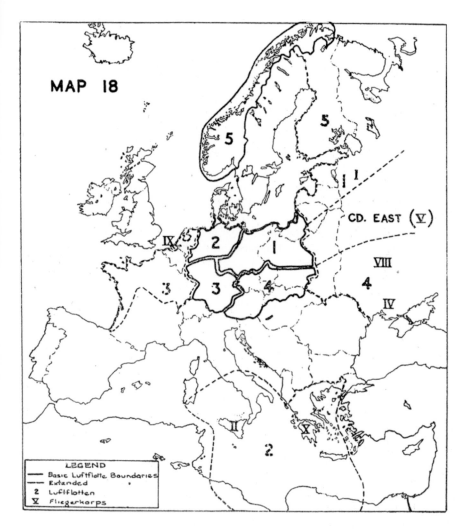

OPERATIONAL AREAS OF COMMANDS
SUMMER CAMPAIGN (JUNE, 1942)

Fliegerkorps VIII, having performed its task in the extreme South of the line, was now moved to the new critical sector of operations. Its move was, in fact, from the southern sector of Luftflotte 4 to the northern sector in that Luftflotte area. This change of location took place at the period when the Germans were about to begin their new offensive on the Kursk front towards Voronezh.

As a result of the move of Fliegerkorps VIII, Fliegerkorps IV was moved to the sector abutting on the Black Sea.

34. The selection of Fliegerkorps VIII to undertake this assault conformed with the now established practice of entrusting this Command, under Richthofen, to the support of the most critical operations in view of its proved experience and efficiency in undertakings involving close-support work on the heaviest scale.

35. The attack on Sebastopol opened on June 2nd, lasting until June 6th, during which time the fortress was subjected to heavy air bombing. On an average some 600 sorties a day were flown with a maximum of over 700 on June 2nd, and some 2,500 tons of H.E. bombs, many of the heaviest calibre[1], were dropped. Nevertheless, it was surprisingly found when the German infantry attacked on June 4th that the fortifications were in general undamaged and the morale of the defending forces unbroken ; however, the weight of the German assault was such that all Russian opposition was overcome in a relatively short space of time.

36. Simultaneously with the operations against Sebastopol an unexpected Russian offensive directed at Kharkov necessitated the immediate transfer of German Air Force units from the Crimea to help stem the advance, and intensive air operations had to be undertaken in order to save the situation. This forestalling action by the Russians not only inflicted losses which were required to be made good, but also delayed preparations then in hand for the launching of the main summer campaign. However, early in June, Flieger-korps VIII was once again moved northwards and set up its headquarters at Kursk, where it was thus situated on the northern half of the operational area of Luftflotte IV. (See Map 18.) Throughout May and June, intensive efforts were made to build up large stocks of bombs, fuel, etc., on the southern front, for which purpose the railways were being worked at maximum capacity. At the same time air reinforcements began to move back to the Russian front, many of them newly-equipped during the previous six months and further strengthened by reinforcements brought back from the Mediterranean following the conclusion of the assault on Malta. Thus, by the beginning of July, German strength on the Russian front had once again been restored to 2,750 aircraft and was therefore equal in strength to that employed during the previous summer. Now, however, 1,500 of these were deployed in the South under Luftflotte 4, leaving only a relatively small holding force of some 600 aircraft on the central front, not more than 375 on the Leningrad front, with a further 200 based in North Norway and Finland.

Operations : July to August, 1942

37. The German offensive opened in the first week of July with Fliegerkorps VIII operating on a relatively narrow front in support of the initial drive against Voronesh. Subsequently its area of operations extended southwards, accompanying the advance of the armoured formations along the Voronesh-Rostov railway in the area east of the Donetz. The close-support forces very quickly followed the rapid German advance down the line of the Don, and the move South of some long-range bombers left only a weak force in the Voronesh area to face considerable Soviet attacks from the North-East against the German flank. Nevertheless the Russians were held at Voronesh without calling upon forces co-operating in the German drive in the South, which received consistent air support from long-range bomber and close-support units.

---

[1] 1,000 kilogrammes.

38. Throughout the rapid German advance down the line of the Don from Voronesh towards Stalingrad and into the Caucasus from Rostov towards Maikop and Armavir, a large proportion of the long-range bomber force was systematically engaged against communications in the enemy's rear. These operations extended over a wide area, including the North Caucasus, where bridges, ferries and railways were heavily attacked. Strategical bombing was also carried out against communications more remote from the scene of military operations, with the object of cutting the supply line between Stalingrad and Moscow, but no attempt was made to bomb towns situated well behind the lines and not subject to immediate threat from the ground. On the contrary, the long-range bomber force was concentrated exclusively on indirect support of the Army, its main task being the dislocation of Soviet communications ; with this in view ports on the Caucasian coast as far as Poti were attacked, and small-scale mining of the Volga was also attempted, together with attacks on Volga shipping as far south as Astrakhan.

39. As contrasted with the offensive against Stalingrad, which was supported by some 1,000 aircraft of all types, the German advance in the Caucasus, once the Don had been crossed, received but little air support until slowed down by hilly country, which hindered the employment of armoured formations. It then became necessary to build up the strength of Fliegerkorps IV, the command controlling operations in the Caucasus, and single-engined and twin-engined fighter units were brought up to bases on a line running approximately West to East through Krasnodar.

Operations : September to October, 1942 (see Map 19)

40. Air policy in September and October was dominated by the inability of the German High Command to secure a decision either at Stalingrad or in the Caucasus. A very high scale of effort was maintained at Stalingrad throughout September by Fliegerkorps VIII controlling the greater part of the forces under Luftflotte 4, particularly by dive bombers which often carried out four or more sorties a day.

41. In spite of continuous operations for four months, the strength of the German Air Force was maintained with remarkable consistency until October at a figure between 2,450 and 2,500 aircraft. A fair number of units, particularly long-range bombers, were withdrawn in August and September for re-equipment, but their place was taken by fresh units with full complements of aircraft and crews. Nevertheless, the concentration of forces in the South left the Moscow and Leningrad fronts weak. It is probable that the Soviet Air Force enjoyed air superiority in this area, and Russian offensives at Rshev and in the Lake Ilmen area necessitated in September the transfer northwards of some units which had been engaged in the Stalingrad battle. However, the reinforcement of the Luftwaffe in the Leningrad sector which took place during September was intended, in conjunction with the reinforcement of the German army on that front, as a preliminary to a full-scale attack, on the assumption that Stalingrad could not hold out for long. By the beginning of October a force of 550-600 aircraft had been assembled on the Leningrad front, but Stalingrad did not fall, and Russian preparations and troop movements, particularly in the Moscow sector and to a lesser degree in the south, compelled the Luftwaffe to redistribute its forces and disperse the concentration at Leningrad. During the last fortnight of October no less than 300 aircraft were withdrawn from this sector.

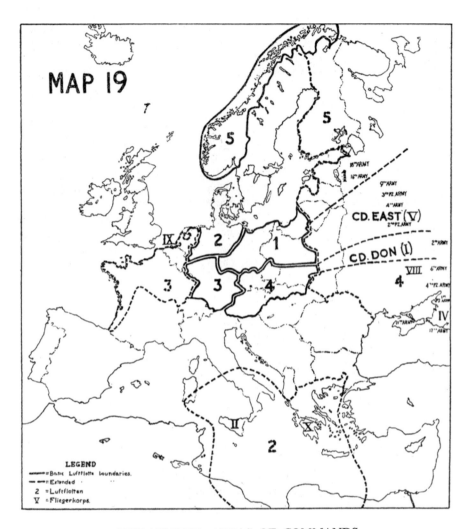

OPERATIONAL AREAS OF COMMANDS
SUMMER CAMPAIGN (SEPTEMBER-OCTOBER, 1942)

In Russia, Fliegèrkorps IV had, by the late summer, penetrated into the Caucasus, while Fliegerkorps VIII was charged with supporting the offensive in the Stalingrad area. Owing to the concentration of Fliegerkorps VIII's forces and to the situation in the Don Basin, it was found necessary to introduce another Command to direct operations in the North of Luftflotte 4's area, on the Voronezh front. Accordingly Fliegerkorps I was brought down from the area of Luftflotte 1 (where it had been operating since the beginning of the campaign) and given the new designation of "Luftwaffe Command Don". It presumably operated directly under the orders of the Air Ministry. Luftflotte 1 was left without any Fliegerkorps staff under it.

The approximate positions of the German armies on the Russian front are shown on this Map.

Stalingrad : German photographs taken during the seige. The aircraft is a Ju.87 dive bomber

G*

42. At this stage the dangers to which the German Air Force in Russia was exposed, became evident. Its supply lines were extended ; it was far removed from the well-developed bases which had been built up during the winter of 1941-1942, and was operating from inferior landing-grounds ; the bulk of its forces were committed to the indecisive struggle at Stalingrad to such an extent that air superiority was sacrificed elsewhere ; close-support units were operating intensively with many crews flying three or four sorties a day and with effects on serviceability of aircraft and efficiency of pilots which must ultimately prove disastrous. At the same time local Soviet offensives and threatened offensives in the North and on the central front necessitated a constant switching of units which allowed no pause for rest and restoration of efficiency.

Operations : November, 1942 to January, 1943

43. The Russian counter-offensive in the Stalingrad area began at the end of October, and was accompanied by preparations and troop concentrations on the Middle Don below Voronesh, where the Germans had only a small defensive force of some 70-80 aircraft to cover a front of 300 miles ; this sector was, however, considered sufficiently important to warrant the further transfer from the Leningrad front of Fliegerkorps I to conduct air operations in this area under the title of " Luftwaffe Command Don." In addition to the frontal attack in the East, the Germans had therefore to face the threat of a flank attack from the North-West. At Stalingrad and in the Don Bend the Air Force was hampered by dislocation of communications, fuel shortage and bad flying weather, and by mid-November the decision had been taken to cease attack and pass over to the defensive.

44. The Soviet advance from the Don Bend to the South-West deprived the Germans of their forward airfields, and necessitated the withdrawal of close-support forces, thus putting Stalingrad outside the range of German single-engined fighters, and giving the Russians air superiority over the encircled German forces. At the same time the strain of continued operations began to be felt, and withdrawals for refitting became imperative. With the opening of the Allied offensives in Libya and Tunisia, further withdrawals became necessary to strengthen the Luftwaffe in the Mediterranean, and by the beginning of December the force in Russia had shrunk to some 2,000 aircraft, of which a considerable proportion must have been unserviceable. The strength of Fliegerkorps VIII and I in the Don area, hitherto about 1,000 aircraft, was reduced to some 650-700 aircraft.

45. After the withdrawal of some 400 aircraft to the Mediterranean it became clear that the German Air Force was unable to meet all its commitments on the Russian front, and activity in the Caucasus area began to decrease. With the movement to other areas of nearly all the long-range bombers and dive-bombers and some single-engined fighters, the initiative in this sector passed to the Russians, who used their numerical superiority in the air to support the Soviet advance across the Elista Steppes towards Rostov and through the western Caucasus towards the Kerch Straits.

46. The encirclement of the German 6th Army at Stalingrad and the virtual encirclement later of the 17th Army in the Kuban imposed a further serious burden on the Luftwaffe namely, air supply of the isolated forces. For this purpose He.111 aircraft were taken from operations and transferred to transport duties. Heavy losses were incurred, due not only to operations in bad flying

weather, but also to sustained Russian attacks on transport aircraft in the air and on the ground. These attacks necessitated the use of fighter escort, thus reducing the number of single-engined fighters available for close support operations. By the end of December there were only some 375 single-engined fighters available on the whole of the Russian front, and this lack of fighter cover may well have been one cause of abnormally high wastage during the last weeks of 1942. Abnormally high wastage was, however, also caused by non-battle losses due to aircraft abandoned on the ground during the retreat and forced operations under adverse weather conditions; when losses of operational aircraft used for transport work are added, wastage in the latter half of 1942 is likely to have been equal to that during the last six months of 1941, which is known to have led to an appreciable weakening of German air striking power in 1942 and which reduced first-line strength to below 4,000 aircraft by the end of the year, after having reached a new peak of 4,800 in July, 1941.

47. The shortage of first-line types at the end of 1942 is indicated by the bringing into operations of second-line units and the use of obsolete types (He.46)[1] and reconnaissance aircraft for bombing. During December the first-line strength of the German Air Force in Russia decreased by some 150 aircraft, in spite of the fact that the Soviet offensive necessitated operations on a scale scarcely lower than before winter conditions set in.

The Campaign of 1942 in Retrospect[2]

48. The seriously weakened condition of the German Air Force at the end of 1942, to which the previous six months campaign in the East had largely contributed, is reviewed in detail in Chapter 9; it will, therefore, suffice here to examine briefly German strategy and tactics and the development of new ideas as to the employment of the Air Force which were becoming apparent by the end of the year.

49. The campaign in Russia in 1942, as in 1941, showed that the Luftwaffe continued to adhere rigidly to its traditional tactics of concentrated attack in close support of armoured ground forces. Singularly successful in the battle of France and in the Balkans, it was clear by the end of 1942 that this policy had failed to produce the expected results on the Russian front. This was due not only to the immense length of the front, which meant that every concentration of forces for attack left the Germans with an exposed flank, but also to the depth of the battlefield. The Soviets exploited these circumstances to the full by withdrawals which extended the German lines of communication until the striking force of the Luftwaffe, drawn far forward away from its supply bases, was attenuated and hampered by maintenance difficulties. Thus the peculiar conditions of warfare in Russia never enabled the established German air strategy of combining the strongest possible close support with heavy attacks on factories and rear supply areas to result in final victory in spite of great initial successes.

50. By the autumn of 1942 failure to achieve hoped-for results was beginning to lead to modification of German tactics and a reorganisation of forces without, however, any suggestion of a radical change. Thus there was a tendency to build up a more flexible organisation on a " functional " basis, with new units

---

[1] This type was a single-engined parasol strut-braced monoplane, which formed part of the 1935 first-line equipment of the Luftwaffe (see page 6).

[2] See also Chapter 9, para. 40 *et seq.*

specially adapted to the tactical needs of the Russian situation. This tendency revealed itself in a greater preoccupation with the problem of defence, precipitated by the Soviet policy to organise winter counter-offences in which the Germans were unable to fight on equal terms. This policy was to lead to the German Air Force in Russia being provided with a balanced force, more equally divided between offensive and defensive functions. For this reason it denoted an advance in tactical conceptions, a sounder if less brilliant strategy, coupled with greater versatility than in previous campaigns.

51. This policy made itself evident by the development of what must be regarded as subsidiary and second-line units. These comprised harassing bomber units equipped with obsolete He.46, Hs.126 and Ar.66 aircraft, whose main function was night operations against Soviet troop concentrations; anti-tank units equipped with Hs.129, Me.110, Ju.87 and Ju.88 aircraft carrying special heavy armament for the defensive role of destroying Russian tanks breaking through the German lines, and finally railway squadrons equipped with special Ju.88 fighter-type aircraft, whose chief task was to cut the main arteries of communications in an effort to cripple Russian offensive operations. All these units represented relatively new categories falling outside the traditional organisation of the Luftwaffe. These experiments and innovations in the main took place at the beginning of July, 1942, after Generaloberst von Richthofen was elevated from the command of Fliegerkorps VIII to the command of Luftflotte 4, and there is some reason to believe that it was he who was a protagonist of the new tactics ; his experience as A.O.C. Fliegerkorps VIII, as the pre-eminent close-support Command, may well have turned his thoughts to the problem of defence with the basic purpose of remedying the defect by which his earlier Russian offensives had been nullified. Events in 1943 were, however, to show that these innovations, ingenious though they were, could not ultimately be effectively developed in view of the growing all-round numerical and qualitative deficiencies of the German Air Force which became so strikingly apparent during the following year.

CHAPTER 8

THE HOLDING CAMPAIGN IN THE WEST, 1941–43

The Air Defence of Germany Against Night Bombing

The Beginnings of Night Fighting

1. In the period immediately before the war, when Germany was already building up her home defence against air attack, entire dependence was placed upon the Flak. The gun, searchlight and prediction equipment was extremely good by the standards of the time, and the Flak regiments were considered to be the élite of the German Air Force. There existed, however, a widespread notion of the value of Flak as a defence against aircraft which was far more optimistic than the facts warranted. This misconception originated from a subconscious assimilation of the propaganda build-up which the Flak had received, as well as on false estimates of the efficacy of searchlight interception and predicted fire ; these estimates had been largely based on results of target practices where training aircraft with low performance had been employed. It was this misconception, too, which led Goering to make his famous claim that no foreign aircraft would ever penetrate to the Ruhr[1].

2. At a conference of service chiefs in the summer of 1939 the possibility of defensive night fighting over Germany was suggested, but in the prevailing spirit of confidence of the time the suggestion was dismissed as belonging to the realms of fantasy. Thus, when the first Royal Air Force bombing raid over Germany took place on the night of 15th-16th May, 1940, the Germans found themselves taken by surprise. On that night the weather over Germany was good, and although searchlight activity was intense, a thick ground haze robbed the Flak of the possibility of any effective action. When British night raids were repeated, small numbers of fighters attempted to intercept such bombers as were illuminated by searchlights ; in this way night fighting began. It became obvious, however, that if the night bomber was to be stopped the Luftwaffe would have to start forming and building up an organised night fighter force.

3. Once the Germans embarked upon the night fighter project they applied themselves to the task with energy and thoroughness, so that by the end of 1942 they had assembled a force with a widespread and efficient ground organisation, and which proved to be a real threat to the operations by Royal Air Force Bomber Command. Thereafter, the battle with the R.A.F. was an ever-recurring cycle of measure and counter-measure, of development and counter-development of radio and radar instruments and tactics.

The Night Fighter Force

4. The German night fighter organisation came into being early in June, 1940, when such aircrew of the twin-engined fighter unit, ZG.1, as remained after operations in the Flanders campaign were despatched with their Me.110 aircraft to Duesseldorf airfield, in the Ruhr area, for training and operational trials in night fighting. The unit, which was reinforced by newly-trained

---

[1] Goering made this speech, published in the German Press, after a tour of German defences in August, 1939.

aircrew, was provisionally known as the *Nacht und Versuchs Staffel* (Night and Experimental Squadron) and its commander, Major Falk, set about the task of developing night fighting tactics with all the energy of the pioneer. It was foreseen that, if the R.A.F. were to embark upon strategic bombing of German industrial areas, its bombers, with the limit in range imposed by their performance at that time, would choose the Ruhr as their main point of attack. Three areas in the Ruhr were therefore cleared of Flak and demarcated on the ground with red lights for experimental operations by the night fighters. The aircraft were controlled from the ground by radio telephony and attacked such bombers as were held in the searchlights.

5. These first operations were attended with some success. A further development in the building of a night-fighter force took place when, on the 17th July, 1940, Goering entrusted General Kammhuber with its organisation and the formation of the first night fighter division. Kammhuber was entirely new to the business of night fighting ; he had created an impression of ability as Chief of the German Air Force Organisation Staff before the war. He had also been the C.O. of a bomber unit in the Flanders campaign and had achieved a reputation for blind flying. Kammhuber's task was now to equip the new Division, to lay the foundations for further expansion, and to create conditions for the technical and tactical development necessary to keep abreast with that of R.A.F. Bomber Command. He applied himself to this task with all the ability and energy for which he had a just reputation.

6. On July 20th, the Night and Experimental Squadron, now with a strength of 23 Me.110's, was renamed Gruppe I of Nacht Jagd Geschwader[1] 1—I/NJG1— and a second Gruppe, II/NJG1 soon followed with an initial strength of 20 Ju.88 C-6's (fighter version armed with two cannon and four machine guns). The Division itself, with headquarters at Zeist in Holland, was at first subordinated to Luftflotte 2[2], but by April, 1941, had been assigned to a newly-formed command of Luftflotte status known as *Luftwaffenbefehlshaber Mitte* (A.O.C.-in-C. Centre). Three months later, on 1st August, 1941, the night fighter Division became Fliegerkorps XII. Major Falk, whose name means " falcon ", had taken command of I/NJG 1 and became known as the " Father of Night Fighting " ; the night fighter force adopted the crest of a diving falcon.

Introduction of Radar to Night Fighting

7. General Kammhuber had himself no knowledge of radar, and his ground organisation, largely drawn from the Flak, had as yet no knowledge of its possible application. In the autumn of 1940 the *Wuerzburg A*, a parabolic reflector ground radar, was introduced, but was largely seized upon by the Flak Command as an aid to fire and searchlight prediction. General Martini, the Luftwaffe Director-General of Signals, however, assigned to General Kammhuber six trained signals companies equipped with this apparatus. In October, Kammhuber set up three night fighter zones in the neighbourhood of the Zuider Zee and Rhine estuary and in the path of the R.A.F. bombers flying to and from the Ruhr. The three zones were contained in an area 90 kilometres in length and 20 kilometres in depth and each was occupied by a searchlight battalion and two *Wuerzburg* radars. The immediate advantage

---

[1] Night Fighter Geschwader.

[2] It will be remembered that Luftflotte 2, under Kesselring, was at this time preparing to strike in the Battle of Britain (Chapter 4).

of the inclusion of radar was that the night fighters could be positioned singly in the zone by being linked through one *Wuerzburg* to a ground control ; a master searchlight was linked to the other *Wuerzburg* and controlled a searchlight cone in illuminating the bombers. The whole area was equipped with a plotting control room, and three night fighters—one in each zone—could be vectored simultaneously. This procedure was known as *Helle Nachtjagd* (illuminated night fighting). Two other similar coastal controlled searchlight areas were later established near Kiel and Bremen.

8. Night fighter successes against the British bombers passing through the coastal searchlight belts were satisfactory, but Kammhuber fully appreciated the limitations imposed on illuminated night fighting by bad weather or cloud conditions ; even 6/10ths cloud created considerable difficulties. He, therefore, concentrated upon the perfection of ground control interception wholly based on radar. The demands he had already made for additional radar equipment eventually bore fruit with the production of the *Wuerzburg Riese* (Giant Wuerzburg) with a radius of action of 60 kilometres. The new ground control interception principle adopted was similar to that of the first experimental controlled searchlight zones in that two radars were employed. In this case, however, the zone could be increased to a circular area with a radius of 60 kilometres to correspond with the sweep of the giant *Wuerzburg*. The course of a bomber through the zone could be followed with one *Wuerzburg*, whilst with the other the fighter could be followed and given vectors to intercept the bomber. The courses of both bomber and fighter were plotted on a table in a control room within the zone. Thus, one fighter could operate within one zone, or " box " ; in order that it should not stray from the " box " when awaiting orders to intercept, the night fighter circled a radio beacon sited within the zone. The procedure was known as *Himmelbett* (literally " four-poster bed ").

The " Kammhuber Line "

9. Late in 1940 the idea was conceived that a chain of these ground control interception " boxes " placed close together, or even slightly overlapping, could form an effective barrier to the R.A.F. bomber, and could be operated independently of cloud conditions. Kammhuber therefore placed a line of " boxes " in front of the Ruhr in such a position that any bombers which took the direct route from England were compelled to pass through the line of " boxes ", in each of which a night fighter was waiting to pounce. This was the beginning of the famed Kammhuber Line[1] (see Map 20).

10. Experience soon taught the R.A.F bombers to avoid this area, where night fighters were always patrolling, and when they began flying to the North and South of the line, Kammhuber replied by extending it to cover the détours. Kammhuber had placed his line of " boxes " in front of the searchlight zones, and encouraged his night fighter force to attempt interception first under radar control, and if that failed to follow into the searchlight zones ; the latter were also eventually equipped with radar. The original Kammhuber line, which first extended no more than 150 miles in a North-East to South-West direction at the end of 1940, was first deepened by the addition of more boxes and then extended until, by March, 1941, it had reached the Danish Border (Map 20, Sketch 3).

---

[1] The name " Kammhuber Line " was applied by the R.A.F. and was not known as such by the Germans.

11. The R.A.F. bombers still countered with détours in their penetrations into Germany, and the raids were now increasing in strength and being aimed at other centres such as Berlin. By March, 1942, Kammhuber had deepened his line up to the coastal areas of Holland and North-West Germany, taking in and re-equipping the original radar-controlled searchlight areas, and had begun extensions South-Westwards towards Paris. By July, 1942, the line had extended to the tip of Denmark, and a further extension to southern Norway was in preparation. The latter could not yet be brought into full operation, however, because the extension of the ground organisation was outstripping the expansion of the night fighter force and the supply of aircraft and trained aircrew. By this time the original unit, NJG 1, had been expanded to a full Geschwader, of 3 Gruppen, and three more Geschwader, NJG 2, 3 and 4 had been added. Total actual strength of night fighters now stood at 250 against an establishmet of 400. Of these an average of 160 were serviceable.

12. Extension and expansion of the Kammhuber line continued throughout the remainder of the year 1942 ; by the closing months it had reached the South-East of Paris, whilst the industrial areas behind the line in Germany were being covered. The whole system was now supported by a network of early warning radar, and large central plotting rooms, which gave a picture of operations throughout the system, had been erected and elaborately equipped and staffed. Thus, the four-engined bomber force which the Royal Air Force now possessed, if it were to penetrate Germany without running the gauntlet of the now formidable night fighter defences, was compelled to make extensive détours, either to the South of Paris or to the North of Denmark. R.A.F. raids which perforce were routed through the line, met with extremely dangerous opposition.

13. Up to that time the bomber stream led by a pathfinder force, a later conception of R.A.F. tactics, was unknown ; the raiding forces, their aircraft flying singly, passed through the line whilst one '' box '' after another vectored its night fighter to the attack with deadly effect. In the middle of 1943, when the workings of the Kammhuber line had been compromised, R.A.F. Bomber Command resorted to the bomber stream, which swamped the few '' boxes '' through which it passed, and thus set the German system of vectoring a new problem. In July, 1943 the electronic jamming of the early warning radar, and the jamming of the Wuerzburg radars of the '' boxes '' with '' window '' metal strips took the whole German defences by surprise. Kammhuber's line, on which untold industrial and military effort had been spent, became an expensive and useless luxury overnight, and it became necessary to reorganise the whole system of night fighter defence. (See Chapter 12.)

Development of Airborne Radar
14. As soon as Major Falk began his night fighting experiments in June, 1940, the want began to be felt for an apparatus which would help in the interception of the night bomber. The only opportunity afforded a night fighter of opening fire on a bomber occurred when the latter was held—often for a fleeting moment —in the searchlights ; there remained the equally unsatisfactory opportunity of stalking the bomber in conditions of clear weather or bright moonlight. In the summer of 1940, an infra-red device was tried out in the night fighters as an aid to detection but, in its state of development at the time it was not satisfactory. Again, late in 1941, a radio-controlled device—the *Uhu* (owl)— attached to the automatic pilot was also tried and rejected. Meanwhile, the

GENERAL JOSEF KAMMHUBER

Born 19.8.96. Entered a Pioneer Battalion August, 1914, transferred to the Infantry September, 1915, remained in the Reichswehr after the war. Transferred to the Air Force October, 1933, employed in the Air Ministry till July, 1935. Head of the Luftwaffe Organisation Staff at the Air Ministry, February, 1938. Commanded KG.51 (long-range bombers) in the French campaign. In July, 1940, he took over the night fighter Division which, in August, 1941, became Fliegerkorps XII. Replaced by Schmid in September, 1943 ; became A.O. for night fighters. Kammhuber was appointed A.O.C.-in-C. Luftflotte 5 in January, 1944 and Goering's Special Plenipotentiary for jet and rocket aircraft in February, 1945. Captured by the Allies 4.6.45.

Heil Hitler ! A pilot has audience with the Fuehrer

189

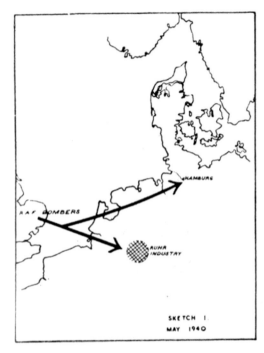

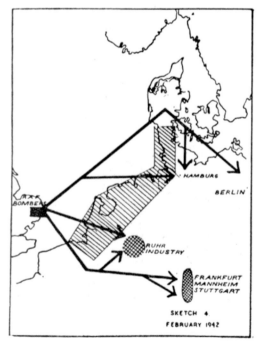

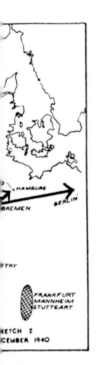

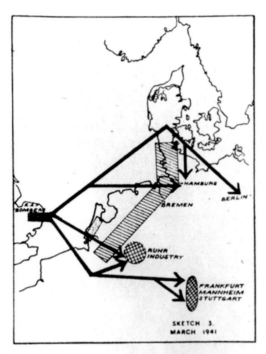

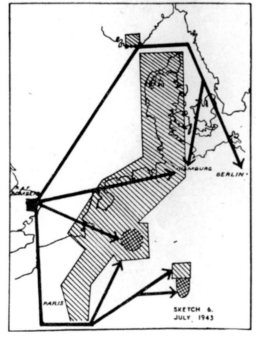

The Ju.88 Night Fighter with Lichtenstein (Fu.G.202) radar interception equipment

expansion of the Kammhuber line and the excellence of German ground radar in the " box " system allowed of vectoring of a night fighter to a distance of 400 yards from its quarry. At that time the R.A.F. bombers confined their attacks to fine weather, and the night fighter aircrews came to regard the ground radar control combined with a final visual attack as being sufficient for their purpose.

15. Kammhuber himself had regarded airborne radar as an aid to final interception as essential to the efficiency of his system of ground radar control. In 1940 he had put forward a technical requirement for an airborne radar, and by July, 1941, the firm of Telefunken had produced an efficient A.I., the *Lichtenstein*, which had a minimum range of 200 yards and a maximum of 3,000 yards in expert hands. Kammhuber persuaded Hitler to give this apparatus top industrial priority, and by the early months of 1942 four aircraft of NJG1 had been equipped with the *Lichtenstein* and were in operation. The immediate reaction was that the aircrews, who followed the fashions set by the aces such at Lent[1] and Gildner, would have nothing to do with A.I. because its cumbersome aerial array caused a reduction in speed of some 25 m.p.h. This attitude prevailed until another ace, Hauptmann Becker, began to achieve a positive success. The majority, however, still regarded the apparatus as no more than a useful aid to attack by visual means. During this period of prejudice, equipment of the operational units naturally depended upon the rate of delivery of the *Lichtenstein* from the manufacturing firms, and most of the units were only partly equipped ; the crews therefore exercised their preference by flying such aircraft as had no *Lichtenstein*. A situation thus arose where the scale of A.I. equipment in the night fighter force was inadequate at a time when R.A.F. bombers were flying singly over German territory and were presenting ideal opportunities for the use of A.I. in conjunction with radar ground control.

16. By 1943, 95 per cent. of the twin-engined night fighter force, now with five Geschwader and a strength of 490 twin-engined aircraft, was equipped with *Lichtenstein* and the prejudice against it had disappeared, largely on account of a lighter aerial array which affected the aircrafts' speeds only little and the improved efficiency of the apparatus itself. As a result of the first use of " window " jamming by the R.A.F. however, the *Lichtenstein*, in common with the early warning radar and controlled interception systems, was rendered useless. Fortunately for them, the Germans already had a new version of *Lichtenstein*—the SN2—operating on another frequency[2] under development, and this apparatus appeared operationally in October, 1943. (See Chapter 12.)

Night Fighter Intruding over England

17. With the founding of the night fighter force on 17th July, 1940, another unit, I/NJG 2, was also formed at Duesseldorf from elements of ZG.76 and ZKG.30, two twin-engined fighter units which had taken part in the Norwegian and Flanders campaigns. This new night fighter unit moved immediately to Amsterdam/Schipol and then a few days later to Gilze Rijen, in Holland and, equipped mainly with the Ju.88 but also with some Do.17's, commenced night intruding operations against R.A.F. Bomber Command airfields in Yorkshire, Lincolnshire, East Anglia and the Home Counties, as well as attacking British bombers returning across the Channel from raids over Germany.

---

[1] See illustration on page 294.

[2] The reasons for the development of this alternative *Lichtenstein* are not yet clear. When its development began, British electronic jamming had not yet appeared, but it is possible that intelligent assumption led the Germans to take this precaution.

18. By September the Gruppe had built up its strength to 36 aircraft, of which some 20 were usually serviceable. Kammhuber appreciated the value and effect of night intruder operations as a part of the defence of Germany, and he planned to raise the strength of the intruder force to considerable proportions ; by March, 1941, he had increased this force to an establishment of 53 aircraft. Serviceability, had, however, not increased in proportion, and still remained at about 20, so that operations over England remained at a constant level. In the autumn of 1941 I/NJG 2 was withdrawn to the Mediterranean, and intruder operations over England ceased. Owing to the rising commitment of night fighting in defence of Germany, and the need for the night fighter force to cover the expanding Kammhuber line, no other unit could be spared to continue intruder operations. Hitler himself gave orders for their discontinuance[1]. Thereafter, R.A.F. Bomber Command was able to develop its bases and night training without interference[2], and was able to deploy its night bombing forces without the inconvenience and wastage which would have been inevitable had Kammhuber's plans been allowed to materialise. As it was, the fact that the R.A.F. was allowed to operate with its bases undisturbed from late in 1941 until early in 1945, when intruder operations were again undertaken—for a brief period of two nights[3]—was an important factor which contributed to the final crippling of Germany.

Air Operations over Great Britain

The Situation in June, 1941

19. At the beginning of the Russian campaign in June, 1941, the German air striking force which had stood opposite Great Britain since the beginning of the Battle of Britain had been largely withdrawn, and such aircraft as remained behind the Continental coasts in the West were those engaged in anti-shipping operations, reconnaissance or fighter defence of occupied territory. It has already been shown in Chapter 4 how, during the remainder of 1941 and the early months of 1942, the Luftwaffe employed its forces in the West in attempting to strangle the seaborne supply of Great Britain ; after the failure of the Luftwaffe anti-shipping forces in the Atlantic and around the coasts of Great Britain, the focus of anti-shipping attention shifted to the Arctic supply routes, by which enormous supplies were being shipped to Russia by Britain and U.S.A. Nevertheless, some of the anti-shipping units, as well as the minelaying force, amounting to a combined strength of some 130 Ju.88's and Do.217's, remained to operate against Great Britain during 1942.

20. Early in 1942, the German Air Force was fully extended on the Russian and Mediterranean fronts and few forces could be spared for a bombing offensive against the British Isles. It must be remembered that at this time the ever-increasing night bombing effort by the R.A.F. over Germany was causing no little anxiety in high German quarters. Added to this, British industry was

---

[1] See Appendix, paragraph 6.

[2] A certain number of scattered attacks on airfields in Great Britain did, indeed, take place between 1941 and 1945, but were not intruder attacks in that the attacking aircraft were not night fighters, but usually bombers or minelaying aircraft which had missed their target and attacked whatever they saw first.

[3] See Chapter 17, paragraphs 30 and 45.

*A Ju.88 Night Fighter with the " Lichtenstein " aerial array
Note the crest of the diving falcon*

The giant " Wuerzburg " radar used in the Kammhubar Line

A Do.17 intruder which set out from Holland to attack Helmswell airfield at 0850 hours on 10th November, 1940. It was attacked by three Spitfires but managed to reach Denmark on one engine, flying at a height of 15 feet above the sea.

The remains of a He.111 raider at Lullington, near Burton-on-Trent (June, 1941)

A He.111 bomber

194

now getting into its stride ; the four-engined bomber was beginning to appear in R.A.F. operational squadrons, the Army was being rapidly re-equipped and expanded after the Dunkirk evacuation, a large-scale programme of first-class airfield construction was in train and the U.S. Air Force was beginning to establish itself. Since May, 1941, Great Britain had suffered negligible disturbance from the air of its industrial effort.

21. After the shifting of the main anti-shipping operations to the Arctic shipping routes, Fliegerkorps IX, operating under Luftflotte 3, remained to continue with minelaying, and also had control of all anti-shipping operations which were continued as scattered attacks on coastwise shipping, convoys and harbours. These operations were supplemented by occasional night bombing raids on such ports as Hull or Portsmouth, where the effort normally did not exceed 30 aircraft. It must be conceded that these attacks were not without their effect since, with aircraft appearing at any point around the British coasts from the North Sea to the St. George's Channel, a considerable and continuous defensive effort in both men and material was made necessary, and large defensive forces that could otherwise have been employed in the Mediterranean theatre were tied down in Great Britain. This defensive effort was perforce increased when, during the summer of 1942, small numbers of long-range bombers operated singly over widespread areas of England in daylight and in cloudy weather, when British fighters could not operate. This effort, directed largely at causing the maximum possible disturbance to industry with the minimum number of aircraft, was also not without its effect. Whilst physical damage to industrial plant was negligible, the time wasted by factory staffs stopping work in the path of each aircraft certainly warranted the German expenditure of effort. German losses in these actions, too, were negligible.

The Reprisal Raids

22. For the Germans, the most difficult situation arose when R.A.F. Bomber Command, perfecting its raiding methods by concentration of attack on one objective in a short space of time, made its first and successful attack on the German city of Luebeck on 28th-29th March, 1942. German public opinion, led by Hitler and the Propaganda Ministry, demanded heavy reprisals against Great Britain in the form of similar attacks on British cities. At that time, the expected victory over Russia having failed to materialise, the necessary Luftwaffe bomber forces were not available in sufficient strength to produce any result that would satisfy the demand for an adequate reprisal. Nevertheless, preparations were made to assemble all possible forces, and the original Luftwaffe pathfinder force, KG.100, was brought back to France and began to practice pathfinder tactics with radio aids to navigation. On the night of April 23rd a force of some 45 long-range bombers, composed of the minelaying and anti-shipping units then available in the West, made an attempt to attack Exeter. On the following night, the first raid having been a failure, the attack was repeated by some 60 aircraft, and similar methods of concentration in time were employed as had been by the R.A.F. over Luebeck. Another heavy attack was delivered by the R.A.F. on Rostock on the night of April 24th-25th at the same time as the Luftwaffe was attacking Bath with 150 aircraft. The latter effort was only achieved by double sorties and by calling in of some of the Bomber Reserve Training Units (O.T.U's.) now largely based in France and Belgium.

23. The R.A.F. raid on Rostock brought a shrill outcry from the German Propaganda Ministry and a speech by Hitler on the 26th, when he threatened " eradication " of all British cities one by one as a reprisal for each and every R.A.F. attack. He spoke of taking Baedecker's guide and of marking each British city off the guidebook as and when it was destroyed. The series of German reprisal raids, thereafter known in Great Britain as the " Baedecker raids ", continued on the same night, the 26th, with another attack on Bath, which was followed on succeeding nights by raids on Norwich and York. German Air Force losses were heavy, especially amongst the Reserve Training Units, whose instructional crews who could ill be spared had been thrown in. The series of raids was perforce brought to a close, to be repeated with heavy losses against Birmingham at the end of July as a reprisal for the R.A.F.'s. successful attack on Hamburg on the night of July 26th/27th.

24. During the succeeding months of 1942 the German Air Force continued minelaying operations at night and reverted to the occasional night bombing attacks on such centres as Newcastle, Sunderland and Canterbury ; in daylight the " disturbance " attacks continued whenever the weather over England was cloudy. At this time, in the summer of 1942, Luftwaffe aircrew training was meeting with difficulties[1] and the small number of units ranged against England could barely replace their losses. With the added difficulty of the rapid improvement of R.A.F. night fighter technique, therefore, large-scale night attacks had to be reduced in their frequency to a minimum. At the same time, too, the strength of the bomber force had fallen to a low ebb ; for instance, the bomber Geschwader KG.2, with 88 crews in January, 1942 had only 23 by September—losses which had been accentuated by such actions as the Allied landing at Dieppe on July 20th.

The Fighter-Bomber in Attacks on England

25. The history of the Battle of Britain and the subsequent *Blitz* on Great Britain of 1940-41 was being repeated in 1942 in the failure of the German Air Force to follow its plan of reprisal raids. The forces involved in 1942 were, it is true, smaller, but in proportion the losses were greater ; where in 1940-41 the night bomber flew practically unmolested over Great Britain, in 1942 the danger from night fighters was becoming ever greater. As after the Battle of Britain, the Germans once more resorted to the employment of the single-engined fighter-bomber.

26. Early in January, 1942, some Me.109's of the two fighter Geschwader based in France for defensive purposes had carried out low-level machine-gunning attacks on ports and towns along the Channel coast of England. By March, small numbers of Me.109's, each carrying one bomb, were frequently flying across the Channel at low altitude—to escape radar detection—and delivering surprise attacks on ports and coastal towns. By June, these attacks began to assume larger proportions and towards the autumn, when the long-range bomber effort was beginning to fall, fighter-bomber attacks became more and more frequent and began to penetrate inland. The two fighter units in France, JG 2 and JG 26, had formed two special fighter-bomber staffeln— one now re-equipped with the FW.190—and were able to put 20 aircraft in the air for these attacks. Once again the British defences over a wide area were severely taxed out of all proportion to the smallness of the German effort.

---

[1] See Chapter 9, paragraphs 12–15.

The Do.217 bomber, used against Great Britain from the autumn of 1941 onwards. Unlike the He.111 and Ju.88, whose heavy bombs were carried externally, it was capable of carrying a heavy internal bomb-load. Its maximum load was 6,600 lb. The above captured example is the Do.217M, one of the last versions of that aircraft to be produced in the war.

A FW.190 fighter

Again, too, these raids frequently took the form of reprisals against purely civilian targets : on a Saturday afternoon in October a particularly heavy attack was aimed against the centre of Canterbury—when the city was at its most crowded shopping period—by some 30 fighter-bombers with a high-cover escort of equal strength, and achieved complete surprise. This attack was followed on the same night by a heavy bomber raid.

27. During the winter of 1942-43 these fighter-bomber attacks continued and were supplemented by occasional small-scale bombing raids at night. The fighter-bomber was obviously the answer to the lack of heavy bomber aircraft and, with its rapidity of attack at low level and its rapid withdrawal, losses to the units concerned were light owing to the surprise achieved. Early in 1943 another fighter-bomber unit equipped with the FW.190—SKG 10—was formed and designed primarily to supplement the anti-shipping forces. With the mounting scale of Allied daylight attack on the U-boat and naval bases on the Atlantic coast, as well as widespread bombing activity over the rest of northern France, the fighters of JG 2 and JG 26 could no longer be spared for offensive purposes, and the new unit, SKG 10, was therefore brought to the Amiens area to engage in bombing attacks on England.

Attacks on England in 1943

28. Early in 1943 the Luftwaffe High Command had decided to put the bombing of Great Britain on a more co-ordinated basis, and with this object in view a new staff, known as *Angriffsfuehrer England* (England Attack Command) was formed. In March, 1943, Oberst Peltz was appointed to the Command from that of the dive bomber formation leaders' course at Foggia. By this time the German bomber force in the West was finding British night fighter defences increasingly dangerous, and a programme of equipping the German bombers with radar tail-warning devices against night fighters was begun. Meanwhile an attempt was made to build up a force of fast night bombers which could outpace the British night fighter. The FW.190's of SKG 10 were at hand and were thrown into night operations, and another Gruppe equipped with the Me.410[1] was added to KG 2—itself equipped with the Do.217—and by June had reached a strength of over 40 aircraft. These two units operated against England, but losses, especially to the FW.190's, were heavy and navigation for the pilots of the latter assumed difficulties which could not be overcome ; several aircraft were in fact lost by landing on airfields in southern England in mistake for the Amiens area.

29. Occasional night attacks by the long-range bombers met with heavy losses, in spite of radar aids to evasion. Towards the end of 1943, Peltz laid plans for attacks of short duration led by pathfinders in the R.A.F. pattern, and a new pathfinder unit was formed for the purpose. The opening of these attacks, which were intended to be short, heavy and devastating, was delayed until larger forces should be available and finally only began in January 1944 (see Chapter 13, paragraph 42).

---

[1] The Me.410 was a development of the Me.110 (twin engined).

PART THREE
The Turn of the Tide
(1943–1944)

CHAPTER 9

THE GERMAN AIR FORCE AT THE END OF 1942

The Collapse of German Air Strategy

Bankruptcy of German Strategy and Policy

1. Following up on the British victory at El Alamein and the expulsion of the German forces from Egypt, the battle of Stalingrad stands out as the essential turning point in the war. On 19th November, 1942, the Russians launched their historic counter attack, cutting the communications of the German army besieging Stalingrad ; on 31st January, 1943, Field Marshal von Paulus, with his remaining force of some 46,000 men, was compelled to capitulate.

2. The defeat was final and irrevocable. Unlike the defeat suffered in the Battle of Britain it left the German High Command with no positive plan, with its resources overstrained, and with no strategic objectives except to cling on, as well as might be, to what had already been won. After their failure in the Battle of Britain, the Germans had still retained their offensive power more or less intact, both on land and in the air ; and they had been able to use this power—in which the Luftwaffe was a leading element—in the service of a strategy which, although over-reaching and wildly ambitious, pursued positive objects : first, to seal the continent of Europe against British influence, then to strike down Soviet Russia, and when the British Commonwealth Armies seemed to be beaten after Rommel's rapid advance to El Alamein in the summer of 1942, to take advantage of the situation and effect a junction in the Levant by means of a two-pronged advance through Egypt and the Caucasus and lay hands on the fuel resources of the Near East.

3. All these hopes were dashed by the twin Allied victories at El Alamein and Stalingrad. Together they marked the bankruptcy of German high policy. Already by the end of 1942 the expulsion of the Axis from North Africa was a foregone conclusion ; the only question was the speed with which it would be accomplished. On the Russian front, although there was at least the posssibility of forming a stable defensive line, the practical question was where and when the Soviet counter-offensive could be halted. On both the Mediterranean and Russian fronts the Germans had clearly been thrown back on the defensive. Simultaneously the magnitude of the Air Force defensive commitment in the West had become fully evident with the entry of the U.S.A.A.F. bombers into the war from bases in Great Britain : after the first all-American bombing raid against occupied Europe in August, 1942, the attack by U.S. heavy bombers on Wilhelmshaven on 27th January, 1943, marked the opening of a new phase in the Allied bombing offensive against Germany, while only three days later the first of the daylight raids on Berlin was undertaken by the R.A.F. A month later, in February, 1943, profiting from exceptionally favourable weather conditions, the famous Anglo-American policy of " round-the-clock " bombing was inaugurated. Politically and psychologically the change in the fortunes of war was reflected in the Casablanca Conference in January, 1943, which set the seal on the military victories of the months immediately preceding by proclaiming the Allied demand for unconditional surrender.

Diminished Resources

4. At this turning point in the war, when German policy was perforce reorientated, and a defensive replaced an offensive strategy, it is essential to halt and survey the position and resources of the German Air Force as it was constituted after three years of inconclusive warfare. The years 1939-42 may, for the Luftwaffe, be described as the years that the locusts had eaten ; during this critical period, when Allied war potential was being rapidly mobilised and built up, its fighting value, due to almost unbelievable optimism in high places, declined both relatively and absolutely. Hence, in many respects, 1st January, 1943, represented a time of crisis for the German Air Force. Its operational strength, the barometer of fighting capacity, had sunk to some 4,000 aircraft ; its initial reserves, to begin with an important adjunct, had fallen away to nothing ; it had failed to bring its equipment up to date by the introduction of modern aircraft types. The fact that it was living, in 1941 and 1942, on its accumulated reserves, that no provision had been made to meet the contingency of a major setback and that the German High Command had resolutely declined to consider the possibility of being compelled to wage a defensive war in the air, was hidden as long as Germany retained the strategic initiative ; but for that very reason the crisis at Stalingrad brought matters abruptly to a head. The strain imposed by the effort, lasting from 5th September to 29th December, 1942, first to force a decision at Stalingrad and then to extricate the surrounded German forces, not only created serious new problems for the Air Force but also clearly and suddenly revealed the long-term deficiencies which had accumulated as a result of strategic miscalculation, lack of foresight and inefficient planning. Not all these problems were a direct consequence of the reverses in Africa and South Russia ; many resulted directly from the fact that the Luftwaffe had from the beginning planned for a series of *Blitzkriegs* of short duration, and in spite of reverses had clung to the belief in a rapid victory even as late as the second half of 1942. By the beginning of 1943, however, this hope could no longer be entertained, and it was consequently imperative to lay down a new programme—a programme for a long war, involving a major shift in the balance between offensive and defensive armament and offensive and defensive policy.

The Prospect of a Long War

5. This decision was faced with reluctance and hesitation, and it is a major criticism of German Air Force policy, that when it was confronted by a new situation demanding clear-cut decisions it proceeded only by way of expedients and half-measures. There were capable personalities on the German Air Staff, such as Field Marshal Milch, who, already as early as the spring of 1942, after the setbacks of the first winter campaign in Russia, had foreseen the imperative need for a radical reorientation of air policy to meet the imminent threat of Anglo-American air attacks on German air potential ; but they were not heeded in time, and even when listened to, their arguments secured only grudging support and half-hearted implementation. At the beginning of 1943, and for many months longer, Hitler and Goering still refused to accept the thesis that the Air Force should sacrifice its offensive potentialities to the exigencies of defence, apparently arguing that Germany's exposed position in Central Europe and her limited war potentialities by comparison with the vast resources of the Allies, did not permit the luxury of a long-term policy.

6. Hence, from the end of 1942, there was a sharp cleavage within the German High Command on all matters of air policy, which had injurious effects on the subsequent prosecution of the air war, particularly as any responsible attempt to view the changed situation with realism was liable to be castigated as " defeatism ". Above all else, no adequate steps were taken to build up a strong defensive air force to oppose the Allied attempt to regain a foothold in western or in southern Europe, although it was evident, after the failure of the German programme of *Blitzkrieg*, that the only hope of securing an acceptable peace was to defeat the expected Anglo-American attempt to open a " Second Front ". The German High Command, isolated in Russia, was out of touch with the overall situation, and unable to take a balanced view ; its energies were concentrated on the prosecution of the war in the East, which was regarded as the primary commitment, and all demands for long-term planning against the threatened war on three fronts were treated as a diversion of effort. Hence, at the critical juncture caused by the defeat at Stalingrad and the débâcle in North Africa, instead of a thorough overhaul of air policy, there was a series of half measures which failed either to resolve the major problems of the present or to provide safeguards for the future.

The Manpower, Training and Aircraft Production situation

Manpower

7. The first problem facing the Air Force was manpower. By the beginning of 1942 the total manpower absorbed into the Air Force, excluding Flak, had risen from 600,000 at the commencement of the war to the maximum figure of 1,100,000. This strength was maintained throughout 1942 and during the first half of 1943, when a decline set in. But already by the end of 1942 major difficulties were arising. The losses incurred in Russia, culminating in the defeat at Stalingrad, had produced a severe strain, and already the Luftwaffe was under compulsion to contribute troops for ground fighting. During the first Soviet winter offensive in 1941-42, it had been necessary to train ground personnel in forward areas to undertake defensive operations in addition to their normal duties, in defence of aerodromes and other key points threatened with attack. At the same time a number of Air Force field regiments were formed, which played a major rôle in the defence of Staraya Russa early in 1942 as part of the command of " Luftwaffe Division General Meindl ", thus undertaking operations of a kind which had hitherto been regarded as the responsibility of the Army. By October, 1942, the decision had been made to extend this organisation, and to build up ground-fighting divisions (*Luftwaffe Felddivisdionen*) to a strength of at least 50,000 men.

8. The adverse results on the normal functions of the Air Force were felt immediately. In order to obtain the necessary men for the Field Divisions, which were intended in fact to reinforce the Army, a number of branches of the Air Force, including signals, were subjected to a 10 per cent. cut in personnel. In addition I.T.W.'s, about twenty of which were situated in France and the Low Countries, had the infantry side of their training emphasised : the intention was without doubt to create a supplementary garrison for western Europe, thus releasing army formations for the active theatres of operations. As the situation in the East deteriorated, however, half were drafted to that theatre

to help build up the Field Division for fighting oh the Russsian Front. By February, 1943 it was evident that the programme for Field Divisions had again been enlarged, and twenty were already in operations in the East. By the spring of 1943, therefore, some 200,000 men in all must have been drafted out of the Air Force into the newly constituted Field Divisions.

9. Already by May, 1943 it was evident that the continual drain of manpower into ground fighting units was having its effect upon the operational efficiency of the Air Force. Some units were not up to strength in the necessary ground personnel, and aircraft serviceability was lowered in consequence. The position was further aggravated by the formation of new flying units, the servicing and maintenance personnel for which were only to be found by robbing existing units. Airfield development in Sardinia—essential as an outpost for the defence of southern Europe—was hampered and limited by lack of ground staff, and the same problem arose when, in spring 1943, it became necessary to develop an Air Force ground organisation in southern France.

10. An attempt to offset falling strength was made with the introduction of a great number of foreign auxiliaries and prisoners-of-war—the latter largely Russian deserters and political converts—who were drafted into Flak as well as ground units ; but this measure itself implied lowered efficiency. Particularly significant was the cut in the signals organisation, to the efficiency of which the early victories of the Luftwaffe had owed much. The drain on manpower, in particular in specialised and trained personnel, who could not easily be replaced, could not fail to react upon the mobility and efficiency of the German Air Force as a whole.

Aircrew and Aircrew Training

11. At the same time as the manpower situation within the Air Force became critical, special difficulties were encountered in the supply of pilots and aircrews. The Air Force had started the war with a large body of fully trained aircrew. The first year of the Russian campaign ate deeply into this body, which had been sufficiently strong to withstand the heavy losses incurred in the Battle of Britain. Particularly in the fighter arm, the reservoir of older trained pilots was used up, and the flow from the schools was no longer sufficient to replace losses.

12. The result, already evident by the early summer of 1942, was contraction and deterioration in the training of pilots and crews. At that time the Reserve Training Gruppen of the single-engined fighter units—the " fourth Gruppe " which each Geschwader had possessed in addition to the normal complement of three operational Gruppen—were disbanded, and in their place three fighter pools were formed, one for the West, one for the South, and one for the Eastern Front respectively. Henceforward operational units at the front had to draw replacements directly from these pools, which were situated at Cazaux, Mannheim and Cracow, and the result was a curtailment in the period of operational training of fighter pilots at the very period when the increased intake of new and inexperienced aircrew required higher standards. In addition, the breakdown of the Reserve Training organisation, which had provided a crewed-up reserve of operational aircraft of a strength approximately one-third of the first line, resulted in a lack of depth behind the first-line establishment.

13. The disruption of bomber training followed later. The first cause was a temporary shortage of aircraft fuel in the summer of 1942, which resulted in a curtailment of flying hours in bombing training. Thereafter the flow of

pupils through the training organisation began to get uneven. But the flow became quite broken and disrupted when, at the end of 1942, numbers of Ju.52 and He.111 aircraft, together with instructor pilots, were removed from the conversion, blind flying and bomber schools to supplement the air transport fleet on the South Russian front supplying the 6th Army at Stalingrad. Pilots nominated for bomber training no longer underwent regular training on multi-engined types at schools, but as an emergency measure were trained by acting as second pilots on Ju.52 transport aircraft.

14. The disruption which followed these emergency measures threw the whole programme out of gear and caused a hiatus in bomber training, resulting in a surplus of partially trained pupils in the elementary training schools and a lack of fully trained crews ready to pass from the advanced training schools into the reserve training units. In an attempt to overcome this impasse, the specialist bomber schools were disbanded and the reserve training units of the bomber Geschwader were made to take over the functions which those schools had heretofore performed. This they were quite unable to do, having insufficient aircraft and instructors to cope with the number of pupils ; ' so pupils were farmed out for training in the operational units themselves. The German bomber force became largely impotent and never recovered. ' Thus Stalingrad which proved to be the turning point in the European war, also proved to be the turning point in the offensive power of the German Air Force.

Aircraft Production[1]

15. The most complex problem facing the Luftwaffe at the time of the Stalingrad crisis was that of production. Udet, to whom the task of building up the Air Force had originally been entrusted, was not equal to the task and was unable to exercise unified control over the whole aircraft industry. Throughout his tenure of the office of *Luftzeugmeister*[2], German aircraft production remained virtually on a peacetime level. In particular no consistent programme was formulated and adhered to ; during the first two years of the war no less than 16 programmes were started, none of which was maintained for longer than 6-7 weeks. The result was that the overall increase in output between 1939 and 1941 was meagre, in the region of 5-10 per cent. ; but so long as a strong reserve was maintained the pinch was not felt. The heavy rate of loss incurred in Russia in 1941 and 1942, however, and the entry into the war of the U.S.A., the most highly industrialised nation in the world, changed all this. German intelligence reports indicated that the combined Anglo-American air forces would have 10-20,000 bombers available by 1942 and 1943. To this threat Udet had no answer, and this failure was in all probability the reason for his suicide in the autumn of 1941.

16. Udet's successor was Milch, who thus regained the position he had lost in 1938[3]. He immediately realised the need for a thorough overhaul of the whole production situation in order to counter the growing strength of the R.A.F. and the manufacturing potential of the Soviet and American aircraft industries, and spent the first three months of his tenure of office, from December, 1941 to February, 1942, in reviewing the resources of the German aircraft industry. The result was the formulation of a programme which, in

---

[1] See also Chapter 2, paragraph 12 *et seq.*

[2] Director-General of Equipment.

[3] See Chapter 1, paragraph 28.

essentials, remained the framework of German aircraft production until the inauguration of intensive U.S. daylight bombing in February, 1944, again enforced a thorough reorganisation.

17. The first necessity was a thorough overhaul of the industrial machine. In the first phase of the war the Germans, counting on a quick victory, do not appear to have given any thought to the organisation of the industry required to support their air force. Speer[1] has estimated that, between 1939 and 1942, he doubled the factory space available for aircraft production, but, through lack of organisation, this increase failed to produce results and there was no commensurate increase in the number of aircraft produced. This was due, without doubt, to the fact that the aircraft industry still consisted of a number of independent firms, each following its own practice without central control. The result was wasteful reduplication and an inefficient use of personnel, which, in view of the critical manpower situation facing Germany, was no longer tolerable.

18. Hence, both to increase output and to economise in manpower, Milch (in conjunction with Dr. Speer of the Todt Organisation) set out to introduce better organised and more efficient industrial methods. The foundation of his plan was a reorganisation of the aircraft industry into a small number of very large complexes. For each main category there were to be one or more large assembly centres with component factories situated within a comparatively small radius. Thus, production of Messerschmitt single-engined fighter was to be carried out at Leipzig, Wiener Neustadt and Regensburg ; the Junkers complex was to be centred at Bernberg, Oschersleben and Halberstadt ; production of the Me.110 was centred at Brunswick. The centre of the Focke Wulf complex was initially Bremen, but due to Allied air attack it was dispersed into two complexes, a western at Kassel and an eastern at Marienburg. At each of these centres there was to be a high capacity assembly line with components fed in from factories in the immediate neighbourhood. Administratively, these centres of production were known as *Ausschuesse*, each *Ausschuss* being under the direction of a chief engineer. The various *Ausschuesse* engaged in the production of one type of aircraft were known collectively as a *Sonderausschuss* under a director responsible immediately to the German Air Ministry, while at the top there were three *Hauptausschuesse*, one for airframes, one for engines and one for accessories.

19. The main defect of this system was that it was peculiarly vulnerable to air attack ; but for a time, until the end of 1943, it worked well, and the result of the reorganisation was a gradual and progressive expansion of output. At the end of 1941 when Milch took over control of the aircraft industry in succession to Udet the total production averaged less than 1,000 aircraft per month (including training types), of which only some 300 were single-engined fighters. Milch, supported by Galland, was the first person in authority to realise the necessity for greatly increasing single-engined fighter output, and in his first programme, presented to Goering in March, 1942, he called for a monthly output of 1,000 fighters of all types by June, 1943. But even Udet's suicide had failed to shake the spirit of complacent optimism which permeated the German High Command, and it was only after overcoming obstruction at all levels that Milch succeeded in obtaining partial acceptance of his demands. Jeschonnek, the Chief of Air Staff, was sceptical of the possibility of finding

---

[1] See paragraph 19.

employment for single-engined fighters above a figure of 360 aircraft a month. Goering and Hitler, on the other hand, both insisted that there must be no sacrifice of offensive to defensive requirements and that bomber production must retain priority, while Hitler added the further stipulation that the output of transport aircraft should be raised to 400 per month, including a large number of troop-carrying machines. It was only when Milch was able to demonstrate that rapid fighter expansion could, as a result of the reorganisation of the aircraft industry, be carried out without detriment to—and, indeed, side by side with the expansion of—the bomber force, that his programme was authorised.

20. Milch's programme, authorised in March, 1942, resulted in an increase of output from under 1,000 aircraft of all types per month at the end of 1941 to about 1,650 aircraft of all types (including 75 transport and 150 training aircraft) at the end of 1942. This figure included about 500 single-engined fighter and 500 long-range bomber types with about 100 dive bombers and 150 twin-engined fighters. By June, 1943, the primary target of 1,000 fighters of all types per month had been reached and surpassed, of which more than 800 were single-engined fighters ; on the other hand only small increases over the 1942 figures had been achieved in the other categories, for reasons which will shortly become apparent.

21. Milch's first programme was only a modest instalment towards fulfilling the requirements of the German Air Force and was deliberately scaled down in order to forestall the objections of the General Staff and of Hitler's entourage. In particular, its provision of fighters was inadequate to Germany's defensive needs, and Milch therefore followed up his first programme, a few months later, with a second programme for the manufacture of 2,000 fighters per month by the beginning of 1944 and 3,000 per month during the summer of that year. In addition, he planned to maintain bomber supplies by an output of 200 He.177's[1] and 750 Ju.88's. Furthermore, the proposed expansion of the Air Force required an extension of training facilities which (as we have seen) had suffered neglect and contraction, and Milch therefore planned a target figure for training types of 500 aircraft per month.

22. These plans, however, failed to secure immediate sanction, since neither Hitler nor Goering was convinced of the necessity for the huge programme of fighter expansion which Milch envisaged. The emphasis at the highest level was still strongly in favour of offensive aircraft. It was consequently only as the Allied air attack on German industry developed after July, 1943 that, under pressure of circumstances, fighter production was given priority, and even as late as April, 1944, Goering was disinclined to accept any diminution of bomber output in favour of fighters. Hence, no provision was made in advance to build up the fighter arm in anticipation of Allied attack and, as Galland has stated, a higher rate of production was only attained at a stage when increasing losses ate up the increased output. Not until July, 1944, was absolute priority given to the fighter arm.

23. Nevertheless, by the end of 1942, in spite of resistance at the top, a fundamental change in the balance of production had been effected. By that time fighter output equalled bomber output, and thenceforward fighter production quickly outstripped bomber production as more and more fighters were required to meet the ever-growing menace of the Anglo-American air attack. This switch-over was not, indeed, intended to take place at the expense

---

[1] Illustration on page 304.

(83331)   H 2

of the striking power of the Air Force ; the bomber force was, in intention, to be maintained and expanded. But factors not allowed for (including the disruption of bomber training, which we have surveyed) intervened, and it proved impossible to maintain the balance of the two arms. Hence, allowing for all exceptions, it is fair to say that the Luftwaffe which, until the end of 1942 had been essentially an offensive striking force, became, beginning in 1943, a defensive force with limited striking power. The point was grasped immediately by General Galland, who informed a conference held in Berlin between 28th January and 3rd February, 1943, that the development of the war situation had forced the Air Force to change over in the main to defensive operations on all fronts, and that in these circumstances the first necessity was to strengthen the fighter force, its main defensive arm.

Aircraft Types and Unit Equipment (see Table 2)

24. The question facing the German aircraft industry, when at the close of 1942 it became manifest that Germany was in for a long war, was not only one of increasing output. There was also the equally important task of improving quality and unit equipment by the introduction of modern aircraft types. The resiliency and high quality of German aeronautical research during the Udet régime is beyond doubt ; already at the conference referred to above Galland was able to speak in detail of five new fighter types—including the Me.262 and He.280 equipped with turbo-jet engines and developing a speed of 480-500 m.p.h. Bomber research was also advanced. But there was also the question of bringing research to the point of series manufacture ; and here, due in part at least to the "economic anarchy" of the German aircraft industry in the early stages of the war, practical results lagged far behind theoretical achievement. Considered in bulk, as the tables opposite show, the aircraft equipment of the Luftwaffe at the end of 1942 was substantially little different from that with which it entered the war. Changes in proportion between types had certainly occurred ; but few obsolescent types had disappeared, few new types had been introduced in appreciable numbers, and for most operational purposes the Air Force was still dependent on established aircraft of long standing.

Fighter Arm

25. The most conspicuous innovation in the fighter arm was the introduction of the FW.190, which first began to appear operationally in the autumn of 1941. Although the increase in production of this type at first was slow, the imperative need for a fighter of superior performance resulted in high priority being given to the FW.190 production programme, with the result that by the end of the year it accounted for more than half the total single-engine fighter output of 500 aircraft per month. In spite of the conflicting claims of the fighter arm with those of the ground-attack (or fighter-bomber arm) then being set up, a high allocation of FW.190 output was reserved for the re-equipment of fighter units. Thus, at the end of 1942, the equipment of the single-engined fighter units was almost exactly evenly divided between the FW.190 and the Me.109. The performance of this latter type had in course of time been improved by the introduction of a series of new versions. The Me.109E, with which the German single-engined fighter force had been entirely equipped in 1940 had already been superseded by the Me.109F and this in turn during 1942 had given way almost wholly to the latest Me.109G with a better performance, particularly at high altitudes.

Equipment of German Air Force First Line Units 1.9.39 compared with 31.12.42

Table 2

	L.R. BOMBERS		DIVE BOMBERS		S.E. FIGHTERS		T.E. FIGHTERS		L.R. RECCE.		TAC. RECCE.		COASTAL		TOTAL	
	1.9.39	31.12.42	1.9.39	31.12.42	1.9.39	31.12.42	1.9.39	31.12.42	1.9.39	31.12.42	1.9.39	31.12.42	1.9.39	31.12.42	1.9.39	31.12.42
He.111	780	310	—	—	—	—	—	—	—	5	—	—	—	—	780	315
Do.17	470	—	—	—	—	—	—	—	280	55	—	—	—	—	750	55
Ju.88 (Bomber) ..	20	520	—	—	—	—	—	—	—	260	—	—	—	—	20	780
Do.217	—	190	—	—	—	—	—	55	—	—	—	—	—	—	—	245
FW.200	—	50	—	—	—	—	—	—	—	—	—	—	—	—	—	50
He.177	—	50	—	—	—	—	—	—	—	—	—	—	—	—	—	50
Ju.86	—	—	—	—	—	—	—	—	—	5	—	—	—	—	—	5
Ju.87	—	—	335	270	—	—	—	—	—	—	—	—	—	—	335	270
Me.109D ..	—	—	—	—	235	—	—	—	—	—	—	—	—	—	235	—
Me.109E ..	—	—	—	—	850	—	—	—	—	—	—	—	—	—	850	—
Me.109F ..	—	—	—	—	—	90	—	—	—	—	—	—	—	—	—	90
Me.109G ..	—	—	—	—	—	570	—	—	—	15	—	25	—	—	—	610
FW.190 ..	—	—	—	—	—	580	—	—	—	10	—	25	—	—	—	615
Me.110 ..	—	—	—	—	—	—	195	365	—	10	—	30	—	—	195	405
Me.210 ..	—	—	—	—	—	—	—	10	—	5	—	—	—	—	—	15
Ar.66	—	—	—	—	5	—	—	—	—	—	—	—	—	—	5	—
Ar.68	—	—	—	—	35	—	—	—	—	—	—	—	—	—	35	—
Ju.88 (Fighter) ..	—	—	—	—	—	—	—	65	—	—	—	—	—	—	—	65
Hs.126	—	—	—	—	—	—	—	—	—	—	195	65	—	—	195	65
He.46	—	—	—	—	—	—	—	—	—	—	100	—	—	—	100	—
FW.189	—	—	—	—	—	—	—	—	—	—	—	130	—	—	—	130
Coastal Types ..	—	—	—	—	—	—	—	—	—	—	—	—	205	135	205	135
Misc.	—	15	—	—	—	—	—	20	—	30	45	—	—	—	45	65
TOTAL ..	1,170	1,135	335	270	1,125	1,240	195	515	280	395	340	275	205	135	3,750	3,960

Note.—The above Tables are based on official German Documents.

209

Milch and Speer

The Me.109G fighter with drop tank (see paragraph 25)

Twin-engined Fighters

26. The position in regard to the twin-engined fighters was less satisfactory. The Me.110, the basic type at the start of the war, had been neglected because of the intention to replace it by the Me.210, and little if any attempt had been made, as in the case of the Me.109, to improve performance by the steady introduction of modifications. But considerable difficulties were encountered in the production of the Me.210, and when the type finally appeared in series production it proved a failure. By this time, however, it was impossible to carry on with the older versions of the Me.110 (fitted with DB.601 engines) owing to its inadequate performance. Thus, at the end of 1942, the Luftwaffe was faced, as an emergency measure, with the need for redesigning the Me.110 by modifying the vulnerable cooling system, removing all external fittings in order to improve the aerodynamics and introducing heavier armament.

27. This check to twin-engined fighter production was serious because it came at a time when the growing weight of R.A.F. night bombing required expansion and improvement of the night fighter force. The Me.410, which was looked to to replace the Me.110 and Me.210, was not yet in series production. Moreover, the bomber arm, which was looking for a fast bomber type to rival the British Mosquito, had its eye on this aircraft, and it was uncertain whether it would ever be made available in sufficient numbers to the fighter force. Hence, the industry was thrown back on improvisation, and produced a modified version of the Ju.88 which proved in practice to be the most successful night fighter employed by the German Air Force. Other bomber types, like the Do.217, were also used on a small scale for night fighting. At the end of 1942, however, the night fighter version of the Ju.88 was only just being developed, output was still small, and the German aircraft industry had serious leeway to make up before its defences against night attack could be considered satisfactory either numerically or qualitatively.

Bombers

28. The position in regard to bombers was in essentials the same as that in regard to twin-engined fighters. The obsolete Do.17 has been eliminated, and its place taken by the Do.217 with a greatly increased bomb load[1]. But, after a fairly quick introduction of this type in the latter half of 1941 and the winter of 1941-42, re-equipment ceased and by the end of 1942 output was waning, and for several reasons, the first of which was the unsatisfactory performance of the BMW.801 engines, the Do.217 did not fulfil its original promise for some time. Thus, 85-90 per cent. of the bombers in operational units at the end of 1942 were still Ju.88's and He.111's, the main change being a steady switch-over from the latter to the former, which now attained its place as the chief bomber type. This reliance on the Ju.88 was, however, not a part of German plans, which envisaged instead the supersession of the current twin-engined bomber types by four-engined bombers which were intended to be the German counterpart of the Flying Fortress. But here, as in regard to twin-engined fighters, the German programme miscarried. The He.177 which, after a series of difficulties, was finally put into operations in small numbers as a transport aircraft in the Stalingrad campaign, proved a total failure and had to be completely redesigned. The Ju.288 which, like the He.177, was to be powered by two pairs of coupled engines, was expected to come into production in 1942 with an output rising to 300 aircraft per month by the end of the year ; but it never appeared.

---

[1] Illustrations on pages 24 and 197.

29. During 1942, production of the older types had been allowed to run down ; it was intended to drop the He.111 altogether while Ju.88 and Ju.87 output had fallen by half. The failure of the new four-engined types therefore created a crisis, and Milch, once he realised that Junkers were unable to put the scheduled Ju.288 programme into effect, had to fall back on the expedient of stepping up the output of existing bomber types. The Ju.288 programme was scrapped and all efforts were concentrated on maintaining adequate supplies of bombers for the present. But the miscarriage of the production plans which Milch inherited from Udet meant a serious hiatus in the German bomber programme ; and when Milch was again able to look from the immediate problems to the future and draw up a long-term plan, he was unable, owing to the delays which had intervened, to anticipate any radical improvement in the German long-range bomber force before about midsummer, 1944.

Close-support Aircraft

30. Still another problem was presented by the ground attack or close-support category and by the whole question of army cooperation, which had special urgency in view of the critical military situation in Russia. The Ju.87 originally designed for " softening up " communications and vital rear areas immediately behind the battle front rather than for direct support of the army in the field, had proved increasingly vulnerable when, in the stress of the Russian campaign, it was thrown into battle in direct support of the fighting troops. In addition, the need had become clear for an aircraft like the Russian Stormovik, specially equipped for combating armoured formations. There was also need for front-line ground strafing and army cooperation aircraft with better speed and performance against increasing fighter opposition than either the Hs.123 or the Hs.126. In this respect, hopes had been placed on the Me.210, and the failure of this type—described by Major Bruecker, an experienced close-support expert, as " the most unsatisfactory aircraft Germany ever built "—thus, had adverse results for the ground attack as for other categories.

31. An attempt to introduce a counterpart to the Stormovik was made with the Hs.129, of which the first and only Gruppe became operational in the Crimean campaign of 1942. But although this aircraft had an excellent airframe, the French Gnôme-Rhône engines were of too low a power and the airframe was not strong enough to be fitted with more powerful engines. Not only were the engines vulnerable and liable to be shot on fire, but they were also very sensitive to dust and sand, and both on the South Russian steppes and in North Africa—where they were tried out for a few weeks at the beginning of 1943—it proved impossible to maintain serviceability. Furthermore, the Hs.129 was only about 22 m.p.h. faster than the Ju.87.

32. Here again, therefore, improvisation was enforced by circumstances. The main expedient was the refitting of the older Me.109 versions (Me.109E and F) either with bomb racks for employment as fighter-bombers, or with 20-mm. cannon which had been the normal equipment of the slower Hs.123. It was also intended to allocate a part of the expanding FW.190 production to the fighter-bomber arm and a start was made at the beginning of 1943. Me.109 and (on a smaller scale) Me.110 was also used, in place of the Hs.126, for tactical reconnaissance, and the FW.189 was turned over for this purpose. But the main result was the retention of the Ju.87 dive bomber, which it had been intended to drop from the production programme. As with the He.111 and the Ju.88, it again fell to Milch to step up output of the Ju.87 in order to maintain operational strength.

The Hs.129 Close-support Aircraft

213

The FW.189 Army co-operation reconnaissance aircraft, employed on the Russian front.

Equipment Situation Summed Up

33. If we attempt to sum up the position of German aircraft production at the end of 1942, the outstanding fact is that, through the failure of the new aircraft which it was intended to introduce and bring out in series by the end of that year, the Luftwaffe was thrown back on a few established aircraft types. Of these, only the single-engined fighters were really up to the requisite standard. The FW.190 was the only completely successful new aircraft introduced on any scale by the Luftwaffe after the beginning of the war, until the introduction of turbo-jet aircraft in 1944. But the Me.109, as modified in the " G " series, was adequate to all the demands made upon it at that period. Here, therefore, except for quantity, the position was satisfactory and, after Milch's reorganisation of the aircraft industry, rapid expansion was possible. In all other categories, on the other hand, progress in modernisation was at a halt, and it was necessary, as a practical expedient, to fall back on established types.

34. This situation, which was clearly unfavourable to the maintenance of qualitative equality, had other adverse repercussions. One reason, for example, for the failure to expand output of the Do.217, which was in itself a satisfactory twin-engined bomber, was undoubtedly the necessity of maintaining and increasing the flow of the Ju.88, because the latter was a general purpose aircraft of high all-round adaptability, which could be used as a stop-gap in many categories in which it had proved impossible to bring out specialised types. Thus, in addition to the " C " fighter version, which could be produced with little modification, a great deal of experimentation began at the start of 1943 in the adaptation of the Ju.88 with heavy cannon as a ground-attack aircraft against tanks and armour, in place of the abortive Hs.129. Similar experiments were also carried out with the Ju.87. The continuance of the He.111, on the other hand, was only to be explained by the fact that the factories were already tooled up, that it was easily turned out, easily maintained and relatively economical in man-hours and material. It could be used satisfactorily on the Russian front for tactical bombing because of the less formidable nature of the Soviet defences ; but it had not the range required for strategic bombing of Russian industry, which lay as far back as Magnitogorsk and Omsk. The failure to produce a long-range heavy bomber adequate in performance and numbers therefore imposed major restrictions on the air war in the East.

35. In sum, therefore, the operational units of the Luftwaffe at the beginning of 1943 were dependent, as to 80 per cent. of their equipment, on six main types : the Ju.88, the He.111, the Me.109, the FW.190, the Ju.87 and the Me.110. Of these, the Ju.88 was preponderant over all others, while three of the main types, the Me.110, He.111 and Ju.87, accounting for 25 per cent. of first-line strength, were by current standards obsolescent. A similar position obtained in regard to transport as to first-line operational aircraft. The six-engined BV.222 flying boats had been introduced in May, 1942, for air transport in the Mediterranean, but was withdrawn and turned over in March, 1943, to long-range sea reconnaissance after prohibitive losses had been incurred among the few available. The Go.244 had been introduced about the same time on the South Russian front, but losses were heavy due to radiator trouble and engine failure, and by October production was finally suspended. The Me.323, first introduced as standard unit equipment early in 1943, was more satisfactory in spite of losses ; but in transport, as in bombers, there was virtually a waste of a year owing to the failure of the types scheduled for 1942. This failure,

215

which resulted in the continued large-scale manufacture and employment of the Ju.52, was particularly serious because the war situation at the end of 1942 made special demands on the air transport fleet. Both in Africa and Russia air transport was at this juncture one of the main methods of supply, and the extraordinary strain imposed on the air transport fleet soon had repercussions throughout the German Air Force.

36. Thus, to the general problems outlined above were added special problems arising directly from the reverses in Russia and North Africa. Of these some were temporary in character and were soon overcome ; but they added to the sense of crisis at the beginning of 1943, and the necessity for diverting effort to cope with them inevitably retarded and adversely affected any attempts to cope with the long-term problems left over as a legacy from the first 40 months of war.

Air Transport and Supply Problems

North Africa[1]

37. In North Africa, the problems encountered by the German Air Force at the end of 1942 were largely the result of difficulties of supply over exceptionally extended and vulnerable lines of communication. It is to these supply difficulties that the failure to build up air strength in Africa to a level sufficient to enable the Luftwaffe to challenge the overwhelming Allied air superiority must primarily be attributed. Between July and September, 1942, ground organisation in Cyrenaica and Egypt was developed on a scale which appeared to allow for the basing of considerably greater air forces in North Africa than had hitherto been possible ; but no appreciable increase took place. This, without doubt, was due to the difficulty—in competition with the conflicting demands of the Army—in bringing forward adequate numbers of ground and maintenance personnel, of building and maintaining stocks, and particularly of maintaining the level of fuel supplies.

38. During the greater part of September, prior to the Allied offensive at El Alamein, German Air Force fuel stocks in the whole of North Africa are believed not to have exceeded 1,200 tons, and supplies at operational airfields in Egypt were never large owing to transport difficulties over the long supply line from Tobruk. Only a few small shipments arrived in October, thanks to the successful interception of the tankers by the R.A.F., and on October 24th, when the Allied offensive began, supplies were only estimated to be sufficient for 10-15 days operations at maximum intensity.[2] An immediate acute shortage was avoided because the daily scale of effort was kept well below the potential maximum, but when withdrawal began and forward supplies were largely lost, the situation deteriorated rapidly. The threat to Axis shipping at Tobruk became so great that supply vessels had to be diverted at Benghazi, and from

---

[1] See also Chapter 6.

[2] Actual supplies of fuel in the forward area in Egypt are not known from German sources, but British estimates made at the time were as follows :—

20.9.42	..	..	..	320 tons.
4.10.42	..	..	..	900 tons.
10.10.42	..	..	..	1,400 tons.
25.10.42	..	..	..	760 tons.
8.11.42	..	..	..	160 tons.

there, owing to shortage of M.T. due to heavy demands at the front, fuel could only be moved forward with difficulty. For that reason no effective air opposition could be provided from airfields in the Benghazi area to harass the Allied advance through Cyrenaica, and on withdrawal to the El Agheila position between November 20th and 24th not more than 50-100 tons of aircraft fuel were available to the Luftwaffe. Moreover, supplies now had to come from Tripoli, which was further away from the operational area than Tobruk had been from the Egyptian airfields ; nor were transport facilities available owing to the lack of M/T.

39. The result was an enforced, and totally uneconomical reliance on air transport. Approximately 200-500 transport aircraft were engaged on the movement of personnel and material to Africa from Greece and Crete during September and the greater part of October, 1942. This total was subsequently reinforced, first as a result of Axis shipping losses and then, in November, in consequence of the Allied landings in Algeria and Morocco which necessitated the opening of a new air transport route operating between Sicily and Tunis. Systematic Allied attacks on this air transport fleet, resulting in losses so heavy as to cause the dissolution or withdrawal of three air transport Gruppin by the end of the year, necessitated the diversion of German single-engined fighters from North African battle to escort duties and to protection and patrol of transport landing-grounds. Similar patrols had also to be maintained over harbours in an attempt to keep seaborne supplies going. In this way the small available fighter force was dissipated, thus contributing to the establishment of Allied air supremacy. Moreover, the same factors affected the long-range bomber position. First in the Eastern and then in the Central Mediterranean, it became necessary to employ these offensive forces almost exclusively on shipping escort in order to maintain essential supplies at a time when Allied shipping in Egyptian and North African ports and large concentrations of troops and aircraft in the battle areas offered profitable targets which were left virtually unmolested.

Simultaneous Problems in Russia

40. It is evident that the problem of supply, which was a decisive factor in the North African campaign, had at the end of 1942 and 1943 increasingly adverse effects on the operational employment and efficiency of the German Air Force in that theatre. The significance of this factor was, however, enhanced by the fact that similar difficulties were present simultaneously in Russia, thus creating an overall problem of growing dimensions. In Russia, also, at the time of the battle of Stalingrad, the German Air Force was operating at the end of long and tenuous lines of communications, subject to serious interference by guerrilla forces. Here again air transport played a major role, and between 1st August and 30th October, 1942, approximately 21,500 transport sorties were flown, covering over 10,500,000 miles and delivering (apart from return loads) some 42-43,000 tons of fuel and equipment[1].

41. By mid-November, when the Russian counter-offensive opened, the strain on the transport fleet was therefore already being felt ; Ju.52 aircraft were already in short supply and the drain on training units began. This strain increased under winter conditions, which reduced serviceability and increased the rate of loss, and became totally abnormal when Hitler and the High Command, instead of retreating from Stalingrad, determined to supply the

---

[1] From records of German Air Ministry (8th Abteilung).

encircled 6th Army by air. Not only was every available transport aircraft drawn in, but special transport units equipped with Ju.52, He.111 and Ju.86 aircraft were rapidly formed at the expense of training units, and finally Hitler ordered the bomber fleet in South Russia (including the He.177's of I/KG. 50) to be used for the transport of supplies. The intolerable strain of winter operations under unfavourable conditions from inadequately prepared airfields was increased by the débâcle in the Caucasus, where the Germans, weakened by having provided reinforcements for the Stalingrad front, had lost air superiority to the Soviet Air Force. Here again, in addition to normal operations, the heavy burden of supplying the 17th Army isolated in the Taman peninsula had to be shouldered.

42. The Stalingrad supply operations involved some 850 aircraft, including 100 He.111's transferred from the Mediterranean theatre, and losses in the period of approximately two months involved amounted to 285 aircraft. Their consequences, in combination with the similar operations going on at the same time in the Mediterranean, were weighty. Goering has since put his finger on one of the most outstanding, when he said : " There died the core of the German bomber fleet ". We have already noted the deleterious effect on the German training programme. Another important consequence of the exceptional scale of transport operations was serious fuel shortage, which began to make itself felt in all spheres of operations about August, 1942, and progressively worsened as the strain of the Stalingrad campaign grew. Severe economy measures had to be instituted, in particular restrictions on all flying behind the fronts, which necessarily had further repercussions on training and thus on the long-term prospects of the German Air Force. In Russia, in the Balkans, even in the West, disciplinary measures were applied to enforce economies " in view of the extremely critical fuel situation ", and in some theatres it was necessary to go so far as to prohibit all flying, including operational flights, not absolutely necessary to the war effort. This critical state of affairs persisted through the spring of 1943, and as late as May and June of that year, rigid and hampering measures of economy were still being enforced. Only the development of the synthetic oil industry in Germany saved the situation, and allowed stocks to be restored ; as a result of the accession of this new source of supply the position was eventually stabilised about midsummer 1943. In the meantime untold harm had been done to long-term plans, and for the Luftwaffe the year 1943 became one of recuperation rather than of renewed effort.

43. This was true especially in regard to aircraft. First of all, the transport fleet had suffered a serious blow, and though it eventually recovered numerically it was mainly by the expedient of taking over foreign types—particularly Italian aircraft after the capitulation of Italy in September, 1943. The German programme, on the other hand, which envisaged replacing the Ju.52 by the Ju.352 had to be scrapped, in order to concentrate on operational aircraft which were more economical to build and of more immediate value.

The Growing Burden of Operational Commitments

The Decline of First-Line Strength

44. With operational aircraft, the introduction of new and more modern types had to be postponed in order to build up strength in all categories. For both at Stalingrad and in North Africa the German Air Force for the first time

came up against a numerically superior opponent, and the rate of loss consequently increased rapidly. This was particularly the case in the Mediterranean theatre, where the Germans for the first time learned the measure of Allied air superiority. In Russia also, the disorganisation consequent on retreat, the strain of intensive operations for excessive periods without rest, the inadequacy of repair facilities, and the high incidence of technical defects, as well as the excellence of Soviet light A.A., all combined to cause heavy wastage by comparison with anything suffered in earlier stages of the Russian campaign. Operational strength had slumped by 18 per cent.—from 4,800 aircraft to only 3,950 during the last six months of 1942—and the rigours of a winter campaign had produced a corresponding decline in serviceability. The problem facing the German Air Force was to make up this leeway at the very time when the reverses in Russia and the Mediterranean required an intensification of air activity in order to stabilise the front. In the winter of 1941-42, in spite of the launching of the first Soviet winter offensive, the Luftwaffe had succeeded in disengaging a major part of its forces in the East for a period of rest and refit, and had thus been able to restore strength and serviceability. In the winter of 1942-43 circumstances prevented the execution of a similar programme on a comparable scale, and units which had fought hard and continuously through the summer and autumn were thrown into the Stalingrad battle regardless of consequences. The result was not only that aircraft strength and serviceability suffered ; but also that an undue strain was placed on pilots, crews and servicing personnel.

The Mediterranean Commitment

45. At the Berlin conference held at the end of January, 1943, to which we have already referred[1], Galland predicted that the centre of gravity for the German Air Force in 1943 would be the Mediterranean. This prognostication proved incorrect. By the end of 1943 strength in the Mediterranean, which over the year 1942 had risen by 50 per cent. to a total of some 1,050 aircraft, had fallen to only 470 aircraft—appreciably less than at the beginning of 1942.

46. This falsification of Galland's expectations was due to the fact that the Air Force, in the state in which it found itself after the reverses at El Alamein and Stalingrad, was in no state to undertake, except for brief periods, a war on three fronts. Instead of growing with its commitments, its strength by the end of 1942 had declined, and it was only able to meet the demands made upon it by frequent transfers of units from one theatre of operations to another and from one section to another of the same front. In face of simultaneous pressure on three fronts only a substantial expansion of strength in all categories, but particularly in interception fighters, could permit a balanced deployment of forces. It had, until approximately the summer of 1942, profited from the fact that it could, by and large, meet its opponents one by one, could therefore concentrate its forces by denuding quiet fronts and quiet sectors, and could thus achieve local air superiority. This advantage, from the beginning of 1943, it no longer possessed ; and it had failed—a failure which marked a turning point in the air war—to use the long respite which it had been vouchsafed to build and man an air force sufficient in numbers and quality for the new phase in operations which it faced in 1943. German air superiority, even with the

---

[1] Paragraph 19.

deftest exploitation of the possibility of concentrating forces at threatened points, which was an inherent advantage of a power operating on internal lines of communication and defending a perimeter, was a thing of the past.

47. The new balance of air strength first became manifest with the launching of the Alamein offensive and the Anglo-American landings in French North Africa, i.e., in October and November, 1942. The German Air Staff, taken up with the question of forcing a decision in Russia, had refused to credit the reports of the building up of overwhelming Allied air strength in Egypt in the summer months and early autumn of 1942—of which German Intelligence was in possession as a result of photo-reconnaissance—and had continued to treat the African campaign as a secondary commitment. The disillusionment, when it came, was therefore all the more serious, and the steps taken to meet the situation threw the whole existing deployment and balance of German air forces into the melting pot. During November, 1942, it was necessary to withdraw no less than 400 operational aircraft from Russia, of which 75 per cent. were long-range bombers. For the first time in the history of the war the Mediterranean became a serious commitment, absorbing almost 25 per cent. of total strength as compared 18 months earlier with only 8 per cent. In the East, on the other hand, strength was reduced to a perilously low figure, having regard to the length of the Russian front and the critical nature of the situation. For their summer offensive in Russia in 1942 the Germans had still been able to assemble a major force of 2,750 aircraft, comprising nearly 60 per cent. of available strength ; nine months later strength in the East had sunk to not more than 2,000 aircraft.

48. These figures make plain the significance of the opening of the North African offensive in the history of the air war in Europe. It was, from the point of view of deployment of forces, a turning-point, compelling the dispersal of strength and thus foiling the principles of maximum concentration on which the early German victories were based. The fact, moreover, that the redispositions which took place at the end of 1942, while substantially weakening the German Air Force in Russia, totally failed to restore it in the Mediterranean to anything approaching air equality, threw a vivid light on its limitations and accentuated its problems. What, the Operational Staff had to ask itself, was the best use for the limited forces available. If over 1,000 aircraft were inadequate to restore the position in the Mediterranean, could more be spared, or was it better to conserve effort and forces and concentrate the largest possible force in the East, where it could most effectively be employed? How far could one front be stripped with impunity for the benefit of the others?

The Russian Front and Air Defence of Germany

49. No answer was found to these questions for the reason that there was no answer. But it is noteworthy that German air strength in the East never again for long rose above the level of 1,600–1,800 first–line aircraft to which it had sunk at the beginning of 1943. The reason was that 1942 had brought a third commitment to the fore, namely, the defence of Germany itself and of occupied territories in the West against Anglo-American day and night bombing. During 1942 it had been necessary to increase the night fighter defences in the West, which rose by 95 per cent. from 180 to 350 aircraft ; and by the end of the year it was evident that a parallel expansion of day fighter defences was an imperative necessity. By the end of the Soviet winter offensive in February, 1943,

almost 70 per cent. of the total German fighter forces were employed on the Western and Mediterranean fronts, and the expansion of the day fighter forces in the West was only just beginning. Between the end of February and the beginning of July, 1943, single-engined fighter strength engaged in the West and in the defence of Germany rose by approximately one-third.

The Changing Ratio of German and Allied Air Forces

50. The winter of 1942-43 was, therefore, a period of crisis in Luftwaffe dispositions. In November, 1942, for the first time since the opening of the Russian campaign in June, 1941, a greater proportion of its total operational strength had to be concentrated on the two Anglo-American fronts than was employed in the East. Thereafter, the odds steadily lengthened ; strength in West steadily rose by comparision with the forces in Russia. But the magnitude of the German commitment in the West only became evident in the course of operations in 1943, and it was only in the second half of 1943 that it assumed such proportions that even the High Command, which had always been inclined to place military operations first, was compelled to give it the highest priority. At the beginning of 1943, although far-sighted Air Staff officers were well aware that the time had come to take measures for the air defence of Germany, the practical problem which weighed heaviest was to stabilise the military situation in Russia and the Mediterranean. Not until some degree of stabilisation on the battle fronts had been achieved was the Air Staff at liberty to devote due attention to the long-term problems facing it. From the point of view of Hitler and the Supreme Command the first necessity was to bring the Soviet advance to a halt. Russia still had first claim on the Air Force, and for that reason it is necessary to turn next to an examination of the Russian campaign and of the part assigned in it to the German Air Force. It was here, that, in the views of the dominating personalities, it was confronted with its most pressing and immediate tasks in the new phase of the war which began in 1943.

221

CHAPTER 10

THE RUSSIAN CAMPAIGN IN 1943–4

The German Recovery after Stalingrad

State of the German and Russian Air Forces

1. By the end of 1942 the Russian Air Force had recovered from the crippling blow which it had suffered at German hands during the summer and autumn of 1941. It had been modernised and strengthened from its own production resources and was also receiving equipment on a large scale from the U.S.A. and Great Britain by way of the Arctic, Alaskan and Persian supply routes. A German estimate of its strength towards the end of 1942 was some 5,000[1] first-line aircraft. The German Air Force on the other hand, with an approximately equal strength was obliged to divide its attention in varying degrees between the Russian fronts, the Mediterranean, attacking England and the Atlantic shipping routes, and defence against the ever-growing bombing of German industry by the Western Allies.

2. A full appreciation of the difficulties which beset the German Air Force during 1943 and 1944 can only be gained by a study of the campaign in Russia, outlined in this Chapter, in conjunction with the other parallel campaigns which Germany was supporting in the Mediterranean and over Germany itself. (Chapters 11 and 12.) It must be remembered, too, that up to the opening of the combined Allied bombing of Germany in the autumn of 1943, in German eyes the Russian front transcended all others in importance[2]. A true perspective of the course of the War up to that time can therefore only be obtained by the reader if he places himself in the position of the Germans— facing the Russians on the eastern front, with the added complication of a deteriorating situation in the Mediterranean, and with the increasing menace of Allied bombing in the homeland.

3. By the late summer of 1943, the Luftwaffe High Command was beginning to realise that a policy of pure army support—4/5ths of the whole German bombing effort on the Russian front had been committed to this policy[3]— could gain no decision against the Russians. The High Command would have preferred to revert to a strategic conception of warfare, where the bomber force could be released from its close-support duties to undertake a bombing of Russian industry and thus prevent the enemy's ever-growing air and ground forces from gaining further strength. With the exception of one interval in June, 1943[4], when a pause in the fighting allowed of a short period of strategic bombing of Russian industry, it was not until after the German failure before Kursk in August of that year that a firm decision was finally taken to re-establish the bomber force as an instrument of strategic warfare. The decision, however, came too late ; by the time it could be implemented the Germans had retreated

---

[1] From German Air Ministry (8th Abteilung) historical records.

[2] The circumstances of the German division of attention between home defence and the Russian front are outlined in paragraphs 39 and 57 of this chapter, and in chapter 13.

[3] From German Air Ministry historical records.

[4] Refer to paragraph 28.

so far as to place Russian industry far beyond the range of the normal bomber. The steady Russian advance left the Luftwaffe High Command with no alternative but to give its full attention to the hard-pressed German Army. The German armed forces were suffering from the Blitzkrieg of their own making, but in reverse, and the Air Force could thereafter spare its long-range bomber forces for little else than a continuous support of the Army.

4. This Chapter will follow the events which led up to the abandonment of the long-established and hitherto successful German Blitzkrieg theory of employing their Air Force as an instrument of army support. The events which followed that failure are merely a recitation of a steady German retirement westwards. Reference to Map 21 during the reading of this chapter will assist in following the course of the campaign.

The German Retreat from Stalingrad (January and February, 1943)

5. The opening of the year 1943 saw the Soviet Command taking advantage of the concentration of German military resources on the Stalingrad battle, and going over to the offensive along the whole eastern front : in the North, the siege of Leningrad was raised on January 18th; on the Moscow front the Russians launched an offensive which brought them to Rzhev and Vyasma before the winter campaign was over, while further South, on the Upper Don, they recaptured Voronezh before the end of January. It was in the South that Russian progress was most rapid ; by-passing the German forces surrounded outside Stalingrad, they swept forward to the line of the Donetz, reaching Rostov, Voroshilovgrad and Kharkov by mid-February and at the same time covering their northern flank by an advance to Kursk. Meanwhile, the Germans were forced to undertake a precipitate retreat from the Caucasus. Mozdok, three-quarters of the way from the Sea of Azov to the Caspian, was recaptured by the Russians at the beginning of January, and only five weeks later Krasnodar exchanged hands, leaving the Germans to defend a narrow bridgehead in the Kuban peninsula.

6. The last remnants of the German forces under General von Paulus, besieged at Stalingrad, capitulated on 2nd February, 1943. During the whole of the siege, and during the period of intensive operations along the whole front from Leningrad to the Caucasus, outlined above, the German Air Force was concentrated in the battle for Stalingrad. From the beginning of November, 1942, the lower Don front had been continuously provided with intensive air support in an attempt to avert the threatening disaster to the German 6th Army. One area after another had to give up aircraft in order to provide the requisite concentration to meet the Russian counter-offensive, with effects on German Air Force dispositions in Russia which are set out in the following table of strengths in aircraft :—

	Mid-October, 1942	Early December, 1942	Mid-January, 1943
Leningrad Front ..	485	270	195
Moscow Front ..	425	480	380
Don Front	545	700	900
Caucasus and Crimea..	495	330	240

7. As the Russian forces swept forward to the mouth of the Don at Rostov and to the line of the Donetz, this process of concentration was carried even further. By early February approximately 950 of a total of some 1,800 first-line

224

operational aircraft available in the East (including the Murmansk front in the far North) had been concentrated in the Don-Donetz sector, comprising almost 53 per cent., as compared with only 36 per cent. two months earlier. Moreover, the majority of aircraft left on the Leningrad, Moscow and Caucasus sectors were army co-operation and reconnaissance types, useful only for the performance of routine duties. Thus, the battle of Stalingrad completely dislocated the dispositions of the German Air Force in Russia, leaving it with unbalanced forces which, except on the main front, were unequal to the tasks confronting them. This disorganisation had been increased by the diversion of bomber units to air transport duties, and was reflected in a widespread decentralisation of operational control, which became most marked when Fliegerkorps VIII—Field Marshal von Richthofen's old command, hitherto the spearhead of every major German offensive—was pulled out of operations and placed in tactical control of air supply, first of the German 6th Army, and then, after the surrender at Stalingrad, of the bridgehead in the Caucasus held by the 17th Army. Its place as a close-support force was taken by an *ad hoc* Command, *Fliegerdivision Donetz*.

8. The German Air Force in this way was left with a cumbersome chain of command, comprising seven headquarters Staffs from Veliki Luki southwards, of which the majority were short-term creations which had sprung up in response to immediate operational and tactical requirements. In these circumstances there was, in German policy, no glimpse of wide strategic planning of purpose ; all efforts were perforce concentrated, under local control, on day-to-day requirements with the simple object of hampering and stemming the Soviet advance so far as locally available means permitted.

9. The concentration in the Don-Donetz sector of the major striking force of the German Air Force in the East, achieved only by the withdrawal and transfer of forces from the Leningrad and Caucasus sectors, resulted in the surrender of air superiority in the latter areas to the Soviet Air Force. Particularly in the Caucasus, where military operations on a major scale were under way, it was evident that the German air elements which remained were incapable of providing adequate cover either over the retreating armies or in the Novorossisk area, which the Germans were developing as a pivot for the defence of the Kuban bridgehead. Moreover, there were certain sectors where air cover was virtually suspended ; thus no striking force was available to oppose the Russian advance across the Elista Steppes, where for a front of nearly 200 miles only a few long-range reconnaissance aircraft were available. The same was true of the exposed northern flank of the Stalingrad salient, where lack of German close-support air forces favoured the rapid Soviet advance to and beyond Voronezh.

10. This sacrifice of outlying sectors was unavailing, since even the strong concentration of units in the Donetz-Rostov area failed during January, 1943, to secure that complete superiority in the air on which the German Army had hitherto been able to rely at the focal points of a major battle. Many factors contributed to this decline of German air power. Firstly, bad flying conditions— to which the Germans were less capable of adapting themselves than the Russians—were responsible for restricting German air activity, grounding the Luftwaffe at a time when the Soviet Air Force was successful in maintaining fighter patrols over German occupied airfields and centres of communications. Secondly, the strenuous efforts throughout the autumn and early winter of 1942 to force a decision at Stalingrad meant that many units had been operating since

the summer of 1942 with little or no opportunity for rest and refit. Hence, serviceability was low, and pilots and crews were suffering from strain and fatigue. The precipitate retreat had, furthermore, caused supply difficulties, and on many airfields there was—largely owing to the concentration of transport aircraft for the supply of the 6th and 17th Armies—undue congestion. As the German Air Force retreated it found itself without an adequate number of air bases ready for immediate use. Loss of forward aerodromes meant lack of operational airfields for short-range close-support units, and the result was inability to provide fighter cover, and therefore a Soviet air superiority over the battle area. Frequent moves of units, involving in many cases the jettisoning of unserviceable aircraft which could not be flown back, was a contributory cause of low serviceability. Finally, there is no doubt that the German Air Force was caught unawares by the strength and mobility of the Soviet counter-offensive and had not taken preparatory dispositions in time ; for an appreciable period all it could do was to extricate itself.

11. The result was that, throughout January, 1943, the scale of effort put up by the Germans in defence of the Donetz line was only moderate in spite of the concentration of air units in this area and in spite of the fact that a number of second-line units were now brought into play as harassing bombers for attacks on Soviet forward concentrations and lines of communication. These units, of which there were eight, were known as *Stoerkampfstaffeln*[1] and were equipped with obsolescent and training aircraft, such as the He.46, He.51, Ar.66 and Hs.126, fitted with bomb racks ; they were auxiliary or supplementary units, thrown together at a moment of crisis as a reinforcement of first-line strength, but they proved a permanent addition and from about March, 1943, were reorganised on a permanent footing, providing the nucleus from which the later *Nachtschlachtgruppen*[2] were formed. Nevertheless, their contribution in the first phase was small ; they were too few in numbers, involving probably only 85-100 aircraft in the whole of Russia, and their offensive capacity was small. Hence, the German Air Force, in spite of its many expedients, failed to halt or even slow down the Soviet drive, which maintained its impetus and on February 5th carried the Russians across the Donetz. This rapid success was clearly unexpected.

12. By the beginning of February the Russians had advanced into the area between Slavjansk and Kramatorsk. On February 16th, Kharkov, the northern bastion of the German Donetz position, passed back into Russian hands, and a week after, Belgorod, 50 miles north of Kharkov, had been recaptured. Most significant of all, a dangerous thrust appeared to be materialising from the North-East towards Dnepropetrovsk and Zaporozhe ; it seemed as though the German position in the Donetz Basin was on the point of collapse and that the German forces might, if they could extricate themselves, be forced to fall back to the Dnieper. However, by February 13th the rearward communications of Manstein's army in the Stalino-Rostov area were cut and the situation was therefore extremely precarious.

13. The Soviet threat to Dnepropetrovsk was more dangerous in appearance than in reality, and it is a measure of von Richthofen's intrepidity and confidence that he left considerable air forces based throughout at Stalino for co-operation with von Manstein, in spite of the threat to their communications, and thus

---

[1] Harassing bomber Staffel.

[2] Night ground-attack Gruppen.

maintained pressure on the flank of the Soviet forces advancing towards Dnepropetrovsk. This measure was based, without doubt, on a realisation that, with the capture of Kharkov and the establishment of a bridgehead over the Donetz, the main Russian effort was spent. A powerful Russian striking force had been built up for the initial Russian attack at Stalingrad and on the Don bend, and for a time the Soviet had all the advantages of an advancing air force ; but by the end of January the Russian forces were fully extended and much attenuated, while the early thaw hampered communications and interfered with the supply of forward elements. From mid-February there were instances of Soviet air units immobilised by lack of fuel, and the further thrust towards Dnepropetrovsk and Zaporozhe was made with inadequate forces and inadequate air cover.

Reorganisation and Recovery of the Luftwaffe Forces

14. It was in the circumstances outlined in the above paragraph that the Germans made fresh preparations and dispositions with three primary objectives in view :—

   (i) The recapture of Kharkov to act as a northern bastion to the southern front.

   (ii) The reoccupation of the Donetz line from Kharkov to Voroshilovgrad, and thence to Taganrog or if possible to Rostov.

   (iii) Maintenance of the Kuban bridgehead. By the beginning of March at latest, the earlier intention to evacuate the bridgehead had evidently been superseded by a determination to maintain a foothold across the Kerch straits.

15. With the above objects in view, Luftflotte 4 was, by mid-February, preparing and operating " within the framework of a new offensive programme ". Widespread reorganisation, necessitated by the failure to hold the Donetz line, was immediately put in hand. He.111 bombers were brought back from transport duties and a special bomber battle unit was formed for the specific task of close support. The chain of command was strengthened and tightened up, and Luftflotte 4, under von Richthofen himself, asserted central control. *Fliegerdivision Donetz,* which had been operating as an independent command under Luftflotte 4, was subordinated from the beginning of February to Fliegerkorps IV. Two weeks later, Luftflotte 4, on Hitler's orders, took over direct control of the air defence of the Crimea, the Kerch straits and the Taman peninsula. In place of the makeshift arrangements which had existed before, Luftflotte 4, with an enlarged area under command, was in this way established in unified control over the whole South Russian front.

16. Having secured unitary control, von Richthofen next restored the fighting efficiency of his forces. His first step was the ruthless elimination of weak and depleted units, of which no less than eight (representing an establishment of 250 aircraft) were withdrawn for resting and refitting during February, leaving their aircraft behind for bringing the remaining units up to strength. The overstrained ground organisation was thus relieved without any diminution of actual fighting strength, and the efficiency of forces actually to be engaged on operations was simultaneously increased. The problem of accommodation on congested airfields was also simplified, and the regrouping facilitated the tasks of maintenance.

227

17. The result was a rapid rise in serviceability, already evident by February 23rd when von Richthofen congratulated the ground staffs on the results of their " self-denying and meticulous work ". A contributory factor, without doubt, was the fact that the retreat had thrown the Air Force back on established airfields, constructed on a permanent basis 12-18 months previously, with good maintenance facilities, and that it was now operating in close proximity to rear bases, like Nikolaiev, at which the re-equipment of close-support units in particular could be carried out at short notice. In addition, at the very time when the Russians were facing supply difficulties through their rapid advance, the German Air Force had withdrawn to shorter and better supply lines with good communications near supply depôts like Poltava. Nevertheless, even if all these considerations are taken into account, the reorganisation and re-establishment of fighting efficiency within the space of 2-3 weeks under continued Russian pressure was a remarkable feat, revealing the resiliency of the Luftwaffe. Not the least notable feature was that the reorganisation was carried through without having to draw appreciably on forces from other fronts or from other sectors of the Russian front.

Last of the Blitzkrieg, and the Luftwaffe's Failure in Russia.

German Counter-offensive and Recapture of Kharkov (21st February to end of March, 1943)

18. Up to February 10th, von Richthofen's forces had been massed in the Rostov area, but he now effected a redeployment in order to comply with the German plan for a concentric counter-offensive operation involving Kharkov and the whole of the Donetz basin. Retaining the bulk of his long-range bombers under control of his own headquarters at Zaporozhe, he divided his close-support units into three main forces, as follows :—

    (*a*) Fliegerkorps I, under General Korten[1], was brought into the northern sector from Borispol (near Kiev) to Poltava on its subordination to Luftflotte 4.

    (*b*) Fliegerkorps IV was based on Dnepopetrovsk in the centre.

    (*c*) In the South-eastern sector, Fliegerdivision Donetz, with powerful close-support forces, was moved on February 20th to the Stalino area.

19. The German armies opened their counter-offensive on February 21st ; in the light of succeeding events, described in later paragraphs of this chapter, this offensive was to provide the last classical example on the Russian front of army-air co-operation on the lines which had won Germany her military victories of 1939 and 1940, and her first successes in Russia. Von Richthofen's forces were thrown into the battle for Kharkov as one coherent whole, with mutual support between the respective commands, and played a major part in providing air support. The main weight of the operations was borne by Fliegerkorps IV, which was allotted the task of supporting the momentum of the advance of the 1st and 4th Panzer Armies towards the Donetz river to the South and East of Kharkov. Fliegerkorps I supported the attack on Kharkov from West and North-West. Fliegerdivision Donetz was at first assigned to the defensive battle on the eastern flank of Panzer Army 1, North-East of Stalino, where it was essential to hold the Russians while the attack on Kharkov

---

[1] See career and photograph page 237.

Rostov

Von Richthofen at a Luftwaffe close-support command post in the field

Moving German supplies for the besieged German Army at Stalingrad by Ju.55 transport aircraft. Russian prisoners are employed.

was developing ; as soon as the German counter-offensive was under way, however, it was switched to the South and East of Kharkov in support of Fliegerkorps IV. As the offensive progressed, co-operation between all tactical commands under Luftflotte 4 increased. Both Fliegerkorps I and Fliegerkorps IV were engaged in the final assault on Kharkov, and were expressly ordered not to pay excessive regard to the line of demarcation between their operational areas. While Fliegerkorps IV was battering its way towards Kharkov, the dive-bomber forces of Fliegerdivision Donetz were employed for the same purpose. The major success of the German counter-attack, the recapture of Kharkov on March 15th, was thus achieved essentially by a concentration of attack by ground and air forces. All available aircraft, including the long-range bombers, were thrown into the battle and were employed in a tactical rôle for close-support on the classical German model.

Luftwaffe Scale of Effort in the Counter-offensive

20. From February 20th to the recapture of Kharkov on March 15th, Luftflotte 4's effort, compared with an earlier average in January of some 350 sorties per day, rose to a daily average little short of 1,000 sorties with a peak figure of 1,200-1,250 on February 23rd. This effort provides an indication of the success of the measures of reorganisation undertaken in the previous three weeks. Too, there is no disputing the skill with which Richthofen handled the forces under his command. In the actual employment of those close-support forces, he had the benefit of the advice of Oberstleutnant Weiss, Inspector of Ground-Attack Forces, who had been detached from Berlin to Luftflotte 4 with the express object of directing the anti-tank units. Particular emphasis was also placed on attacks on Soviet railways which, in view of an early thaw affecting road transport, were the Russians' only reliable means of bringing up reserves and supplies. For these attacks on railways, special units (9/KG 3, 14/KG 27 and 9/KG 55) were detached from the long-range bomber Geschwader and equipped with Ju.88 C-6 aircraft, fitted with heavy cannon. The main factor behind Richthofen's success, however, was extreme flexibility, coordination and concentration—the latter secured by the creation of temporary *ad hoc* battle groups to support the spearheads of attack by military formations, such as the SS Division Reich which led the assault on Kharkov. " Massive concentration ", " drastic concentration ", " concentration of all forces to the highest degree ", were phrases which resounded through Luftflotte 4's battle orders ; another factor was the reservation by von Richthofen to himself alone of the right to switch the main effort from one Fliegerkorps to another in accordance with the tactical situation. Both Fliegerkorps I and Fliegerkorps IV were instructed to make sure that their subordinate units could be brought to bear immediately in either command's operational area.

21. After the fall of Kharkov this concentration of effort was kept up until Belgorod was taken, thus strengthening the German hold on the Donetz line. By the end of March, however, when the spring thaw interrupted further operations, German air effort slackened markedly, and the offensive was at an end. In this offensive, in which the forces of Luftflotte 4 under Field Marshal von Richthofen played an important—perhaps a decisive part, the Germans had achieved their main objectives. The energy with which the air operations were directed and executed showed that, even after the disasters of the previous two months, the Luftwaffe was still a factor to be reckoned with. Nevertheless, in the light of succeeding events, it is important to realise the limitations of the

Germans' success. In the first place, they failed—partly owing to the fact that they started too late and were halted by the thaw—to carry the offensive northwards from Belgorod to Kursk, where the Russians remained in possession of a consolidated salient which outflanked the new positions which the Germans had established on the Donetz. In the second place, the concentration of forces in the battle for Kharkov had allowed the Russians time to consolidate their bridgeheads over the Donetz further to the South in the regions of Chuguev and Izyum ; German armoured groups, with air support, were thrown against these bridgeheads but without success, and the Russian defensive line in this area remained unbroken during the whole of March. Thus, when the battle for the Donetz Basin subsided at the beginning of April, the Soviet forces still retained certain vantage points. The latter were to prove their importance when, three months later, at the beginning of July, the summer campaign of 1943 began.

German Offensive in the Kuban Peninsula

22. When, at the beginning of April, 1943, weather conditions made a continuation of intensive operations on the Donetz front impossible, the Soviet Command was able to maintain pressure in the Kuban, to the East of the Crimea, and this situation compelled the Germans to redispose their air forces in the new theatre. The German reaction in this area presumably had the aim of retaining the bridgehead of the Taman and Kuban peninsulas as a springboard for a resumption of offensive operations against the Caucasus. During the first half of April, the Germans concentrated a powerful striking force of some 550-600 aircraft in the Crimea, and on April 17th they launched a series of heavy blows. However, it is clear that Soviet reconnaissance had observed the concentration on the Crimean airfields, and that the Soviet Command had assembled adequate forces to meet the German threat ; hence, the Germans were unable to secure tactical air superiority. On the other hand, the Soviet Air Force, by attacks on German supply traffic in the Black Sea and across the Straits of Kerch, forced the Germans to maintain defensive forces in the Crimea which, operating under conditions of numerical inferiority, suffered considerable losses. German long-range bombers were also compelled early in May to carry out a series of attacks on Black Sea ports, where it appeared that the Russians were assembling troops and transport for an amphibious operation against the Crimea.

23. The scale of operations over the Kuban should not be underestimated. Soviet pressure there throughout May compelled the Luftwaffe to maintain a scale of effort in that sector averaging some 400 sorties per 24 hours, which was more than that exerted at the same period over the Tunisian bridgehead[1]. The battle for the Kuban was, in fact, a struggle on the same scale as the battle for the Tunisian bridgehead, and a German defeat foreboded results scarcely less significant than the loss of North Africa—viz., a Soviet reconquest of the Crimea, placing the growing Soviet bomber force within easy reach of the Rumanian oilfields. For this reason the German Air Force, in spite of its need for rest, could not afford to neglect the Kuban battle. This commitment, too, was so heavy as to preclude major operations elsewhere, and the German failure to loosen the Soviet stranglehold on Novorossisk necessitated the postponement of other plans.

---

[1] See Chapter 11, paragraph 15.

German Preparations for an Offensive against Kursk[1]

24. From the beginning of May, the German Air Force concentration in the Crimea was gradually reduced and dispersed without having achieved any success, and a general shift of forces began. Probably to meet the threat of possible Soviet offensives, the available forces were redistributed fairly evenly over all sectors from Smolensk southwards. During June, on the other hand, German dispositions took more positive shape, and it became clear that two main concentrations were being established on either side of the Russian salient at Kursk. Simultaneously, Fliegerkorps VIII was relieved of its transport duties in the Crimea and brought back as an operational command in the Kharkov/Belgorod sector. The appearance of this famous headquarters staff, with its long experience of intensive close-support operations, was a pointer to the initiation of an offensive. A second indication was the appearance, about the beginning of May, of a new command, Luftflotte 6, on the central sector of the Russian front between Smolensk and Orel, covering the northern flank of the Kursk salient. This latter command, formerly Luftwaffe Command East, was led by General von Greim.

25. Another important change, which met with violent opposition on the part of General von Manstein the Army Commander, was the sudden transfer, in the middle of June, of Field Marshal von Richthofen from his command of Luftflotte 4 to that of Luftflotte 2 in the Mediterranean[2]. After the disaster at Tunis there began an increasing tendency to reinforce the Mediterranean at the expense of the air forces in Russia. The transfer was made at Kesselring's urgent request, and Goering assured von Manstein that the move implied no change in the method of conducting air operations on the Russian Front. Oberst Schulz, von Richthofen's Chief of Staff retained his post under the latter's successor, General Dessloch, and thus ensured a continuity of method. Dessloch had led Luftflotte 6 in the Polish campaign of 1939, and after holding Flak commands in the West and in Russia, had returned to the command of flying units and had frequently deputised for von Richthofen.

Strength of the German Air Force before the Kursk Offensive

26. By the end of April, after the abortive Kuban offensive, first-line strength of the Luftwaffe on the Russian front had been reduced to 2,100 aircraft, although it was quickly restored to a figure of approximately 2,500 by the return of units from rest and re-equipment. Its ability to mount a force of this size for the third consecutive summer's operations in the East, despite its increased commitments in the Mediterranean, was possible as a result of the remarkable recovery in total first-line strength which took place in the first six months of 1943. After having fallen to under 4,000 aircraft at the end of 1942, its overall first-line strength had risen by June, 1943, to almost exactly 6,000 aircraft, a size which it never succeeded in reaching at any other period of the War. This is to be attributed largely to the impetus given to single- and twin-engined fighter output in face of the crippling lack of day fighter strength revealed during 1942, and with the impending threat of the full-scale entry of the U.S.A.A.F. into the European war coupled with the ever-growing weight of the R.A.F. night bombing offensive. Simultaneously, both long-range bomber and dive-bomber strength was appreciably increased, and the newly-formed ground attack (*Schlacht*) category, equipped with FW.190 fighter-bombers, was now in the field. In addition, moreover, the Luftwaffe second-line force of special units employed in the East had been expanded and furthermore, the satellite

---

[1] Further details of the manner in which this offensive was planned at high level appear in paragraph 12 of the Appendix.

[2] See also Chapter 11, paragraph 17.

Rumanian and Hungarian Air Forces operating in the East, although still small in numbers, had been equipped with modern German aircraft. This policy of re-equipping satellite air forces was in part a means of overcoming the dislocation of the German Air Force training programme already noted, quicker results being possible by retraining experienced satellite crews to German aircraft types than by producing new German crews. The operational value and efficiency of the second-line and satellite units was, however, doubtful, although adequate for defensive operations on static sectors of the front. They could therefore be used to release first-line Luftwaffe units for supporting the spearheads of German attacks.

27. This great expansion in first-line strength was not accompanied by a similar improvement in its quality, primarily on account of training difficulties which made it impossible to maintain an output of crews commensurate with that expansion. Single-engined fighter strength now stood at 1,800 aircraft, but some 800 of these were now absorbed in the West, including defence of the European coast from Norway to the Bay of Biscay, whilst a further 450 were employed in the Mediterranean, where Allied air superiority required intensive fighter defence involving heavy wastage, which absorbed the bulk of single-engined fighter replacements. On the Russian front, single-engined fighter strength could consequently not be raised higher than some 600 aircraft, which was little more than that of July, 1942 ; the situation was, however, now greatly different since not only had German military strategy been compelled to revert to the defensive, but Soviet air strength had by now grown appreciably both in quantity and quality. This fighter weakness in the East was therefore now a limiting factor for all other aircraft categories, which could no longer operate efficiently and without disproportionate losses unless provided with fighter cover. Already, therefore, at the beginning of the summer campaign of 1943, the effects of Allied air pressure in the West and in the Mediterranean were making their influence felt in the East. More than ever before, the German Air Force was obliged to rely on rapid transfers and quick concentrations—in themselves a cause of serious strain over any considerable period—to achieve its objects, but it had no longer any prospects of securing lasting control of the Russian skies.

Opening of the Kursk Offensive (June, 1943)

28. After an enforced lull due to adverse weather conditions, operations by the Luftwaffe on the Russian front began in the latter part of June with a series of heavy raids on industrial targets in the Soviet rear. These latter included the tank works at Gorki (250 miles East of Moscow), the rubber works at Jaroslavl (150 miles North-East of Moscow), oil refineries at Saratov (400 miles East of Orel) and oil depots at Astrakhan at the mouth of the Volga. These attacks, carried out almost nightly during the second and third weeks of June, were clearly intended to strike a major blow at Soviet war potential immediately before the resumption of offensive land operations. They were seconded by sustained and fairly intensive low-level attacks on Soviet airfields and rail communications immediately behind the front line between Orel, including particularly violent raids, by night and day, on Kursk. Once again the Germans were following their familiar pattern of *Blitzkrieg* in the same way as French airfields had been intensively bombed in May, 1940, before the opening of the Battle of France, and British airfields, ports and industrial centres had been attacked in August, 1940—as a preliminary to the invasion of England.

29. The Soviet Air Force replied to these attacks of June, 1943, with several heavy raids on Orel and a series of night-attacks on the railway stations at Briansk, Roslavl and Gomel, through which German reinforcements were being transported. There was, thus, no element of surprise about either the probable time or place of the opening of the summer offensive, which began at dawn on July 5th with German attacks simultaneously on either side of the Kursk salient. General Jeschonnek, the German Chief of Air Staff, had not hesitated to mass the major part of German air power in the East, as well as all available reserves, in support of the offensive, in the conviction that the battle could only succeed if accorded the strongest possible backing by the Air Force. At least 1,000 first-line aircraft—i.e., 50 per cent. of the forces available for the whole Russian front from Murmansk to the Sea of Azov—were thrown in, and although this force was only two-thirds the size of that employed 12 months earlier for the advance on Stalingrad and into the Caucasus, the area of operations in 1943 was much more restricted, permitting an even greater concentration of effort. Hence, German air activity on the opening days of the offensive was on a remarkable scale, in the region of 3,000 sorties per 24 hours, with the dive bombers flying as many as five or six missions a day. By the end of the first week of operations the scale of effort had sunk by half, but a high average was maintained during the whole of July amounting to approximately 1,000 sorties per 24 hours. The German effort was, however, equalled by the Soviet Air Force which was fully prepared for the weight of the German attack ; the German Air Force, in spite of all its efforts, failed at any stage to secure decisive air superiority.

Failure of the Kursk Offensive (5th August, 1943)

30. This transfer of initiative from German to Soviet hands was a decisive factor in the air war in the East ; indeed, it was by steadily maintaining the initiative in face of immense German pressure that the Russians brought the German advance to a halt. About July 10th, the Germans had scored a definite initial success on the southern flank of the salient, in the region of Belgorod, by a concentration of close-support forces, in which the Ju.87 played its traditional rôle of cutting a path through the Soviet defences for the advancing troops. On July 15th, however, the Russians launched a counter-attack against Orel from the North, and this diversion compelled the Luftwaffe to weaken its concentration on the southern flank by the transfer of aircraft to the Orel area in order to check the Soviet advance. Immediately there followed a secondary Russian offensive on the Lower Donetz front. Here again, the Germans had considerable grounds for anxiety, since the concentration of first-line aircraft in the Kharkov-Belgorod area had left this sector weakly defended, principally by Rumanian and Hungarian units, and the Luftwaffe was thus forced to move further elements away from the main battle zone around Belgorod, this time to the southern front. In this way Soviet tactics enforced, from about July 20th, a dispersal of the available German air forces over three main areas (Orel, Belgorod and Stalino) and the undertaking of three distinct operations instead of the planned concentric attack on Kursk. Instead of a concentrated force of 1,000 or more aircraft, therefore, the Germans were from that time operating with three small forces each comprising about 450 aircraft. In these circumstances there was no question of wresting the initiative from or securing air superiority over the Soviet Air Force.

31. The failure of the German Air Force in face of the superiority of Soviet air planning and tactical skill in the conduct of air operations, was a major factor which enabled the Russians to halt the German drive against the Kursk salient and to go over to the offensive on their own account ; the German High Command had relied upon air power to break open a way for its armoured units[1]. By July 17th-18th the Russian front line on the northern flank of the salient had been re-established ; on July 21st-22nd, the Germans began a withdrawal from their wedge on the southern flank ; and on July 23rd, Stalin was able to announce the collapse of the German offensive. By August 4th, Orel was in Russian hands and on the same day Belgorod was recaptured. The reconquest of Orel and its fortified region marked the end of the first period of the summer campaign, and a radical change in the military situation. With the liquidation of the Orel salient the way was opened for the great Russian offensive of 1943.

Repercussions in the Air Staff : Jeschonnek's Suicide

32. After a long period of success, the whole German policy of concentration of offensive air power in support of the Army had been rendered bankrupt. The failure of the Kursk offensive, which Jeschonnek had backed with all available Luftwaffe strength, following upon the German defeat in North Africa, caused even Hitler to turn against his Chief of Air Staff. Relations between Jeschonnek and Goering had already been strained since the previous year, and earlier in 1943 the latter had suggested to Hitler that Jeschonnek should be replaced as Chief of Air Staff and be given command of a Luftflotte. This arrangement would have suited Jeschonnek, who was worried by his inability to resist Hitler, and he had already discussed with von Richthofen the possibility of the two exchanging their appointments. Hitler had refused to hear of such an arrangement ; now he declared in a speech that there was something wrong with the Luftwaffe, either in its technical development or its leadership—on reflection he considered it to be the latter. Jeschonnek, in a vain hope of transferring the blame elsewhere, drew up a list of Goering's mistakes, in which he pointed out that such mistakes had been made as a result of decisions which Goering had taken contrary to his own advice. Jeschonnek handed this document to von Below, Hitler's adjutant, but it was suppressed. A few days later Jeschonnek had a stormy telephone conversation with Hitler, in which it became obvious that he had lost both Hitler's and Goering's support and that he alone was being held responsible for the failure of the Luftwaffe. Hitler concluded the conversation with " —you know what is left for you to do now ". Jeschonnek shot himself.

33. It was given out to the World that he had died of a chronic disease, but this deceived nobody on the Air Staff, since Jeschonnek's reign was clearly at an end ; the policy he had backed had failed and his removal from office was already a foregone conclusion. Thanks to the fact that he had taken his own life, he had saved Hitler—as Udet had saved Goering—from admitting that his choice of a senior officer had been at fault.

---

[1] German aircraft losses, which in June had totalled 487, rose to 911 in July, and in August were 785. These monthly German Air Ministry figures cover the whole of the Eastern Front. As, however, the main German air effort on that front was in support of the operations outlined above, it may safely be assumed that the bulk of these heavy losses occurred in those operations. Soviet ground defences were responsible for a large number of German losses, particularly in the close-support categories.

GENERALOBERST KORTEN

Born 26.7.98. Entered a Field Artillery Regiment as a cadet in September, 1914. Served in a Pioneer Battalion during the war of 1914-18, and remained in the " Reichswehr " after it. Transferred to the Secret Air Force in April, 1934, becoming General Staff Officer to the Secretary of State for Air till October, 1936. Appointed Chief of Staff to the C.-in-C. Air Forces in Austria, Generalleutnant Loehr, in April, 1938. Appointed Chief of Staff Luftflotte 3, February, 1940, for the Western campaign ; Chief of Staff Luftflotte 4 in January, 1941 for the Balkan and start of the Russian campaign ; then A.O.C. Luftwaffe Command Don (Fliegerkorps I) in August, 1942. In June, 1943, Korten was appointed A.O.C.-in-C. Luftflotte 1, and in September he became Chief of Air Staff in succession to Jeschonnek. Died from injuries received in the attempt on Hitler's life, 25th July, 1944.

237

FIELD MARSHAL VON GREIM

Born 22.6.92. Entered a Royal Bavarian Railway Battalion as a cadet in 1911. Served in the Artillery as an observer at the beginning of the 1914-18 war, transferring to the Flying Corps as a pilot in October, 1916. Commanded Jagdstaffel 34 and Jagdgruppe 10. Active in " Sports " flying training, 1927-34. Entered the Secret Air Force January, 1934. Appointed Inspector of Fighters and Dive Bombers April, 1935 ; Inspector of Equipment and Safety February, 1936 ; and head of the Personnel Section of the Air Ministry, June, 1937. In February, 1939, von Greim became O.C. Flieger-division 5, later Fliegerkorps V, holding this post during the Western and Russian campaigns. Fliegerkorps V was renamed Luftwaffe Command East in April, 1942, and Luftflotte 6 in July, 1943. Appointed C.-in-C. of the Luftwaffe on 26th April, 1945 in succession to Goering. Committed suicide on being taken prisoner in June, 1945.

Korten as Chief of Air Staff

34. After Jeschonnek's death it was rumoured that von Richthofen would be the new Chief of Air Staff. Those who knew him, and knew his relationship with Goering, did not think this likely, however, as Richthofen was far too powerful and would have excluded Goering from any share in the leadership of the Air Force. After a good deal of discussion General Korten, who, it will be remembered, had only taken over the command of Luftflotte 1 in February of that year (paragraph 18), was appointed as Jeschonnek's successor.

35. Korten assumed command in September, 1943, but only on the understanding that his former assistant in Luftflotte 3, Koller[1], should be posted to him as chief of the Operations Staff. Koller, who at this time was Chief of Staff to Sperrle, A.O.C. of Luftflotte 3 in Paris, fought hard against the transfer ; he even induced Sperrle to put his signature to an unfavourable report which, however, did not succeed in deceiving Goering. Korten and Koller, close friends, arranged from the first that Korten's task would be to keep Goering in a good humour, whilst Koller should represent Korten's " tough " side— to be hard, objective and uncompromising with Goering, and only to fall back on Korten's protection when an impasse was reached. The primary objective of this partnership was indeed for a time achieved ; Goering again had confidence in his Chief of Air Staff, and Hitler's faith in the Luftwaffe— although not in Goering—was restored. Korten made prompt use of the power gained by his diplomacy.

Korten's Reforms

36. The new Chief of Air Staff was an upholder of the importance of strategic bombing and of fighter defence, and was on the side of the " defensive clique " which had slowly been gaining ground since the previous year. It was, therefore, natural that he should attempt to reverse the policy pursued by Jeschonnek of giving priority to the demands of the battle fronts and of maintaining the offensive at all costs. His aim was to reduce Luftwaffe operations in support of the Army to a minimum, and to relieve the situation by putting Germany in a position to defend herself whilst making the utmost use of her offensive forces in strategic bombing operations. This reversal of policy demanded changes, both in Air Staff organisation and in the composition of commands in the field.

37. The organisational changes which Korten brought about may be summarised in Koller's own words :—

> " We tried to split up the vast organisation of Obd. L. (*Oberkommando der Luftwaffe*—C.-in-C. Luftwaffe), to group all the parts which were necessary to the conduct of the war under a military command, and to detach them from the unessential sections of the Air Ministry ".

The result of this attempt was the new organisation which Koller was to take over when he himself became Chief of Air Staff 10 months later, and which was to remain unchanged in its essentials until the end of the war. The new organisation embodied the *Oberkommando der Luftwaffe* (High Command of the Air Force) which comprised the *Fuehrungsstab* (Operations Staff), *Waffengenerale* (Air Officers in Command of the various arms such as fighters, bombers, fighters, etc.), the Quartermaster-General's department and the Director-General of Signals (including Signals Intelligence).

---

[1] See illustration on page 406 for Koller's career.

38. One change long overdue was the formation of the new Ground Attack Command which had hitherto been subordinated partly to General Galland as Air Officer for Fighters, and partly to the Air Officer for Bombers ; in this way the Ground Attack arm was relieved of a double subordination in its fighter and bomber-type aircraft. Oberst Hitschhold, the new A.O.C., developed the arm on up-to-date lines, devoting particular attention to the anti-tank units and to their re-equipment with the FW.190 instead of the now obsolete Ju.87.

Plans for a Strategic Bomber Offensive against Russia

39. Korten's proposals for reducing the close-support forces in Russia and forming on the one hand a strategic bomber force and on the other a strategic fighter defence were rapidly developed. The latter proposal—to which weight was lent by the growing strength of Anglo-American air attacks on the Reich—was implemented by September, 1943, when ZG 26 and 76[1] and JG 3, 11, 53 and 27[2] were recalled from the Russian battle zone and employed for defence of the Reich. Korten's other proposal, to build up a strategic bomber force, encountered more substantial opposition, both from the *Oberkommando der Wehrmacht* (Supreme Command of the Armed Forces), which still thought in terms of maximum air cover for the armies in the field, and from Hitler himself. In the end, however, Korten's view prevailed, and in November, 1943, profiting from the unfavourable weather conditions which limited air activity, bomber units began to be withdrawn from close-support operations in the East for re-training, and a special pathfinder unit (II/KG 4), was set up. Control of the whole scheme was vested in Fliegerkorps IV, which ceased to operate as a close-support command early in December, and commencement of the new operations was scheduled for February, 1944. In collaboration with the Minister of War Production and the Intelligence Department, a comprehensive programme for attacking Soviet production and reserves of material was worked out ; it was considered possible, by a careful selection of key targets, to eliminate 50–80 per cent. of Soviet productive capacity, which amounted, in current German Intelligence estimates, to 3,500 tanks and 3,000 front-line aircraft per month.

Blitzkrieg In Reverse : The Russians Assume the Offensive (August, 1943 to May, 1944)

Russian Offensive of the Dnieper (August to December, 1943)

40. It is now necessary to return to the fighting in Russia and to follow air operations there from the end of August, 1943, at the time of the failure of the last major German attack on that front which produced the repercussions described above. During the remaining four months of 1943, air operations on the Russian front were dominated by the same factors which had been decisive in the closing stages of the battle for the Kursk and Orel salients, namely, German numerical inferiority and Soviet strategic initiative. After the reverse at Kursk, the German Air Force continued to operate hard in defence of the line of the Donetz ; but its forces were excessively extended, and with the initiative in Soviet hands it was compelled to adopt a makeshift policy of switching its units and its main effort from one sector to another of the front at the dictate of Russian pressure. It had, in fact, no margin of reserve.

---

[1] Twin engined fighter units.   [2] Single engined fighter units.

41. Its main forces, comprising some 900 aircraft, were at the beginning still concentrated in the area from Kharkov southwards in two groups, of which one faced East, covering the line Stalino–Taganrog, the other North-East opposing the Russian advance on the Dnieper via Kharkov and Poltava. After the fall of Kharkov and the evacuation of the Kharkov airfields on August 23rd, units from this area withdrew to air bases in the regions of Dnepropetrovsk, Krementschug, and Mirgorod for defence of the Dnieper line. But this concentration in the South, although essential so long as the Germans were determined to hold on to the Crimea and the land approaches to the Crimea along the shores of the Sea of Azov, meant a dangerous weakening of the northern flank of the great Ukrainian salient, which the Russians were quick to exploit. Through air reconnaissance the Russians were well aware of these weaknesses—which were reflected in parallel weaknesses in armoured ground forces—and planned their offensives accordingly. These reached maximum intensity in September, after long pressure had finally worn down German resistance in the Donetz Basin.

42. On August 27th and 28th, Soviet forces overran the whole area between Stalino and Taganrog, necessitating a strengthening of Fliegerkorps IV (which was entrusted with air operations on the southern extremity of the front) at the expense of Fliegerkorps VIII covering the Poltava–Kharkov sector. This reinforcement was, however, not quick enough to save Taganrog, which fell on August 30th. Meanwhile, after the Russians had recaptured Kharkov on August 23rd, they aimed a further offensive in a South-westerly direction from the Orel area towards Konotop ; for the Luftwaffe, this necessitated further transfers of units, which left the adjacent sector from Kiev to Chernikov virtually without air cover. Thus, the gradual concentration southwards of German close-support forces weakened air support on the central front, where on a line of 350–400 miles, only some 500 aircraft, including a high proportion of reconnaissance and army cooperation types, were available. Russian progress in this sector therefore encountered little air opposition, and Briansk and Smolensk fell to the advancing Soviet troops on September 17th and 25th, respectively.

43. The air situation in the East remained fundamentally unchanged in October when the Soviet forces, which had obtained bridgeheads across the Dnieper at the beginning of the month, began a major assault with the aim of occupying the Dnieper Basin. For about a week from October 20th, the German Air Force operated intensively against the Russian advance from Kremenchug (on the Dnieper) towards Krivoi Rog. All long-range bombers available on the whole southern front were concentrated for this task, many units flying in one day two sorties in this area followed by a third in the Kiev sector, 175 miles to the North, and there is little reason to doubt that air support on this scale, amounting to some 1,200 sorties per 24 hours for a period of 4–5 days, played an appreciable part in halting the Russian advance short of Krivoi Rog. But, once again, this concentrated and effective air effort was only possible as a result of substantial reinforcements at the expense of the central front. The consequent weakening of the German Air Forces between Kiev and the Pripet Marshes, in conjunction with a parallel shift southwards of ground forces, facilitated the Soviet breakthrough at Kiev, which was captured by the Russians on November 6th ; a rapid advance followed in a broad salient to Zhitomir. The critical situation resulting from the Soviet

241

advance to Zhitomir necessitated an immediate redisposition of German air as well as ground forces. Aircraft were switched from the Dnieper bend, where bad weather was now hampering air operations, for support of the counter-attack against the southern flank of the Russian salient, which began on November 15th, and carried the Germans back almost half-way along the road from Zhitomir to Kiev.

44. This small German defensive success, following on that at Krivoi Rog, virtually ended the period of operations beginning with the Russian capture of Orel in August, for bad weather conditions now curtailed air operations throughout the southern half of the front. But the position in which the Germans found themselves was very unsatisfactory. Kiev remained in Russian hands and the Russians had substantial bridgeheads across the Dnieper further South. In addition, the position in the Crimea, which had been cut off since the Russian advance to the Perekop Isthmus at the end of October, was precarious and constituted an abnormal and unproductive drain on German Air Force resources, for although the forces isolated there were small, comprising with Rumanian units some 185 close-support aircraft, they were forced to undertake defensive activity on a scale equivalent to that of the whole German Air Force in Italy at the same period, and wastage was consequently high. Furthermore, the Luftwaffe had the unwelcome commitment of protecting supply shipping proceeding to the Crimea from Rumanian ports and of escorting transport aircraft operating from Odessa and Nikolaiev.

45. Thus, in spite of the German retreat along the whole front, the Luftwaffe, with limited forces at its disposal, was as much extended in December as it had been in August. In spite of Russian pressure and major successes on the central front, the greater part of the Luftwaffe forces, comprising 1,150 out of 1,750 first-line aircraft, or approximately 64 per cent., was still engaged South of Kiev. This concentration, precluding effective air intervention elsewhere, was necessitated by the overriding need to hold the Russians at a distance from the oil resources of Rumania. The Germans were able to achieve a number of short tactical successes against advanced and vulnerable Soviet spearheads, but Luftwaffe intervention was now no longer on a scale or of a character formidable enough to exert direct influence over the broad outlines of strategy. At best it delayed the Soviet advance ; at worst it involved heavy wastage due to the employment of unescorted bombers and dive bombers in massive daylight raids over the front line, without compensatory results ; but in the main its effectiveness was frittered away in close-support operations which followed no strategic plan and were undertaken less in pursuance of a higher policy than at the behest of local military commands in the field.

Failure of Korten's Strategic Bombing Scheme (March, 1944)

46. Pressure from the Army Commanders through Hitler, and the events on the Russian front from August, 1943 to the end of December, 1943, outlined above, precluded any withdrawal of the bomber forces for their training for the proposed strategic bombing offensives—planned for February, 1944. The training scheme under Fliegerkorps IV was, in fact, only completed by March/April, 1944 ; by then, however, further Russian progress on the ground, forcing an evacuation westwards of German Air Force ground organisation, had carried many important targets, including Gorki, outside the range of the He.111. Re-equipment of units from He.111 to He.177 had, indeed, been

envisaged ; but this was held up by continued technical difficulties and—disregarding the brief appearance of KG 50 at Stalingrad at the end of 1942, which was a fiasco—the first He.177 unit did not appear on the Russian front until the summer of 1944, by which time the fuel situation had deteriorated to such an extent as to preclude sustained large-scale bomber operations.

Consequences of Failure

47. The failure of Korten's scheme seriously affected the fighting capacity of the German Air Force in Russia during the winter campaign of 1943-4 and throughout the spring of 1944. In the first place, the withdrawal of fighters which had taken place in the autumn of 1943 to bolster up the defences of the Reich was never made good, and the Russians could henceforward operate with impunity over the German lines. In the second place, Fliegerkorps IV—although occasionally thrown into action in support of the army at Hitler's command in moments of crisis—was to all intents and purposes out of the battle, with a corresponding decline in offensive power. Hence, the Air Force, which had been inadequate to sustain the weight of the Soviet summer offensive, was still less able to operate effectively against the winter offensive which followed. This became evident already at the end of December, when the Russians, having built up reserves, renewed their offensive West of Kiev, necessitating considerable immediate redisposition on the part of the Germans, by the transfer from the Lower Dnieper sector of 100 close-support aircraft (including all Hs.129 anti-tank units), whilst long-range bombers remaining in the South were, without moving their bases, subordinated for operations to Fliegerkorps VIII. The resultant scale of effort was, however, low (averaging only some 300-350 sorties per day) due in part to adverse weather, but in part also to the poor state of airfields, low serviceability and dislocation due to frequent moves of units. Furthermore, the move back of aircraft parks and supply depôts to central Poland, which now ensued, had adverse effects on maintenance and serviceability, which could not be kept up to standard at a distance of 400 miles over congested communications.

48. When, in the course of January, 1944, Russian pressure spread all along the front, with simultaneous offensives on the Leningrad, Rovne, Smela and Nikopol sectors and an expansion of the Soviet bridgehead in the eastern Crimea, it found the German Air Force throughout Russia weakened by long overdue withdrawals for rest and refit, by the reservation of Fliegerkorps IV for the planned strategic bombing operations, and by the employment of a proportion of the remaining bomber force on transport duties. While this latter commitment was in no wise comparable to the Stalingrad commitment a year earlier, by the beginning of February, when the regular Ju.52 transport service was primarily engaged on supplying the Crimea, He.111 bombers were being used to supply three Army Corps and to this burden the supply of the 6th Army, isolated in the Nikopol bridgehead, was added on February 5th. Thus, the Germans were thrown back in the main on their close-support forces at the very time when, in view of improvement in the quality and quantity of the Soviet fighter force, they had planned to withdraw Ju.87 dive-bomber units for re-equipment with the FW.190, and FW.189 units for re-equipment with the Me.109.

49. The strain under which the Luftwaffe, fully extended all along the line, was operating became manifest with the launching of the Russian offensives into southern Poland and Galicia which carried the Soviet advance to Tarnopol

by April 15th. This advance found the main forces of the Luftwaffe in South Russia concentrated in the Ukraine, East of the Lower Bug, in the expectation of further Russian pressure from the Krivoi Rog area towards the Dnieper estuary, in combination with an offensive from North and East to clear the Germans from the Crimea. Consequently, the initial German reaction, as the Russians advanced to the vital Lwow-Odessa railway, was weak, particularly as the bomber force, which alone could be switched without change of base against the new offensive, had sunk by the end of March—consequent on the disengaging of Fliegerkorps IV—to only 165 immediately available first-line operational aircraft in the whole of Russia, all of which had to be made available in the Ukraine. Furthermore, due to Russian pressure along the whole front, it was impossible to concentrate forces, which were broken up into small combat groups in order to provide a modicum of air cover against a numerically superior opponent ; in consequence, there were no forces to spare from any sector North of the Pripet Marshes. It was not until March 17th that all the forces under Luftflotte 4 in the South—i.e., units of both Fliegerkorps I and of Fliegerkorps VIII—were concentrated against the Russian spearheads, but by that time it was too late.

Russian Thrust to Rumania and Fall of the Crimea (March-May, 1944)

50. By a broad outflanking movement, the Russians were by mid-March threatening the Rumanian oilfields ; an incidental consequence of the Russian advance was political unrest in Hungary, against which German bombers had to be concentrated at Vierine, and single-engined fighters from the Balkan area at Belgrade and Nish, with a view to a " demonstration " against Budapest and support for airborne landings in Hungary and Bulgaria. More immediately important, however, were the consequences in the Ukraine, where the concentration of forces of Fliegerkorps I and Fliegerkorps VIII in the Yampol area left only the depleted and inefficient Rumanian Air Corps to support the defence of the line of the Lower Bug, which the Russians were crossing between Troitskoe and Voznesensk. Thus was facilitated the rapid Soviet advance from Nikolaiev, captured on March 28th, to Odessa, which the Russians occupied on April 10th. On the northern flank, also, between the Carpathians and the Pripet Marshes, the German Air Force was too weak to offer serious resistance to the Russian offensive in the Brody/Tarnopol area, of which the spearhead was aimed at Lwow. Having cleared the Black Sea littoral as far as the mouth of the Dniester, the Russians were also well placed for a major effort in the Crimea, which could now only be supplied either by air or by sea from Rumanian ports.

51. This imposed a heavy extra commitment on Fliegerkorps I, although there was no attempt to reinforce the small detached Crimean Command, which with only about 85 serviceable aircraft out of a total of 160 of all types, including Rumanian and other satellites, flew 2,400 sorties during the first week of the Russian assault. Nevertheless, Soviet air superiority was complete, and after the fall of Simferopol, the capital of the Crimea, on April 13th, the German Air Force was soon squeezed onto the few remaining airstrips at Sevastopol, which came under concentrated bombing and strafing from the Soviet Air Force, supported from April 17th by artillery fire ; by the 20th, the main airfield was no longer serviceable. In these circumstances wastage was particularly severe, amounting to 200-250 aircraft, mainly single-engined fighters, in the month's assault between April 8th and May 9th, apart from aircraft

which it was impossible to evacuate after the loss of the last remaining airstrip on May 8th. The evacuation of the Crimea also imposed a heavy strain on Luftwaffe units based on the Rumanian mainland. Torpedo-bombers from the western Mediterranean, twin-engined fighters which had been engaged on air defence of Austria, and a few FW.190's from the Balkans, amounting in all to 70-80 aircraft, were moved in haste to Rumania to provide added protection for evacuation convoys against Soviet naval and air opposition. Following upon Soviet night bombing of Constanza—the sole remaining large reception port for traffic from the Crimea—a Staffel of night fighters was also brought up. With these additional forces, the evacuation of the Crimea was eventually carried out with greater success than might, at one stage, have been anticipated.

52. With the Russian re-occupation of the Crimea the Soviet winter and spring offensive virtually came to an end (the front line at this time is shown in Map 21). In Northern Rumania it proved possible for the Germans to build a defensive front West of Iasi ; in Galicia the impetus of the Soviet drive died down, and although Lwow continued to be threatened, the city remained in German hands. Nevertheless, as at the end of the spring and autumn campaigns of 1943, the Russians finished the campaigning season with spring-boards in their hands for the next offensive. There were no natural defences to hold up an attack on eastern Poland, and the line of the Dniester, the natural defence of Rumania, was outflanked from the North. The Russian occupation of the Crimea exposed the Rumanian seaboard to amphibious attack, the threat of which remained a serious preoccupation for the Luftwaffe, while Rumania itself lay exposed to Soviet bombing from the East, and Anglo-American bombing from Italian bases. Along the whole eastern front the Russian position was such as to cause the German High Command continuous disquiet, and throughout May, 1944, nervousness over Soviet preparations for a new offensive necessitated regular bombing operations against vital points in the Soviet railway network, including Veliki-Luki in the North and Kiev in the South, while special operations were undertaken against railways between the Crimea and the mainland in order to impose maximum delay on the transfer to the mainland of troops no longer required in the Crimea.

German Air Force Redisposition on the Russian Front (May, 1944)

53. During May, 1944, considerable German redisposition took place with a view to a renewal of active operations at the beginning of the summer campaign. This indicated that defence of the Rumanian oilfields was still the major German preoccupation, and that they were in the unenviable position of having to sacrifice to this commitment the defence of Poland and therewith of Germany's *Lebensraum*[1] in the East. During the remainder of that month some 750 first-line aircraft, representing about 40 per cent. of the total on the whole eastern front, were concentrated in Bessarabia and Rumania, while the Rumanian Air Corps had already been extricated from the Ukraine and moved back to Rumania for overdue restoration of strength and serviceability. The change in the war situation was, however, best revealed by the fusion of the Russian and Balkan fronts and by the development of a new defensive network in the East of the Reich territory. Due to the rapid advance westward of the Russian front, two new Luftwaffe defence commands were now set up, with the titles " O.C. Fighters East Prussia " and " O.C. Fighters Upper Silesia ".

---

[1] A term much used by the Germans from about 1934 onwards, meaning "living space".

I*

These were contiguous authorities, separated roughly by the line Posen-Warsaw-Brest Litovsk, and they extended eastwards as far as Lwow in the South and to a line Vilna-Libau in the North. From Lwow southwards, on the other hand, Luftflotte 4—with headquarters at Rzeszow (90 miles west of Lwow)—was in undivided control. Its sphere of command, however, now no longer extended only to the battle-front, where Fliegerkorps I and Fliegerkorps VIII were still in tactical control, but also covered the air defence of Rumania and eastern Hungary, which were now threatened with sustained Anglo-American bombing in support of the Russian offensive.

54. This was an unwieldy command, for the mountain barriers and difficult communications prevented the quick interchange of forces (which had been a feature of operations in the Ukraine) between Fliegerkorps VIII North of the Carpathians and Fliegerkorps I defending the Dniester line South of Iasi. The two Fliegerkorps were now also distinct as regards ground organisation and supply, and the fact that the supply route to Rumania now ran through Hungary was one reason for placing the area East of the River Theiss under Luftflotte 4 control. The extension of the area of Luftflotte 4 over the Balkans was, however, necessitated primarily by Anglo-American air attacks on Danube ports and shipping and the mining of the Danube, which began in May in support of the Russian operations in the Crimea. These attacks revealed the need for unitary control of the fighter forces in the area, in order to obtain maximum employment of all available fighters—including those formerly committed exclusively to the Russian front—against long-range bombing from Italy. They reflected also the shrinkage of the battle front, which already made feasible a fusion of commands and necessitated the introduction of a system of air defence of the Balkans which simultaneously looked East and West. This was the result of the great Russian advance across the Ukraine in 1943 and 1944 ; but it was also the result of the Anglo-American victories in the Mediterranean. Nothing, however, more graphically symbolised the shrinkage of the battle fronts than the inauguration, on 2nd June, 1944, of American " shuttle " bombing across Europe to Russia and back to the 15th Air Force bases in Italy : the policy of shuttle bombing exploited at one and the same time the immensely increased strength of the U.S.A.A.F., the capture of an Anglo-American foothold on the Continent in Southern Italy, and the great Russian advances in face of the weight of German ground and air opposition, which were the outstanding features of operations in 1943.

Conclusion

Effects on the Eastern Front of the Mediterranean and Western Front Air Operations

55. It is no reflection on the achievements of the Soviet Air Force in 1943 and 1944 to point out the contribution which the simultaneous campaigns in the Mediterranean and the development to full strength of U.S.A.A.F. bombing of the Reich made to its victories. The history of the Russian campaigns of 1943 and 1943-44 is the clearest tribute to the tactical skill with which the Soviet Air Force exploited its air superiority, extending the smaller German Air Force opposed to it by constant and ever-shifting pressure up and down the front. But that air superiority, although registered in the victory at Kursk in

July, 1943, was only in part of Russian making. Without the pressure exerted by the Anglo-American air forces in the West and in the Mediterranean, the balance in the East would perforce have been radically different, just as the ground opposition to the landings in Sicily and Italy would have been radically different if the bulk of German divisions had not been tied down by the struggle in Russia.

56. Again and again through 1943 the inability of the German Air Force to make available reinforcements for the eastern front made itself felt ; it had no margin of reserves. In particular, its expanding fighter production was absorbed by the Anglo-American fronts, the fighter strength—which alone could assure air superiority—dwindled in Russia ; the total increase in single-engined fighter strength during 1943 went to the West and the South, and the Russian front was regularly starved of fighters. For that reason, the great successes of 1943 must be credited to the combined effort of Allied arms. A mark of the new times was the German decision, even before the Russian summer offensive of 1943 began, to move von Richthofen and his senior staff officers to the Mediterranean front in Italy, thus depriving the Russian front of its most experienced commanders and of the very persons who were responsible for the air contribution to the victorious counter-offensive at Kharkov in the spring of 1943.

57. The fact that for the Germans the Russian front lost its absolute priority after September, 1943, was indicated by the concentration of the most modern aircraft types on the Anglo-American fronts. Thenceforward, the East had to be content with its quota. Numerically, at the time of the launching of the German offensive against Kursk in 1943, the East still absorbed the greatest proportion of the available forces—over 40 per cent., as compared with 30 per cent. in the West, and about 15 per cent. in the Mediterranean—but by the beginning of 1944 even the numerical preponderance had gone, and first-line strength in the East had dropped to some 1,800 aircraft as compared with 2,600 operating in the West and in the defence of Germany against Anglo-American air attack. Hence, the failure of the German Air Force in Russia was merely a symptom of the growing air power of the Allies. This failure is, however, only fully apparent in the succeeding two chapters, where we turn from the eastern to the Mediterranean campaign, and then to the problem of defending German war industry from air attack.

(83331)

I*2

CHAPTER 11

THE MEDITERRANEAN CAMPAIGN, 1943–4

The Last Phase in North Africa (1st January to 12th May, 1943)

The German Air Force at the End of 1942

1. By the end of 1942 the position of the German forces in North Africa had been relatively stabilised. The German High Command was still faced with major problems of supply, and it had been compelled to reinforce the Mediterranean theatre on a scale which adversely affected its broad strategic planning ; but by vigorous measures it had recovered from the first shock of the Allied landings in French North Africa and had established an unexpectedly strong defensive position. In the West, the initial Allied thrust toward Bizerta and Tunis had failed, and the Allied air forces were faced with the problem of building up a ground organisation in an unfavourable terrain with inadequate communications. This problem was only gradually overcome, and in the meantime the German Air Force, which had shown considerably energy and capacity in developing airfields and ground organisation in Tunisia, was able to hold its own against numerically superior forces, particularly as the tardy Allied decision to release the latest types of Spitfire for the Mediterranean— contrasted with the immediate allocation of FW.190's from the Channel area— gave the Germans for a considerable period the advantage of technical superiority type by type. In the East, the voluntary German withdrawal from Agheila to the strong Buerat position materially eased German supply difficulties, while it also enabled the Luftwaffe to operate, not from second-rate desert landing grounds, but from old established and well-maintained airfields in the vicinity of Tripoli. The British Desert Air Force, on the contrary, like the British Eighth Army, was operating at the end of extended supply lines, and was compelled by supply and airfield problems to halt from time to time and consolidate its position before attempting another leap forward.

2. These conditions were all peculiarly favourable to the defence, and it is evident that the German High Command hoped that the natural obstacles confronting the Allies on both flanks of the German North African stronghold would offset Allied material superiority and produce a stalemate. The history of the North African campaign so far had, after all, been a tale of victorious armies on both sides unable to exploit their victories owing to insuperable difficulties of communications and supply ; the Germans could therefore not unreasonably count on their shorter supply lines and the possession of the ports of Tripoli and Tunis as a major factor in their favour. This advantage, however, was regarded solely from the point of view of defence. There is no evidence whatever at this stage indicating will and ability to go over from the defensive to the offensive ; and offensive actions undertaken in February, 1943, were both of a limited and local character, planned solely to maintain the integrity of the German defensive positions. Success in either case would have loosened the Allied stranglehold of the Tunisian strongpoint and postponed the final assault. Owing to the strained supply situation, the Germans had neither the material nor the manpower to do more ; they could not follow up a tactical success with a strategic offensive.

3. In these circumstances, therefore, the outcome of the North African campaign from the beginning of 1943 depended fundamentally on a solution of the problems of supply which faced both opponents. The ability of the Allies

to launch an offensive to drive the Axis from North Africa was conditional upon their ability, in the face of German opposition, to build up their own supplies and consolidate their forward positions—a problem of administrative organisation which is not within the province of this volume to describe—and upon the disruption, by Allied action, of the German lines of communication in order to cripple German powers of resistance. The predominance of these supply problems is reflected in the dispositions in the Mediterranean theatre at the beginning of 1943, as shown in the following table :—

German Air Force Dispositions, Mediterranean Theatre, 1st January, 1943

	Tripoli-tania	Tunisia	Italy, Sicily, Sardinia	Greece and Ægean	Total
L.R. Bombers	—	—	270	75	345*
L.R. Reconnaissance	5	—	30	20	55
Dive Bombers	20	20	10	—	50
Ground Attack	30	5	—	—	35
S.E. Fighters	70	90	35	15	210
T.E. Fighters	10	15	45	—	70
Tactical Reconnaissance ..	15	10	—	—	25
Coastal	—	—	—	10	10
Total	150	140	390	120	800*

4. It will be seen from the above dispositions that the Luftwaffe in North Africa relied upon two small tactical groups, equipped preponderantly with single-engined fighters, whose main task was the interception of Allied raiders and the protection of harbours and communications. A small ground-attack force of Ju.87's and FW.190 fighter-bombers was available for close-support, but no attempt was made to base long-range bombers in Africa. These were held at bases in Sardinia, Sicily and the Eastern Mediterranean for attacks on Allied convoys and North African disembarkation ports like Bône and Philippeville, and for escorting air transport convoys. Similarly, the bulk of twin-engined long-range fighters was based in Sicily to cover German sea traffic proceeding to Tunis. These dispositions are not explained simply by supply and maintenance difficulties limiting the size of the forces which could be based in Africa, although these difficulties played a part ; on the contrary, they were undoubtedly due to a clear realisation that the issue in North Africa would be decided by control of the Mediterranean, and that the main task for the Luftwaffe was to dispute Allied mastery of the Mediterranean and to ensure the maintenance of Axis supply traffic across the Sicilian straits.

5. In these circumstances, therefore, the course of air warfare in Africa was only of secondary importance, the most notable feature being the ability of the Luftwaffe to maintain the strength of its close-support forces in Africa at a figure of 300-330 aircraft from the beginning of January to the middle of April. This, and the average high serviceability was a co siderable achievement in face of the absolute Allied numerical superiority and tie subjection of Axis forward airfields to Allied air attack. It was secured by diverting a high proportion of single-engined fighter output to the Mediterranean theatre, the flow of single-engined fighter replacements to the Mediterranean having risen from some

* There were in addition a further 90 aircraft of L.R. Bomber units employed on coastal operations, supply duties (FW.200), or not actively engaged in N. Italy.

150 aircraft a month at the end of 1942 to 260 a month in April, 1943. This achievement, although it meant a disproportionate drain on single-engined fighter replacements at a time when the German Air Force as a whole was engaged on a large-scale programme for re-equipping and expanding the single-engined fighter arm, succeeded in its immediate object. For three months the Luftwaffe was able to operate effectively in Africa, and it was only in the second week of April, when it fell back to the few remaining airfields East and South-East of Tunis, that the Allied air forces re-established the complete air supremacy which they had enjoyed at Alamein.

The Allied Offensive Reopens

6. The Allied offensive, which had come to a halt in December, 1942, when the Germans withdrew from the Agheila to the Beurat position, reopened on 15th January, 1943 and resulted in the Allied capture of Tripoli on January 23rd. Air operations during this battle were on a considerable scale, and German Air Force losses relatively high. By the time of the withdrawal from Tripolitania to Tunisia, single-engined fighter strength was down to 75 aircraft with serviceability as low as 45-50 per cent., while of the fighter-bomber force only about 10 aircraft out of 25 were serviceable. But the German Air Force, cutting down effort to 40-50 sorties per 24 hours, made the most of the lull which followed whilst the Eighth Army was moving up against the Mareth position, and thus quickly restored strength and serviceability. At the same time, it profited from the respite to carry through a reorganisation in which the forces hitherto divided between Tripolitania and Tunisia were placed under a single operational command, known as *Fliegerkorps Tunis*.

7. This change permitted greater flexibility in the employment of forces on either flank, as circumstances required, and was undoubtedly a factor contributing to Luftwaffe success in the face of a superior enemy. Its effectiveness became evident in mid-February, when the possibility of an Allied breakthrough from central Tunisia towards Sfax, threatening to divide the armies of Rommel and von Arnim, compelled the German Command to launch a counter-attack to widen the Gafsa-Sfax bottleneck. In support of this operation a considerable Luftwaffe force was moved down from northern Tunisia to the Kairouan-Sfax area, and on February 14th some 360-375 sorties were flown in support of the successful German thrust towards Feriana and Sbeitla. An effort of approximately 250 sorties per 24 hours was maintained on the following two days, and the scale of air support only fell thereafter as a result of exceptionally bad flying weather. Meanwhile, however, the German Command energetically exploited its success in central Tunisia by opening an offensive, beginning on February 26th, against the Allied First Army in the North. Here also, in spite of its notable contribution to the success of the thrust towards Sbeitla, the Luftwaffe provided effective support with the small forces available, averaging some 150 close-support sorties per 24 hours for the first four days in operations.

8. The German close-support in North Africa thus proved unexpectedly resilient and effective, and even after three weeks of sustained operations following the opening of the Eighth Army attack on the Mareth Line on March 19th, its strength was still over 300 aircraft, of which 60 per cent. were serviceable. Having regard to its limited size, it accomplished with success the tasks committed to it, maintaining a high average scale of effort at all periods of operational activity. From a force of the size allocated, the German armies

251

could not have hoped for more efficient support, and its history is a classic example of what may be accomplished, in the face of a superior enemy, by a small, compact force of high morale and efficiency, although outnumbered. But the fate of the German contingents in North Africa was dependent less on *Fliegerkorps Tunis*—which held out with tenacity and determination until the last three weeks of the campaign, by which time the deterioration of the ground situation had seriously impaired its ground organisation—than on the long-range bomber forces which alone could impede the Allied build-up and disrupt Allied preparations for attack. It was the failure of the long-range bombers which decided the issue.

Eclipse of the Bomber Force

9. This failure—the first clear indication of the insufficiency of the German bomber force in the new conditions of war—had many causes. First in importance was the inability to recover from the severe losses incurred in the intensive operations during the month following the Allied landings in French North Africa on 7th November, 1942. During December three Gruppen, representing an establishment of 90 aircraft, had to be withdrawn for rest and refitting, and by December 31st, long-range bomber strength had dropped from a peak of 310 aircraft to 270, of which only some 55 per cent. were serviceable. These enforced withdrawals continued throughout the winter months, and were only partially offset by the return of re-equipped units to operations. This failure to maintain the flow of newly rested units was due to the dislocation of the training programme, which had occurred in consequence of the Stalingrad commitment. Particularly weighty was the closure of specialised schools, which cut down the supply of highly-trained torpedo-bomber crews. Hence, the operational efficiency of the torpedo-bomber arm, as well as its operational strength, underwent an eclipse. Compared with an establishment of 90-100 aircraft, strength at no time in the first four months of 1943 exceeded 50-60, and by early April serviceability fell to such a degree that not more than 5-10 crewed serviceable aircraft were available at any one time for operations.

10. The main German weapon for attacking Allied supply convoys, the torpedo-bomber, in this way failed totally in its allotted task. The remainder of the German bomber force in the Mediterranean suffered scarcely less seriously from the same factors. In addition, shortage of specialised and modern convoy escort aircraft—a factor almost inevitable in an air force built up expressly for land warfare—necessitated the misemployment of the German bomber force for escorting German convoys. How far this diversion to escort duties impinged upon the orthodox offensive duties of the long-range bomber force is seen in the following analysis of long-range bomber sorties during the first four months of 1943 :—

Daily Average Effort	Attacks on Convoys	Attacks on Ports	Convoy Escort	Ground Targets Tunisia	Miscellaneous	Total
January	11	5	12	1	6	35
February	8	2	11	—	6	27
March	8	4	13	13	12	50
April	2	5	11	15	11	44
Average daily sorties January – April, 1943	7–8	4	12	7–8	8–9	39

11. The above table reveals that one-third of the total bomber effort during the first four months of 1943 was expended on escorting Axis convoys across the Mediterranean. It also reveals the low average effort maintained by a force which never fell below 200 aircraft. Moreover, it will be noted that a high proportion of Ju.88 effort in March and April was employed in night operations against ground targets in the battle area. This was necessitated by the failure of the African-based Ju.87's and Hs.129's against strong Allied fighter opposition ; but it meant the diversion of aircraft from strategic bombing at a time when the Allied supply ports in Algeria offered targets of the first importance. Nothing is more notable than the failure to maintain any appreciable effort against the Allied disembarkation points. This was due partly to the widespread dispersal of aircraft as far East as the Aegean in a mistaken endeavour to interfere with Allied shipping throughout the length and breadth of the Mediterranean instead of concentrating on the operationally vital area. It was due also to the difficulty of maintaining adequate supplies and servicing facilities on advanced bases, particularly in Sardinia.

12. These factors made it difficult to assemble a powerful striking force at any one point. They were aggravated, but not until the end of March, by heavy Allied attacks on Sardinian airfields, inflicting considerable aircraft losses and resulting in a steep decline in serviceability, which necessitated the withdrawal of units to the Italian mainland ; thereafter Sardinia was used mainly as an advanced landing ground. Yet none of these factors was as important as the deterioration in quality after the best aircrews had been used up in the intensive operations of November and December. By the beginning of 1943 this deterioration was so pronounced that a large proportion of the extraordinarily small effort against ports and convoys was abortive : owing to inadequate training, the inexperienced crews increasingly failed to locate their targets.

13. The total eclipse of the long-range bomber and torpedo-bomber force in the early months of 1943 materially facilitated the Allied preparations for the final assault which began on March 19th. By failing to prevent, or even appreciably hinder, the Allied build-up, the German Air Force permitted the establishment of overwhelming ·Allied material superiority. On the other hand it failed to provide adequate protection for German sea and air transport. This was due to overall fighter weakness, the result of the failure to carry through an adequate programme of fighter expansion in 1942. The Me.110 and Me.210 aircraft employed for escorting sea and air convoys were no match for the Allied fighters, and the numbers of Me.109's available were too small to carry out this task effectively, except at the expense of close-support. When it proved necessary, as the Allied ring round Tunis and Bizerta was drawn tighter and Allied interference with Axis supply traffic correspondingly increased, to divert an increasing proportion of the single-engined fighters of *Fliegerkorps Tunis* to escort duties, the result was impairment of the close-support effort ; indeed, in the last weeks of the African campaign the problem of providing adequate fighter screens, patrols and escort not only for convoys but also for reconnaissance aircraft and close-support units, assumed insuperable dimensions.

14. By mid-April these difficulties were enhanced by problems of servicing and maintenance, which became acute when all elements of the Luftwaffe in Tunisia were thrown together on a small number of airfields near Tunis and Bizerta. Vulnerable to Allied attack, which reduced serviceability, often

prevented from taking off by standing Allied fighter patrols, and beset by maintenance and fuel shortage problems, the performance of the aircraft of *Fliegerkorps Tunis* declined markedly in the last three weeks.

15. Gradually units were withdrawn in whole or in part to Sicily in order to avoid losses on the ground. The first withdrawals were bomber reconnaissance types and dive bombers ; but later fighters also were transferred, flying daily to advanced landing grounds in Tunisia. At the beginning of May, strength in Africa had fallen to some 200 aircraft, of which all were fighter types. In the following 12 days it declined even further, until at the end all landing grounds were overrun, and all attempts to provide air cover for the evacuation had to be made from Sicily. But due to the disorganisation resulting from piecemeal withdrawal of fighters from Africa, these efforts were weak and unsuccessful. In the last days of the North African battle the German Air Force in the Mediterranean although still comprising over 800 aircraft, was an effete force, completely unable to achieve effective intervention : its influence in the last days of the campaign was nil, and Allied aircraft and naval craft were able to patrol with impunity off Cape Bon, preventing evacuation and reducing the defeat of German arms in Africa to a disaster.

The Invasion of Sicily (14th May to 17th August, 1943)

Reorganisation after the Collapse in North Africa

16. The collapse of Axis resistance in North Africa left the Luftwaffe faced by a multiplicity of problems which absorbed its attention, to the detriment of other commitments, throughout May and June. First in importance was the restoration of the strength and serviceability of flying units exhausted in the North African battles. Next was the reinforcement of the Mediterranean theatre, in view of the proved insufficiency of the forces allocated in the early months of the year. In addition, there was the strategic problem of redisposing the available forces to meet the multiple threats of Allied landing operations. This necessitated the strengthening and development of ground organisation, particularly in outposts such as Sardinia, to provide adequate servicing for the redistributed flying units. It also required careful appreciation of the probable direction of the main Allied thrust, in order to operate the available forces with maximum economy and effect.

17. To meet the new situation a reorganisation and strengthening of the German Air Force operational commands was carried through without delay. In the first place, the Mediterranean theatre, hitherto centralised under Luftflotte 2 commanded by Kesselring, was divided into two separate commands, each of Luftflotte status, Luftflotte 2 now covering only Italy and the Central Mediterranean, and the other (Luftwaffe Command South-East), S.E. Europe including Greece, Crete and the Balkans. This division beyond doubt was precipitated by the possibility of Allied landing operations in either area and in order to ensure greater ease in the conduct of operations. Simultaneously, the Luftwaffe headquarters staff in the Mediterranean, which had shown itself lamentably wanting in ability and energy, was strengthened by the transfer of energetic and experienced officers from Russia. Field Marshal von Richthofen[1] himself took over command of Luftflotte 2 in the Central

---

[1] See Chapter 10, paragraph 25, for the parallel reorganisation in Russia.

254

The Me.323 transport aircraft, used extensively in the supply of Tunisia from Sicily

General Galland (right) leaving the headquarters of KG.54 at Catania (Sicily).

A Luftwaffe Staffel (Squadron) commander and his Ju.88.

Mediterranean. Under him, in command of Fliegerkorps II, was General Buelowius formerly in command of an army cooperation corps in Russia. Tactical command in Sicily was given to Generalleutnant Mahncke, previously commanding *Fliegerdivision Donetz* and as such responsible for driving the Russians back beyond Kharkov in March, 1943. Apart from these and other staff officers from Russia, Generalmajor Harlinghausen was relieved of command of the Mediterranean bomber units and replaced by Oberst Peltz, a coming man who earlier in 1943 had been charged with the conduct of operations against England[1]. At the same time General Galland, Inspector of Fighters and Ground-Attack aircraft, was detached to the Mediterranean on an extended tour of duty with the task of speeding up the supply of fighter pilots and aircraft and restoring efficiency and morale.

18. These measures are an indication of a set determination to oppose the expected Allied landing attempts with the best personnel and forces available. They show, perhaps more graphically than anything else, that the German Air Force appreciated that the Allied attack, when it came, would be on a scale demanding first rate experience and ability. No effort was spared to strengthen the German Air Force in the Mediterranean to the maximum possible extent in anticipation of the invasion of the European continent which was clearly regarded as inevitable. Hence, in a period of only $1\frac{1}{2}$ months, an increase in strength was achieved, amounting to 440 aircraft, or more than 50 per cent., with a corresponding rise in serviceability. This increase is set out by type and by area in the following comparative table, which shows strength in the Mediterranean on the morrow of the loss of North Africa and on 3rd July, 1943, when the air operations began which heralded the assault on Sicily :—

	14 May, 1943			3 July, 1943		
	Central Med.	Eastern Med.	Total	Central Med.	Eastern Med.	Total
L.R. Bomber	260	40	300	260	40	300
Dive Bomber	—	—	—	—	65	65
Ground Attack	70	—	70	150	—	150
S.E. Fighter	180	10	190	380	70	450
T.E. Fighter	120	5	125	100	10	110
L.R. Recce.	45	30	75	60	45	105
Tac. Recce.	20	—	20	25	25	50
Coastal	—	40	40	—	50	50
Total	695	125	820	975	305	1,280

19. The reinforcements brought up during May and June, 1943, besides revealing the importance attached to the defence of southern Europe, indicated that the German Air Force had well and truly learned the lessons of Allied air superiority in the African campaign. The paramount importance of adequate fighter defences was now a guiding principle, and it is notable that 260 out of 440 additional aircraft available (or almost 60 per cent. of the reinforcements) were single-engined fighters. In addition the Ju.87, which had proved too vulnerable in the later stages of the Tunision fighting, was relegated to the eastern Mediterranean, which was beyond the range of Allied single-engined

---

[1] See Chapter 8, paragraph 28 *et seq.*

fighters. Instead, a serious effort to improve the quality of close-support was made by the transfer from the West of additional FW.190 fighter-bombers, hitherto engaged on harassing attacks against South and South-East England. The increase in single-engined fighter strength was achieved without drawing units from other fronts ; but two newly-formed units, probably intended to strengthen the fighter defences of the Reich, had to be sent to the Mediterranean, which also received a disproportionately high percentage of Me.109 and FW.190 replacement aircraft direct from the assembly plants. The Mediterranean allocation of single-engined fighter types during the period 1st May-15th July, 1943 is calculated to have exceeded 40 per cent. of total production ; on the other hand, no expansion of long-range bomber strength took place. A number of units were withdrawn for rest and re-equipment, and their place taken by others recently refitted ; but it proved impossible to remedy fully the deficiencies caused by the heavy losses in Russia and the Mediterranean at the end of 1942. Nevertheless, the force of 300 bombers available was considerable enough, if only its fighting efficiency could be restored : this was the task facing Peltz, and on his success or failure depended the weight of resistance to the Allied invasion fleets.

20. After the end of the North African campaign the German Air Force had almost two months in which not only to complete its redispositions, but also to hinder Allied preparations for the assault by attacks on shipping and invasion ports. In both respects it signally failed to make the most of its opportunities. Through a skilful use of " cover plans " and of diversionary tactics, the Allies kept the German High Command guessing where the main blow would fall, and thus brought about a wide dispersal of Luftwaffe forces which went far to offset the increased strength available. For an appreciable period the Germans believed that the main Allied attack was likely to be directed against Greece or Crete, and as a result aircraft strength in the eastern Mediterranean, very weak at the time of the Axis collapse in Tunisia, was by the end of June more than doubled. A similar threat led to the doubling of the forces in Sardinia. Furthermore, much effort was diverted to the building up of a ground organisation in southern France, which was also believed to be threatened, and in the course of June and July an appreciable force was stationed in this area. How these multiple threats reacted on German dispositions is clear from the following table :—

	14.5.43	1.6.43	14.6.43	3.7.43	10.7.43
Sardinia	80	80	115	175	115
Sicily	415	275	315	290	175
Central and S. Italy	200	360	290	345	460
S. France and N.W. Italy ..	—	80	80	165	135
Greece and Crete	125	185	220	305	265
Total	820	980	1,020	1,280	1,150

21. The remarkable fact emerging from the above table is the extraordinarily slight fluctuation, in spite of the rapid increase in the total force available, in the combined strength of the German Air Force in Sicily and southern Italy. This amounted to 615 aircraft on May 14th and had only increased to 635 aircraft at the date of the invasion of Sicily. This failure to build up the German

Air Force in the region finally chosen for the Allied assault, while partly the consequence of Allied air attacks on Sicilian airfields, making Sicily untenable as a long-range bomber base, was the direct result of the necessity for providing against potential Allied threats to other areas, which the Germans were never able completely to discount. Even in the last week, between July 3rd and 10th, Allied air attacks on Sardinia helped to maintain German uncertainty as to the direction of the impending blow.

22. If one factor restricting German resistance to the initial assault on Sicily was a dispersal of forces, the other was a failure to make full use of the respite after the end of the North African campaign. No serious attempt was made at any time to interfere with Allied preparations. This failure was due in large measure to successful Allied bombing of Sardinian and Sicilian airfields during June, which drove the Luftwaffe off the bases from which concentrations in North African ports could most effectively be attacked. The long-range bomber force was driven back first to central Italy, and then in part to northern Italy and southern France ; and although an attempt was made to use Sicilian and Sardinian airfields as advanced landing grounds, the scale of effort inevitably declined. Sporadic long-range bomber operations, mainly against Bône and Bizerta, took place in May and June, but the attacks were half-hearted and the Luftwaffe failed to maintain a consistent long-range bomber effort by night.

23. Thus, as in the closing stages of the North African campaign, the outstanding weakness remained, the failure of the long-range bomber force to intervene effectively at any stage in operations. Although the Germans at no time had less than 250 to 300 bombers available, only on few occasions did more than 50 to 60 aircraft reach the target area, the average being 25 to 30, and results were negligible. This weakness, although attributable in part to low service-ability averaging only 55 per cent. of strength, was primarily due to the persistent shortage of fully-trained crews, which had now become endemic. Owing to the serious crew situation only some 50 per cent. of the serviceable aircraft could be manned at any one time, thus reducing the scale of effort on any one occasion to between one-third and one-quarter of total bomber strength. Furthermore, the incompletely trained crews failed to press home their attacks or even to locate their targets, and losses—due often to faulty navigation were disproportionately high, amounting almost regularly to 10-15 per cent. of the force engaged.

24. Hence, the Allies were able to complete their preparations for the assault on Sicily virtually undisturbed, and the operations against Lampedusa and Pantelleria early in June provided a valuable clue to the low fighting value of the German Air Force, in spite of its numerical recovery. In these operations no attempt was made to interfere either with the Allied bombing which broke the island defences, or with departure ports or the fleet at sea, although the latter was sighted at an early stage by reconnaissance aircraft. It was only after the Allied occupation of the islands on June 11th and 12th that Luftwaffe activity increased, with attacks on shipping lying offshore. For these attacks the Germans relied principally on FW.190 fighter-bombers with fighter escort ; the long-range bomber effort remained weak, amounting only to some 25 Ju.88 sorties per night, in spite of excellent targets available. The same long-range bomber weakness was evident later in the month, as Allied preparations reached their culmination : during the whole fortnight preceding the invasion of Sicily only two long-range bomber attacks were carried out against North African ports.

259

Allied Landings in Sicily

25. An intensive Allied bombing offensive, which began on July 3rd and continued without respite for a week, gradually wore down the German fighter defences. Between July 3rd and July 10th—the day of the assault—German Air Force strength in the central Mediterranean was reduced by over 100 aircraft, half of which were lost in Sicily, whilst many Sicilian airfields were made unusable. Hence, all serviceable FW.190's had to be withdrawn from Sicily to the Naples area, using Sicilian airfields thenceforward as advanced landing grounds only. At the same time single-engined fighter strength in Sicily was reduced from 185 aircraft on July 3rd to 100 aircraft on July 9th, the decrease including about 50 aircraft transferred to Calabria and Apulia to avoid the weight of Allied bombing. A similar weakening of the German Air Force by Allied bombing occurred simultaneously in Sardinia, where in the course of one week's operations the serviceability of the fighter-bomber force was reduced from 55 per cent. to 35 per cent. of strength. Thus, Allied attacks, which prevented the use of Sardianian airfields as advanced landing grounds for long-range bombers, also weakened the single-engined fighter and fighter-bomber forces available in Sardinia for transfer to Sicily as soon as the invasion of Sicily began.

26. When the invasion of Sicily began on the night of July 9th-10th, Luftwaffe defences were therefore already seriously weakened. The withdrawal of fighter-bombers to the Naples area meant that this force, on which the Luftwaffe relied for attacks on landing craft and beaches, was based some 200 miles away from the scene of operations. A proportion of single-engined fighters was likewise outside effective range, some elements having been withdrawn to the Italian mainland and others remaining isolated in western Sicily, since even after the Allied landings between Pachino and Gela had taken place, the Germans considered that these might be feints to cover a main landing in the West, and therefore held air forces in the Palermo area.

27. In these circumstances the Luftwaffe reaction to the Allied assault was hesitant and lacked coordination, its effort being dissipated between the Gela–Licata and the Syracuse–Pachino areas. At the same time the weight of the Allied air attack on the Sicilian airfields necessitated the diversion of a large proportion of the German fighter forces still left on the island to defence, thus effectively diminishing the scale of offensive operations. Hence, the scale of effort in the early stages reached only a moderate level. Between July 10th and July 12th an average of some 275 to 300 sorties per 24 hours by all categories was maintained, 50 per cent. being by night. In face of overwhelming Allied air superiority even this mediocre reaction was not maintained, and thereafter the average effort fell to only about 150 sorties per day, including fighters and fighter-bombers based in southern Italy and Sardinia which moved forward daily to landing grounds in Sicily. As early as July 12th the scale of effort was adversely affected by the evacuation of advanced airfields, and the consequent disorganisation of ground staff and the servicing organisation ; by July 19th Allied bombing had reduced the serviceability of fighters and fighter-bombers in Sicily and southern Italy to 35 per cent. of actual strength. In these circumstances the German Air Force had no alternative save to withdraw. By July 16th only 120 aircraft (of which not more than 30 were serviceable) remained in Sicily, and by the 18th the total had sunk to 25. All

that remained of the German and Italian Air Forces in Sicily were some 1,100 destroyed or damaged aircraft abandoned on the ground : of these, approximately 600 were German.

Defeat of the Luftwaffe in Sicily

28. With this total defeat, the Luftwaffe was virtually eliminated. A small force, comprising some 50 FW.190 and Me.110 fighter-bombers and 50 to 60 single-engined fighters was maintained in the toe of Italy for support of the troops fighting a rearguard action in the Catania area. But fighting at extreme range, with limited airfield facilities, and vulnerable to Allied air attack, this small force was a negligible factor. Only in the last phase of operations, from August 14th to 17th, when it was necessary to provide cover for the evacuation of the remnants of the German troops from Sicily, was there an increase of effort, and single-engined fighter sorties, which previously had averaged only about 60 per 24 hours, rose to an average scale of 150 sorties per day. But, from the time of the evacuation of the German Air Force from Sicily, which took place on July 22nd, the Air Force command was less concerned with the battle which was continuing than with effecting recovery from the costly reverse which it had suffered in order to be ready for the defence of the Italian mainland. Every effort was thus made to restore strength and serviceability, and at the end of July, two single-engined fighters, two fighter-bombers and one twin-engined fighter Gruppe, all badly mauled in the Sicilian fighting, were withdrawn for re-equipment. Simultaneously, other units remaining on operations reduced their scale of effort, so as to conserve aircraft and build up strength.

29. Meanwhile on the Italian mainland, airfield development was carried on apace so as to have adequate bases ready for the recuperated units. The Germans were well aware that they could not expect a respite such as had followed the conclusion of the African campaign, and their preparations for the defence of the Italian mainland could therefore not await the conclusions of the Sicilian campaign. Nevertheless, the drastic losses inflicted in Sicily could not be made good, and when the Allied forces—after under three weeks' halt—crossed the Straits of Messina and landed at Reggio on September 3rd, German Air Force strength in the Mediterranean had fallen from the peak figure of 1,250 aircraft at the beginning of July to only 880 aircraft, the lowest figure since the loss of Tunisia in the middle of May. This decline, which marked the end of any attempt by the Luftwaffe to contest Allied air superiority in the Mediterranean, was partly due to the extraordinarily heavy wastage suffered in the Sicilian campaign ; but a second factor had by now come into play. During August, units representing an establishment of 210 aircraft were withdrawn, and all but one were transferred to the western front. The Mediterranean had now finally and irrevocably lost its priority.

The Allied Invasion of Italy (3rd September to 1st October, 1943)

Strength of the German Air Force in Italy

30. With a Luftwaffe force of only approximately 625 aircraft covering the whole of the western and central Mediterranean area, including southern France, Sardinia and Corsica, as well as Italy, a major reaction to the Allied landings on the toe of Italy was out of the question. There were only about 120 single-engined fighters and 50 fighter-bombers in the whole of central and southern Italy, and the few low quality airfields in Calabria, exposed to Allied

261

bombing, were inadequate to hold an appreciable close-support force. Thus, the effort on September 3rd, when the Allied forces landed at Reggio, was only in the region of 110 fighter and 40 fighter-bomber sorties, the latter in the landing area, with a proportion of the fighters providing escort and the remainder maintaining defensive patrols over German airfields. The long-range bomber force, now concentrated in the Foggia area, was not employed at all against the landings. Instead, on the night of September 2nd-3rd, about 35 aircraft attacked a convoy off the North African coast, and on the night of September 6th-7th, there was a further heavier but ineffective raid by about 80 aircraft on Bizerta. This use of the bomber force, in conjunction with the weak reaction to the Allied landings in Calabria, indicated that the Germans were awaiting a more dangerous threat than an Allied invasion of the very tip of the Italian peninsula ; and this was proved by the vigorous and immediate reaction when, on September 8th, the Allied invasion fleet sailed into the Gulf of Salerno.

The Salerno Bridgehead

31. There is no doubt that the German Air Force made an all-out effort to liquidate the Allied bridgehead at Salerno. For ten days the close-support forces maintained the high average of two sorties per serviceable aircraft, beginning with some 170 sorties on September 8th and rising to a peak effort on the 13th in support of the counter-attack by the German ground forces, which seriously threatened the bridgehead. The FW.190 fighter-bombers, which operated effectively against shipping and landing craft, were supported by Me.109's equipped to carry 21-cm. mortars. Most significant of all, however, was the revival of the long-range bomber force. On the night of September 8th-9th approximately 155 bomber and torpedo-bomber sorties were flown, and a further effort of 100 sorties was attained on the night of September 10th-11th. This effort was stronger than anything attained since the operations against Malta in March, 1942. In addition, two new weapons, the radio-controlled bomb and glider-bomb were successfully introduced in daylight operations by specially equipped Do.217 bombers: on an average one hit with either the " FX " or " Hs.293 " type of missile was attained per 15 sorties.

32. This high effort was only possible at the expense of the southern front, where the Eighth Army was left to advance with virtually no Luftwaffe opposition. Their rapid progress, by forced marches, eventually liquidated the threat to the Salerno bridgehead. After September 17th, the approach of Allied ground forces to the airfields of Foggia, the evacuation of which by the Germans was completed by September 25th, rapidly eliminated Luftwaffe activity against the Salerno area. By September 21st all remaining fighter and fighter-bomber units had withdrawn at least as far as the Rome and Viterbo areas and, fighting at extreme range, were unable to afford appreciable air support. Furthermore, half of the forces were moved north to the Pisa area to cover the evacuation of Sardinia and Corsica, which was one of the immediate consequences of the Salerno landing and of the Italian capitulation. With the occupation of Naples on October 1st, the Allied hold on southern Italy was stabilised, since Naples provided the necessary harbourage for maintenance of supply. With the occupation of the Foggia airfields, on the other hand, the Allied bomber forces had at length secured a major base on the continent of Europe, and henceforth threatened Germany from the south.

Effect of the Collapse of Italy

33. The German failure to liquidate the Salerno bridgehead thus marked a stage in the Mediterranean war. The Germans had failed in their main purpose, and the collapse of Italian resistance—militarily unimportant, but politically significant—reflected this failure. The Allies had a firm lodgement in Italy, but on the other hand the Germans possessed naturally strong defensive positions between Naples and Rome. Hence, a rapid Allied advance by a frontal attack was unlikely, and the necessity for keeping strong German close-support air forces in Italy correspondingly small. On the other hand, Germany was now vulnerable to air attack from Italian bases, and consequently there were added reasons for strengthening the fighter defences of the Reich at the expense of the Italian front where, owing to the difficult terrain, adequate defensive measures were possible without calling upon the Luftwaffe for intensive operations.

34. The Italian capitulation had furthermore created a precarious situation throughout the eastern Mediterranean. The whole German position in the Balkans, Ionian Islands and Aegean was compromised by the defection of Italian garrisons on the numerous islands which were of primary importance for the strategical and tactical defence of the eastern theatre, and the Germans were confronted with the possibility of immediate Allied occupation of key points from which an attack on the Balkan mainland might be launched. Hence, after the failure to liquidate the Anglo-American bridgehead at Salerno, interest turned away from Italy. Following the Allied occupation of Naples, a static period set in, and from mid-October the seasonal deterioration in the weather imposed a further limitation on air operations. Italy had sunk to the level of a secondary theatre in the air war, and the primary German interest in the Mediterranean was to restore its shaken position in the Ionian Islands and the Dodecanese, the outer bulwarks of its Balkan bastion.

German Air Force Operations in the Eastern Mediterranean (21st September to 17th November, 1943)

The Germans Re-establish their Position

35. The German reaction to the threat in the eastern Mediterranean was systematic, vigorous and effective. Although only limited air forces were available they took advantage of the inevitable delay in the establishment of Allied air power in Apulia and of the fact that the areas affected lay for the most part beyond the effective range of Allied fighter aircraft and—operating almost at will—proved a valuable asset for the recovery of key points. Between the Italian capitulation on September 8th, and October 3rd, reinforcements amounting to 110 aircraft were moved into the eastern Mediterranean theatre, comprising long-range bombers from the western front and Russia, single-engined fighters from Austria and army cooperation units from Russia ; as a result the total Luftwaffe strength in the area rose from 235 to 345 first-line aircraft, at approximately which strength it remained stable.

36. The first German objective was the island of Cephallonia, covering the entrance to the Gulf of Corinth, which was attacked on September 21st with strong air support, mainly by Ju.87's which, profiting from the absence of Allied air opposition, flew some 120 sorties from the bases in N.W. Greece, representing approximately three sorties per serviceable aircraft. The Ju.87's

played a similar role of eliminating artillery defences in the attack on Corfu, the main fortress on the eastern side of the Straits of Otranto, which followed without delay on September 24th. On the following day, the dive bomber effort was switched against Split, the most important port on the eastern shores of the Adriatic, which after the bombing of battery positions was quickly carried by assault. Thus, in under a week the Germans, by energetic and systematic use of the small air component available, re-established their position on the eastern side of the Adriatic, assuring the supply route through the Adriatic to Greece and the Aegean and forestalling the danger of an Allied invasion of the Balkans across the Straits of Otranto, which seemed imminent after the Allied occupation of Apulia.

37. Attention was then immediately turned to the Aegean. Here the Germans were substantially aided by the lamentable Allied failure to take the opportunity of the Italian capitulation to throw a task force into Rhodes. Hence, Rhodes, where a negligible German garrison with no air support whatever reasserted control as early as September 12th, became available as a base for short-range aircraft, including single-engined fighters and dive bombers. These were quickly moved in after the conclusion of the Adriatic operations on September 27th, and it was the possibility of using Rhodes—which had lain open to Allied assault with no Luftwaffe protection whatever from the Italian defection on September 8th-27th—which enabled the German Air Force to intervene with maximum effect against the minor Dodecanese islands, Kos, Leros, Samos and Syros, which had passed into Allied hands.

38. The operations against Kos and Leros, which re-established the German position in the eastern Mediterranean until the end of the war, were models of what a small but intrepid air command could achieve against an irresolute opponent without effective air support. The major share of the German Air Force in the success of both operations stands out beyond all doubt. Yet, this success was achieved, not as has sometimes been suggested—by use of overwhelming air power, but by fully exploiting a favourable situation with a small force maintaining only a moderate scale of effort. Both at Kos and at Leros Luftwaffe activity was slighter than had been expected. The total effort in the two days' operation for the reduction of Kos amounted to under 300 sorties, including 65-75 Me.109 sorties of a defensive character ; the main weight of the attack on October 3rd and 4th was borne by Ju.87's which flew 140-150 sorties. Operations against Leros began immediately after the recapture of Kos. Long-range bombers and Ju.87's maintained a combined average effort of 60 sorties a day against fortifications and gun positions throughout the remainder of October, and meanwhile further forces, up to a total of 300 aircraft of all types, were moved up for the assault which began on November 12th, when 90-95 Ju.52's dropped 500 parachutists.

39. As in the operations against Kos, the German Air Force concentrated its efforts against Allied artillery and A.A. positions. These operations, although exceedingly effective owing to the lack of Allied air opposition, were only moderate in scale ; during the five days of the attack, only 675-700 offensive sorties were flown and the weight of bombs dropped in this period did not exceed 600 tons. The recapture of Leros, effected by close air and army cooperation, eliminated the Allied threat to the Aegean ; Syros and Samos were both evacuated without a fight, and all danger from this quarter ceased.

The Static Phase in Italy : Cassino and Anzio (October, 1943 to July, 1944)

The Luftwaffe Conserves its Effort

40. Contrasted with the determination and energy displayed in restoring the situation in the eastern Mediterranean, as evidenced by the rapid sequence of operations between September 21st and November 16th, the German Air Force in Italy virtually ceased to operate after the stabilisation of the battle front north of Naples at the beginning of October, and it became clear that for the Germans Italy had become a secondary commitment. Ground operations were of so limited and local a character that they would scarcely have been assisted by massive air support, and the German Air Force after incurring heavy losses in pilots and aircraft during the Sicilian campaign, was not prepared to squander its forces on ineffective operations. Hence, in conformity with the military situation, a policy of strict conservation of effort was enforced, once the Allied advance had brought its armies into difficult country. Taking into account periods of bad weather, which precluded operational flying, single-engined fighter and fighter-bomber sorties in the battle area did not exceed a combined daily average of 30-35 per 24 hours during November and December. More significant, however, was the low scale of long-range bomber effort, in view of the obvious desirability of hampering the movement of Allied supplies to Italy. Between October 15th and December 5th, long-range bombers in Italy only operated eight times, including six raids on Naples, one on Maddalena (Sardinia) and one on Bari, flying a total of some 400 sorties. This was an average of 55-60 sorties per week by a force of 145 to 185 bombers, or scarcely more than one sortie every two weeks per serviceable aircraft. Moreover, a large proportion of this effort was abortive. In a raid on Naples on the night of October 23rd-24th only 15 to 20 out of 90 aircraft airborne were reported over the target ; and although major damage was inflicted at Bari on the night of December 2nd-3rd through a chance hit on an ammunition ship, only 30 out of 100 raiding aircraft actually bombed the target area. Better results were achieved by the anti-shipping force of torpedo and glider-bombers based in southern France for attacking Allied supply convoys. But, although this force achieved tangible results in all its operations, it was only at the cost of appreciable losses, amounting on occasion to 20 per cent. of the aircraft operating, which necessitated 'long periods for rest, retraining and re-equipment ; consequently, after four operations in October and November it remained totally inactive until 10th January, 1944, when a convoy was attacked off Oran.

41. The long period of stalemate in Italy, besides leading to a rapid decline in Luftwaffe activity, was also used as an occasion to transfer units to other more active fronts. In spite of the low scale of effort, no appreciable recuperation took place in single-engined fighter strength, since the overriding need for fighters for the defence of the Reich absorbed the expansion in fighter production, leaving no surplus for Italy. The already small FW.190 fighter-bomber force was further weakened by the withdrawal for re-equipment of the fighter-bombers evacuated from Sardinia, which eventually moved to the western front. Finally, during the course of December the entire long-range bomber force in North Italy, representing an established strength of 180 aircraft, was withdrawn in preparation for reprisal raids on England. Thus, German Air Force strength in the Mediterranean, which by October had already declined by nearly 40 per cent. from the peak figure of July, fell rapidly until by January it comprised

only 575 aircraft of which only 370 were available in the central and western Mediterranean area. The stages in this decline are seen in the following table :—

	1 July, 1943			1 October, 1943			1 January, 1944		
	Central and W. Med.	Eastern Med.	Total	Central and W. Med.	Eastern Med.	Total	Central and W. Med.	Eastern Med.	Total
L.R. Bombers	260	40	300	220	70	290	85	35	120
Fighter Bombers and Ground Attack	150	—	150	15	—	15	15	—	15
Dive Bombers	—	65	65	—	70	70	—	—	—
S.E. Fighters	380	70	450	140	45[1]	185[1]	200	65[1]	265[1]
T.E. Fighters	100	10	110	—	10	10	—	10[2]	10[2]
L.R. Recce.	60	45	105	30	25	55	35	20	55
Tac. Recce.	25	25	50	10	40	50	20	35	55
Coastal	—	50	50	15	45	60	15	40	55
Total	975	305	1,280	430	305	735	370	205	575

Renewal of Effort at the Anzio Beachhead

42. Such was the situation on 21st January, 1944, when, contrary to German anticipations, the Allied command attempted to resolve the deadlock on the Italian front by a large-scale landing operation behind the German lines. After the difficulties encountered by the Allies at Salerno, there is little doubt that a second operation of the same sort was not expected during the winter months ; and due to the weakness of German air reconnaissance, which had degenerated into routine weather and sea patrols over unvarying routes, the Allied landing at Anzio achieved complete surprise. German Air Force strength in the Mediterranean had fallen by nearly 200 aircraft since the Salerno landing. Due to the withdrawal of the long-range bomber force from northern Italy, the weakness of fighter-bomber units and the necessity for employing a large proportion of fighters on defensive operations in North Italy (where German communications were suffering serious dislocation through incessant bombing), the German Air Force in Italy, with a minimum defensive force, was in no way prepared to deal with a large-scale operation.

43. As always, German Air Force reaction to a major strategic threat was prompt and energetic. Between January 23rd and February 3rd some 140 long-range bombers were rapidly moved to Italy from N.W. Germany, France and Greece, including aircraft which, as late as the night of January 21st-22nd, had been on operations over London. Simultaneously, the anti-shipping force in southern France was reinforced by 50-60 additional Do.217's and He.177's operating with radio-controlled glider-bombs, and these were able to operate against shipping off the Anzio beachhead by using advanced landing grounds in Italy. There was, on the other hand, no immediate strengthening of close-support forces in Italy. Some 50 single-engined fighters were moved down from

[1] Excluding 60 S.E. Fighters in Rumania and Bulgaria.
[2] Excluding 35 Night Fighters in Bulgaria and Rumania.

northern Italy to the battle area by February 23rd, but there was no reinforcement from outside until the end of February, when 40 single-engined fighters were transferred from the western front for support of the third German counter-attack. Fighter-bomber strength never exceeded 30-35 operational aircraft, and failure to reinforce the fighter-bomber force was one of the most striking features of the whole campaign against Anzio. Nevertheless, the overall increase in strength by 1st March, 1944, was substantial, amounting to nearly 35 per cent. since the Allied landing ; at the peak, Luftwaffe strength in the Mediterranean rose to 750-775 aircraft, of which 600 were in the central Mediterranean, and approximately 475 available directly for operations in the Anzio area.

44. Operations against the Anzio beachhead fell into four phases. In the first phase, before the Germans had recovered from their surprise and before ground troops had moved up against the beachhead, the main reaction was by long-range bombers, which were assigned the task of hindering the Allied build-up by attacks on supply shipping. The burden of these operations fell on the torpedo and glider bombers which in all carried out over twenty attacks on shipping off Anzio, beginning with an effort of 150 sorties on the nights of January 23rd-24th and 24th-25th ; but, unable owing to strong Allied fighter opposition to operate in daylight, these units were no longer so effective as at Salerno—they had, moreover, in the meantime suffered crippling losses of experienced crews—and the proportion of hits or near misses to total sorties fell sharply. Moreover, they were unable to sustain their initial effort. Thus, when the German ground forces delivered the first counter-attack on February 3rd, the support received from the German Air Force was inadequate. Between February 3rd and 15th, seven attacks on shipping off Anzio took place, but the highest number of sorties on any one night was only about 50, of which 20 were by Do.217 and He.177 operating with Hs.293 radio-controlled glider-bombs[1], while the Ju.88 units now assembled in North Italy proved incapable of more than small harassing attacks, mainly on ground targets, with forces rarely exceeding 10-15 aircraft. Daylight attacks on shipping by fighter-bombers were even less effective. Apart from one successful operation on January 24th against three Allied hospital ships (two of which were damaged and one sunk), shipping losses attributable to fighter-bomber action in the period January 23rd-February 15th amounted to only one landing craft burnt out and two further landing craft damaged.

45. The first German counter-attack, on February 3rd, was launched under bad weather conditions—probably a deliberate decision in order to cut down the vastly superior Allied air opposition to a minimum—and Luftwaffe support was therefore small, the poor quality airfields available for the close-support units being in most cases unserviceable. When the counter-attack was renewed on February 16th, weather conditions were good and—all available forces having been concentrated against Anzio to the detriment of the air defence of northern Italy and of support of the Armies fighting in the South near Cassino—fighter and fighter-bomber effort was at the maximum. Flying five sorties per serviceable aircraft on February 16th and four sorties per serviceable aircraft on February 17th, the small force of 20-25 serviceable FW.190's flew 160-170 sorties in two days. Single-engined fighters on escort

---

[1] See Chapter 13, paragraph 37 *et seq.*

and patrol flew some 300-350 sorties in the same period. But in the face of overwhelming Allied air superiority—the Allied effort on February 17th amounted to over 1,700 sorties—this effort could not be maintained and from February 18th onwards German Air Force operations quickly lost their initial aggressiveness and impetus. No similar air support was available for the third German counter-attack which began on February 29th. This was carried out in bad weather conditions, regardless of the German Air Force, because it was realised by the Germans that further delay would result in changes in the relative strength of the ground forces disadvantageous to themselves. Hence, air activity was negligible, the close-support effort by fighters and fighter-bombers for the whole period of four days (March 1st-4th) amounting to only 120 sorties while the long-range bombers operated only twice and then on a very reduced scale. Already by March 1st, however, Kesselring had realised that the elimination of the bridgehead was impossible, unless two fresh and experienced divisions could be made available, and since these were lacking, he decided to go over to the defensive with the object of preventing the Allied forces from breaking out in the direction of Rome.

46. Although the operations for the elimination of the Anzio beachhead were unsuccessful, the Germans nevertheless, by energetic air and ground action, defeated the strategic threat implicit in the Allied landings and—profiting from the failure of the Allied command to exploit its initial success—had no difficulty in tying down the Allied forces within a narrow perimeter which, instead of developing into a major threat to the German positions in the South, developed into an embarrassing and unprofitable Allied commitment. The three German counter-attacks, throwing the Allies on to the defensive, stabilised the situation ; and the operation must, from the Allied point of view, be adjudged a failure. Instead of an opening up of the Italian front, there was, from the beginning of March, a reversion to the position of deadlock, and the Allies were forced to undertake a difficult and unpropitious frontal attack at Cassino. The Germans were, therefore, able to return to the purely defensive policy of the previous winter, radically curtailing the scale of air support and again withdrawing surplus Luftwaffe elements for operations elsewhere.

47. Approximately 60 Ju.88's which had moved to northern Italy at the time of the Anzio landing, returned to North-West Germany, and some 40 single-engined fighters were transferred from central Italy to the Balkans now under a serious threat from Anglo-American bombers based at Foggia. Some attempt to bolster up the fighter defences of Italy was made by the organisation of a small Italian Fascist Republican Air Force under German control ; but little came of this project, and the scale of effort in April, 1944, fell even below that during the earlier stages of the Italian campaign. A few harassing bombers, both Italian Cr.42's (manned by German crews) and Ju.87's were brought in to replace the long-range bomber force, which sank into total inactivity ; but their sporadic activity at night over the front-line area was too insignificant to achieve anything. Hence, even when the Allied Fifth and Eighth Armies reopened their offensive on May 11th, and crossed the Rapido and Garigliano rivers, the German Air Force made no serious attempt to increase its scale of effort, and even before the Allied occupation of Rome, on June 4th, it had practically ceased to intervene in the fighting.

Renewed Allied Offensive (11th May to 19th July, 1944)

Eclipse of the Luftwaffe in Italy

48. The German Air Force was, of course, by this time completely outnumbered and outclassed, and could not even defend its own airfields : it was, for example, bombed out of Piacenza with heavy losses on May 14th, and a few days later the same fate overtook it at Viterbo. Its elimination was complete, and as constituted it had no hope whatever of operating with any effect against the overwhelming weight of Allied air power. But there were, in addition, two other important contributory reasons for its total ineffectiveness. The one was fear of further Allied outflanking landings on either the Adriatic or the Tyrrhenian coast, which made the German Air Force Operational Command unwilling to commit all its few available forces in the frontal battle in the South. The other, overshadowing all else in importance, was the clear realisation in Berlin of the imminence of major Allied amphibious operations against the West coast of France, perhaps combined with simultaneous landings on the French Mediterranean littoral.

49. Even before the battle for the Anzio beachhead was decided, the overriding need to prepare against the expected Allied invasion of occupied western Europe had begun to influence German Air Force policy and operations in the Mediterranean. The first sign in the change of emphasis was the withdrawal to northern France of Fliegerkorps II, the command hitherto in charge of tactical air operations in Italy. This was followed, early in March, by the withdrawal of Fliegerkorps X, the Command hitherto controlling operations in Greece and the Aegean. This withdrawal reflected not only the decrease in strength in the eastern Mediterranean theatre from some 300 aircraft at the beginning of December, 1943, to only about 115 aircraft in March, 1944, but also the fusion of the Balkan and South Russian fronts under Luftflotte 4, to which reference has already been made. Fliegerkorps X now took over command of the anti-shipping units in western and south-western France. Simultaneously, the anti-shipping units in southern France, which at the time of the operations against the Anzio beachhead, were temporarily under command of Luftflotte 2 and of Field Marshal Kesselring, again came under independent control.

50. Thus, from March, 1944, there was no longer any Fliegerkorps organisation in the whole Mediterranean area. These changes indicated the extent to which the centre of gravity for the Luftwaffe had moved from the Mediterranean to the western front. The same fact was illustrated by the refusal to make reinforcements available even after the link up of the Allied Fifth Army with forces in the Anzio beachhead on May 25th and the rapid advance on Rome ; the German High Command feared to deplete its anti-invasion forces in the West or to decrease the fighter defences of the Reich. The long-range bombers remaining in North Italy were carefully conserved, evidently so that they would be available for immediate transfer to the West, and at the end of May even the few remaining FW.190 fighter-bombers were withdrawn from operations and sent to North Italy to restore readiness against possible Allied outflanking landings, which it was thought might coincide with the invasion of western France. When, after the fall of Rome on 4th June, 1944, all the remaining single-engined fighters from the central Italian battle area were moved back to North Italy for air defence, the German Air Force ceased to play any part in the Italian campaign.

(83331)

K

Widespread Repercussions of the Mediterranean Campaign, 1944

Effects of the 1943 Campaign on the Luftwaffe

51. Few contrasts in the course of the air war are more remarkable than the change in the importance of the Mediterranean theatre in the twelve months between July, 1943 and July, 1944. Compared with a total of 1,280 aircraft at the beginning of July, 1943, strength in this whole area had by the beginning of July, 1944, sunk to only 300 first-line aircraft, and the Mediterranean had, in fact, ceased to count in German Air Force calculations since the end of 1943. This was due, without doubt, to a clear realisation that the Italian campaign could not in the nature of things result in decisive strategic decisions, and that—confronted with an overall shortage of aircraft—the German Air Force could, without serious risk, sacrifice the Italian front to the overriding needs of the western and eastern theatres. Once the situation in the eastern Mediterranean, which after the Italian capitulation had threatened to undermine the German hold on the Balkans, had been restored, the German Air Force therefore carried through a drastic thinning out of its Mediterranean forces. Events proved the correctness of the calculation that it was possible to fight a successful defensive battle without air support in favourable terrain ; it was only in April, 1945, after the German collapse in the West, that the German defences in Italy broke down. But these facts should not be allowed to obscure the significance of the Mediterranean campaigns of 1943 in the history of the air war. Although the Allies never succeeded in turning their Mediterranean victories into a major strategic success, the strain imposed on the German Air Force by its unsuccessful defence first of Tunisia, then of Sicily and last of Italy, had important results which were felt on all battle-fronts.

52. The Mediterranean campaigns of 1943 were a drain on the German Air Force which interfered with all its plans for recovery and expansion, and therefore vitally affected its capacity both to defend German industry from air attack and to oppose and withstand the Allied landings in Normandy on 6th June, 1944. It was not only at Stalingrad but in the Mediterranean that the cream of the German bomber force perished ; and it was the continued drain of crews and aircraft against superior Allied opposition in the Mediterranean which, long after Stalingrad, reduced German offensive power to a nullity. It was in the Mediterranean that the Allies took the measure of the new anti-shipping force, including the He.177 and Do.217 glider-bombers which the Germans had built up in 1943, and inflicted such heavy losses that, by the time of the Normandy landings, it had ceased to be a dangerous threat. But it was above all else the heavy wastage imposed on the expanding German fighter arm which was the outstanding feature of the air war in the Mediterranean in 1943. Not less than 850 German operational aircraft were totally destroyed in the central Mediterranean area alone during July, 1943, of which approximately 600 were single-engined fighter types. This heavy fighter wastage was one of the first major checks arresting the steady increase in fighter strength up to June, 1943. The necessity, three times in only six months, of rebuilding its Mediterranean fighter defences seriously interfered with the scheduled programme of the German Air Force's expansion ; the high rate of fighter replacements absorbed by the Mediterranean, amounting in July, 1943, to some 350 aircraft, ate into surplus production and slowed down the formation of new units. Later in the year, it is true, the situation was reversed, and the Mediterranean theatre, no longer accorded high priority, had to be content

with the modest quota. But by this time direct attack on the German fighter industry had succeeded the effective but indirect attack on German single-engined fighter strength : the first phase of the attack on German aircraft production, beginning with the raids on Regensburg and Schweinfurt in mid-August, 1943, maintained the restrictions on German fighter expansion which the Mediterranean campaigns had first imposed.

Conclusions

53. Looked at from the point of view of the general history of the German Air Force, the Mediterranean campaigns of 1943 and 1943-44 had, therefore, three main results. The success of the Sicilian landings, in the face of the best opposition which the Luftwaffe could put up, established for all time the overwhelming superiority of the Anglo-American Air Forces over the German ; never again was the issue in doubt. Secondly, the methods so successfully employed to eliminate German air opposition to the invasions of Sicily and Italy provided a model in air tactics for use when the time came for the Normandy landings. Thirdly, the wastage imposed at a crucial phase in the long-term preparations of the German Air Force to wage a defensive war seriously upset all German plans for expansion, and—although not preventing—materially delayed the build-up of the German fighter force. The ultimate consequences of this were twofold. On the one hand, the German Air Force had not adequate forces to oppose the Allied air attack on the German aircraft industry which commenced after midsummer, 1943. On the other hand, partly as a result of the delays imposed by the Mediterranean campaign, partly through the destructive attacks on aircraft assembly plants which followed—the German Air Force failed in its plans to build up overwhelming air defences with which to meet and defeat the long awaited opening of the " Second Front ". In both of these respects, the superiority established by the Anglo-American air forces in the Mediterranean in 1943 was a cardinal factor, from the results of which the German Air Force never fully recovered.

(83331)

K 2

CHAPTER 12

THE DEFENCE OF THE REICH, 1943–44

Effects of the Anglo-American Bombing Offensive

The Change in Balance of Forces

1. The extraordinary change in the balance of forces in the Mediterranean which was an outstanding feature of the period July, 1943-July, 1944, resulting in a decrease in German first-line air strength in that theatre from 1,280 to 475 aircraft, was the direct consequence of the launching of an all-out Anglo-American air offensive against German war industry. From early in 1943 until the Allied landings in Normandy on 6th June, 1944, the combined Anglo-American air attack on the Reich was the dominating factor in the air war. It resulted, as we have seen, in the reduction of German Air Forces in the Mediterranean to a size at which their influence over the course of operations became negligible. It resulted in the transfer from Russia to Germany of single-engined and twin-engined fighter units at the very moment when the growing superiority of the Soviet Air Force required a strengthening of German fighter opposition. And, above all else, it enforced a change-over from bomber to fighter, from offensive to defensive equipment, which irrevocably altered the whole composition and character of the German Air Force.

Increase in Home Defence Fighter Strength

2. The development of the Anglo-American air offensive entailed a closely coordinated and highly integrated employment of night and day bombing, which taxed the defensive efforts of the Luftwaffe and confronted it with a complex series of problems, many of them technical and scientific. In the first phase, until approximately July-August, 1943, R.A.F. night bombing was the more serious problem. Thereafter, until October, the main effort was directed against the threat of U.S.A.A.F. daylight bombing ; and in this respect, a defensive success was scored against deep, unescorted daylight bombing missions which severely curtailed the scale and scope of U.S.A.A.F. daylight attacks, until the introduction of the Thunderbolt and Mustang long-range fighters in January, 1944, completely transformed the air situation. Meanwhile, the use of " window " jamming by the R.A.F. at night from July, 1943, had completely dislocated the existing German night fighter system,[1] and had created new scientific and tactical problems, both for aircraft and for A.A. defences. Simultaneously, a further strain was placed on the German defences by the inauguration of day and night bombing from Italian bases after the Allied occupation of Foggia and its satellites in October, 1943. The multiplicity of threats and the rapid development of scientific devices and counter-devices throughout this period drove the Germans to a series of expedients, which complicated the picture—in any case far from simple ; at one phase, for example, twin-engined night fighters were employed against daylight bombers, at another single-engined night fighters were introduced and, after a brief success in this capacity, became less effective through the Allied use of countermeasures, and were eventually turned over to daylight defence.

---

[1] See also Chapter 8.

3. Throughout this long and complicated story of measures and counter-measures, one factor alone remained stable : the continuous and rapid build-up in strength of the fighter defences of Germany and Western Europe, which amounted during 1943 to approximately 235 single-engined fighters and 370 twin-engined fighters. The gross overall change in the distribution of fighter aircraft on the three main fronts during 1943, illustrated in the following table, shows therefore a rapidly growing preponderance in air defence, absorbing nearly the total gross fighter expansion of 1,680 aircraft :—

Area of Operations	Type	1.1.43	1.1.44	Difference
Germany (incl. Austria) and the Western Front (incl. Denmark and South Norway).	S.E.F.	635 ⎱ 1,045	870 ⎱ 1,650	+ 605
	T.E.F.	410 ⎰	780 ⎰	
Mediterranean and Balkans ..	S.E.F.	210 ⎱ 280	320 ⎱ 365	+ 85
	T.E.F.	70 ⎰	45 ⎰	
Russian Front	S.E.F.	395 ⎱ 445	345 ⎱ 425	− 20
	T.E.F.	50 ⎰	80 ⎰	
TOTAL	—	1,770	2,440	+ 670

4. The figures set out above indicate how, during 1943, the fighter defences of the Reich were, under ever-growing Allied pressure, expanded to such an extent that, by the end of the year, they almost equalled the whole fighter force of the German Air Force on all fronts at the beginning of the year. Similar changes occurred in Flak, which with the spreading of the battlefields through the Russian, Balkan and African campaigns, had by 1942 been widely dispersed to the detriment of air defence. In 1943, this process of dispersal was reversed, and it has been calculated that by the end of that year the requirements of the Western Front air defences contained approximately :—

68 per cent. of the total single-engined and twin-engined fighters (1,650 aircraft).

70 per cent. of the total Flak personnel (900,000 men).

75 per cent. of the total heavy A.A. guns (principally 8.8 cm.).

55 per cent. of the total automatic A.A. guns (principally 20 mm.).

5. The extraordinary increase in strength in the West was accompanied by a redistribution of forces within the western defensive zone. The growing threat to German war industry, coupled with the rapid loss of air superiority over the western occupied territories to the Allied air forces, necessitated the concentration of fighter defences within Germany at the expense of France, Holland and Belgium. By the beginning of 1944, 75 per cent. of the force of 1,650 fighters opposed to the Anglo-American bombing offensive was concentrated within Germany, with the remainder spread out widely between Norway and the Loire estuary. The result was not only inability to defend the occupied territories in the West and in 1944 to defend the " V-weapon " sites on the Channel coast, but also a radical weakening of the forces available to oppose the initial stages of the Allied landings in Normandy

in June, 1944.   Apart, therefore from its direct effects on German war industry—these will be considered at a later stage—the Anglo-American air offensive in the West in 1943 and 1944 had the following results :—

(a) By necessitating the withdrawal of German fighter units to defence of the Reich, it relieved pressure on the Russian and Mediterranean fronts.

(b) By enforcing the concentration of productive capacity on fighter types, it brought about the weakening and eventually the eclipse of the long-range bomber force.   In particular, twin-engined night fighter expansion could only take place at the expense of the bomber arm.

(c) By compelling the Luftwaffe to exert every effort in defence of war industry, it inflicted a rate of wastage which limited numerical expansion and resulted in a rapid decline in performance and quality.

(d) By forcing the Germans to withdraw the bulk of their fighters from the West to Germany, it facilitated the immediate establishment of complete Allied air superiority over the beachheads in Normandy at the time of the invasion in June, 1944.

The R.A.F. Night Bombing Offensive

The Situation Early in 1943

6. The main problem facing the German Air Force at the beginning of 1943 was still the R.A.F. night bombing offensive. The Germans were well aware of the build-up of the U.S.A.A.F. day-bomber force which had been proceeding in England during 1942, and it was known that the Americans were practising large-scale formation flying. But it was not until 27th January, 1943, when Wilhelmshafen was bombed, that the first American daylight attack on German territory took place ; and this raid by only 64 Fortresses was on so small a scale as to assuage fears. Already in May, 1942, on the other hand, the R.A.F. had sent out over 1,000 bombers on one night ; moreover, the forces employed contained an ever-increasing proportion of four-engined bombers which soon completely replaced the old twin-engined types. Thus, whereas the daylight attacks of the U.S.A.A.F. remained limited both in number and in penetration, the night attacks of the R.A.F. had, by the end of 1942, become ever stronger and more successful.

7. These attacks had, as has been seen[1], been met in 1942 by the development, under General Kammhuber, of the classic system of a chain of G.C.I. stations extending from Denmark to the Paris area.   This system achieved a fair measure of success, reflected in Bomber Command's rate of loss on night operations, which rose from 2.5 per cent. of sorties in 1941 to 4 per cent. in 1942. But by the end of the year, Bomber Command had devised and put into execution a series of tactical counter-measures, which made their effects felt particularly noticeably when, after a certain respite in the winter of 1942-43, large concentrated attacks on the Ruhr began in the spring of 1943. The novelty of these operations lay in the use of pathfinders to mark the target and in the concentration of the following bomber stream which attacked within a period of 30-40 minutes. This tactical method had the desired result, as will be seen later, of dislocating the current

---

[1] See Chapter 8, paragraphs 9–13.

German Flak organisation and therefore of minimising losses to A.A. Similarly, it reduced losses to G.C.I.-controlled night fighters. As a result of the concentration of the bomber stream, the narrow night-fighter zone in the West was quickly penetrated, and the number of fighters that came into actual contact with the bombers was correspondingly reduced. The narrower the width of the bomber stream passing diagonally through the G.C.I. area, the fewer the number of controls that could have bomber aircraft within their range ; the shorter the period in which the bombers passed through each G.C.I. area, the fewer the number of possible interceptions which could be effected.

" Wilde Sau " Single-engined Night Fighters

8. These measures necessitated a reorganisation of German night defence, although still within the framework of Kammhuber's G.C.I. system. This system was extended in two directions : first, the night fighter zone was deepened by the development of a second, more easterly belt of ground stations and secondly, the system of control was developed so that two or more night fighters could be brought into action simultaneously in any one night fighter sector. This necessitated the construction of new night fighter bases and the expansion of the night fighter force in the West. But, even so, the G.C.I. system was peculiarly susceptible to saturation tactics, and was very uneconmical, since it necessitated the wide dispersal of fighters over the whole defensive belt, of which only a few could be brought into play against any one threat. Hence, already by the early summer of 1943, two measures had been adopted which fell outside the scope of the classic system. The one, which went back to 1942 in origin, was the equipping of night fighters with airborne radar (*Lichtenstein*), freeing the pilots to some extent from their dependance on ground control and enabling fighters directed *en masse*—and no longer individually—on to the bomber stream to pick out and keep contact with their targets. The second measure, which owed its introduction to the initiative of Major (later Oberst) Herrmann, was known as *Wilde Sau*[1], and was intended to supplement the controlled night fighting (Himmelbett) system. Under the *Wilde Sau* system single-engined fighters were employed in close cooperation with searchlight teams, primarily for air defence over the target ; in place of ground control, a system of pyrotechnic and other visual signals was used to guide the aircraft to the bombers. At the same time, a new method was introduced (*Zahme Sau*)[2] for throwing stronger twin-engined night fighter formations against the bomber stream during its outward and homeward flight. Thus, night fighting developed from closely controlled operations in small night fighter areas to a coordinated operation over large areas.

The First Use of " Window "

9. Such in broad outline was the picture of German night defences when, on the Hamburg raid on the night of 24th-25th July, 1943, " window " was first dropped by Bomber Command with the object of saturating the German G.C.I. system, interferring with enemy airborne A.I. and dislocating gun-laying for the Flak and radar control for the searchlights. The result was so satisfactory in that Kannhuber's night fighter defence system as built up over the previous three years collapsed completely, while R.A.F. losses to Flak showed

---

[1] = " Wild Sow ".　　　　[2] = " Tame Sow ".

an immediate decline. The night fighters also suffered an undisputed setback, and the Germans were compelled to evolve a fresh interception technique whilst their research staffs were working out new technical countermeasures.

10. It is not true to say that the German signals organisation was taken by surprise when the British first employed " window ". About a year previously engineers at the Technical Office of the Luftwaffe had studied the question, and early in 1943 experiments had proved that the metal strips could be a menace to the whole defensive radar organisation. This information was conveyed to General Martini, the Director-General of Air Force Signals, who duly passed a report to Goering. Goering was so upset that he ordered immediate destruction of the document and the taking of utmost precautions to prevent the British from learning of the discovery. It was, therefore, extremely difficult at that time for the Luftwaffe Signals Organisation to work out countermeasures, since the danger of the metal strips being picked up after experimental flights was very real. When the Hamburg raid took place there was general consternation at no countermeasures being ready, and Goering placed the full blame on General Martini.

11. The night fighter force was fortunate in the experiments which had been carried out under Hermann's aegis in freelance night fighting, and a rapid development of this practice, which was quickly extended from single-engined to twin-engined fighters, tided them over the period until new and more efficient A.I. apparatus of frequencies beyond those jammed by " window " could be introduced. In the autumn of 1943 the single-engined night fighter force, which began with one Geschwader (J.G.300) was rapidly expanded : two new Geschwader (J.G.301, 302) were formed and towards the end of the year, all single-engined night fighters were concentrated into a new Command, Jagddivision 30, which was commanded by Oberst Herrmann and, at the beginning of 1944, was placed directly under the operational control of the newly-formed Luftflotte Reich. In all they amounted to approximately 100 aircraft.

Recovery from the Effect of " Window "

12. The system worked out by Oberst Herrmann provided a framework which was rapidly filled in from August, 1943 onwards, with results which cannot be described as unsatisfactory ; indeed, for a period it seemed as though the introduction of " window " by forcing the Germans to discard their rigid G.C.I. system, had actually brought about an improvement in night fighter defence. Individual control was abandoned, and instead a scheme of fighting over target areas was developed, using both single-engined and twin-engined fighters in large numbers. These aircraft were directed by a special radio running commentary on the air situation which provided general directions to the night fighters for locating the bomber stream in the vicinity of the target. To assemble the fighters in fair strength a system of radio and visual beacons was used, the aircraft being directed to orbit these beacons until the target was determined, whereupon they were despatched with all speed to the target area to intercept with searchlight cooperation. The Flak at the target was usually given a ceiling above which the fighters operated.

13. From this time onwards the actual basing of night fighter units became a matter of small importance ; for example, cases occurred in which a unit based in northern Denmark intercepted Allied raiders over Stuttgart. The whole of

(83331)

K*

German night fighter tactics were characterised by great flexibility and skill in bringing the largest possible opposition to bear. Consequently, while losses to Flak declined there was, as a sequel to the introduction of " window ", no noteworthy permanent decline in the rate of loss to night fighters ; the overall rate of losses sustained by Bomber Command on night operations during 1943 amounting to 3.6 per cent., of which three-quarters (i.e., 2.7 per cent.) were attributed to fighters, as compared with 4 per cent. of which slightly more than half (2.2 per cent.) were attributed to fighters in 1942.

The Radio Battle of Measure and Countermeasure

14. The energetic German reaction to " window " and the new impetus to night fighting through the introduction of the new tactics therefore forced Bomber Command, in the later months of 1943, to devise countermeasures. Thenceforward (until the establishment of the Allies on the continent in the autumn of 1944) the history of night fighting became largely one of the technical ingenuity of the signals organisations of both adversaries. These technical countermeasures necessarily involved minor tactical changes ; but the system of large-scale, loosely controlled night fighting over a wide area introduced around August, 1943, was at no time fundamentally modified ; in spite of all countermeasures it was still the best available answer to the heavy " thousand bomber " raid.

15. Bomber Command's first reaction to *Wilde Sau* was to shorten its attacks to 15-20 minutes' duration, and this was quickly followed by the development of feint or " spoof " routes and attacks, and the use of the " Mandrel " airborne jamming screen. The intention—and frequently the result—was to send the enemy to the wrong area, at the same time not allowing him sufficient time to reach the real target in large numbers. The German answer to these measures was to improve the overland plotting system, so as to bring the fighters into the bomber stream as soon as possible after landfall had been made and to keep them there to and from the target. In these circumstances, the German Observer Corps immediately became of the highest importance ; and measures were taken to increase the efficiency of the reporting service by a general change-over from sound locators and visual range-finders to electrical range-finders. The introduction of improved radar search gear led to the development of a new radar reporting service, which was intended eventually to replace entirely the old sound and visual reporting service. *Wassermann* and *Mammuth* long-range radar equipment was made available in increased quantities ; plotting and transmission were centralised and simplified ; and a special raid tracking organisation, operating a network of intercept stations, listened to all forms of transmission from bomber aircraft in order to provide material for the running commentaries. The first transmission used by the Germans was the I.F.F. left on or switched on in R.A.F. bombers over enemy territory. When this was eliminated by strict enforcement of aircrew discipline, other transmissions such as " Monica " and " H2S " became available. Simultaneously, with the attempt to use radiation from Allied bombers for early warning and plotting, airborne homers were developed to assist the night fighters in finding the bomber stream and to enable them to close at least to A.I. range ; thus, the *Flensburg* apparatus was developed to home on " Monica ", *Naxos* for " H2S ". At the same time, an endeavour was made to produce an A.I. set not susceptible to jamming ; and with the delivery to operational units

of the new version of *Lichtenstein*, "SN2", which took place between the early autumn of 1943 and the beginning of 1944, new and usable airborne radar became available.

16. The effects of these measures were seen from the beginning of 1944, when the German night fighter force appeared to have mastered the problems confronting it. The new plotting and control system quickly proved its worth ; it was a formidable defensive organisation with few weaknesses capable of exploitation. In spite of "spoof" raids, which scored frequent successes as diversions, thereby reducing the overall average rate of Bomber Command losses, it was by no means unusual for the German defences to inflict casualties amounting to 8-9 per cent. of the aircraft engaged on a particular night bombing mission ; and this rate of loss, although not sustained, was sufficient, if inflicted once or twice a month, to act as a serious check to Bomber Command operations. Particularly impressive and effective in this way were the losses inflicted on the nights of 24th-25th and 30th-31st March, 1944, when 72 out of 810 aircraft raiding Berlin, and 94 out of 795 aircraft raiding Nuremburg were shot down, representing a wastage of 8.8 and 11.8 per cent., respectively. This menace was maintained during subsequent months, until the Allied invasion of the Continent and the rapid Allied advance across France and the Low Countries, dislocating the German early warning system, completely revolutionised the whole situation to the detriment of the German Air Force. Even in July, 1944, however, at the height of the battle for Normandy, the German night fighter defences succeeded in inflicting an overall rate of loss on Bomber Command aircraft attacking targets in Germany—exclusive of bomber support, Mosquito and minelaying operations—amounting to 3.8 per cent. of sorties, and the effectiveness of the night fighter force was again demonstrated as late as the night of July 28th-29th, when in operations against Stuttgart and Hamburg 8.4 per cent. of the force attacking these targets was lost. On this occasion, however, due allowance must be made for the unusual lightness of the night.

17. The first six months of 1944 thus witnessed—in a surprising reversal of fortunes since the introduction of "window"—what the objective historian must concede to be a success for the German night fighter defences, and there is abundant evidence that responsible Luftwaffe officers believed at this stage that, sooner or later, Bomber Command would be forced to abandon its large-scale night attacks, relying instead on increased use of Mosquito aircraft, against which no satisfactory defence had been devised. The success was due in part to the steady expansion of the twin-engined night fighter force, which increased in size by 50 per cent. from some 550 aircraft in July, 1943, to about 775 aircraft in July, 1944, apart from the supplementary use of single-engined night fighters. It was due also to gradual conversion from Me.110 and Do.217 to Ju.88 aircraft and from the older Ju.88 types (R-2 and C-6) to improved sub-types (G1 and G-6) giving an improved performance. Another important factor was the installation of heavier armament, including 30-mm. forward cannon and 20-mm. upward-firing cannon. But the most effective and most important measure was the extensive development of the early warning system, in combination with running commentary, which has already been described. By the beginning of January, 1944, this system had reached a point at which it was again possible to revert—this time on a large scale—to route interception, the earlier scheme of target interception having largely been defeated by Bomber

Command countermeasures. Instead of waiting until the target became known, night fighters were thenceforward fed into the bomber stream as early as possible, and by February, 1944, this procedure had been so far developed that fighters flew half way across the North Sea to meet the approaching bombers. The widespread bases used by the German Air Force in combination with the early warning enabled the night fighters to converge from all directions in force on to the bomber stream, and at the same time further improvements allowed relatively small formations to be given simultaneous individual local control, thus making successful interception of multiple raids possible and thereby counteracting the Allied use of diversions.

18. The sum total of these measures constituted a formidable and flexible defence against strategic night bombing. But for a change in Allied bombing policy from the spring of 1944 onwards, when night attacks were directed mainly against targets in Western Germany, France and the Low Countries as part of the preparations for the landing on the Continent in June, 1944, they might well have had a considerable deterrent effect on deep penetration raids into Germany. As it was, the attacks on " fringe " targets imposed limitations in the extent to which the German defences could be fully put into effect, and to the Germans it appeared that they had successfully diverted Bomber Command from targets in the heart of Germany. Such operations when carried out had, nevertheless, to be confined to bad weather conditions. This itself was an advantage to the defence, since it was soon aware that major night attacks of this type need not be anticipated in the moonlight period, and the assault on targets deep in Germany—particularly on Berlin—was in practice undertaken for three weeks out of four by Mosquito aircraft. On the other hand, the confining of deep heavy bomber raids to dark night periods made the use of free-lance single-engined night fighters unprofitable, since these aircraft (without search gear or control) could only operate successfully on clear nights in cooperation with searchlights. From about the end of 1943, therefore, the units of Jagddivision 30 were more and more held back for daylight operations against U.S.A.A.F. four-engined bombers ; but their withdrawal from night operations was amply compensated by the expansion of the twin-engined night fighter arm and by the adaptation for twin-engined fighters of the methods of Oberst Herrmann.

19. The twin-engined fighter force was strong and flexible enough to put up a reasonable defence against the Bomber Command threat, except for Mosquito raids, the increasing scale of which was a major German preoccupation in the spring and summer of 1944. Against the Mosquito the Luftwaffe had no adequate defence ; the He.219 was in many ways a first-class aircraft, but its performance was not sufficiently good for this purpose, and only some 30 He.219's in all were available for operations, output having been seriously affected as a result of the successful attack on the assembly plant at Vienna-Schwechat on 23rd April, 1944. In spite of occasional heavy losses, Bomber Command kept up intermittent heavy attacks in weather unfavourable to the defence throughout the first half of 1944, but the problem of carrying out sustained concentrated attacks with maximum forces on single objectives had reached major proportions.

20. By midsummer, 1944, therefore, the twin-engined night fighters had become the strongest and most efficient arm of the German Air Force, comprising 15 per cent. of total first-line strength. This expansion and efficiency

R.A.F. bombers leaving England at dusk.

Ju.88 Night Fighter with the " Lichtenstein " SN2 and the " Flensburg " homer (aerial array on leading edge of wing).

GENERALLEUTNANT GALLAND

Born 19.3.12. In 1932 started training as a pilot with the German Air Pilots' Training School. Entered the Air Force 1934. Commanded a Close Support Staffel in the Condor Legion in Spain, May, 1937, to June, 1938. During the Polish campaign was a Staffel commander in II/(Schlacht) Lehrgeschwader 2. Afterwards was Officer for Special Duties with J.G.27, until he became O.C. III/J.G.26 in June, 1940 and O.C. J.G.26 in August, 1940. Claimed over 100 kills as fighter pilot. Appointed Inspector of Fighters at the German Air Ministry in December, 1941 in succession to Moelders. Relieved of post January, 1945. O.C. Jagdverband 44 (Me.262 fighter unit) February, 1945. Captured by the Allies 5th May, 1945.

282

was itself a tribute to the threat which Bomber Command night operations constituted to the German war effort, and implied a diversion to a purely defensive commitment of production capacity and aircraft, which might otherwise have been used for building up the Ju.88 bomber force. In addition, it necessitated an extensive ground organisation absorbing manpower on a considerable scale, and severely taxed German scientific research and manufacturing capacity ; already in August, 1943, it was estimated that—apart from normal airfield and servicing personnel—no less than 32,000 personnel were required to man the night-fighter control system on the western front alone. However, the Allied advance from Normandy across France to the borders of Germany introduced a new phase. Deprived of its early warning system, no longer able to manoeuvre its forces over wide areas and already severely hampered by fuel shortage, the German night-fighter force entered on a period of rapid decline from which recovery was in the circumstances impossible. Its share in the final defence of Germany was inevitably small. This was, however, a result less of inherent defects than of the rapid changes in the military situation which deprived it, from August, 1944, of the prerequisites of success. Until overtaken by military events, the German night-fighter force managed, with reasonable success, to compete with Allied countermeasures, and functioned efficiently. How the situation changed after the Normandy landings remains to be seen ; it is the last—and most dismal—chapter in the story of the Luftwaffe's effort to defend the Reich from Allied air attack.

21. It must be remembered, however, that strategical considerations played a big part in deciding the tactics of Bomber Command's offensive from the beginning of 1944 onwards. After the Battle of Berlin, the requirements for deep penetration attacks declined. To the extent that these proved necessary, they were carried out, though sometimes at heavy cost, and the German defences never really succeeded in deflecting the Command from its purpose, however hazardous the operations were made. If the night bomber offensive had been required to proceed on the old terms, new methods could have been devised, such as the conversion of three groups to Mosquitos and the retention of two Lancaster Groups, each capable of saturation raids on individual targets. The radio countermeasures and skilful diversionary and tactical routing employed by Bomber Command enabled the offensive to go forward, and the fact that it was thought better to accept a diminution of attacks, during light-moon phases, in 1944, rather than recast the Command in a form less useful to subsequent operations, should not be regarded as a German victory. Moreover, the resources devoted to night defence inevitably detracted from those available to combat the powerful daylight offensive. These facts in no way detract from the fine performance of the German night-fighting arm during this phase, but it would place it in the wrong perspective to give it credit for decisive results

Flak and Searchlights Policy
22. The factors which governed the evolution of the German night fighter force also affected the employment of Flak and searchlights which—in contradistinction as has been seen[1], to the British practice—were from the beginning an integral part of the Luftwaffe and therefore closely co-ordinated in tactics and employment with the fighter arm. Allied countermeasures were directed scarcely less to disrupting German Flak and searchlights than to

---

[1] Cf. Chapter 2.

disorganising night fighter defences. Moreover, already long before the beginning of large-scale night and day bombing of targets in Germany, the initial German reliance on A.A. artillery as the primary target defence had proved unsuccessful, while the demands of the battle fronts—which always received priority consideration so long as Jeschonnek was Chief of Air Staff—had adversely affected the Flak situation within the Reich. This was illustrated by the decision, taken (largely for political reasons) as late as December, 1942, to transfer German Flak units to Italy to bolster up Italian Flak defences. In all, some 150 batteries (100 8.8 cm., 20 automatic and 30 searchlight batteries) were transferred before the decision was reversed in the spring of 1943. Such transfers and the heavy demands of the eastern front absorbed a large proportion of mobile units, and in this way the Flak within Germany lost the mobility so necessary for the rapid formation of strong points, which was one of its outstanding potential assets. A further point was that the Flak defences had not, by the end of 1942, been brought into line with the latest scientific developments ; approximately 30 per cent. of the heavy batteries were without ranging apparatus and only 25–30 per cent. of the guns had their own radar.

23. Thus, at the beginning of 1943, the Flak defences of Germany were in need of strengthening and reorganisation and this need was intensified when Bomber Command introduced saturation tactics. The Flak, emplaced in single batteries, was not able to cope with the concentrated attacks, which were launched in particular against targets in the Ruhr in the spring of 1943. Up to this period, the defensive system had been based upon a division of Germany's industrial towns into sectors, each containing up to 30 searchlights and possibly twice as many heavy and light guns, and each sector was responsible for the defence of its own area. The method of defence was to concentrate all searchlights in each sector on a single hostile aircraft and to direct gunfire into the apex of the cone of searchlights. This system of visual fire, limiting in practice the number of gun engagements at one time to the number of sectors in the Ground Defence Area, was necessarily ineffective against attacks concentrated in time and numbers ; the higher the concentration achieved by Bomber Command, the fewer the aircraft engaged by Flak, and consequently not only was there a rapid decline in the number of losses to Flak, but it became possible to saturate and swamp the ground defences. In the course of 1943, therefore, a thorough-going reorganisation of German Flak was carried through, resulting in the discarding of the old scheme of " sector " defence. Instead, Flak was concentrated into *Grossbatterien*—large batteries, comprising 2–3 single batteries of the earlier pattern—at all large and important targets. In particular, the defences in the Ruhr, comprising approximately 200 heavy (8.8 cm.) batteries at the end of 1942, were practically doubled by bringing in all mobile reserves, including railway Flak, and the number of guns in a single battery was increased to six and eventually to eight. Simultaneously, increasing numbers of 10.5 cm. guns and the first 12.8 cm. static batteries came into operation in western Germany.

24. The switch-over to *Grossbatterien* solved some of the outstanding problems consequent on the introduction by Bomber Command of the pathfinder technique and of saturation tactics. From the summer of 1943 also, operations by massed *Grossbatterien* proved particularly effective against U.S.A.A.F. daylight attacks, particularly when carried out in clear weather allowing visual ranging. At night, also, the introduction of close co-operation

between Flak, searchlights and night fighters under the *Wilde Sau* system, brought improved results. But the introduction of '' window '' by Bomber Command in July, 1943, seriously—and, indeed, permanently—affected the efficiency of German Flak defences at night. Controlled fire at night was almost completely disrupted, and fixed box barrages alone remained feasible. Measures were, of course, immediately taken to overcome the jamming of radar and by the end of 1943 ranging was again possible ; but the quality of the locating henceforth 'remained inferior. By the end of 1943, furthermore, the increased use by the R.A.F. of bad weather conditions for large-scale raids was interferring with the effective operation of searchlights. The only answer, for the Luftwaffe, was to build up still further the Flak arm, to increase the weight of Flak opposition and above all to carry forward the process of concentrating the widely-dispersed defences around primary objectives which had begun in 1943. It was a policy of making up in quantity what had been lost in quality through the disruption by Allied electronic countermeasures of the established defensive system.

25. This build-up of Flak went on steadily from about August, 1943, to June, 1944, and was facilitated by the new outlook at Air Ministry which characterised Korten's tenure of the post of Chief of Air Staff. The problem was one not only of productive capacity and output, but also of manpower. This latter problem was solved, partly by decreasing the numbers of Flak personnel per battery, but mainly by drawing upon new sources of manpower, the chief of which were :—

(a) The *Reichsarbeitsdienst*, or Labour Service, which manned approximately 200 batteries within Germany in the period after August, 1943.

(b) The *Luftwaffenhelfer*—an approximate equivalent of the A.T.C.—providing some 75,000 students from secondary schools for assisting at the batteries.

(c) Female personnel (approximately 15,000) for staff duties.

(d) Russian P/W volunteers (approximately 45,000) and Croatian soldiers (approximately 12,000).

26. Through the opening up of these supplementary resources, it proved possible almost to double the numbers of personnel available—though not without adverse effects on quality—and thus to provide manpower for the expansion which was necessary to meet the growing scale of air attack, by day and by night, on the Reich. The armament of individual batteries, which in 1943 had been stepped up to 6–8 guns per battery, was in the first half of 1944 increased to 8–12 guns per battery, and searchlight batteries—in order to provide a bigger field of illumination for night fighters—were stepped up to 16 searchlights. In accordance with the new policy of giving first priority to the defence of the Reich, units were brought back from the East in order to undergo re-equipment for home defence ; thus, on the evacuation of the Crimea, the Flak division formerly located there was transferred to Upper Silesia. Railway Flak was moved back from French territory to the Reich, and additional railway Flak units were formed in order to provide better defence for trains against the increasingly insistent low-level attacks which already in the spring of 1944 were disrupting communications between Germany and the West in preparation for the Normandy landings. The main feature, however, was the stepping up of the output of weapons, which allowed rapid expansion

amounting in the early part of 1944 to 30–40 new heavy batteries, about 10 light batteries and 12 searchlight batteries per month. This expansion was concurrent with improvements in ammunition and the introduction of larger calibre guns, so that, as the numbers of batteries grew, an increasing proportion of high performance guns (8.8 cm. Flak 41 and 12.8 cm. Flak 40) became operative. Finally, anti-aircraft liaison officers (*Flakeinsatzfuehrer*) were installed in each Jagddivision to co-ordinate Flak operations.

27. Unlike the development of Flak defences in 1943, which was largely a reaction to R.A.F. night operations, the development and expansion in 1944 was largely necessitated by the growing weight of U.S.A.A.F. daylight attacks on industrial targets in the heart of Germany, in particular the attack on the aircraft industry in the spring of 1944 followed by the inauguration of crippling raids on the German synthetic oil plants.[1] This transfer of effort had two causes : first, the menacing character of the U.S.A.A.F. daylight raids ; secondly, the fact that R.A.F. jamming measures still severely limited the efficiency of German Flak at night, making it more profitable to concentrate on daylight defence. Hence, the Flak, which at night was largely inoperative, from this period began to score an increasing number of victories by day, particularly in defence of synthetic oil plants, and the proportion of U.S.A.A.F. losses to Flak steadily rose. After the first attacks on the synthetic oil industry, smaller Flak units were dissolved and reconcentrated round the main plants at Leuna, Poelitz, Brux, Blechhammer, Wesseling, Gelsenkirchen and Ludwigs-hafen, the plan being to bring up 300–400 guns, rising to 600 in the case of the biggest plants, including a large number of 12.8 cm. guns. These defences provided a formidable obstacle to U.S.A.A.F. attacks, and their effectiveness can be gauged from the fact that out of 766 aircraft despatched to attack Leuna in 10/10th cloud on 25th November, 1944, no less than 209 (i.e., 27 per cent.) returned with Flak damage, apart from bombers actually shot down by Flak in the course of operations.

28. The defence of oil targets—imposed by the threat to Germany's fuel supplies—was at the expense of general defensive commitments, and the concentration of Flak around the main synthetic oil plants weakened opposition elsewhere. Another factor affecting Flak defences of the Reich was the need to prepare against the expected Allied landings on the French coast, which led to the building up of the forces in France under Flakkorps III. This necessitated the transfer of approximately 3,500 light and medium guns to the French coast before the landings on 6th June, 1944, followed immediately after June 6th by a further 50 light batteries and 140 heavy batteries, including the bulk of the mobile railway Flak. Thus, the Normandy landings which (as we have seen) quickly ruined the German night fighter defences, also adversely affected the Flak defences of the Reich, drawing off considerable forces. The effects were not felt immediately, because the first weeks of the invasion of the Continent brought a noticeable respite in Anglo-American air activity over Reich territory ; but after the Allied breakthrough and the advance across France and the Netherlands, the Flak organisation, like its day and night fighter forces, was confronted by insuperable problems, particularly as from that time forward the attack by the U.S. 8th and 15th Air Forces and by Bomber Command was supplemented by continuous activity on the part of the Tactical Air Forces against shallow targets and communications in the rear

[1] See Chapter 15, paragraph 9.

of the German armies. This concentration of Allied air power, including light bombers and ground-strafing fighters against Reich territory opened a new phase with problems of its own, not least for the Flak which now, in addition to the long-standing defence of strategic targets, had ever-increasing commitments in defence of river crossings, road and rail communications, and in opposition to the threat of Allied airborne and paratroop landings.

The U.S.A.A.F. Day-bombing Offensive

Growing Threat of American Attacks

29. The threat from U.S.A.A.F. daylight bombing, which from the beginning of 1944 was a most serious menace to German war potential, had gradually come to a head during 1943, enforcing a progressive switch of emphasis from night to day defence, the effects of which have already been observed in the operational deployment of the Flak artillery. Whereas the night fighter defences, had, by the beginning of 1944, largely come up to German expectations, the day fighters, in spite of more rapid expansion and constant increases in the size of battle units, failed to secure any lasting success. Hence, after midsummer of 1943 an increasing proportion of Luftwaffe effort, productive capacity, planning and organisation was devoted to the problem of defeating the threat of deep-penetration raids in daylight and precision bombing of industrial targets.

30. It was after the middle of July, 1943, that the German Air Force, realising that daylight bombing was an immediate threat to Germany's capacity to prosecute the war, was compelled to take radical countermeasures. During the first six months of 1943, extending from the first U.S.A.A.F. attack on targets in German territory on January 27th to July 17th, U.S.A.A.F. activity had been largely of an experimental character. Of the 40 Fortress raids in this period, 27 were directed against U-boat bases and supply depôts, the remainder against miscellaneous industrial targets and airfields, whilst the weight of attack still fell on military targets in the occupied territory in the West. Moreover, operations were still on a modest scale, averaging 80-100 Fortresses over the period, rising to a peak of 250-300 in July. In this period, therefore, the Luftwaffe Operations Staff—still committed under Jeschonnek's régime to maximum support in the East and on the Mediterranean front—was content to leave defence in the hands of the small single-engined fighter force of approximately 250-300 aircraft based in France and the Low Countries. These units, operating on traditional lines, scrambled regularly against the bombers, intercepted in small formations with no serious attempt at tactical coordination, and made a determined effort to shoot down the bombers, even when the targets were in occupied territories. The result was to reveal the total inadequacy of traditional tactics against American formation flying. In the first place, the normal armament of the German fighters—which, in the case of the Me.109, was still only two machine guns of 7.9 mm. calibre and one of 13 mm. calibre— was inadequate against the heavily armoured and defended Fortresses. In the second place, the Germans were tactically unable to concentrate their forces, which were spread out thinly in a weak defensive screen from the Heligoland Bight almost to Biarritz, against the strong Spitfire escorts which accompanied the early Fortress raids against shallow targets ; hence, they went in to the

attack in a position of overwhelming numerical inferiority—normally only 15-20 fighters against a strongly escorted bomber formation—and incurred disproportionate losses. The resultant German fighter weakness facilitated the extension of Fortress raids beyond escort range ; and unescorted bombers, relying upon formation flying and coordinated fire-power as a defence, flew first to the Paris area, then into the northern French industrial area beyond Lille, and even to Holland, incurring minimal losses. The German Air Force, in a first attempt to bring tactics into line with new conditions, sought at this stage to withhold attacks until the fighter escort had left the Fortresses ; but owing to the inadequacy of German fighter armament the rate of loss inflicted on the U.S. bombers was far below expectation, and it seemed as though unescorted bombers, flying in close formation, could range far and wide with impunity.

31. It was in these circumstances, encouraged by the earlier successes, that the 8th U.S. Air Force based in England decided both to step up the scale of heavy bomber attacks and to extend the range of unescorted raids deep into Germany. This phase of U.S.A.A.F. operations extended, with intermissions, from 18th July to 14th October, 1943. The unescorted heavy bomber raids on the Reich were supported by medium bombers which carried out simultaneous attacks on airfields and other targets in occupied territory, with the intention of diverting at least part of the German fighter reaction from the main operation ; the medium bomber attacks were kept up with the object of wearing down and baffling the fighter defences, even on days when there were no major raids. Thus, in the period 18th July to 17th August, 1943, 9 heavy and 14 medium bomber raids took place, and the German reporting and controlling organisations frequently experienced great difficulty in differentiating in good time between major raids and diversions, with the result that a diversion often provoked a considerable fighter reaction before its true nature was recognised. With technical improvements in the reporting and controlling systems, however, the Germans overcame in large degree this difficulty ; in the period between August 18th and October 7th, when medium bombers operated on 29 days, the policy of ignoring such raids and reserving effort for major attacks on the Reich was applied with some success. In the same way, it was a cardinal feature of German Air Force policy—dictated by Goering himself and maintained in spite of the criticism of Staffel and Gruppe commanders, who saw the need for the moral benefit of occasional victories over Allied fighters—to avoid entanglement with the Allied fighter escort and to hold back attacks, where possible, until the Fortress formations were unescorted. This policy was dictated not merely by the desire to avoid unnecessary losses, but also by the overriding consideration that the bombers were the greatest menace, and that American precision bombing constituted a major threat to German war industry.

Special Measures and Technical Developments for Defence of the Reich

Moves to Counter the Daylight Bomber

32. It was the series of U.S. heavy bomber raids on targets within Germany, beginning on 18th July, 1943, and culminating in the deep thrust to Schweinfurt and Regensburg on August 17th, which awakened the German High Command

to the seriousness of the danger and provoked the energetic reactions which—under the direction of Generaloberst Korten—gave a new orientation to German air policy. The defeat of the daylight bomber now became the first concern of the Luftwaffe and in quick succession a series of measures and expedients was adopted, some only to be discarded as failures, which revealed the urgency of the problem and the necessity of sacrificing to it all other considerations. Some of these measures reached back in inception to the spring of 1943, to the period of the heavy raids on Bremen and Wilhelmshaven in March, but it was when Korten took over the post of Chief of Air Staff after the death of Jeschonnek that all were developed and coordinated, and it is therefore desirable to consider them together in chronological sequence, thus demonstrating the gradual evolution of German day fighter defences and their adaptation to the new circumstances and to the threat consequent on the inauguration of deep penetration raids into the heart of Germany. They may be summarised under the headings of production, dispositions, tactics and armament, in the following order :—

(a) Pre-requisite for all else was single-engined fighter expansion on a major scale. This was possible because Milch's 1942 programme of increased fighter output had, by June-July, 1943, taken full effect, total fighter output being well in excess of the target figure of 1,000 aircraft per month, including a high proportion of Me.109's and FW.190's. Between November, 1942, and July, 1943, German single-engined fighter production rose from about 480 to 800 aircraft per month, and including repaired aircraft, about 1,000 single-engined fighters were available monthly as replacements and for expansion. Hence, a considerable increase in first-line single-engined fighter strength took place between 1st January and 1st July, 1943, raising the actual (first-line) strength by 500 aircraft from a total of 1,250 to some 1,800 aircraft ; there were, of course, no reserves, as production was just keeping pace with expansion and replacements. The increase in output was, however, arrested after that date by the inauguration of U.S. daylight attacks on aircraft assembly plants, thus limiting further expansion at the very time when the American threat was growing more serious. Moreover, the extraordinarily heavy fighter wastage incurred at this period in the Mediterranean absorbed a large proportion of the new production, and offset the expansion, imposing limits on the numbers of aircraft available for defence of the Reich.

(b) As the seriousness of the threat to German industry became manifest, the Luftwaffe was therefore faced by the necessity of a far-reaching redisposition of its fighter forces. As early as July, 1943, two Gruppen of J.G.3 were transferred from Russia to Germany and the fighter defences of North Norway were weakened to build up the western defences. The process thus begun continued apace during August, September and October. As we have seen, the Russian, the Balkan and finally the Italian fronts were denuded of single-engined fighter cover ; in addition to J.G.3, J.G.27, J.G.11 and J.G.53 were assembled in the Reich as a reinforcement of the defences against daylight bombing. Hence, first-line single-engined fighter strength in Germany and the western occupied territories, which had been about 635 aircraft on 1st January, 1943, and rose to about 800 aircraft on July 1st, amounted by October 1st to approximately 975 aircraft capable of a very high scale of effort against unescorted bombers penetrating deeply into German territory.

(c) The reinforced single-engined fighter arm was supplemented, on many occasions, by twin-engined night fighters. This practice of employing night fighters against daylight raids began in March, 1943, before the single-engined fighter defences had been strengthened ; but it was still employed, for example, against the Schweinfurt raids on August 17th and October 14th, on both of which occasions approximately 90-100 sorties were flown by night fighters, and it is obvious that the intention was not merely to increase numerical opposition but also to take advantage of the night fighters' inherent advantages of range and endurance. Although the use of night fighters by day inevitably meant heavier losses, including highly-trained night flying crews who could ill be spared, the practice was therefore kept up, in spite of its potentially adverse effects on opposition to R.A.F. night raids. Not only could twin-engined fighters keep up the attack long after single-engined fighters had been compelled to land to re-fuel or re-arm, but also twin-engined aircraft, based far from the scene of operations could be brought up, in this way increasing defence in depth.

(d) Similar advantages for single-engined fighters were sought by a scheme introduced about May-June, 1943. This scheme involved stocking up a number of airfields within an area extending from the Pas de Calais eastwards to the Rhine and beyond, and south-eastwards towards the Swiss frontier, probably supplemented by a similar organisation covering the approaches to N.W. Germany via Holland. Each airfield envisaged for the scheme was to be permanently in a position to re-arm, re-fuel and service up to 30 fighters landing in the course of pursuit of U.S. aircraft. This made it possible for short-range aircraft to fly two or even three sorties against one raid, and at the same time greater flexibility of the daylight defences and a rapid concentration of aircraft against a particular raid were secured.

(e) The scheme outlined went hand in hand with, and was beyond doubt intended to facilitate, a radical change in single-engined fighter tactics. The methods of interception still in use on the eastern front, and used earlier in the West, under which individual units scrambled independently on receiving local warning of the approach of hostile bombers, had proved both costly and ineffective. By the summer of 1943 it was patent that the only prospect of success lay in concentrated attack by coordinated forces. This was secured by rapid expansion of the ground organisation, particularly of the Signals Intelligence service and of radar, by the development of a network of fighter control stations all over the Reich, and by centralisation of operational control from the Corps through the Division to the individual unit. The fighter Divisions, which had the immediate responsibility for the operations of subordinate units, received notice from Corps head-quarters and from their own plotting stations of the course of the raid, from the moment when the bombers began to formate in

England. The early warning system thus allowed them to prepare, and if necessary to redispose their units, and to bring them together at fixed assembly points (e.g., Hannover or Brunswick) at a pre-determined altitude in advance of the arrival of the bombers. Thus, in place of weak and scattered interception by dispersed formations of 15-20 fighters, which had been the rule at the beginning of 1943, concentrated formations of 50, 80, 100 or even 150 aircraft under control of the Divisions through the network of fighter control stations, were now thrown in to the attack.

(*f*) To make the most of the new tactics, the first essential was improved armament, since each fighter, no matter how big the formation, had to attack separately once within close firing range, and each had to face the combined fire power of the American bombers flying in close battle formation. Hence, the fire-power both of the Me.109 and of the FW.190 was stepped up. The former, in place of one 13-mm. and two 7.9-mm. machine guns was re-equipped with two 13-mm. machine guns and one 20-mm. cannon ; the FW.190, originally armed with two 13-mm. machine guns and two 20-mm. cannon had its cannon doubled and retained its two 13-mm. guns. These improvements lessened the discrepancy between the armament of the German fighters and that of the U.S.A.A.F. bombers ; but the combined fire-power of the American aircraft flying in close formation and trained in mutual defence, was still formidable, and called for special measures to break up bomber formations, thus mitigating the effects of cross-fire from the bombers and allowing German fighters to pick off stragglers.

(*g*) The first measure introduced for this purpose by the Germans was air-to-air bombing, first reported in N.W. Germany in May, 1943. But this expedient had obvious inherent defects, and was discarded after only four or five weeks of experiment, having failed to secure the desired results. Instead the Germans turned to the 21-cm. rocket mortar—a widely available infantry weapon, easily fitted to aircraft— which quickly proved its value as a means of breaking up bomber formations. This weapon came into general use in the German fighter force in the latter part of July, 1943, and its employment was rapidly extended. In the first place it was mounted on single-engined fighters, the number so equipped and available in Germany and Western Europe increasing rapidly to a total of 110-130 aircraft by the end of October, 1943. More significant, however, was the decision to re-equip twin-engined day fighter types (Me.110 and Me.410) with rocket mortars, the twin-engined fighters being able to mount four mortars per aircraft instead of two in the case of single-engined fighters. During August, September and October, Me.110 units were recalled from the Russian front, the Bay of Biscay and the Mediterranean, and were transferred to N.W. Germany ; in addition they were reinforced by a newly-formed Me.110 unit with some 50 aircraft, and by a long-range bomber unit (KG 51) withdrawn from the East and re-equipped with Me.410 aircraft carrying 21-cm. mortars against U.S.A.A.F. bombers. Thus, by the end of October, 1943, at least 150-175 twin-engined fighters equipped with rocket mortars were available. These aircraft were based in western

Germany behind a single-engined fighter screen in France, Belgium and Holland, and were held back until the American bomber formations were beyond the range of their fighter escort ; they normally refused battle with escorted bombers, their rôle being to attack unescorted formations in deep penetration over Reich territory, to break them up and thus to create an opportunity for single-engined fighters to press home their attacks.

Temporary Success Against Daylight Bombers

33. The effects of the tactical and technical innovations reviewed above, and of the rapid reinforcement of the daylight defences of the Reich, were seen between August and October, 1943. Particularly effective against unescorted bombers was the 21-cm. mortar, which was fired from outside the effective range of the American 0.5-in. machine guns, which had provided a formidable defence against orthodox attacks. The introduction of twin-engined fighters armed each with four mortars thus went far to restore equality between defence and attack, particularly when backed up by the increased weight of single-engined fighter operations, and it was in these new circumstances that the German defences scored their first major success. This was against the double raid on Schweinfurt and Regensburg on August 17th, when apart from the twin-engined fighter effort, over 500 sorties were flown by single-engined fighter units based in France, the Low Countries and N.W. Germany, the result being the loss of 60 bombers out of 376 taking part, or approximately 16 per cent. This reverse led to a revision of American bombing policy, lasting from August 18th to October 7th, during which period only three out of 15 heavy bomber raids were against targets in Germany. At the same time, the necessity under the new conditions for continuous escort was realised by the Americans and the development of long-range fighter cover began. Thus, on September 27th, a Fortress raid on Emden was given continuous Thunderbolt cover, and this raid was also one of the first to employ pathfinder technique for daylight bombing through cloud. But, owing to limitations on fighter range, escorted raids could only reach fringe targets in Germany, and limitation of operational activity to such attacks meant therefore the abandoning of the planned programme of a systematic onslaught on German war industry deep in Reich territory. Hence, after a series of attacks by medium bombers on German single-engined fighter bases in occupied countries, intended to weaken the German single-engined fighter defences, the policy of deep unescorted penetration was resumed.

34. The renewed deep penetration raids, carried out with extraordinary determination on October 8th-10th and October 14th met the full vigour of the reorganised German fighter defences with the result that severe losses were again experienced. In what was a decisive engagement, determining the whole future of unescorted bombing, the Luftwaffe proved equal to its task, and the whole range of its tactics was fully exploited. Single-engined fighters made successful interceptions over very long distances ; areas denuded of fighters were reinforced by switching units from neighbouring sectors not directly threatened ; and both day and night twin-engined fighters were employed in considerable numbers, full use being made of the rocket mortar weapon. Moreover, the German Air Force proved that, in spite of severe losses, it was able to maintain a high rate of effort in consecutive operations. Thus, its greatest success was scored on October 14th, when well over 500 sorties were

flown against U.S. bombers raiding Schweinfurt, losses inflicted on the raiders amounting to 60 out of 294 aircraft, or more than 20 per cent. of the American force engaged. The overall U.S.A.A.F. rate of loss for the four days (October 8th, 9th, 10th and 14th) was 11 per cent.

Additional U.S. Penetrations from Italy

35. This rate of loss was prohibitive, and the Schweinfurt raid of 14th October, 1943, was the last of the series of unescorted deep-penetration raids into Germany. The German success was undeniable, and the 8th Air Force was forced to call a halt and revise its tactics. But the period from October 15th to the end of 1943 saw the development of another threat, in the form of 15th U.S.A.A.F. bombing from Italy, which allowed the German Air Force no respite and necessitated a build-up of fighter defences in South Germany and Austria. Moreover, the 8th Air Force was quick to recover from the shock administered on October 14th, and although no attacks comparable to that on Schweinfurt were carried out during the remainder of 1943, much effort was devoted to the tactical innovations designed to overcome the temporary German success. The first of these was the development of continuous fighter escort by relays to and from the target. The second was the increasing use of instrument bombing through cloud. The latter expedient was particularly effective in the winter months at the end of 1943, and serious limitations were imposed on the orthodox German single-engined fighter force which was neither trained nor equipped for blind flying. Hence, the Germans decided to employ the single-engined night fighters—whose period of usefulness against R.A.F. night raids had passed—for the interception of bad-weather missions. But against the fully escorted raids into N.W. Germany which were typical of this phase of operations, success was meagre, and generally limited to occasions when the fighter escort failed, due to weather conditions or for other reasons, to locate the bomber formations.

The Shock to the Germans of the Escorted Bomber : Appearance of U.S. Long-Range Fighters

36. The decisive factor, enabling the U.S.A.A.F. to resume its attacks on German industry deep in Reich territory, was the appearance at the beginning of 1944 of Thunderbolts and Mustangs with a range far in excess of anything previously experienced. The rapid development in the latter months of 1943 of the new American long-range fighter—in itself an astounding feat of energy and productive capacity—took the Germans completely by surprise ; its appearance was, said Goering, " a tragedy ". When the first appearance of the fighters over Hannover was reported, the report was received by Goering himself with incredulity and the reporting centre concerned was reprimanded. But when, shortly afterwards, the A.O. for Fighters, General Leutnant Galland, accompanied by his Chief Inspector, Oberst Trautloft, took off on operations to observe the performance of the German fighters, he was chased by four Mustangs back to Berlin. From this stage forward the die was cast. The Luftwaffe for the first time had no answer to the daylight bombing threat. The twin-engined fighter equipped with 21 cm. mortars, which had already been proved exceptionally vulnerable to U.S. fighters in the autumn of 1943, became obsolete. As a desperate remedy, *Sturmstaffeln* were formed, manned by picked crews inculcated with a spirit of determination and recklessness and encouraged to ram Allied bombers rather than return to base without a victory. The inception of the scheme dated back to the winter of 1943-44 ; but it was

Oberstleutnant (Wing Commander) Lent, the night fighter ace, is congratulated by Hitler after decoration with the Diamonds to the Knight's Cross.

Funeral of Lent ; Goering takes the salute

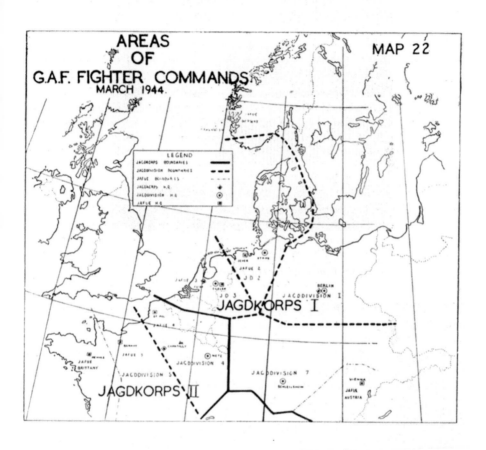

AREAS
OF
G.A.F. FIGHTER COMMANDS
MARCH 1944.

MAP 22

LEGEND
JAGDKORPS BOUNDARIES
JAGDDIVISION BOUNDARIES
JAFUE BOUNDARIES
JAGDKORPS H.Q.
JAGDDIVISION H.Q.
JAFUE H.Q.

JAGDKORPS I

JAGDKORPS II

JAFUE DENMARK

JAFUE 2
J D 2
J D 3
JACDDIVISION I
BERLIN

ST POL
JAFUE 4

JAFUE 3
CHANTILLY
METZ
JACDDIVISION 4
JACDDIVISION 7
VIENNA
JAFUE BRITTANY
JACDDIVISION 5
SCHLEISSHEIM
JAFUE AUSTRIA

not until July, 1944, that the first *Sturmgruppe* (IV/JG.3) went into action. But the very conception of the *Sturmstaffel*, with its emphasis on the destruction of bombers, was in itself an indication of the failure of the Luftwaffe to adapt its tactics to the new situation. In accordance with orders from Goering, the weight of attack was still thrown against the American bomber formations, and, partly to conserve forces, the German fighters were instructed to avoid the American fighter escort. The result was, as the Kommodore of J.G.6, pungently said, that " the safest flying that was ever possible was that of an American fighter over Germany ". Nor were the psychological results insignificant ; the German pilots developed a sense of inferiority, the American pilots a marked attitude of superiority ; and soon the latter, who at first had proceeded with due caution, sought out and attacked the German fighters and prevented them from approaching the American bomber formations.

37. It was under such conditions that, in February, 1944, the U.S.A.A.F. was able to revert, on a scale hitherto unknown, to the attack on German fighter aircraft production and assembly plants, which had been virtually suspended since October, 1943. Already at the beginning of the month, attacks on targets in Western Germany—e.g., the raids on Brunswick and Frankfurt on February 10th and 12th—had resulted in major German losses, averaging about 10 per cent. of the fighters engaged. Between February 20th and 25th this success was follows up by an all-out attack on the German aircraft industry, targets attacked including the Ju.88 plants at Bernberg, Aschersleben and Halberstadt, Me.109 assembly at Regensburg and Erla/Leipzig, FW.190 production at Tuetow and Oschersleben, the Me.110 plants at Gotha, Brunswick and Fuerth, the Messerschmitt factories at Augsburg and He.111 production at Rostock. These attacks are estimated to have resulted in an immediate loss of production, between 20th February and 1st April, 1944, of 1,000 aircraft. In addition they demonstrated the absolute superiority of the U.S.A.A.F. German losses were at the prohibitive rate of 10-15 per cent., and even at this heavy cost they were unable to prevent the 8th and 15th Air Forces from reaching and attacking their targets. Galland, the most energetic and efficient German expert, realised the failure of German tactics, particularly of the policy of concentrating opposition against the bombers, and sought to develop special " high altitude " fighter units, the first of which made its appearance in April or May, to engage the American fighter escort ; but he was hampered by the conservatism of his superiors, particularly Goering, and unable to secure approval for a reorientation of German fighter policy. Hence, the American fighters continued to operate with impunity, and after the middle of March the heavy bomber attack on the German aircraft industry was supported by long-range fighter missions against airfields and depôts with the object of wiping out aircraft on the ground, thus preventing recovery from the blow struck between February 20th and February 25th.

38. The appearance of the American long-range escort fighter and the attacks on the German aircraft industry thereby made possible thus inaugurated a new and decisive phase in the air war. Every aspect of the German war effort was affected by the American success in overcoming the obstacles to daylight precision bombing, which had beset its policy between the end of October, 1943 and January, 1944. This was seen when, from May, 1944 onwards, the American attack was switched from aircraft to oil, and the German Air Force, which had just faced a threat to its productive capacity, was confronted by the danger of

inadequate fuel supplies restricting operations. The heavy wastage incurred in defence against American daylight raids also resulted in a serious shortage of experienced pilots, with immediate repercussions on the fighting efficiency of the defensive forces, and from April, 1944 onwards, it was necessary to take emergency measures and comb transport, reconnaissance and ultimately even bomber units for aircrew capable of rapid retraining on fighter-type aircraft. But the essential requirement was more fighters, more aircraft, to contest the U.S.A.A.F. air ascendency, to protect the aircraft and synthetic fuel industries, and finally to restore fighter strength on all the battlefronts, which had been depleted far below the bare minimum in order to meet the demands and requirements of the daylight defence of the Reich.

Reorganisation of German Home Defence Commands

39. The whole of the organisation of the Luftwaffe, on the eve of the Allied landings in Normandy, was thus charged with a sense of crisis and emergency, which was heightened by the knowledge that the Allied landings would bring with them, as an inevitable concomitant, further heavy demands on the single-engined fighter forces, which in the occupied territories of the West had by this time been reduced to 170 aircraft, of which only about 50 were available in N.W. France. The consequence of the American deep escorted daylight raids was therefore to enforce far-reaching reorganisation (see Map 22). First, in point of time was a thorough reorganisation of the chain of command, to secure more effective control and employment of the fighter defences. This went back to 30th January, 1944, when Luftflotte Reich was set up under Generaloberst Stumpff and the seven Fighter Divisions (Jagddivisionen) were regrouped under two Jagdkorps, with the intention at a later date—never implemented—of calling a third Jagdkorps into existence in southern Germany[1]. Secondly, there was a new scheme (*Windhund*) for the rapid retraining of bomber pilots to fighter aircraft. But most important of all were the steps taken to improve and speed-up fighter output. This reorganisation had two facets. The one was to bring about at the earliest possible moment the introduction of reaction-propelled aircraft (Me.163, Me.262) in order to contest the American qualitative superiority ; but this was delayed by the damage to plants, which has already been noted, and subsequently—as will be seen later— by long-drawn-out controversy between the advocates of bombing and the advocates of fighting as to the use to which the new jet types were to be put. More immediately effective were the steps taken to expand the production of orthodox fighter types. These resulted in the displacement of Milch, who had been Director-General of Air Force equipment since December, 1941, and the transfer of aircraft production to Speer, who appointed Sauer to the head of a newly-formed Fighter Staff (*Jaegerstab*), set up in March, 1944. Under Sauer's energetic leadership a remarkable recovery was effected from the effects of the American attack on the aircraft industry by such methods as dispersal of plants, and from June, 1944, the output of Me.109's and FW.190's went ahead by leaps and bounds. Plans were laid for an increase in the production of fighters of all types to a total of over 5,000 aircraft per month ; and although for some months Goering and Hitler resisted the reduction in the output of bombers and miscellaneous types which was necessary to achieve this target, by July 1944 even they were won over and bomber output was cut down, apart from the new jet types absolute priority being given to fighter aircraft.

---

[1] For further details of the reorganisation in the Chain of Command to meet the impending Allied landings in Normandy, cf. Chapter 13.

40. Thus, primarily as a result of U.S.A.A.F. daylight bombing, a complete change had come over the German Air Force by midsummer, 1944. Before we proceed to the next phase of operations, which opened with the Anglo-American landings in Normandy on 6th June, 1944, it is therefore necessary to halt and to review—by comparison with the position at the beginning of 1943—the character and the composition, the dispositions and the potentialities of the German Air Force as it was constituted on the eve of the long-awaited opening of the " Second Front ". Such a survey, revealing its strength and weaknesses, will enable us to assess its fighting value in the final phase of the war, which extended from 6th June, 1944 to 5th May, 1945.

The Defence against Strategic Bombing and its Effects on the German Military Effort

41. The very considerable elements of the German fighter force and Flak engaged in the defence of German industry against Allied strategic bombing represented a formidable proportion of Germany's striking force. The absorption of fighters has already been discussed, and as regards Flak, some 30 per cent. of the total output of German artillery in 1944 consisted of Flak guns together with 20 per cent. of the output of the heavier calibres of ammunition for Flak shells. One-third of the optical industry was engaged in the production of aiming devices for Flak and other anti-aircraft equipment.

42. Between 50 and 60 per cent. of the armament production capacity and the electro-technical industry was engaged in the production of radar and signals equipment for defence against bomber attacks. Consequently, there was a shortage of army signals equipment of all types, whilst the radar requirements of the Navy were likewise only partly met. In the case of the Luftwaffe, 50 per cent. of the valves produced for their requirements were diverted to home defence needs.

43. The fighting power of the German Armed Forces was thus considerably weakened by reason of the priority given to defence, reflecting Hitler's conviction that the best defence was in Flak rather than in fighters, a view opposed not only by members of the Luftwaffe Higher Command but by Speer. Moreover, the consequences of these defensive operations need to be considered in terms of military strategy. The Allied air offensive in the summer of 1944 succeeded in its purpose of eliminating the enemy's supplies of liquid fuel and it succeeded with a far smaller cost in casualties than would have been incurred had there been no resort to the bombing of industrial capacity. In addition, a decisive victory was scored in rendering abortive the massing of these ground and air defences and thereby preventing their deployment in a more destructive rôle.

PART FOUR

Decline and Fall of the German Air Force
(1944–1945)

CHAPTER 13

THE GERMAN AIR FORCE ON THE EVE OF THE SECOND FRONT
(January–June, 1944)

The General Situation at the Beginning of 1944

Grounds for Optimism

1. In many respects the German Air Force at the beginning of 1944 was giving signs of new life after the rout it had suffered in the Mediterranean and on the Russian front during the summer and early autumn of 1943. First-line strength, although not fully recovered to the peak of July, 1943, was again rising, thanks to the efforts of Milch in stepping up production, and a vast improvement had occurred in all categories as compared with 12 months earlier, as will be seen from the following table :—

			First-line Strength	
			1st January,	1st January,
Category			1943	1944
Long Range Bombers	..	..	1,135	1,580
Ground Attack	..	..	270	610
Single-engined Fighters	..	..	1,245	1,535
Twin-engined Fighters	..	..	495	905
Long Range Reconnaissance		..	400	425
Tactical Reconnaissance	..	..	275	330
Coastal	..	..	135	200
Total ..	..	..	3,955	5,585

2. There were other ostensible grounds for satisfaction : the fuel situation was showing a marked improvement, thanks to output from synthetic oil plants being at its peak, and reserves were in consequence being rapidly built up to a level higher than any reached since the summer of 1941 ; this was assisted, however, not only by the seasonal decline in operational activity, but also by a certain conservation of effort aided at this juncture by the fact that heavy Allied daylight raids deep into Germany had, for the time being, been discontinued. Training during 1943 had also shown a remarkable improvement over 1942, following General Leutnant Kreipe's appointment as Air Officer for Training in June, 1943 ; the numerical output of crews, increased according to programme to meet existing deficiencies and at the same time the anticipated expansion of first-line strength in 1943, had, during the year, been fully up to schedule.

3. At the same time, new and improved types of aircraft were beginning to come forward, which were calculated to offset the disadvantages of inferior performance from which the Luftwaffe was increasingly suffering vis-à-vis the more modern equipment of the Allied air forces, particularly in the West. Thus, the FW.190 was being rapidly introduced into the single-engined fighter force, and at the same time into the ground attack units in place of the obsolete

301

Ju.87; the Ju.188 was beginning to come off the production line—together, at last, with the long awaited He.177—to improve the quality of the long-range bomber force, while the Me.410 and He.219 were also now appearing as improved twin-engined fighter types, the latter the nearest equivalent to the British Mosquito. Moreover, a beginning had been made with the jet-propelled Me.262, although it was not destined to appear in operations until the autumn of 1944.

4. Further, the cessation of daylight bombing raids deep into the Reich, and the fact that British night bombing was now being mainly confined to targets in western Germany following the Luftwaffe's night fighter successes of the summer and autumn of 1943, afforded justifiable reasons for confidence that at last the fighter defences were proving a match for the Allied heavy bomber forces[1].

5. There were, consequently, certain solid grounds, for the Germans, for feeling that things were beginning to take a turn for the better, although it was recognised that in face of the vast resources of Allied air power, the Luftwaffe would still be far from adequate in the steadily deteriorating strategic situation of Germany, with the certainty that the coming summer would see the long awaited Allied landing in the West.

Elements of Weakness

6. Despite the successes gained in the autumn of 1943 against American unescorted daylight bomber raids, it was clear that the Allied bombing threat, both by day and by night, constituted the most immediate menace threatening Germany, the effects of which at this stage have already been reviewed in Chapter 12. The concentration of fighters in Germany and the West which this threat entailed meant that, despite an increase in first-line strength of some 1,600 aircraft during 1943, there could be no improvement in the forces available on the main battle fronts in Russia and in the Mediterranean by January, 1944, a fact clearly shown by the distribution of forces in the following table :—

	First-line Strength	
	1st January, 1943	1st January, 1944
Western Front	} 1,445	{ 1,410
Defence of Reich		{ 1,225
Eastern Front	1,530	1,710
Mediterranean and Balkans	855	505
Non-operational	125	735
Total	3,955	5,585

7. In spite of the favourable factors, there were, therefore, considerable grounds for disquiet as to the situation with which the Luftwaffe could expect to be confronted when faced with the full weight of Allied military strength from East, West and South, particularly in the air, in 1944. To observers in a position to form a sound judgment, it was patent that the resources of the Luftwaffe would be totally inadequate to meet the demands which would be imposed on it. Nevertheless, it was impossible for Milch and his production chiefs, as always during the war, to persuade Hitler and the General Staff to

[1] See Chapter 12, paragraphs 17–19.

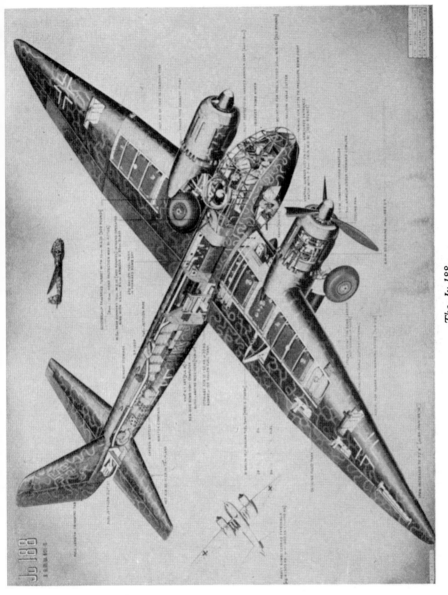

The Ju.188

This type was actually a much-improved version of the Ju.88, with a far better performance and armament (compare illustrations of the Ju.88 on pages 23/99).

303

The He.177

This four-engined bomber (with two coupled engines driving each propeller) was one of Germany's great failures in aircraft design. Its maximum bomb load of 15,400 lbs. was high, and it had ample internal bomb-stowage space, but its performance was mediocre. In the attacks on England in January to April, 1944 (see para. 40), the He.177 often carried two 2,500 kilogramme bombs—the Luftwaffe's heaviest—which were too large to be carried internally and were hung on the external carriers under the wing. Its maximum range was 2,850 miles.

The Focke-Wulf fighter assembly plant at Marienburg before and after attack by the U.S. 8th Air Force.

afford still greater priority to aircraft production until events finally forced their hand ; moreover, the improvement in training output masked vital weaknesses in the training organisation, amongst which was the fact that such improvement had only been achieved by a reduction in flying training hours and consequently in quality of crews. The following paragraphs review these and other factors as they affected the preparation by the Luftwaffe to meet its greatest test.

<hr>

The Allied Attack on the German Aircraft Industry

The Fighter Assembly Plants

8. As has already been seen[1], the aircraft production programme at the beginning of 1944 was still based on Milch's schedule for an increase in output drawn up in 1942, although the inability of either Hitler or Goering to visualise the future need for fighters had prevented priority being given to this category until after July, 1943. Nevertheless, the improvement in all-round first-line strength at the beginning of 1944 was the direct outcome of Milch's efforts.

9. By July, 1943, single-engined fighter production had reached a new peak of 1,050 aircraft per month (725 Me.109's and 325 FW.190's) and had led to a substantial increase in first-line strength. The recognition by the Allied Intelligence of this fact and of its consequences—if permitted to continue—upon American plans for daylight bombing, brought about the first bombing offensive against the fighter assembly plants. In this offensive the large-scale attacks on Me.109 and FW.190 production at Regensburg, Wiener Neustadt and Marienburg in August and October were outstanding. The strength of the German fighter defences did not, however, permit these costly undertakings to be maintained ; nevertheless, they were not without effect, for apart from the damage caused, they also brought home the necessity for greater dispersal of the aircraft industry. Consequently, fighter production remained somewhat below the 1,000 mark for the remainder of 1943, and did not recover to the former figure until February, 1944, resulting in the loss of some 4,000–5,000 aircraft on the planned programme covering the period.

The U.S. Long-Range Fighter and the Assault on the German Aircraft Industry

10. It was at this point that the whole situation was violently changed in February, 1944 : (a) by the appearance of the American long-range day fighter, and (b) by the renewal and intensification of the attack on the aircraft industry, which coincided. The long-range escort fighter at a stroke capsized German defensive air strategy, for the Luftwaffe Planning Staff had been lulled into a false sense of security during the winter of 1943-44 on the assurance of the Research and Development Branch that such an aircraft was a technical impossibility ; the views of this body had, moreover, deprived the Luftwaffe of the advantage of developing this type of aircraft. Its appearance at the shortest notice in large numbers meant that the German defensive commitment had overnight been magnified beyond all expectations ; it cast existing plans and schedules for aircraft production and training into the melting pot. Added to this, the weight and accuracy of the February assault on the aircraft industry brought a new and forceful realisation of the meaning of Allied air power and the extent of the threat to German war industry as a whole ; in these February attacks alone, 23 airframe and 3 engine factories were hit, and the weight of bombs was only slightly less than in the whole of the previous bombing of aircraft plants.

<hr>

[1] Chapter 9, paragraph 16 *et seq.*

G.A.F. A/C. ACCEPTANCES BY TYPE.
Dec. 1943-Dec. 1944

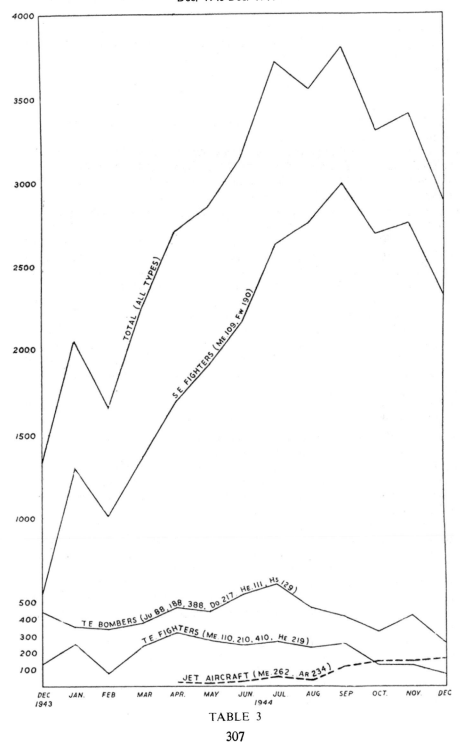

TABLE 3

Two high-performance aircraft of the German Air Force. The Ta.152 (above) developed by the Focke-Wulf company, was delivered to operational units in small numbers only, and the Do.335 (below) had not passed the final development stage by the time the war ended. Note the two in-line engines and the rear propeller.

Setting up of the Jaegerstab[1]

11. Such a situation called for desperate measures and it was in these circumstances that a *Jaegerstab* was set up. It functioned under Speer's Ministry for Armament and War Production, in which Saur was charged with the responsibility of effecting an immediate further dispersal of the industry and simultaneously an expansion of aircraft production to the maximum possible. Even at this juncture, however, it was impossible to secure full priority for the fighter programme against Hitler's obstinate demands for a stronger bomber force with which to retaliate. Throughout March, April and May, 1944, the Allied bombing offensive continued on the heaviest scale, with the main weight directed against airframes, particularly Me.109 and FW.190 targets, while engine factories were also receiving serious attention. By the end of April, with dispersal schemes coming rapidly into operation, the industry was, however, already becoming a less attractive bombing target.

12. While the immediate purpose of the *Jaegerstab* was to take over responsibility for all future aircraft production, and in particular fighter output, a revision of existing programmes with a view to the pruning of sub-types and the introduction of simplified methods was an extension of its functions which logically followed. At this time the number of aircraft types and sub-types in simultaneous production was about 200, a figure which the *Jaegerstab* reduced to 20. However, it was not until July that Saur was at last able to obtain Hitler's consent to a reduction in bomber output in favour of an all-out drive for fighter production.

Success of the Jaegerstab

13. The achievement of the *Jaegerstab* in attaining its objective was astonishing and beyond all expectation, it completely defeated the aim of the Allied attacks to knock out aircraft production in that the attacks led directly to an upward revision of future programmes and encouraged a more vigorous dispersal policy. While these operations did, in fact, cause a loss to production of a further 4,000 fighter aircraft, acceptance of single-engined fighters in March exceeded the January level of 1,300, and were followed in April by an increase of 25 per cent.; thereafter, output continued to mount rapidly until a peak of nearly 3,000 was reached in September (1,605 Me.109's and 1,390 FW.190's), and, although a decline then set in, the level remained at 2,700–2,300 until the end of the year. (See Table 3.) Consequently, in December, 1944, the number of aircraft produced was still higher than at any time previous to May, 1944, and was nearly twice as high as in the previous December. For the whole of 1944 single-engined fighter output was nearly 300 per cent. greater than for 1943, while twin-engined fighters also showed an increase of 50 per cent., in addition to which the bulk of the Ju.88 production was absorbed into the night-fighter force from July onwards. Much of this accomplishment was due to the intense development of the FW.190 production complexes during the year. Whereas output of the Me.109 rose from 930 in January, 1944, to 1,600 in September, that of the FW.190 in the same period jumped from 380 to no less than 1,390, a most remarkable increase.

Loss of High Performance Aircraft

14. It will be noted that the expansion was confined to stock types and that no aircraft of higher performance (with the exception of jet and rocket-propelled aircraft) were introduced. The failure of many of these to appear is

---

[1] Fighter Committee.

309

attributable to the effects of Allied bombing. Thus, series production of the Focke-Wulf Ta.152, considered to be a better fighter than either the Me.109 or FW.190 in speed, ceiling and above all, endurance, was planned to begin in October, 1944. The fact that large-scale production of this aircraft never got under way was partly due to Allied air attacks on the aircraft industry and transport, although probably the most influential factor was the determination of the *Jaegerstab* to produce the maximum possible number of aircraft if necessary at the expense of improvements in performance. Again the Do.335 was delayed by an attack on the Dornier plant at Manzel in March, 1944, which destroyed all the production tools ; neither of these aircraft got beyond conversion units and therefore failed to appear in operations. The Ta.154, a counterpart to the Mosquito, had also to be scrapped after the sole plant for the preparation used for glueing plywood sections was put out of action by air attack ; finally, the He.219 never recovered from the bombing of the factory at Vienna-Schwechat in April and June, 1944, although it did reach the operational stage in small numbers in a single night fighter unit.

15. The advantages which might have been expected to have accrued from this huge expansion in fighter production never, in fact, materialised for reasons given below in this chapter and in later chapters of this book. It is sufficient here to state that the switching of the Allied air offensive against the synthetic oil plants was the most important factor in crippling the ability of the Luftwaffe to play a major rôle from August, 1944, onwards[1]. The Luftwaffe suffeied from no shortage of aircraft in the last six months of the war, as shown by the strength of the single-engined fighter force, which rose from 1,535 aircraft on 1st January, 1944, to a peak of over 3,000 by mid-November, and was still at 2,275 by the end of the year[2]. Similarly, the twin-engined fighter force grew from 900 to 1,290 aircraft in the same period. At the same time, combat losses and non-operational flying wastage did not account, together with these increases, for the whole of the vast output for 1944, and the fact that first-line strength did not reach still greater proportions is attributable only to heavy losses of aircraft on the ground largely by the Allied low-level strafing and, to a lesser extent, by bombing. In all, probably some 9,000 aircraft are to be accounted for in this way.

16. Second only to the fuel crisis, and in part deriving from it, a factor in the failure of the German Air Force to exploit the resources at its disposal was the failure of the training organisation to produce crews adequately trained to a standard remotely approaching that of the Allied pilots to whom they were opposed. The reasons for this failure are dealt with later in this chapter, while its consequences and effects are to be seen in steadily declining fighting value of the Luftwaffe as a whole, and particularly the day fighter force in the course of 1944[3].

Jet Aircraft—Fighter or Bomber ?

17. In the final stages of the war it was upon jet-propelled aircraft that the Luftwaffe came to place its main hopes. The Me.262 had been developed as early as 1937 and was flown experimentally in 1941, but was then rejected, since the need for it then was not apparent, and perhaps because it involved too many

---

[1] See Chapter 15, and Chapter 14 (paragraphs 21, 25 and 27).

[2] See Chapter 17, paragraph 1 and footnote to 19.

[3] See paragraphs 23–29 below, and Chapters 14 (paragraphs 22–23) and 17 (paragraph 4).

THE LUFTWAFFE'S TWO MAIN JET TYPES

Me.262.   It had a maximum speed as a fighter of 525 m.p.h. at 22,960 feet, and a range of 750 miles.   Its armament was four 3 cm. cannons.

Ar.234.   This aircraft had a maximum speed of 472 m.p.h. at 19,700 feet (service ceiling 31,150 feet).   Its bomb load was 2,200 lb.

311

The Me.163 liquid fuel rocket-propelled fighter. Designed by Dr. Lippisch, of Messerschmitt's, it had an extremely rapid rate of climb. It was intended as an intercepter for the high-flying U.S.A.A.F. daylight bombers over Germany. The two-wheel undercarriage was jettisoned after take-off.

The He.162 intercepter fighter. Powered by a B.M.W. turbo-jet with a static thrust of 1,760 lb., it had a maximum speed of 520 m.p.h. at 19,700 feet. Its armament consisted of two 20-mm. or alternatively two 3-cm. cannons.

complications for practical use ; its introduction would also have required the extensive re-training of pilots. The intensification of Allied bombing from 1943 onwards, however, urged the necessity of developing a new type of exceedingly fast interceptor fighter, and production of the Me.262 accordingly began in March, 1944 ; output numbered 16 in April and rose to 28 in June and 59 in July, when the Ar.234 also began to appear in small numbers.

18. Both types had been demonstrated before Hitler at Insterburg in East Prussia in the winter of 1943-44 and it was at this time that it was suggested that the Me.262 could carry a 1,000-kg.[1] bomb load. Hitler, still obsessed with the idea of offensive air warfare, subsequently ordered that the Me.262's, when they appeared, were to be developed as high-speed daylight bombers ; he thereby precipitated a controversy which raged throughout the remainder of 1944 as to the most suitable employment of this aircraft. Hitler's decision was violently opposed by Galland and other responsible senior officers of the Air Force who saw in the jet aircraft the ideal answer to Allied daylight bombing, but the order could not be reversed. Consequently, the re-training and re-equipment programme was largely overshadowed by this policy for the remainder of the year, and in the autumn of 1944 no less than nine former long-range bomber units were in process of conversion to the Me.262.

19. Nevertheless, Galland was successful in maintaining his standpoint to the extent that the Me.262 did actually first appear in operations as a fighter, and he was able to set up a special experimental Me.262 fighter unit commanded by Major Nowotny in the autumn of 1944 ; thus, it came about that no less than 50 Me.262's were being employed as fighters in October, a greater number than were at the time available for bomber units.

20. Although during the winter of 1944-45 a jet fighter Geschwader was in process of being formed, it was not until the final throes of catastrophe had been reached that it was finally decided to throw the whole of the German jet resources into fighter defence : at the end of March, 1945, when dissolution and disintegration were already becoming apparent in the Air Force. Hitler raised the whole jet programme out of the normal Luftwaffe channels and placed it in the hands of the S.S. General der Waffen, S.S. Dr. Ing. Kammler, who was appointed " General Plenipotentiary of the Fuehrer for jet propelled aircraft " with authority to exercise administrative control of personnel for jet units, of the build-up of ground organisation and the allotment of aircraft. This " Fuehrer programme " entailed the withdrawal of jet bomber units from ground attack operations and their employment for strategic fighter defence ; in this capacity they became increasingly active, although not noticeably effective, and certainly very expensive owing to the pilots being untrained and inexperienced in new tactics. In any event, Germany was then tottering to her final collapse and it was too late for such tardy measures to be any longer of significance except to emphasise for the last time the deplorable effects of Hitler's interference in Luftwaffe matters.

The Me.163 and He.162

21. The introduction of the Me.163 (rocket propelled) and He.162 (single jet) fighters also formed part of the *Jaegerstab's* plans for the rapid development of new high performance aircraft for air defence. The development of the Me.163 had already been envisaged simultaneously with the decision taken in

---

[1] Actually, the Me.262 never carried more than a 500-kg. load.

the winter of 1943-44 to put the Me.262 and Ar.234 into series production, and in June the first aircraft began to appear in an operational unit (J.G.400) : by September output had reached 35 and was increased to 60 in October and finally to 90 in December, by which time 45 of these aircraft had become operational. Although this unorthodox aircraft possessed a remarkable performance, particularly in climbing powers, its endurance was short, and for various reasons it proved unsatisfactory. It was accordingly dropped from the production programme from January, 1945 onwards and its place taken by the He.162.

22. The He.162 (*Volksjaeger*)[1] was a remarkable aircraft in that it was designed, tried out and adopted for large-scale production in less than four months. In September, 1944, a programme was drawn up for an output of 1,000 aircraft by the following April, a figure which was again stepped up in December following the decision to abandon the Me.163. Great hopes were pinned on this small mass-produced fighter, but it was destined never to be operationally employed, and teething troubles delayed its coming into production in large numbers before the end of the war. Subsequent examination of the aircraft by Allied technical establishments showed that it was aerodynamically unsound and could never, in fact, have been an effective operational aircraft, and the Me.262 and Ar.234 remained the only satisfactory jet aircraft used by the German Air Force.

Training

Recovery of Training

23. The training situation at the beginning of 1944, as already mentioned, contained solid grounds for satisfaction, the output of crews during 1943 having more than doubled that for 1942, as the following figures show :—

	Crews	
	1942	1943
Reconnaissance (Advanced Pilot's Certificate)	192	464
S.E. Fighter	1,662	3,276
Night Fighter (Advanced Pilot's Certificate)..	239	1,358
Ground Attack	537	1,264
Bomber	1,962	3,231

Thanks to the co-operation of all the authorities, the A.O. for Air Force Training, General Leutnant Kreipe, had been enabled to raise the effective exploitation of aircraft and personnel to a degree hitherto deemed impossible ; new records had been broken in aircraft hours, and the increased output of trained personnel had been achieved in spite of a fall of 20 per cent. in basic personnel. A steady output had been ensured by regular allocations of fuel, although the allocations could with advantage have been higher.

Shortage of Operational Aircraft

24. There were certain shortcomings which marred this rosy picture, and the year 1943 saw the development of difficulties which were to prove insuperable during the latter part of the war. One of the most serious was the shortage of new types of operational aircraft for training purposes, and it

---

[1] " People's fighter ".

was already recognised that unless this shortage was made good, both the extent and quality of training would sink to a dangerously low level. Thus, in the Advanced Fighter Schools there were, at the beginning of 1944, only 235 Me.109's against an establishment of 480, while in the '' C '' twin-engined pilot schools deliveries of Ju.88's had fallen seriously behind, and in the Bomber Observer schools not a single Ju.88 had been delivered in the last three months of 1943. Early in 1944 strong recommendations were put forward to remedy this defect, even at the expense of delivery of such aircraft to the front, and the heavy fighter losses which had occurred since the beginning of 1944 gave added emphasis to this point and at the same time rendered most urgent a further rapid expansion of the output of fighter pilots.

Lack of Instructors

25. A further weakness which had made itself felt during 1943 was a shortage of flying instructors, and, in an endeavour to remedy this a short series of courses for potential instructors had been instituted. The supply of instructors, however, never became plentiful and was a frequent cause of anxiety. General Galland, the A.O. for Fighters, was constantly critical of the lack of instructors, and particularly of the fact that no long-term planning had been made beforehand to meet the increased demand for them when it was decided to increase fighter output so steeply during 1944. In fact, Galland went so far as to assert that the output of fighter pilots sufficed only for replacement, leaving nothing for expansion. Furthermore, much dislocation of flying training had already been experienced in the latter part of 1943 from increasing Allied air attacks. Constant transfers of schools and training units interrupted programmes and courses ; during 1944 this problem was accentuated and caused increasing concern.

Deterioration in Quality

26. Despite these difficulties, by dint of improvisation and cancellation of unessential training, it was possible to produce sufficient personnel for operational needs, and numerically the Air Force did not at any point suffer from a curtailment of training programmes. It was in quality of output that the great weakness lay. Whilst the maximum results had been obtained with the minimum material, Kreipe was fully aware that in other circumstances the quality of output would have been higher and that British training standards were on a far higher level. Whereas German night-fighter pilots had 110-115 flying hours, British pilots had as many as 200-220 hours, while the disparity in single-engined fighter pilot was even more marked with a steady reduction in flying hours ever since the autumn of 1942.

27. As losses at the front began to rise in 1943 and 1944, so the standards of training fell, and the pilots sent to the front during the latter part of the war lacked general flying experience ; moreover, although the shortage of operational aircraft in training units improved out of all recognition in 1944 (fighter O.T.U's. and Advanced Fighter Schools had respectively some 1,000 Me.109's and FW.190's at their disposal by the autumn of 1944) the fuel was then no longer available in sufficient quantities. Other factors which contributed to the lowering of quality in aircraft crews were that the Luftwaffe was now no longer able to train its flying personnel in southern France and Italy and consequently the weather played an important part in programme fulfilment in the absence of special summer and winter schedules. Again, both

General Hitschold (A.O. for Ground Attack) and Galland maintained that there was a certain lack of coordination between the schools and the front, so that pilots proceeding to O.T.U's. would find practices different to that which they had been taught. Finally, the few flying hours allowed during training resulted in pilots on operations being too concerned with the technicalities of flying and unable to concentrate on gunnery and tactics ; this in turn imposed increased preoccupation on the more experienced unit and formation leaders and so further detracted from efficiency.

28. Thus Field Marshal Sperrle, commanding Luftflotte 3 in France, found in July, 1944, that with rare exceptions only his Gruppe and Staffel commanders had operational experience exceeding six months. A small percentage of other personnel had an average of three months, while the majority of pilots had seen active service for as little as 8 to 30 days.

29. The full extent of the effects of these shortcomings and weaknesses, some of them avoidable and others not, but all impossible to remedy at short notice in such an advanced stage of the war, made themselves felt disastrously in the campaigns with which the German Air Force came to face from 1944 to the conclusion of the war, as will be seen in the following chapters. Second only to the shortage of fuel, these shortcomings were to a large extent to nullify the prodigious effort of the aircraft industry in producing the material wherewith to sustain the struggle ; neither could the situation be improved despite the most strenuous efforts to increase training output up to midsummer 1944, when in April, May and June the output of pilots exceeded the thousand mark, including 800-900 fighter pilots. The numbers could be achieved, but not the vital element of quality.

Policy and Preparations to Meet the Anglo-American Invasion of Europe

Reorganisation of Commands[1]

30. The first step towards the building up of the necessary Command organisation to meet the Allied landings which, without a doubt, would have to be faced during the coming Summer of 1944, manifested itself in the return of General-Major Peltz from Italy, in August, 1943, in order to resume his Command of the bomber force on the western front. Peltz was accordingly given command of Fliegerkorps IX controlling all long-range bomber units based in northern France and the Low Countries, and notably reinforced at the same time by the withdrawal of the whole of the long-range bomber force from Italy to the western front.

31. It was not until February, 1944, that the next step was taken, this time also at the expense of the Italian theatre, by the transfer of Fliegerkorps II with its Commander, Buelowius. This move did not, as in the case of Fliegerkorps IX, result in any change of intensification of activity in the West ; the Command, as the most experienced now available in close support operations, remained throughout the next few months solely engaged on preparatory measures for operations, particularly with the development of airfields, communications, supplies and ground organisation generally, with a view to the time when it would have to undertake its vital rôle in opposing the Allied landings.

---

[1] Refer to Map 23, page 328.

32. The third major step occurred in the middle of March when the Luftwaffe Anti-shipping Command, Fliegerfuehrer Atlantik, operating long-range aircraft from bases in South-West France, was upgraded to the status of Fliegerkorps. Once again this development was at the expense of the Mediterranean theatre, whence Fliegerkorps X under General Leutnant Holle was transferred to this Command. Holle was selected for this task in view of his long standing experience in anti-shipping operations, not only in the eastern Mediterranean, but previously also from 1941 to 1943 when he was in charge of similar Commands in Norway as Fliegerfuehrer North and Fliegerfuehrer North-East. This measure reflected the German appreciation of the important rôle which anti-shipping operations would inevitably take in opposing a major Allied landing ; moreover, to meet these his Command was in due course to be substantially reinforced by the development and expansion of anti-shipping units intended for this purpose.

33. These measures completed the basic preparation for the conduct of operations on the western front and finally eclipsed the Mediterranean as a major theatre of Luftwaffe operations ; at the same time the torpedo-bomber units based in southern France, where they were strategically placed in order to guard against an Allied landing in that area, or alternatively on the western front, came under the control of Flieger Division 2 which was subordinated also to the new Fliegerkorps X. A further measure for the defence of southern France was the setting up of a small Fighter Command for that purpose known as *Jafue* South France.

Preparations for Operations

34. Fully appreciating the vital part the German Air Force would be called upon to play in repelling the Allied invasion, particularly in its early stages, the Luftwaffe High Command began during January and February, 1944, to make active preparations for exploiting all available Luftwaffe resources to the full. While it was realised that Allied air superiority would inevitably be overwhelming in numbers, and that the burden of the defensive campaign in Russia, as well as of continued fighter defence of the Reich, would severely limit the air forces which the Germans could put into the field when the moment came, it was nevertheless hoped that the advantage of shorter range would to some extent enable the Luftwaffe to offset this adverse preponderance. The measures adopted by the German Air Force to make use of its limited resources were far-reaching in the extreme ; preparations had to be made for the rapid transfer of flying units to the area endangered, training units had to be prepared for operating in emergency and fighter units had to be trained and equipped to enable them to operate as fighter bombers should the necessity arise. To the latter end Budowius devoted much time to the inspection of fighter units scheduled for reinforcement in the West, laying special emphasis on the training and instruction of formation leaders, while unit commanders were, so far as conditions allowed, sent to the envisaged operational area in order to familiarise themselves with their particular tasks, and to acquaint themselves at first hand with the intended operational airfields and landing grounds under development. The training on a limited scale of long-range bomber units for operations by day was also put in hand.

35. So far as supplies and other administrative requirements were concerned, no important difficulty arose. In particular, bomb and ammunition stocks were plentiful and so also were German fuel supplies ; increased production and

strict economy measures had resulted during the winter and spring of 1944 in raising stocks of aircraft fuel to no less than 420,000 tons, with a further Supreme Command reserve of about 120,000 tons, so that altogether, about 540,000 tons was at the disposal of the Air Force for all purposes[1]. So far as Luftflotte 3 was concerned, stocks of aircraft fuel in France and the Low Countries by the end of May exceeded 20,000 tons, sufficient for at least a full month's supply for intensive operations. However, while material resources seemed adequate, the manpower situation was already beginning to cause difficulties by early May ; the expansion of the fighter arm and the generally difficult replacement situation with regard to aircrew hampered the reorganisation of bomber units, while the further development of Air Force station commands and airfield detachments had at the same time to be limited owing to lack of personnel.

36. As a result of the efforts outlined above, the Luftwaffe ground organisation in the West could, on the eve of the Allied landings be regarded as substantially satisfactory in all major respects, and everything was ready for the reception of the intended reinforcements whenever the emergency should arise ; there was, however, no actual move to transfer flying units in readiness for the event, due primarily to the predominant need for maintaining the fighter defence of the Reich, but also partly owing to uncertainty as to where the main blow would fall, and also to prevent needless loss and damage to aircraft by Allied air attacks previous to the landing.

Development of the Anti-Shipping Forces

37. In June, 1943, the German Air Force specialist anti-shipping forces stood at the lowest level of strength and efficiency which had yet been reached. This was due in large measure to the attrition of the torpedo bomber units in the Mediterranean during the winter and summer of 1942-43, as a result of which, only two Gruppen comprising some 50 Ju.88 torpedo-carrying aircraft were available for offensive operations.

38. Accordingly, a large programme for the expansion of the anti-shipping force was put in hand and the development of new weapons urgently pressed forward. By the autumn of 1943 the He.177 was at long last becoming operational and three new units were formed, one equipped with the He.177, the others with Do.217's, all of them using remote control missiles, viz., either the Hs.293 glider bomb and/or the FX. radio-controlled bomb. These measures were accompanied during the winter of 1943-44 by the re-equipment and development of KG.40 in South-West France for undertaking operations of a more offensive character than armed reconnaissance and U-boat cooperation for which it had long been employed, and further He.177's were allocated to this unit.

39. Simultaneously, a further expansion of the anti-shipping force was projected, this time by the conversion of an existing long-range bomber unit for torpedo operations, by which means it was hoped that by June, 1944, there would be a balanced force of some five Gruppen of torpedo-bombers and a similar number of units operating with remotely controlled missiles ; experiments were also undertaken with a view to the development of the Me.410 as a torpedo-carrying aircraft possessing higher speed and greater manœuvrability than the Ju.88, but for technical reasons it was found that this aircraft did not prove suitable for such employment.

---

[1] See Chapter 15.

The Hs.293 radio-controlled Glider Bomb. (Above) on the FW.200 and (below) on the He.177. (See also illustration on page 324).

The " Mistel " pick-a-back combination of fighter and explosive-laden Ju.88 (see paragraph 40).

The Ju88 S. A faster and more powerful version of the Ju.88, equipped with the same B.M.W.801 radial engine as used in the FW.190. This type was employed largely in the specialist pathfinder unit (see paragraph 42).

40. In addition, among all these preparations for anti-shipping warfare a completely new innovation was also devised. This consisted of a "pick-a-back" type of composite aircraft known as the *Mistel*[1] consisting of a Ju.88 heavily loaded with explosive charges surmounted by a Me.109, so arranged that the pilot in the latter controlling the two aircraft coupled together could release the Ju.88 at close range against the selected target. The intention was to use these novel weapons against battleships or other major Allied naval units supporting the landing; however, only very small numbers became available in time and such operations as were carried out proved wholly abortive.

41. Thus, there was every hope that a strong force of up to 450 aircraft would be available to meet the Allied seaborne assault, a powerful and formidable complement to the long-range bomber force; but circumstances were, in fact, to be such that the full expansion envisaged could not be achieved owing to interruption of the bomber programme in favour of concentration on fighters in the spring of 1944. In consequence, by April, 1944, the total anti-shipping forces had been built up to not more than 200-250 aircraft, and even this strength could not be maintained, sagging to approximately 190 aircraft by early June; further, those units engaged on operations during the winter of 1943-44 incurred heavy losses, the torpedo-bomber units in particular proving notably vulnerable with average losses of 15 to 25 per cent. of the aircraft attacking their targets. Thus, there came about an acute shortage of crews with the highly specialised training and experience necessary for the effective employment of the torpedo-bomber arm in particular, which was to prove an insuperable obstacle to the achievement of any substantial success when the time came for them to be committed against the Allied landing.

Bombing Operations Against Britain

42. The reinforcement of Fliegerkorps IX from Italy in December, 1943, resulted in an increase in the bomber forces under its command to a strength of some 550 aircraft, composed mainly of Ju.88, Ju.188 and Do.217's; there were, however, also 35 of the new He.177's for the first time available for long-range bombing operations against the British Isles, 20 Me.410's and 25 FW.190's also employed for bombing. It has already been noted in Chapter 11 to what extent the German bomber arm in the Mediterranean had declined in efficiency and striking power due largely to the fundamental lack of experienced crews: Peltz's force was, therefore, by no means as formidable as its numbers would suggest. He realised that the standard of training amongst his bomber crews was not high enough to permit of an efficient and concentrated bombing of targets vital to the British and Allied war effort. Recognising this deep-seated weakness, he made considerable efforts to emulate the example of the R.A.F. Bomber Command by the formation of specialist pathfinder units with crews specially trained in navigation assisted also by a form of radar-radio ground control. It was hoped that the short-comings in the operational efficiency of the bomber force as a whole could be overcome by resort to this technique, in which an elaborate target-marking system, employing clusters of parachute flares and ground markers, was devised.

43. Operations against Britain began with an attack on London on the night of 21st January, 1944. There is little reason to doubt that the offensive then started was launched on Hitler's special orders and had, as its object, far

---

[1] Mistletoe.

more a measure of reprisal against the heavy night bombing attacks on Germany and to provide propaganda for home consumption which it was felt was badly needed. It is clear that the bombing offensive which developed mainly against London could, at that stage, do little if anything to contribute in any useful way to the hindering of Allied preparations for the launching of their assault. The attack on January 21st came far short of expectations ; the pathfinder technique failed and few aircraft succeeded in reaching even the general target area of Greater London, where not more than 30 tons of bombs fell, whilst a further 270 tons were scattered round the surrounding countryside at large. It was not, therefore, until after an interval of eight days that the attack was resumed on January 29th, with a similar lack of success ; two further operations up to February 13th produced even more unsatisfactory results. On February 18th, a considerable improvement took place, when 175 tons were dropped in the target area and a greater measure of success continued to be achieved up to the end of that month, and from then until the final raid on London on April 18th about 50 per cent. of the total number of aircraft operating on any one night were able to reach the target area. The scale of effort dwindled progressively, however, and whereas about 270 sorties were flown on January 21st, not more than 100 to 140 were carried out in any of the subsequent operations.

44. Dispersed among the raids on London were two attacks directed against Hull and a third against Bristol, but once again the increased range led to major navigational errors and it proved impossible to identify the target in any of these operations ; in the case of the Bristol attack a fairly good concentration of bombs fell near Weston-super-Mare some 20 miles away from the target.

45. While these operations did not in themselves have any major bearing on the preparations of the German Air Force to hamper or frustrate Allied plans, they are of importance in the disastrous effects which they entailed for the whole of bomber force on the western front. While actual losses due to the British fighter and A.A. commands amounted to some 135 aircraft destroyed, approximately 6 per cent. of the total sorties flown, heavy additional losses were at the same time incurred ; these must, in part at least, be attributed to the inefficiency of the aircraft crews, but were also swollen by the successful Allied low-level attacks on bomber base airfields. By the beginning of April, the actual strength of the bomber units of Fliegerkorps IX scarcely exceeded 200 aircraft, in many cases units having fallen to 50 per cent. or less of establishment and by the end of April a further drop of 170 aircraft had taken place. The reason for this catastrophic decline is to be found in the major change in German policy which had come about during the course of these operations, namely, the decision to concentrate all possible resources on fighter production. In due course it was to lead to the virtual elimination of the Luftwaffe bomber force, such aircraft of suitable bomber type, e.g., the Ju.88, as continued to be built, being required largely for the maintenance and still further expansion of the night fighter defences. Consequently, with no stock of reserve aircraft, losses could not be replaced and the only important outcome of this fruitless campaign against England was to leave Luftflotte 3 with a mere 130 bombers, exclusive of the anti-shipping force, with which to resist the Allied invasion.

46. It was not until the last week of April that air operations against the United Kingdom began to be directed against Allied preparations, when two attacks on April 23rd and 25th were directed mainly against the Portsmouth

area and shipping concentrations observed in the Solent and Poole-Swanage areas. Although approximately 100 and 130 sorties respectively were flown on these occasions, which were followed by smaller operations on three succeeding nights, all proved wholly ineffective although representing the maximum effort which the then depleted bomber force could attain ; their failure was attributed to interference with navigational aids by British countermeasures and the very effective jamming of the pathfinder procedure upon which everything depended. It was, therefore, recognised that unless this difficulty could be overcome, further attacks of this nature could only hope to be successful under moonlight conditions when still greater losses would have had to be accepted. One further and more determined attack was made on major fleet units at Plymouth, on the night of April 30th, when the Fliegerkorps IX effort was supplemented by some 15 specialised anti-shipping aircraft of Fliegerkorps X with " Fritz-X " 1,400-kg. radio-controlled bombs ; once again, however, no important objective was hit. After this attack no further operations with missles of this type were undertaken against the United Kingdom.

47. One of the chief handicaps in assessing both the area and scale of the Allied build-up for the invasion was the shortage of photographic reconnaissance of the British Isles. The strength of the defences had long prevented any attempt during 1943 or the early part of 1944 to obtain such cover, and it was not until the middle of April that efforts were made to fill this gap. Even so, it was extremely limited in extent; the main effort over southern England had to be restricted to coverage by short-range reconnaissance aircraft over the South and South-West Coast, but long-range reconnaissance of Scapa Flow and northern Scotland was also increased. No attempt was made by reconnaissance aircraft to penetrate overland and, in fact, by the end of May there was a falling off in the scale of effort compared with the situation at the beginning of the month. Lack of frequent cover prevented any reliable estimate being made of the progress of Allied preparations ; in many cases vertical overhead pictures could not be taken owing to the strength of the defences and in consequence it was frequently impossible to obtain more than occasional distant, oblique photographs of objectives. The failure of German air reconnaissance at this time is outstanding, and contrasts vividly with the strength and activity of their reconnaissance forces during the early stages of the war both on the western front and in the East ; this failure was a major factor in the inability of the German High Command to formulate any accurate ideas as to the direction from which the assault would be undertaken, and it consequently contributed to a widespread dispersal of German forces throughout the western front from Brittany to the Low Countries, Denmark and Norway.

German Air Force Dispositions

48. The general dispositions of the German Air Force in the West during the period leading up to the Allied landings have already been made clear, namely, the concentration of the bomber force under Fliegerkorps IX in northern France and the Low Countries, with the anti-shipping forces under Fliegerkorps IX in northern France and the Low Countries, with the anti-shipping forces under Fliegerkorps X in southern and south-western France. The fighter forces in the West were subordinated to Jagdkorps II and during the whole of this period were purely defensive against Allied day bombers operating over north-eastern France and Belgium, Fliegerkorps II continuing to play an inactive role. At 1st January, 1944, the total strength of the single-engined

The " Fitz-X ", 1,400-kilogramme radio-controlled bomb.   Carried by Do.217's, this type of bomb was used in an unsuccessful attack on warships at Plymouth on the night of 30th April, 1944.

The Hs.293 radio-controlled glider bomb

fighter force in the West did not exceed 130 aircraft, and throughout the spring of 1944 the heavy weight of Allied day bombing of Germany compelled all available forces to be employed for defence. So great was this pressure that, by the beginning of March, the already weak fighter force in France and Belgium had been reduced by 40 aircraft withdrawn to Germany for this purpose, while a further 85 fighters had also been moved back from Holland. It was not, in fact, until the beginning of May when the strength of the single-engined fighter defences of north-eastern France and Belgium could again be raised once more to a total of 135 aircraft ; this, moreover, was a defensive measure against the growing weight of Allied attacks on the area in question, in association with the offensive against the V.1 flying bomb sites, and amounted in no way to preparations to meet the Allied landing. In fact, no major redisposition of fighters of any kind took place in an attempt at least to have ready on the spot a force of some potential striking power to operate in an emergency. This may have been partly due to the continued uncertainty of Luftflotte 3 up to the very last as to Allied intentions, the possibility of landings either to the east or west of the Seine estuary having to be envisaged. Consequently, the close-support forces available for Fliegerkorps II on the eve of the invasion were still substantially smaller than its forces in the Italian theatre in July, 1943, when it failed to operate effectively in defence of Sicily.

49. Particularly outstanding was the weakness of the ground-attack units available in France ; towards the end of May a small reinforcement took place but there were, in fact, no more than some 75 FW.190 fighter-bombers at the disposal of Fliegerkorps II to meet the invasion, contrasting strongly with the situation on the eastern front, which continued to absorb no less than 600 aircraft of this category. No attempt was made to draw on this substantial force in the East, due to the desperate need for meeting the Russian threat at all costs, and, in particular, to prevent penetration into East Prussia and Rumania ; as already indicated, the general policy was to fill this gap by the adoption of fighter units for this purpose, an unsatisfactory arrangement due to lack of the necessary training and combat experience, and uneconomical in that it reduced substantially the number of fighters available for solely defensive purposes. Thus, it may be said that, so far as close-support forces were concerned, the German Air Force was content to adopt a policy of waiting on events, a fact which inevitably imposed serious limitations on the reaction possible in the initial stages of operations ; subsequent events were to show that whatever more active measures might have been taken in anticipation of events, the weight of the Allied air forces was to be such that, no matter what strength the Luftwaffe committed for battle, its forces must in any event have been ineffectual from the start and subject to crippling losses.

CHAPTER 14

THE INVASION AND THE FLYING BOMBS

The Allied Landings in France and the Advance to the German Border
(6th June to 20th September, 1944)

The General Strategic Situation

1. As indicated in the previous chapter, the German High Command up to the last was undecided as to the point where the Allied landings were likely to take place. The staff of Luftflotte 3, the Operational Air Command on which fell the burden of defence in the West, was of the firm opinion that landings were to take place in the Dieppe and Seine Bay areas, and air opinion generally was inclined to favour the area between Le Havre and Cherbourg. But although by early June it was clear that the Allied assault, wherever it might be launched, could not be long delayed, the urgent needs of home defence and the military situation on the Mediterranean and Russian fronts made it impossible for the slender forces of the Luftwaffe already in France and the Low Countries to be reinforced. Home defence remained up to the eve of the assault the prime commitment of the German fighter force, while in other theatres German air strength was already far from adequate to meet the diversity of its tasks. By now the Russians had already advanced into Rumania as far as Jassy, and the Crimea was lost. But although Russian progress was temporarily halted, it was a period of uneasy lull in which great anxiety was felt concerning the possibility of Russian landings on the Bulgarian coast. The need to strengthen the defences of the Rumanian oilfields was pressing and, above all, there was the necessity of hampering Russian preparations for a new offensive. These considerations had led during May, 1944, to the transfer to the Russian front of units from South Germany, Austria and North Italy and there was therefore little left in those areas which could provide reinforcement for the West.

2. In Italy, the Allied offensive which had opened in mid-May had taken the German Air Force completely by surprise, half of its single-engined fighters in the battle area having been moved to North Italy only a few days before the offensive was opened ; thus, faced with overwhelming Allied air strength, the German close-support force in Italy, which for long had never been strong enough to play an effective part in the campaign, had been virtually eliminated.

3. Luftflotte 3 in the West was in this way in the unenviable position of having to face the Allied invasion with a force very limited in strength, and with the close-support Command under its direction (Fliegerkorps II) disposing of forces substantially smaller than those held in the Italian theatre in July, 1943, when no effective operations in the defence of Sicily had been possible owing to decisive Allied air superiority. There was no doubt that this inability to build up in advance its forces in France was bound to impose severe limitations on German Air Force reactions in the initial stages of operations.

Dispositions on the Eve of the Landings[1]

4. On June 5th, Luftflotte 3 possessed a total force of some 800 aircraft, of which not more than 170 were single-engined fighters, distributed between South and South-West France and Belgium, with the main concentration

---

[1] See Map 23 and Chapter 13, paragraphs 30–33.

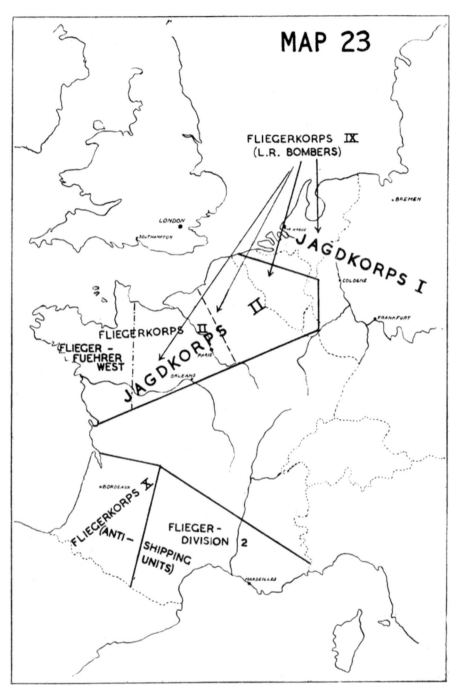

DISPOSITION OF FORCES UNDER LUFTFLOTTE 3 IN FRANCE
AT THE TIME OF THE ALLIED LANDING IN NORMANDY
(6th JUNE, 1944)

North-East of the Seine. The anti-shipping forces of Fliegerkorps X (units operating with radio-controlled missiles) and Fliegerdivision 2 (torpedo-bombers) were based at such distant bases as Bordeaux, Toulouse and Marseilles ; in all, these amounted to some 200 aircraft, a potentially formidable force, but were suffering from deep seated weaknesses owing to a high proportion of inexperienced crews. The long-range bomber force of Fliegerkorps IX, based in northern France and the Low Countries and already waning in strength, could muster no more than some 130 aircraft. The ability of both the above-mentioned Fliegerkorps to maintain a sustained effort was very much in question, having regard to the decision taken earlier to concentrate all resources of production and manpower to the strengthening of the fighter-force. On 5th June, 1944, the disposition of the German Air Force was approximately as follows :—

	L.R. Bombers	Ground Attack	S.E. Fighters	T.E. Fighters	L.R. Recce	Tac. Recce	Coastal	Total
South and South-West France (South of 46°)	180	Nil	15	20[1]	15	Nil	5	235
France (West of Seine to 46°)..	90	75	50	35[1]	35	25	Nil	310
France (East of Seine) and Belgium ..	30	Nil	105	90	10	Nil	Nil	235
Holland..	25	Nil	Nil	—[2]	10	Nil	Nil	35
	325	75	170	145	70	25	5	815

[1] T.E. day fighters.

[2] The night fighter units in Holland were subordinate to Luftflotte Level.

5. The scanty strength of the ground attack units will, in particular, be noted ; it was not for any lack of such aircraft that the ability of the Luftwaffe to strike against the Allied landings in their earliest stages was hampered, but rather to the policy dictated from the highest level whereby not a single ground-attack aircraft was moved from the Russian front, where some 550 were being held in readiness to repulse the Russian onslaught then thought to be imminent. The weakness of the reconnaissance forces, particularly of tactical reconnaissance units, was most outstanding, and moreover, the night-fighter units of Luftflotte 3 in eastern France and Belgium were not intended for use against landing forces. Thus, it will be seen that out of Luftflotte 3's total strength of 815 aircraft, not more than some 600 could be regarded as the actual striking force which could be thrown in against the Allied landings on " D " Day.

The Luftwaffe's Reaction to the Landings

6. It is clear that no major reaction could be initiated against the early and most critical phase of the landings on " D " Day itself, and it is true to say that the German response was barely perceptible. The scale on which Allied air cover was provided made any question of the employment of the German bomber or anti-shipping force by day unthinkable, and the total Luftwaffe effort amounted to less than 100 sorties, of which 70 were flown by single-engined fighters. With the onset of darkness, however, a major effort was directed

against the beachhead, mainly by the long-range bomber and torpedo-bomber forces ; some 175 sorties were flown, the majority being accounted for by units of Fliegerkorps IX, while the anti-shipping effort amounted to little more than 25 per cent. of the total. The latter were the units which Goering had designated " the spearhead of the anti-invasion forces ", but the cutting edge proved dull and little was, in fact, accomplished. During their approach flight they suffered casualties not only from Allied night fighters but also from German Flak, and their reception over the beachhead was such that in many cases attacks had to be broken off prematurely.

Reinforcements

7. Preparations already made beforehand for the sending in of fighter reinforcements on a major scale were put in hand immediately, beginning on June 6th and continuing throughout the next few days ; over 200 fighters were flown in from Germany during the first 36 hours and a further 100 by June 10th. During the same period the anti-shipping forces were reinforced by 45 torpedo-carrying Ju.88's moved from Germany to southern France together with 70 long-range bombers transferred from Italy to Belgium and a further 20 from Germany ; thus, by the end of a week the total force directly engaged against the Allied invasion had reached some 1,000 aircraft of all types. This effort was to prove the maximum which could be attained ; from that time onwards the heavy losses and wastage suffered from all causes were to result in a steady decline.

8. The effect of these reinforcements was to bring about a considerable improvement in the German air effort, the close-support effort on June 8th reaching a peak of over 500 sorties of which the single-engined fighter force accounted for some 400, the remainder being by ground-attack and twin-engined day fighters ; similarly, the bomber effort on the night of June 7th-8th rose to over 200 sorties evenly divided between the anti-shipping and bomber units.

The Course of the First Week's Operations

9. Whatever plans may have been drawn up for the employment of the close-support force against the Allied landing, it had been shattered from the start by the weight of the Allied air attack. From the first the Luftwaffe was forced on to the defensive, much of its effort consisting of ineffective sorties and of defensive operations in rearward areas against Allied attacks on its airfields and ground organisation. The dislocation caused by Allied air action not only against airfields but against communications, ground installations, supply dumps, transit depots and aircraft parks, the superior Allied cover over the beachheads and the standing patrols maintained over German air bases which frequently prevented such reconnaissance aircraft as were available from taking off, not only disorganised the Luftwaffe but also denied any possibility of obtaining a full picture of the ground situation and so to plan operations accordingly. Operations soon deteriorated into a succession of temporary measures designed to alleviate the trials of the Luftwaffe itself, while the needs of the now hard pressed ground forces became only a secondary consideration.

10. The lack of specialised ground-attack units, which remained without reinforcement, resulted in the diversion of a considerable proportion of the single-engined fighter force to those duties, thereby weakening appreciably the ability of the force as a whole to fulfil its proper functions. Four days after the Allied landing no less than 150 single-engined fighters, equivalent by then

to 25 per cent. of the total fighter strength engaged, had been diverted to ground-attack operations. The effort, however, was hardly worth while, for with pilots untrained for this work it was not possible to reach more than a low level of efficiency, while further strong elements of the remaining fighters had to be diverted to provide the necessary escort.

11. This unsatisfactory state of affairs could not be permitted to continue, and on June 12th orders were issued from Berlin that all single-engined fighter units employed on fighter-bomber operations in France were to revert at once to fighter operations. The order of the previous day from Luftflotte 3 that all aircraft were to be fitted as quickly as possible with bomb racks, since bombing was considered the primary task and the shooting down of aircraft only secondary, was thereby reversed. The new orders now insisted that all fighters were to be used for concentrated operations against Allied air forces over the main point of ground fighting in order to clear the skies of Allied air opposition. Thus, strong differences on air policy as between Luftflotte 3 and Berlin had already arisen and this conflict was immediately followed by the withdrawal of Fliegerkorps II from the battle area. Jagdkorps II then assumed direct control over all fighter operations in France, so that Buelowius and his Command, on which so much reliance had been placed, was early relieved of his duties. The first major crisis had already arisen.

12. With the long-range bomber force also, things were not going well. As early as June 14th it was decided that owing to the Allied anti-aircraft, searchlight and balloon defences, which constituted an impenetrable barrier, only high-level bombing was possible. From great heights, however, targets were impossible to find in the confined areas of the beachheads, and, in fact, from the night of June 12th onwards the whole of the long-range bomber force went over to minelaying operations in an attempt to strangle the movement of Allied shipping and to prevent the movement ashore of supplies. From that date onwards, throughout the remainder of June and most of July, a long sustained period of sea mining operations was undertaken which included also the dropping of circling torpedoes ; almost every night without a break an average of some 60-70 such sorties were flown and in sum the total effort for the six weeks was considerable, amounting to between 1,500-2,000 sorties, equivalent to the laying of 3,000-4,000 mines. While their accumulative effect was considerable and caused difficulties and delay to the Allies in the handling of landing craft and shipping, nevertheless, it was clear that this policy could not hope to be decisive in its results and that the most that could be hoped for was to retard the build-up of the Allied forces ashore. Such operations, moreover, had the advantage of being the only type of activity which the bomber force could carry out with reasonable prospect of success and at the same time incur casualties on a relatively low scale ; having regard to the weakness of the force available it was in all probability the most effective use which could have been made of it.

13. The anti-shipping force proved to be even less effective. The lack of training on the part of the torpedo-bomber crews operating from distant bases in the South of France was immediately apparent, and low serviceability meant that these operations could not be more than on a minor scale. After operating 30-40 sorties on each of the first two nights, activity was suspended and a major effort was not again achieved until the end of the first week, and on this occasion only six aircraft reached the target area. Similarly, the Do.217's and He.177's,

although operating most nights, but with relatively weak forces, achieved conspicuously little success. It was clear that few effective results were to be expected from these forces, on which so much hope had been placed. At the end of the first week there was dissatisfaction and all-round disillusionment of the hopes which had been placed on the part to be played by the Luftwaffe in preventing the Allies from gaining a lodgment on the Normandy beachhead.

The Situation by the end of June

14. Throughout the remainder of June the Luftwaffe continued to fight an increasingly uphill battle. With the departure of Buelowius and his Command some attempt was made to step up the scale of fighter operations, which for a few days became much more aggressive, but the strength and serviceability of units was already waning, and great difficulty was being experienced in bringing up replacement aircraft owing to the movement back of the main transit depôts of Le Bouget and Toul ; these had to be withdrawn, owing to the weight of the Allied air attack, to Wiesbaden, Cologne and Mannheim. In consequence, the strength of many units quickly fell to only 65 per cent. of establishment, while losses from all causes had resulted in the withdrawal from operations of no less than five single-engined fighter units for re-equipment only 10 days after the Allied landing, and these losses could only be made good by bringing forward some of the few remaining units still left for defence over Germany itself.

15. On the withdrawal of Fliegerkorps II, the main fighter force came under the direct control of Jagdkorps II with a subsidiary Command under " O.C. Fighters, Britanny ", covering air operations in the Cherbourg Peninsula, but air support for the German forces in this latter area had to take second place to the greater need of providing all possible help to the German troops endeavouring to contain the main bridgehead in Normandy. By now the German Air Force, driven by Allied bombing and ground attack from its main airfields near the scene of operations, had been forced back to the Paris area and was operating at a range no less than that of the Allied air forces based in southern England : a further initial advantage had been lost. Although some attempt was made to concentrate a strong defensive force over Cherbourg on June 24th and 25th it was too late and too weak to prevent the fall of the port ; at the same time increasing pressure by the Allies in the Tilly-Caen area was causing anxiety and called for the maximum possible air cover for the protection of road traffic. As the ground fighting became more intense in this sector at the end of June, some recovery was possible with the overcoming of the difficulties and delays in bringing up replacement aircraft and by the return of units from re-equipment ; there was consequently some increase in fighter strength, and for a short period at the turn of the month the daylight effort rose to some 500-600 sorties. However, the formations used were so small and so scattered that little was achieved and complaints from Army commanders became more frequent. " In order to be able to stand up to the present pressure " complained the Commander of a Parachute Corps, " it is necessary for our fighters to operate over the battle area at least for short periods of the day ". As it was, the efforts to undertake such operations resulted only in heavy losses, sometimes up to 10 per cent. of the forces engaged.

16. At this stage yet another change was to take place among the ranks of officers commanding the Luftwaffe in the West, and on July 1st Buelowius now reappeared to take over Jagdkorps II in place of Junck, on whom no doubt

the strain and lack of success during the past few weeks had been telling. Once again there was a short-lived but perceptible increase in activity and aggressiveness, but at the same time the change served to emphasise the lack of continuity in the close-support command in France.

The Effect of Operations in Normandy on Defence of the Reich

17. It is opportune at this stage to review the situation which had developed in Germany as a result of the shift of fighter forces to the western front. Immediately before the launching of the invasion, single-engined fighter strength employed on the defence of Germany totalled approximately 700 aircraft, to which there were added a further 165 twin-engined day fighters. Although during June certain single-engined fighter units had to be withdrawn from France for re-equipment, the situation in the West was such that it was impossible to add these to the fighter force defending the Reich, and further transfers to the West had to be made in order to take their place in the support of the land battle. At the end of June the disposition of the single-engined fighter force was as follows :—

Western Front	425
Norway	40
Defence of the Reich	370
Eastern Front and Balkans	475
Italy	65
Non-Operational	60
Total	1,435

The weak forces available for defence against the bombing of Germany were thus clearly inadequate to meet the growing intensity of the Allied bomber forces operating both from the South and the West in the development of the offensive against oil ; it was in South Germany alone that the fighter defences were maintained at anything approaching an adequate level, approximately one-third of the total home defence force being deployed to cover this area, and it was therefore possible to put up relatively strong opposition such as that encountered by the U.S. 15th Air Force in its raid on Vienna on June 26th. This situation was to continue throughout the remainder of July and August, notwithstanding the increasing havoc being steadily wrought by the Allied bombing forces in their operations against the German synthetic oil installations.

Operations during July

18. During the early part of the month much of the close-support effort had to be expended on demonstrations in support of the morale of the German ground troops, and there was increasing attention given to relatively minor tasks, e.g., the combatting of Allied artillery-spotting aircraft ; moreover, the relentless Allied air pressure meant that the effort expended had increasingly to be devoted to defensive patrols over the lines of communication. Thus, the frittering away of forces on such secondary tasks substantially reduced those available for operations in the main battle area, and no attempt could be made to use the close-support fighters to cover the German counter-attacks. The strain of long and sustained operations on a force so completely outnumbered inevitably resulted in temporary exhaustion after 2-3 days of all-out effort. This was a fact which Buelowius had to face after spurring on his units to

increase their activity to the full on July 4th and 5th ; serviceability, due to disorganisation and the heavy burden thrown on ground crews in particular, dropped away heavily as a result of such operations. A spell of bad weather provided a welcome breathing space and by the middle of July a marked recuperation had occurred, bringing back serviceability to about 65 per cent. of strength, which continued to be maintained at around 450 aircraft ; for the rest of the month there was little appreciable change in the general close-support situation. The inadequacy of German resources was once again demonstrated when, in the third week of July, the British and Canadian forces succeeded in breaking through south-east of Caen and east of the Orne, and also when later, towards the end of the month, the Americans thrust through to Coutances and beyond. No attempt was made to interfere with the heavy Allied daylight bomber attacks preceding these operations and the Luftwaffe found itself unable to impede in any way the Allied onrush both in Brittany and to the Seine. A few fighter aircraft were at this time fitted with 21-cm. rocket mortars for daylight operations against tanks and troops, but their small numbers and the lack of experienced formation leaders imposed severe limitations on any policy to switch over to more aggressive and offensive types of operations.

19. The bombing offensive against oil which had begun in May, now began to make itself felt by the withdrawal on July 7th of the He.177's and FW.200's of the anti-shipping forces, comprising in all some 90 aircraft, from South-West France to Germany and Norway. Owing to poor serviceability, these units had been able to play little part in anti-shipping operations, and they were consequently not greatly missed ; nevertheless, it was an ominous portent of the consequences developing behind the front to Luftwaffe fuel resources. The withdrawal of these aircraft made Fliegerkorps X, the Command controlling them, redundant, and shortly afterwards it was disbanded. The situation as regards the anti-shipping force in early July was, therefore, that its strength had been cut down to no more than 130 aircraft, of which about 100 were Ju.88 torpedo-bombers, and the eclipse of units operating with remotely-controlled missiles was nearly complete. As for the torpedo-bomber force itself, despite relatively high serviceability it was incapable of playing any important rôle in anti-shipping operations, due to shortage of crews and lack of experience.

20. The Allied breakthrough in Normandy in the third week of July caused the first interruption of the steady mining operations by the long-range bomber force. On the night of July 17th-18th and again on the night of 24th-25th, this force was diverted against troop and tank concentration and other land targets ; 100 and 120 sorties were flown respectively but with little effect, and mining operations were resumed and continued up to the end of the month. During the first five nights of August the bomber force once again intervened against ground targets, primarily traffic centres, in an attempt to impede the Allied advance out of the Avranches area into Brittany and Anjou ; it was, however, powerless to stop the flood, and fuel shortage compelled it to be grounded for the remainder of the month apart from a brief resumption of minelaying in the Siene Bay on August 17th-18th, an operation which seemed to have no bearing on the ground situation and was correspondingly ineffective.

The August Rout

21. August, which was to prove a black month in the history of the German Air Force in the West, opened ominously with the beginning of the disbanding of torpedo-bomber units formed earlier in 1944 ; but it was not until August 11th

that the full realisation of what was happening on the home front with the ceaseless Allied offensive against the German oil industry became apparent. On that date, Luftflotte 3, on instructions from Berlin, was forced to issue orders to all subordinate commands and units imposing serious restrictions on flying activity of all kinds ; fighters were in consequence permitted to undertake unrestricted operations only in defence against Allied heavy bombers, while reconnaissance, a vital necessity at that time, could only be carried out when essential for the general conduct of operations. As for the bombers and ground-attack units, their operations were specifically limited to such actions as could be considered decisive after the closest scrutiny, while all heavy four-engined aircraft were grounded except after special permission for their flights had been obtained. For the first time a general curtailment of Luftwaffe operational activity had been ordered ; previously there had been occasions when the overall fuel shortage had restricted transport and training activity, and sometimes local shortages had imposed brief limitations on operational activity, but an order of such drastic scope had never before been issued.

22. During the previous month there had been obvious signs of the failure of the emergency fighter training scheme to provide pilots of sufficient skill and experience. The restrictions now imposed seemed to point to the virtual elimination of the Luftwaffe as a factor of military importance in the future continuation of operations in France. Such was the situation during the first fortnight in August, the time when the German Army was being forced into a rapid retreat across the Seine and on Paris following the failure of the counter-attack on Avranches. Although every effort had been made, including the use for the first time on the western front of 30-40 night fighters for ground strafing operations, and the employment once again of long-range bombers against ground targets, all efforts had failed, and the close-support force was practically exhausted. By August 14th only 75 serviceable single-engined fighters were available for operations at first light, but although the effort achieved on the following day was some 250 sorties, it could not be maintained. Faced with impending disaster, the Germans decided, in the emergency, to throw in four new fighter units, some of them manned entirely afresh and re-equipped after earlier decimation in France—once more at the expense of strategic fighter defence. Again, this access of new units was to prove of little avail since the pilots were almost wholly lacking in battle experience.

23. With the headlong retreat of the German Army continuing, much dislocation of the Air Force ground organisation ensued from the enforced transfer of units back to new bases ; moreover, the new crews were proving not only ineffective but also, as a result of their inexperience, incurred severe losses in the heavy air battles which took place on August 17th and 18th. Norwithstanding the almost hopeless situation it was, however, necessary to do something to endeavour to cover the Army's retreat, and accordingly a further reinforcement of two fighter units was moved in to France from Germany about August 20th. Consequently, full-scale effort was again able to reach about 300 sorties on August 23rd, but at the same time units were then being moved back towards the Belgian frontier. The respite was, however, short and on August 29th, with the Allied troops now approaching Soissons and Rheims, Buelowius had to order his units to withdraw behind the line of Dunkirk-Charleville on the same day, and thus the close-support force finally

335

departed from French territory. At this stage, despite reinforcements, his single-engined fighter strength mustered no more than approximately 420 aircraft disposed as follows :—

Brussels Area	..	..	..	..	..	75
Antwerp and Eindhoven		..	..	..	..	65
South-East of Brussels..		..	..	..	..	95
Namur to Mezières	..	..	..	..	..	75
Metz, Nancy and Verdun	..	..	..	..	110
						420

These new dispositions placed the bulk of the close-support forces approximately 160-170 miles from the fighting still continuing on the Lower Seine, and 120-140 miles from the Upper Seine-Rheims area. Although the German fighters were thus compelled to operate at the limit of their range, nevertheless, they were for a brief spell able to enjoy greater immunity from attack on their airfields by Allied aircraft. Accompanying the retirement of the fighter forces, the long-range bomber and night-fighter forces, hitherto based in Belgium and North-East France, were also moved back to bases in Holland and North-West Germany, and with all units from the West withdrawing towards or within the Reich frontiers, a radical redisposition and reorganisation became necessary which for the time being virtually discounted all serious air operations.

The Allied Landing in Southern France.

24. On August 15th the Allied landing in southern France had occurred and added to the general discomfiture of the German Air Force in the West. This had by no means come as a surprise, in view of the strong concentrations of invasion craft located by reconnaissance aircraft in Corsican harbours and the intensive bombing of airfields, communications and strong points along the South coast of France and in the Rhône Valley during the second week of the month. The immediate effect of these attacks had been to force the withdrawal of the anti-shipping units still based in the Marseilles area first to Orange and Valence and thence to Lyons, Tavaux and Dijon ; it was, however, recognised by the Germans that with the weak forces available, comprising only some 65 Ju.88 torpedo-bombers and 15 Do.217's operating with radio-controlled missiles, little air resistance could be offered to the new Allied assault. It was also impossible at this stage to afford any further reinforcement of this new theatre of operations beyond the transfer of one fighter unit from northern Italy. On August 16th and 17th some 70 sorties were flown each day, but in spite of the concentration of Allied shipping off St. Maxine, St. Raphael and Cavallière, the torpedo-bomber units paradoxically complained, as previously off Normandy, of a lack of suitable targets, nor were their sufficient flare-dropping aircraft for illuminating sea targets for night attack. By August 21st all Luftwaffe activity in southern France had ceased, the fighter units moving northwards to the Metz area while the anti-shipping units returned to Germany to pass into final oblivion.

The Air Situation in September

25. By early September the air situation in the West could scarcely have deteriorated further, and to all intents and purposes the Luftwaffe was a spent and exhausted force with seemingly little future prospect of recovery. After a

A section of Rheine airfield (near Osnabrueck) after Allied bombings

The Allied paratroop landings near Nijmegen

brief stay on Belgian airfields the fighter forces were compelled early in the month to withdraw finally into Germany, but the lack of servicing facilities and fuel at new bases resulted in such dislocation that no serious attempt at operations could be made. Heavy losses of aircraft were also suffered owing to the abandoning of unserviceable aircraft and, during transfer of units, as a result of Allied low-level attacks ; moreover, the newly-occupied airfields were also lacking in Flak protection and were thus further exposed. Lack of transport during the retreat had, in addition, led to the loss of equipment and ground staffs, and hampered the bringing up of fuel and bombs. Unified control had at least temporarily lapsed and, further, there had been signs of a break in discipline and morale ; responsible commanders and officers had in certain cases departed by air, leaving their ground elements without leadership to carry out the rearward transfer, thus contributing to the heavy losses of men and material. As regards the long-range bomber force, its ability to intervene at this stage was hampered by fuel shortage and, inadequately provided with trained crews, continued to shrink, having a strength in the West at the beginning of September of only some 175 aircraft, all of which, however, had to be grounded temporarily at this critical juncture.

26. The course of events on other fronts must also at this stage not be overlooked. In the East, Rumania had been lost and the German Air Force had withdrawn to Hungary. Greece was also in process of being abandoned and units were being withdrawn into Yugoslavia, while Finland also was evacuated by the Luftwaffe and units transferred from there to the Baltic States and East Prussia. The contraction of the ring round Germany was thus proceeding apace and a widespread reorganisation of the main Commands on all fronts had become inevitable. In the West, Luftflotte 3 was degraded on September 21st to the status of Luftwaffe Command West, a development foreshadowed by the replacement of Field Marshal Sperrle by General Dessloch in August, 1944 ; it now became subordinate to Luftflotte Reich, which thus assumed control over both strategic and tactical operations in the defence of Germany, thereby greatly extending the sphere of Field Marshal Stumpff's responsibilities. In Norway, Luftflotte 5 was also degraded at about the same time to the status of a Luftwaffe Command, and similarly in Italy Luftflotte 2 relinquished its functions to a '' Luftwaffe General in Italy '' ; in the Balkans also a general reshuffle of Commands took place, numerous subsidiary Commands in this area being grouped together under '' Luftwaffe General North Balkans '' covering northern Yugoslavia and '' Luftwaffe General in Greece '', both of them being subordinate to Air Force Command South-East. This extensive regrouping resulted in a great concentration of forces which should, theoretically, have added to flexibility and effectiveness in the defence of Germany, but in practice this advantage was offset by the desperate fuel shortage, the steady decline in fighting value, and congestion and increased vulnerability of airfields.

The Allied Airborne Landing at Arnhem

27. It was at this stage of a general redisposition and reorganisation of forces that the Allied airborne landings in Holland took place on September 17th. Complete tactical surprise was achieved and German air opposition on the first day of the operation was virtually negligible, only some 50-75 sorties being flown against the powerful Allied defensive fighter screen. However, during the week which ensued from September 18th until the Allied withdrawal from Arnhem

on September 25th, practically the whole of the German air effort in the West was diverted against the airborne landings, defence of the Reich becoming a secondary consideration. It was appreciated that the objective of these landings was to gain crossings over the Lower Rhine and Waal in order to open up a thrust into North-West Germany. Consequently, reinforcements were thrown in from the strategic fighter defence of Germany, amounting to some 320-350 single-engined fighters, almost double the force in the immediate area of the landings. Bad weather, unsuitable airfields and the now inevitable fuel shortage all combined to restrict air operations to a maximum of some 250 fighter sorties a day, but the situation was judged sufficiently serious to warrant the return of the long-range bomber force to operations for the first time for more than a fortnight, about 100 sorties being undertaken on two nights when operations were possible. The latter were directed against Eindhoven as a communications centre and against the main group of airfields immediately behind the airborne landing area. This, however, was the last appearance in strength of the long-range bomber force in the West; Fliegerkorps IX was withdrawn from operations on September 22nd and thereafter relegated to the status of a Training Command for the conversion of bomber pilots to fighters.

28. It cannot be said that the German Air Force was able to play any prominent part in the German success in preventing the exploitation of these airborne landings. The difficulties from which it was suffering at this stage have already been noted, but nevertheless the reaction achieved was the first sign of the very remarkable recovery which was to make itself obvious over the next few months. As had so frequently occurred on other fronts in the past, the Luftwaffe once again was to show a surprising capacity for recovery as soon as Allied pressure was sufficiently relaxed; the pause on the West wall which then followed gave it the breathing space so desperately needed. In spite of the disasters on the fighting fronts, fighter production in Germany was still rising by leaps and bounds and the new jet aircraft were on the point of coming into service; the remarkable revival in the fortunes of the Luftwaffe which consequently took place during the last three months of 1944, and the methods whereby it was attained, are described in the following chapter.

Ever since June, 1941, Luftflotte 3 had been the operational Command responsible for the conduct of operations on the western front against Great Britain. The long-range bomber forces subordinated to Luftflotte 3 had throughout this period been under Fliegerkorps IX, with the exception of the anti-shipping units in South-West France which came under the independent control of Fliegerfuehrer Atlantik.

The fighter forces up to 1943 had been under Fighter Command West (Hoehere Jafue West), when, consequent upon a general reorganisation, the Command was upgraded to that of Jagdkorps II, the strategic defence of Germany being entrusted to Jagdkorps I both for day and night fighters (compare Map 25).

This map shows the German Air Force dispositions in the West at the beginning of June, 1944. Fliegerkorps IX continued to control the long-range bomber force in northern France and the Low Countries, while Fliegerkorps X, transferred from the eastern Mediterranean, had assumed the functions of Fliegerfuehrer Atlantik; this Command was responsible for the operation of He.177, FW.200 and Do.217 aircraft operating with remotely-controlled missiles (the Hs.293 glider-bomb and FX radio-controlled bomb). In southern France, the torpedo-bomber units came under the control of Fliegerdivision 2.

340

Under the general control of Jagdkorps II, the close-support forces (mainly day fighters) were subordinated to Fliegerkorps II, formerly in Italy, to which Fliegerfuehrer West (or Jafue Brittany) was in turn subordinated.

The Flying Bomb Campaign (12th June, 1944 to 30th March, 1945)

Origins of the Flying Bomb

29. The Flying Bomb, known to the Germans as the FZG76[1] and to the world as the V1[2], finally came into operation, against England, on the night of 12th-13th June, 1944, six months later than the Germans had planned. At that time, with the Luftwaffe bomber force seriously depleted, the Germans were fortunate to be able to bring to bear a weapon which replaced their bomber force and at the same time diverted a considerable portion of Allied air effort for countering the weapon at a time when the invasion of the Continent had only just opened. When, in December, 1942, the first trial V1 was launched at the German research station at Peenemuende, its eventual rôle of replacing the bomber force was certainly foreseen by some. The possibility that Germany would shortly be forced to reduce its bomber production in favour of a defensive fighter programme on a tremendous scale was certainly not foreseen, and it was largely fortuitous that, when the Luftwaffe was being forced on to the defensive by the scale of Allied air attack, the Flying Bomb was ready for operations.

30. The first powered Flying Bomb to take to the air was launched from Peenemuende on Christmas Eve, 1942, and it flew a distance of 3,000 yards. In July, 1943, a bomb flew for a distance of 152 miles and impacted within half-a-mile of its intended target. This success encouraged the General Staff to order the urgent development of the weapon, and they provisionally fixed 15th December, 1943, for the commencement of flying bomb operations against England. Preparations were placed in the hands of the Luftwaffe General of Flak.

Preparations for Operations

31. The selection and training of the necessary troops for handling and launching the weapon were put in hand immediately with the formation of Flak Regiment 155(W)[3] and its drafting to Zempin for training, under its Commander, Colonel Wachtel. Parallel with these preparations, plans for the construction of launching sites were being pushed ahead in France. The scheme, drawn up by the Air Ministry, envisaged 64 main launching sites and 32 reserve sites in a belt facing England and stretching from Cherbourg to the outskirts of Calais. Construction work entailed the building of storage and assembly accommodation and a launching ramp on each site, as well as eight heavily protected supply centres each capable of holding a stock of 250 flying bombs. By late September some 40,000 workers of the Todt organisation were engaged on this work.

---

[1] Fern Ziel Geraet = Long-range target apparatus.
[2] Vergeltungswaffe 1 = Reprisal weapon No. 1.
[3] W = Wachtel, after its Commander.

341

The R.A.F. Delays the Programme

32. During the summer of 1943 British Intelligence had come to know of the Flying Bomb research and experimental work, and heavy R.A.F. raid on the Peenemuende research station in August of that year caused some damage to the experimental equipment. At the same time the extension of the training site at Zempin was suffering from shortage of materials and from the delays in selecting and posting of recruits for the new Flying Bomb Regiment. In France, meanwhile, bombing attacks began to be directed against rail communications, and the delivery of supplies of construction material was thereby delayed. In addition, the large numbers of foreign workers were constantly stopping work when Allied aircraft passed overhead.

33. The first training shoots at Zempin eventually took place on October 16th, and the first battery of trained men of Regiment 155(W) left for the Calais area on the 21st to take part in the final installation of the sites. By early November the Germans were still hoping to have 88 sites in France ready for the planned date. In the middle of December, however, the opening of determined and heavy R.A.F. bombing attacks made it clear that the system had been compromised and accurately plotted. A large proportion of the sites was soon either completely destroyed or severely damaged, so that any possibility of their operation in the near future was out of the question. Furthermore, any attempts at repair only brought repeated destruction from bombing. It was obvious to the Germans that a new system of more carefully hidden or even of mobile sites would have to be devised, and that the opening of Flying Bomb operations would have to be considerably delayed. With their knowledge of the Allied preparations in England for an invasion of the Continent, they realised that any new construction programme must be put in hand with all possible speed.

34. There is no doubt that, had the Germans been allowed to develop their plan unmolested—and it is rather typical of German mentality during the war that they laid their plans without consideration of probable enemy opposition—a combined assault on London and southern England by the Luftwaffe bomber force and the Flying Bombs would have taken place late in 1943, and there is no doubt that its effect could have been disastrous. To this end, tactical exercises with combined bomber and Flying Bomb organisations were being held in December under the aegis of Luftflotte 3. As it was, the bomber assault, opening on January 21st, had to take place by itself, with results which are described in Chapter 13.

Fresh Preparations

35. After the disaster with which the first system of launching sites had met, work was immediately begun on a new system which had more regard for British photographic reconnaissance and Intelligence. The utmost security precautions were therefore taken, and the new sites were much simplified and cleverly camouflaged. At the same time a new chain of supply for the transport of the bombs from Germany was organised.

36. The deployed strength of the Regiment in the proposed operational areas was meanwhile being steadily increased as more trained crews became available, and by March, 1944, the Regiment, with a strength of 5,700 men, was stationed near the various sites which it was to use ; for security purposes the sites were not to be occupied until immediately before operations began.

A Flying Bomb (FZ976 or V1)

A Flying Bomb on its launching ramp

A Flying Bomb carried by the He 111.

M*

By the beginning of June the majority of the new simplified sites were ready, and few had been subjected to any premeditated bombing by Allied aircraft. By then, however, another complication had arisen in the widespread Allied bombing of communications in northern France in connection with the invasion operations.

Supply of Flying Bombs

37. At a conference at the end of December, 1943, the production figures of flying bombs were laid down as 1,200-1,400 a month for the period of January to March, 1944, rising to 4,000 a month by May.

The Opening of Operations

38. With the launching of the invasion on 6th June, 1944, the flying bomb system was still not ready for operations. The C.-in-C. Forces West was urging the start of operations in the belief that the Allies would thus be forced to divert some of their air strength from Normandy and the bombing of Germany, and would thus relieve the pressure on the German Army and Air Force at the beachheads, as well as on German industry at home. In view of this pressure from C.-in-C. Forces West, the Flying Bomb Regiment had no alternative but to accept the order to begin operations on the night of 12th-13th June. They fully realised that, with the lack of many items of equipment, including lighting on the sites and a shortage of the special fuel, operations could not assume a large scale for some days.

39. The opening operation had envisaged the firing of salvoes of Flying Bombs, directed from all sites, against London ; such bomber aircraft of Fliegerkorps IX—under the Command of Peltz—as could be made available were to attack London at the same time in accordance with the plan often practised by Luftflotte 3. It was, indeed, planned that two salvoes should be fired on the opening operation, one at 2300 hours and one at 0400 hours ; each salvo was to be timed so that all Flying Bombs would impact in London simultaneously. At zero hour on the night of June 12th, however, so many sites reported themselves unserviceable that the plan for the salvo had to be abandoned ; instead, such sites as were ready for action were to maintain a harassing fire until 0300 hours. That night seven sites were in action and launched a total of 10 flying bombs, four of which reached England—one in London itself.

40. After this preliminary failure, operations were temporarily suspended for a necessary investigation ; after three days, however, enough sites were ready for the operation to be reopened, and on the night of June 15th, 55 sites were able to launch a total of 244 missles. Thereafter, operations continued on a scale of an average of 120 to 190 bombs during each period of 24 hours and by June 29th, 2,000 had been launched against England, and mainly London. During this time a British reaction was not, of course, lacking. Defences on a prodigious scale had been erected between the Kent and Sussex coasts and London. Ground defences included an A.A. coastal belt, and a balloon barrage around the outer London suburbs of the greatest density that had ever been assembled. The channel area and the intervening space in England were left free for fighter action, and the R.A.F. Tempest, with a speed of 50 m.p.h. faster than that of the Flying Bomb, was employed with considerable success. During this period and subsequent months a considerable

Allied air and ground defensive effort was perforce diverted to the combatting of the missles in the air and to the photographing and bombing of the launching sites. New sites of the simplified design were meanwhile continually under construction, and various decoy devices were employed by the Germans, including dummy sites and ramps, and lights to simulate the launching of bombs at night—the latter on lorries which continually moved about the country.

41. The Allied bombing of the new type of site certainly did not meet with the success of its previous effort, and the Flying Bomb launching programme was but little disturbed. The defences in England, however, were having increasing success and a large proportion of the missiles was being brought down in open country. It was in the field of supply that the effects of Allied air attack began to make themselves most apparent. The transport and supply organisation broke down to an extent which precluded any operation to the full capacity of the Regiment. A rationing of missiles to the sites had soon to be instituted, and this resulted in some days of intensive launching activity and others of comparative calm. Largely as a result of this shortage and partly as a result of unforeseen technical defects in launching, a planned rate of fire of one bomb from each ramp every 26 minutes was reduced to an average rate of one every 1-1½ hours.

The German Retreat and the End of the First Operation

42. By the early days of August it had become obvious that the new weapon was not going to have the expected decisive effect in the war. Furthermore, it became obvious that many of the launching sites would have to be evacuated in face of the advance of the British and Canadian armies. Work on new sites in the area South of the Somme was therefore called off, and work was begun on a further system of sites placed as far North into Belgium as the range of the Flying Bomb would allow. During August the Regiment began an orderly retreat northwards, but by the end of the month and when Amiens was captured, the retreat began to assume the character of a rout. For lack of transport one site after another was abandoned, its equipment as far as possible destroyed.

43. On September 1st at 0400 hours, the first Flying Bomb operation against England came to an end as the last remnants of the Regiment retreated from France ; on the next day the Regiment had been declared non-operational. In its period of operational life between June 12th and August 31st it had launched 8,564 Flying Bombs against London with the employment of some 6,500 men and 150 officers ; of the Flying Bombs, 1,006 crashed after take-off. In addition, 53, of which nine crashed, were launched against Southampton.

The Second Phase—Airborne Launching

44. Experiments at Peenemuende had resulted in the evolution of a method of launching the Flying Bomb from aircraft. The He.111 bomber was found to be most suitable for this purpose, and the Flying Bomb was slung on a carrier placed under the wing between the engine and fuselage. By a simple release gear, the missile could be successfully launched from a height of 1,500 feet and, aimed in the direction of a target like London, its chances of impacting in a built-up area were considerable.

45. Early in September, therefore, aircrew were withdrawn from several semi-defunct bomber units, mainly from the Russian front, and after a short course in launching were posted to a reconstituted KG.53 in North-western

Germany. Under conditions of the utmost secrecy, such elements of KG.53 as were ready began to operate from Venlo airfield on the German-Dutch border and to launch Flying Bombs at night over the North Sea against London. In this they met with some success, and by November the aircraft available for these operations had been planned to reach Geschwader strength of about 100. By December elements of two Gruppen with a total of some 20 crews were available ; these were operating from the Hamburg-Bremen area, to which they then had retired from Holland. Losses due to accidents and to R.A.F. action were heavy, but nevertheless the launchings continued until the advance of the Allied armies towards North-West Germany precluded further operations. Such German figures as have become available show the following launchings of Flying Bombs from aircraft in this phase of operations :—

September	..	..	..	..	177 on 13 nights
October ..	..	..	..	..	282 on 20 nights
November .	..	..	..	..	316 on 13 nights
December 1st-13th	..	..	..		90 on 6 nights

Continental Operations and the Third Operation against London

46. When, at the close of the first Flying Bomb operation against England early in September, Flak Regiment 155(W) was declared non-operational, such strength as remained to it—some 3,500 men—was reassembled and taken away from the responsibility of the General of Flak. The LXV Army Corps now obtained control after much intriguing in higher quarters, and, taking over the remnants of the Regiment, began a type of long-range artillery action against the British and American fronts and rear areas, particularly Brussels, Antwerp and Liège. Early in 1945, however, the S.S. obtained control of Flying Bomb operations, and the original Commander, Oberst Watchel, was brought back into operational control. Meanwhile, a modified version of the Flying Bomb with wooden wings and spars and a range of action increased from the original 152 miles to 220 miles had been developed at Peenemuende. This increased range once more opened the possibility of action against London from Holland, and to that end three new sites were erected near Delft and began operations early in January. Extension of these operations by bringing in further batteries from the Rhineland was now planned, but could not take place in view of the drawing up of a scheme for the eventual evacuation of Holland. On March 30th, the S.S. ordered the suspension of all secret weapon operations. In this third phase of attack on London only 275 Flying Bombs of the new type had been launched.

CHAPTER 15

THE ATTACK ON THE GERMAN OIL INDUSTRY: THE CRIPPLING OF THE LUFTWAFFE

German Fuel Resources, 1939-44

Review of the Situation in 1944

1. As has been seen in Chapter 13, Germany was faced in the spring of 1944 with the vital need of concentrating all possible resources for the defence of the Reich against the Allied day and night air bombardment. Further, the Allied invasion in the West, to be supported by massive air power, still lay in anticipation, while in the East the need for preventing further Russian advances had become paramount, and the Luftwaffe was battling against long odds of numerical inferiority. This critical situation postulated the development and expansion of the fighter forces to the utmost possible extent at the expense of offensive striking power, and, as already seen, led to the setting up of the *Jaegerstab*[1]. Yet, despite the great reinforcement of German fighter strength which this accomplished, it was completely nullified by the devastating onslaught on German oil resources which successfully prevented the fighter defences from being employed, except on a severely restricted basis, for the purpose for which they were built up. Before considering further the scope, intensity and effects of the Allied bombing of the German oil industry, it is necessary first to review briefly the fuel position during the war up to the Spring of 1944.

Outbreak of War to the Russian Campaign of 1941-42

2. At the outbreak of war in 1939, German production capacity of aviation fuel was inadequate to provide the anticipated requirements for war, and over a period of at least two years beforehand substantial supplies had had to be imported. The greater part of these imports was allocated, not for current consumption, but to the " Supreme Command of the Armed Forces Reserve ", so that by September, 1939, this reserve amounted to 355,000 tons, equivalent to about three months' consumption under war conditions. The brevity of the Polish campaign in 1939 and of operations in Norway and in the West in 1940 was such that no restrictions of any kind were imposed on the use of aviation fuel ; the demands of all branches of the Air Force were fully met up to the spring of 1941. At this date, limited measures were taken to curtail consumption in order to build up stocks in preparation for the attack on Russia.

3. During the first 12 months of the Russian campaign the German Air Force was able to sustain its maximum effort, again without any restrictions except in isolated cases where purely local supply difficulties were encountered. However, it was realised that the unexpected duration of the fighting in Russia, with the prospect of a further major campaign in the East in the summer of 1942, coupled with the great distances over which fuel had to be transported, would make stringent economies in consumption inevitable in the future. The heavy fighting in Russia which continued into the autumn and winter of 1942 came also to be accompanied by a further heavy expenditure of fuel on account

---

[1] See Chapter 13, paragraph 11 *et seq.*

of the Mediterranean campaign; there was in consequence a substantial depletion of stocks, and in September a critical position was reached when Air Force reserves of aviation fuel fell to less than two weeks' requirements. This situation was not, however, permitted to interfere with operations in these two main theatres, and the necessary economies had therefore to be made elsewhere; as was to happen repeatedly in the future, the flying training branch was the first to feel the pinch and suffered a considerable reduction in its quota of aircraft fuel. Restrictions were also imposed in the case of transport and communications flights, while on the relatively inactive western front, offensive operations were restricted to times when weather conditions were most favourable.

4. At the beginning of 1943 the position began to be somewhat eased by the increasing output from the synthetic plants, but as operations intensified with improving weather, the supply position began to deteriorate in the same manner and at the same time as in the previous year. Once again operational activity was maintained to the full at the expense of the flying schools.

The Effect on Training and Engine Testing

5. In June, 1943, General Leutnant Kreipe was appointed Air Officer for Training. Before taking over the post he demanded an assured monthly allocation of 50,000 tons of aviation fuel in order to carry out his duties adequately, and although he did in fact receive no more than 30,000 to 35,000 tons a month, until that autumn he was able to carry out the prescribed programme with this amount. As has been seen in Chapter 13[1], a considerable improvement in the output of aircrew from training establishments was actually achieved during 1943 as compared with 1942. While the output in terms of numbers was able to meet requirements, training had in the circumstances to be curtailed, in consequence of which the quality of output inevitably declined and much final training which normally should have taken place in O.T.U's. had to be carried out after the posting of crews to operational units.

6. Apart from the training organisation the aircraft industry also suffered severely by the reduction of its allocation of fuel for bench-testing and flight-testing, particularly from the summer of 1943 onwards. These reductions proved costly and were reflected in growing operational inefficiency; such was the effect of the curtailment of these supplies that eventually only one aircraft in five made the proper acceptance flight, the others being flown for 20 minutes and then sent direct to the front.

Increased Synthetic Production

7. During the winter of 1943-44 the aviation fuel situation underwent a considerable improvement due to increased production from synthetic plants and a simultaneous reduction of consumption during the winter months. During that period the most strenuous efforts were made to consolidate the position to the utmost. In this respect substantial results were achieved, and fuel stocks rose from a relatively low level of 280,000 tons in September, 1943, to 390,000 tons by December, and reached a peak at the end of April, 1944, of no less than 574,000 tons. Thus, when the Allied air offensive against the German oil industry began, the German Air Force stock position was stronger than it had been at any time since the summer of 1940.

---

[1] Paragraph 23 *et seq.*

8. These substantial stocks, gained by limiting consumption as well as by the normal excess of production over consumption during the winter, led to the formation of a series of reserves. Whereas there had always been at least in theory a "Supreme Command Reserve", it was decided that in addition there should be set aside the *Fuehrer Reserve* which, nominally at least, could only be broached at the express orders of Hitler himself. The designation of this reserve was such that it helped to ensure that the stocks thus set aside would only be used in exceptional circumstances. There were, in addition, certain private reserves built up by several of the Luftflotten as a routine precaution against any unexpected interruption or unexpected consumption which might occur. These three systems, existing in the spring of 1944 for making provision against future eventualities, had the effect of at least attenuating the length of time in which a stoppage of output could bring about a total stoppage in operations.

The Attack on German Fuel Resources

9. It was in these circumstances that the Allied bombing effort came to be directed against the German oil targets, opening with heavy attacks by the U.S. 8th Air Force on May 12th and 28th-29th, when over 2,500 tons of bombs were dropped on the main synthetic oil plants at Leuna, Poelitz, Bohlen, Luetzkendorf, Magdeburg, Zeitz and Ruhland, responsible together for about 40 per cent. of the total estimated output of synthetic oil. These attacks were followed up during June by R.A.F. Bomber Command and the U.S. 8th and 15th Air Forces, and by June 22nd the attacks had been so successful that they had brought about a loss of 90 per cent. of the aircraft fuel production, which fell from 195,000 tons in May to not more than 52,000 tons for the whole of June. In the following three months the output fell still lower, the figures being 35,000, 16,000 and 7,000 tons respectively, but the foresight shown in accumulating reserves during the favourable early period of the year provided sufficient stocks to enable the Luftwaffe to cover approximately three months of maximum operational effort. As a consequence, the full severity of the crisis was not felt before August.

10. In particular, the Luftwaffe's resistance to the Allied landings in Normandy was in no way limited by any lack of fuel, neither had serious shortages occurred in France during the first two or three months ; moreover, the supply position was also eased by the heavy losses in aircraft. However, by August drastic measures had to be taken to conserve available supplies. The Luftwaffe High Command was then compelled to impose what were described as " far reaching limitations upon operations " ; only fighter operations in air defence were permitted to continue unrestricted ; even reconnaissance flights were limited and the support of the Army by bomber and low-flying operations was permitted only in " decisive situations ". Further, night fighter operations had shortly afterwards to be cut down in order to allow greater quantities of fuel to be made available for daylight operations, while the acute shortage of fuel undoubtedly hastened the decline and disbandment of the bomber units already being broken up at about this time.

11. As a result of this critical fuel shortage in the autumn of 1944, the Luftwaffe was unable to derive any advantage from the fact that its first-line strength had reached a peak almost equalling that attained in the summer of 1943, with a production of aircraft averaging 3,100 a month, mainly of fighter

GERMAN PRODUCTION, CONSUMPTION & STOCKS OF AVIATION FUEL
1940 — 45

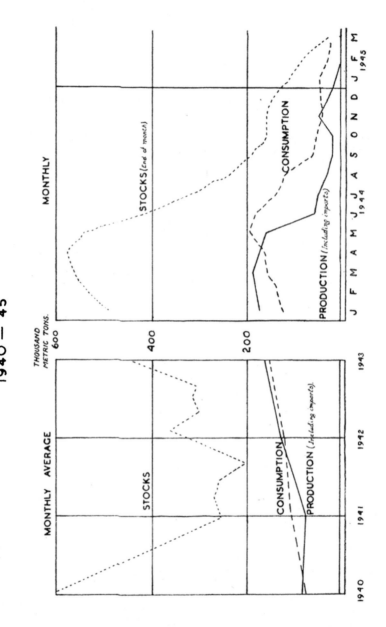

A forward fuel dump

The Leuna sidings

types, in the last quarter of the year. It was the decline in fuel production and the diminishing prospect of its satisfactory restoration which made necessary a further drastic revision in the aircraft production programme. All efforts were directed to increase the output of jet-propelled fighters—the He.162 was designed, tried out and adopted for large-scale production in the remarkably short time of about four months—the concentration on these jet aircraft being due not only to their superior performance but also to the fact that they required only low grade fuel.

12. By November, 1944, the shortage of fuel in all operational areas was causing units to be grounded for long intervals, while in the West the position was, if possible, even tighter, as stocks were being assembled in preparation for the Ardennes counter-offensive. However, towards the end of the month supplies were becoming more abundant, due not so much to the reduction in consumption as to a small but important recovery in production. The Allied bombing offensive had continued inexorably up to September, when for a time no German oil plants of any kind were operating. The fact that the Allied strategic bombing forces failed to maintain their offensive against oil targets, and so consolidate the advantageous position then attained, resulted in the production of aircraft fuel rising to 18,000 tons in October and to 39,000 tons in November and these quantities were sufficient to inject the Luftwaffe with new life. Thus it was possible for German aircraft to appear once again on an appreciable scale in support of the Ardennes offensive and to carry out the New Year's Day attack on Allied airfields on the western front, intruder operations against Bomber Command airfields in England and the operations connected with the Remagen bridgehead (Chapter 17).

13. The final phase of the Allied bombing offensive began in the middle of December when, with an improvement in weather conditions, operations could once more be resumed against those installations now back in production—thanks largely to the tremendous efforts of Geilenberg, who had unlimited facilities placed at his disposal by way of manpower and materials to counteract the devastation of bombing. This renewal of the offensive opened with a remarkable series of consistent operations by the U.S. 15th Air Force directed at the immobilisation of the Silesian synthetic plants and also of the one at Brux ; these were accompanied by heavy R.A.F. night bombing attacks, carried out with great accuracy and success, on Poelitz, Leuna and Brux, while the U.S. 8th Air Force continued its operations by day. With these developments the final outcome of the Allied oil offensive was no longer in doubt. By March, the remaining stocks of fuel were almost exhausted and by the beginning of April practically the whole industry was immobilised, while during the month most of its constituent units were rapidly overrun by the Allied ground forces. With the whole German war machine on the point of collapse so that repair and dispersal schemes could no longer be implemented, the task of dislocating the German oil resources had been completed and the remnants of the Luftwaffe, grounded with empty tanks, were unable to play any part in the closing stages of the German collapse.

The Rumanian Oilfields

14. In considering the offensive against the German oil industry, it must not be forgotten that the offensive against the Rumanian oilfields formed part of the general scheme of Allied operations. The first air attack on Ploesti was made from North African bases on 1st August, 1943, but failed to achieve

tactical surprise. Consequently it was possible for the Germans to inflict heavy losses on the attacking force ; moreover the damage to installations was not as great as expected, although the main achievement of the attack was to eliminate permanently the surplus of effective refinery capacity. This costly operation was not repeated until the spring of 1944, since no consistent effort against the Rumanian oilfields could be made until the U.S. 15th Air Force became established on the airfields at Foggia, and long-range fighter escort could be provided. However, the attacks on Ploesti in the spring and early summer of 1944 only achieved indifferent results, and Rumanian refinery production staged a substantial recovery in July and the early part of August. At this time the effects of the mining of the Danube were, in fact, far more disturbing to the Germans, causing dislocation of shipping transport and thus creating a greater bottleneck. It was not until the middle of August that the 15th Air Force succeeded in delivering a number of successful attacks against the leading active plants in the Rumanian oilfields ; these successes were rapidly followed by the Russian occupation of the oilfields and of Ploesti itself.

15. The loss of the Rumanian oil industry had a far-reaching and immediate influence on the situation. Apart from the loss of productive capacity, it also released the strength of the U.S. 15th Air Force from its most onerous commitment, and led to the immediate intensification of attacks against other targets within operational range. Thus, the weight of the 15th Air Force effort could be added to the already crippling blows being dealt against the German synthetic plants from the West and its attention could be directed to the elimination of the otherwise inaccessible Silesian synthetic industry. This switch of air power at that particular moment was of the greatest importance in that it accompanied the heavy assault from the West, now at its peak, and thus enabled the whole of German synthetic oil production to be brought to a complete standstill in the middle of September.

Defence of the German Oil Industry

Policy and Strategy

16. To complete the review of the Allied bombing assault on the German oil industry, it is necessary to examine German policy and strategy in the defence of these vital targets, both from the point of view of the German fighter force and also of the Flak defences. It has already been shown how the increasing need for defence of the Reich against Allied day and night bombing had, during 1943 and the early part of 1944, constituted an ever-growing dilemma for the German Air Staff as to the distribution of its inadequate fighter forces between the tactical needs of supporting the Army at the front and the simultaneous defence of German industry against strategic bombing. This problem was to become increasingly acute during 1944, with the ring closing in steadily on Germany from all sides, and notwithstanding the remarkable expansion of the fighter force which occurred in the face of seemingly almost insuperable difficulties. The opening of the attacks on the German synthetic oil targets in the middle of May, 1944, was, in fact, no more than a further development of Allied bombing strategy which, during the earlier part of the year, had been directed primarily against the German aircraft and friction bearing industries ; whilst these latter attacks had not achieved the success which appeared likely at the time, the assault on the oil industry in contrast struck at the most vital and sensitive part of the whole German war economy.

Fighter Defence

17. In order to view the German reaction to the Allied air offensive against oil it is necessary to examine the strength and disposition of the German fighter forces at the beginning of April, 1944, that is to say, while the Allied strategic bombing offensive was in full swing but had not yet been directed against the synthetic oil plants. At 1st April, 1944, the German single-engined fighter force comprised 1,675 aircraft, disposed as follows :—

	Aircraft
Defence of the Reich	850
Northern France and Low Countries	135
Norway	30
Italy	145
Eastern Front	515
Total	1,675

It will be seen that approximately 50 per cent. of the total force was then engaged against the Allied strategic day bombing of Germany ; moreover, this force was supplemented by a further 110 twin-engined day fighters, while no less than 500 night fighters out of a total of 615 in this category were also engaged against the night bombing offensive. Thus, 55 per cent. of the total German fighter resources were directly committed to the defence of German industry.

18. Little or no appreciable change occurred in these dispositions up to the time of the Allied landings in Normandy in June, except that the steady expansion of first-line single-engined fighter strength due to rise in output was fully absorbed in strengthening the defences of Germany, and such withdrawals as could be made from operational fronts, e.g., Italy, were ruthlessly made.

19. It has already been shown in Chapter 14 how the necessary reinforcement of the weak German fighter strength in the West was only possible at the cost of a serious reduction in the force which could still be reserved for the strategic defence of Germany ; by the end of June, 1944, the single-engined fighter force, now somewhat reduced in strength to little more than 1,500 aircraft owing to the severe wastage encountered in operations in the West, was almost evenly divided as between the defence of the Reich and the western and eastern fronts. Thus, when the second phase of the attack on German oil plants began in July, no attempt could be made to put up anything approaching serious fighter opposition.

20. The increasing weight of assault during July and August once again brought about the enforced weakening of tactical support in the field, even in face of the critical situation then developing in France, in an attempt to stave off the complete elimination of the German oil plants ; even so, owing to lack of numbers and also to want of skill, nothing effective could be done to bring the Allied air attack to a halt. It thus came about that the whole of German synthetic oil production was brought to a complete standstill by mid-September.

21. From that time to the end of the month it was clear that there was no halting the advance of the Allied armies towards the Rhine, nor were there in fact suitable airfields in the Rhineland area to accommodate more than a fraction of the still considerable numerical German single-engined fighter

strength ; moreover, the acute fuel shortage then prevailing effectively prevented any attempt being made to employ the whole of the force available at more than a fraction of its potential effort. There remained the faint prospect that, with the Allies' rapidly lengthening lines of communication and the inevitable supply problems arising therefrom, a breathing space might be won in which to reassemble and re-deploy the fighter force.

22. Thus, at the end of September, the decision was taken to leave not more than a small force of some 300 single-engined fighters to support the German Army in the West covering the approaches to the Rhine, while no less than 1,260 aircraft (including 25 Me.163's) were allocated to the defence of the Reich out of the total single-engined fighter strength, now risen again to some 1,975 aircraft. To provide this vast access of strength for the defence of the oil installations, even the fighter force on the eastern front had to be reduced to no more than 375 aircraft. On top of this, 900 twin-engined night fighters were now available against the night bombing offensive, and altogether 70 per cent. of the total German fighter strength was now earmarked for the defence of the oil industry.

23. At that stage, General Galland, A.O. for Fighters, evolved a plan by which, instead of fighter strength being as heretofore dissipated by frequent weak attempts at interception, it would be built up to deal a series of concentrated attacks against the daylight raids. Training and preparations with this object in view were pressed forward, and with the formidable force now at his disposal, Galland was able on November 12th to inform the Operations Staff that the fighter force was ready to undertake this operation termed *Der Grosse Schlag* (the big blow)[1]. The few occasions, however, when it was possible during the autumn of 1944 to secure the large-scale employment of the fighter force did not bring the success which had been hoped for ; some 500 sorties were flown against an attack on Leuna on November 2nd, but the interception was not resolutely pressed home, and although 63 U.S.A.A.F. aircraft were brought down, not more than some 15 are thought to have been destroyed by fighters. The peak efforts occurred on November 21st and 25th with similar results, and thereafter the division of the single-engined fighter force to close-support tasks in connection with the Ardennes offensive prevented a large defensive effort from being maintained.

24. The Ardennes offensive had the effect of completely reversing the situation as regards the deployment of the single-engined fighter force, Hitler insisting on its maximum employment for the support of this last desperate offensive and attempt to drive back the Allied armies from the borders of Germany. Thus, by the end of December the strategic fighter defence had once again been reduced to not more than 520 aircraft, of which 45 were Me.163's, while over 1,200 were now committed to the fighting in the West ; an attack on Allied airfields on 1st January, 1945, was carried out by between 750 and 800 of these, resulting in severe German losses both of aircraft and crews.

Flak Defences

25. The defence of the oil plants in central Germany, which were regarded as the most important, was put in the hands of the 14th Flak Division, and the serious nature of the task which this Division had to fulfil was duly impressed on its commanding officer. When appointed to the Command on 17th May,

---

[1] See Chapter 17, paragraph 18.

1944, he received visits from various personalities, who included Field Marshal Milch and Reichsminister Speer, and was informed that if his Division failed in its duty to defend the plants in its area the reserves of liquid fuel would be exhausted, the Army and the German Air Force would be immobilised and the war lost by September, 1944.

26. The area to be defended was centred upon Leuna, a district which also included an important part of Germany's production of fixed nitrogen, explosives and synthetic rubber, all of them dependent upon the synthetic oil plants. At that time the Division had at its disposal 374 guns, of which 104 covered the Halle-Leuna area and 174 the Leipzig-Bittefeld area. From May onwards these defences were continuously strengthened and the number of heavy guns defending Leuna eventually exceeded 460 ; these additions, however, could only be made good by depleting the defences of Berlin and the Ruhr and by the withdrawal of Flak units from Eisenach, Weimar, Chemnitz and Dresden, leaving these cities undefended. Yet these immensely strong defences failed to achieve their object and although numerous Allied aircraft were damaged, the number of those destroyed were wholly disproportionate to the effort involved. Moreover, the vast expenditure of ammunition brought about in due course an acute shortage, which in turn affected the fighting fronts.

CHAPTER 16

THE EASTERN FRONT: THE RUSSIAN ADVANCE INTO POLAND AND THE BALKANS (June–December, 1944)

Situation in June, 1944

German Air Force Dispositions

1. As has already been seen in Chapter 10, the winter campaign of 1943-44 had virtually come to an end with the Russian occupation of the Crimea during April, and the succeeding lull had been taken up largely with re-dispositions in anticipation of a renewal of operations for the summer campaign. The reorganisation of commands had been concerned mainly with a strengthening of the southern front covering the approaches to Rumania with its oilfields, and to the Balkans, the bulk of the close-support forces being subordinated to Luftflotte 4 on that sector. The opportunity afforded by the lull had also been taken of strengthening and re-equipping units, with the result that all categories were, by June, well up to strength. In particular the process of converting Ju.87 dive-bomber units to FW.190's for ground attack operations was proceeding apace, while a long-range bomber Geschwader was being re-equipped with the He.177—although destined never to take part in operations. The general picture, in effect, contrasted strongly with the absence of any comparable forces with which to oppose the Allied landings in the West.

2. Despite the Russian gains in territory, the vast eastern front, over 1,500 miles in length[1], still extended in the far North along the Finnish frontier to the Gulf of Finland, where German Air Force operations still came under Luftflotte 5. The main front continued from Narva on the Gulf of Finland along the eastern boundaries of the Baltic States, air operations on this sector being under the control of Luftflotte 1, while the main approach to Germany across White Russia and Poland was in the hands of Luftflotte 6, its area being divided in the centre by the Pripet Marshes in the South. As already indicated, Luftflotte 4 covered the approaches to the Carpathians and the Balkans[2]. The total forces of the Luftwaffe over this vast extent of territory totalled nearly 2,100 aircraft which were disposed as follows :—

	L.R. Bombers	Ground Attack	Night Harassing Units	S.E. Fighters	T.E. Fighters	L.R. Recce.	Tac. Recce.	Coastal	Total
Luftflotte 5	—	20	10	30	15	10	15	5	105
Luftflotte 1	—	70	95	105	15	25	40	10	360
Luftflotte 6	370	100	45	100	30	35	95	—	775
Luftflotte 4	35	390	75	160	45	45	80	15	845
Total ..	405	580	225	395	105	115	230	30	2,085

[1] See Map 21.
[2] See map 24.

It will be noted that the main concentration of long-range bombers was on the central front, in contrast to the relatively strong ground-attack and fighter forces in the South, and that strength on the main front from the Gulf of Finland to the Black Sea amounted to nearly 2,000 aircraft. There was, in addition, a small mixed force of some 150 aircraft under Luftwaffe Command South-East covering Jugoslavia, Albania, Greece and Bulgaria, but at this time independent of the operational commands on the eastern front.

The Russian Summer Campaign

The Main Offensive

3. Contrary to expectations, the Russian summer offensive opened on June 10th with a major assault on the Finnish frontier in Karelia along the Gulf of Finland, which led to the capture of Viborg by the 20th. Initially, no attempt was made to reinforce the weak Luftwaffe forces available owing to a reluctance to weaken the main front to support the Finns, but the rapid deterioration of the situation soon led to the transfer of 50 dive bombers and single-engined fighters from the Narva front to central Finland.

4. When the main Russian offensive began on June 23rd on the central front, the German Air Forces North of the Pripet Marshes had already been somewhat denuded by events in the Gulf of Finland, the more so in view of the withdrawal of a further 50 fighters to Germany to strengthen the weakened defences against Allied day bombing following upon the large-scale transfer of units to Normandy. By July 3rd, Vitebsk, Mogilev and Minsk had already fallen to the advancing Russians ; the need for reinforcement of the central front was paramount and every aircraft which could possibly be spared from other fronts was hurriedly thrown in.

5. From defence of Germany, 40 single-engined fighters were immediately brought back, and a similar number was transferred northwards from Luftflotte 4, but the main call was for ground-attack aircraft to operate against the Russian columns. No less than 85 FW.190's were accordingly taken from the already depleted Italian front, thereby removing the last potential striking force for army support in that theatre, a force which it was destined never to regain ; 40 more were transferred from Normandy, despite the critical situation resulting from the establishment of the Allied bridgehead where, however, they had been unable to play an effective part, while a further 70 were moved North from Luftflotte 4. Thus, some 270 aircraft had, by the beginning of July, gone to ease the strain on the already cracking central front.

6. These forces were totally inadequate to stem the rout ; on July 12th, the Russians advanced 21 miles on the Baltic front, Vilna fell on the 13th, followed by Pinsk and Grodno ; South of the Pripet marshes the retreat was also now under way, and Brest-Litovsk, Lublin, Lwow and Przemsyl were all lost between July 24th-28th. Such was the state of disintegration that all possible forces had to be thrown in, even at the risk of laying open the Carpathian and Balkan fronts in Rumania, and Luftflotte 4 was stripped of the remainder of its close-support forces in the effort to stem the tide ; there was nothing further left to be committed to the battle.

7. By the end of July, therefore, a remarkable change had come over Luftwaffe dispositions on the Russian front, and the losses suffered during July had more than offset the reinforcements received, reducing strength on the main front from the Baltic to the Black Sea to some 1,750 aircraft which were now thus disposed :—

	L.R. Bombers	Ground Attack	Night Harassing Units	S.E. Fighters	T.E. Fighters	L.R. Recce.	Tac. Recce.	Total
Luftflotte 1 ..	—	155	110	70	—	30	35	400
Luftflotte 6 ..	305	375	50	215	50	55	110	1,160
Luftflotte 4 ..	30	—	35	30	40	25	40	200
Total ..	335	530	195	315	90	110	185	1,760

8. Moreover, the widespread transfers necessitated not only by the move of units from other fronts, but also by continual retreats and changes of base, had resulted in widespread dislocation accompanied by a serious decline in serviceability ; thus, despite the substantial strengthening of the central front, the average daily effort could not be raised to more than 500-600 sorties which was wholly inadequate to relieve the hard-pressed and harassed ground forces.

Developments in the Balkans

9. It was at this critical moment that the Balkan front suddenly flared up. The weakness of the German Air Force in Rumania had already been demonstrated in the Allied attacks from Italy on the Ploesti oilfields on July 9th and 15th, when the total fighter effort put up was unable to exceed 50 sorties, half of which were by Rumanian units, and on July 22nd the reaction had been even less. Thus, the transfers of fighters from the southern front to the Polish and Galician sectors were already being reflected.

10. It was in the political arena, however, that the main German preoccupation now came to lie. By the end of July, it was becoming clear that the neutrality of Turkey could not be relied upon to last much longer ; the expected Turkish move necessarily entailed measures on the part of the Luftwaffe in anticipation of its consequences. Accordingly, the staff of Fliegerkorps II, relieved of its command in France, was transferred on July 31st to Bulgaria purely as a defensive and security measure in view of the fact that no sufficient forces were any longer available with which to undertake offensive operations.

The Rumanian Coup d'Etat

11. A state of inactive uneasiness thereafter ensued on the southern front until the Rumanian *coup d'état* occurred on August 23rd, accompanied by a Russian offensive across the River Pruth. Taken by surprise, the Germans immediately despatched air reinforcements to the new seat of trouble ; 40 Ju.87's were moved to Zilistea from as far away as the Esthonian front, while 30 FW.190 fighters were also transferred from North of the Carpathians. Attempts were also made to move troops by air transport to Bucharest, but as most airfields, including Baneasa, were now in Rumanian hands, and Otopeni (still held by the Germans) was rendered unserviceable by American bombing, results were very limited and insufficient to restore the situation ; an effort to

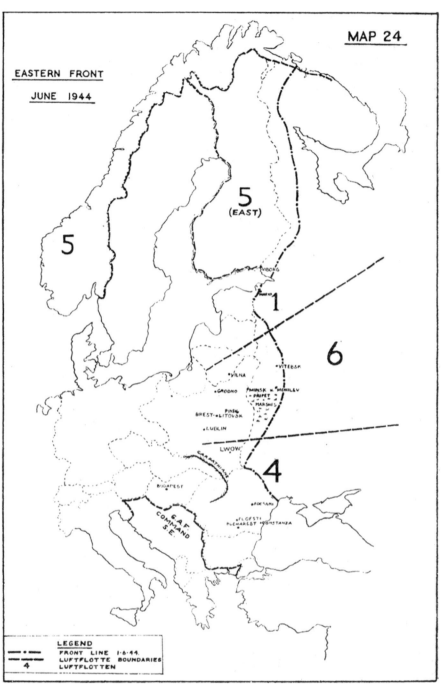

The front line is shown approximately as at the opening of the Russian summer offensive (see also Map 21). Luftflotte 5 (East) continued to control air operations in Finland and N. Norway, and Luftflotte 1 still covered the Baltic States. The area of Luftflotte 6 extended over the whole of the White Russian and Polish Fronts as far as the Carpathians, while Luftflotte 4 extended from Galicia to the Black Sea along the line of the River Pruth. In the Balkans the independent Luftwaffe Command South-East was still responsible for operations in Jugoslavia, Albania and N. Greece.

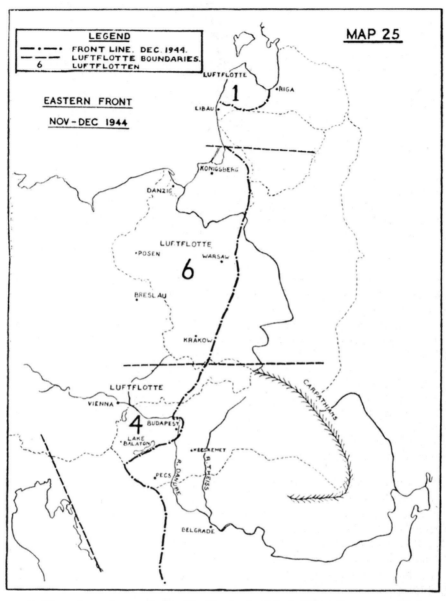

Luftflotte 1 was by now isolated in Courland, while Luftflotte 6 now covered the whole of the main front from the Baltic coast of East Prussia to Slovakia. Luftflotte 4 was now responsible for operations covering the approaches to Austria both in Hungary and Jugoslavia, with Fliegerkorps I subordinated in Hungary against the advance in Budapest, and Luftwaffe Command S.E. in northern Yugoslavia also subordinated to it.

transport airborne troops from Jugoslavia had to be cancelled on August 25th owing to bad weather, shortage of trained crews and lack of serviceable Me.323's. Thus, the endeavour to regain Bucharest by air transport failed and similar operations at Ploesti and Foesani had to be called off ; a final attempt to restore the situation in the capital by the bombing of Bucharest on the same day also failed to secure results.

12. It was clear that the situation had rapidly got out of hand and that all attempts to hold up the Russian advance would be fruitless with the limited resources available. Constanza was captured on the 29th, Ploesti on the 30th and Russian forces entered Bucharest on the 31st. There was nothing left but to save what could be saved from complete catastrophe, and to evacuate all elements of the German Air Force mainly to Hungary as quickly as possible, destroying airfield installations, equipment and stocks before leaving. Such units as were moved to Bulgaria enjoyed only the briefest stay, for on September 6th Bulgaria declared war on Germany and the Balkans had to be given up for lost after less than a fortnight from the beginning of the collapse.

13. By mid-September the eastern and south-eastern fronts had become fused with the Russians, now on the borders of Jugoslavia, and Luftflotte 4's area of command was extended in early October to cover the Luftwaffe forces in the Banat, in the northern part of that area. This, however, provided little access of strength, and the reorganisation failed to compensate for the paucity of air forces on the southern flank for which still no reinforcements were forthcoming. Further, it was at this juncture that the fuel shortage made itself felt in the East as in the West and all operations had to be ruthlessly cut down ; only the most economical conduct of operations with minimum forces was permitted in Luftflotte 4's area due to the strained aircraft fuel situation, and the implication of this may be gauged from the fact that on the whole eastern front on September 11th only 250 German sorties could be flown against a Russian effort of 2,000-2,500. The Russian air preponderance was thus so overwhelming that German Air Force opposition in the Balkans, as elsewhere on the front, was unable to affect the general development of the military situation.

The Eastern Front from October to December

14. On the northern and central sectors, the landslide had in the meantime, continued unabated. The cease-fire had been sounded in Finland on September 4th, the Russians had reached the Baltic near Liba on October 9th and Riga had fallen on the 13th, followed closely by the arrival of Russian troops in East Prussia. In the Balkans, Belgrade had been captured on the 20th[1].

15. By now the impetus of the Russian advance in Poland and the Balkans had for a brief spell spent itself, and the main centre of air activity was confined to the Baltic-East Prussian front, where Luftflotte 1 in due course was to become cut off and isolated in Latvia. However, the stringent fuel situation had resulted in the grounding of almost the whole of the long-range bomber force, thereby denying a useful source of close support to the exhausted German armies, except for the continued but insignificant employment of four special " railway attack " squadrons. Even so, other operational flying had also to be seriously curtailed, and not more than an average of some 500 sorties were being flown, of which 125-150 were accounted for in the area south of the Carpathians.

---

[1] See Map 25.

16. In the latter area considerable reorganisation had now become necessary. In mid-October, General Oberst Dessloch again assumed command of Luftflotte 4, after a brief spell in the West as A.O.C. Luftflotte 3 following the dismissal of Sperrle, and at the same time the whole of the forces of Luftwaffe Command South-East were now taken under his command. These forces were now available in the Pecs area to operate against the Russians advancing up the Danube from Belgrade, although appreciably weakened following the withdrawal of units during the evacuation of southern Jugoslavia, Albania and northern Greece. The remainder, comprising the bulk of Luftflotte 4's scanty forces, were now assembled under Fliegerkorps I in the Kecskemet area, covering the approaches to Budapest. However, under the new organisation either sector could now be easily reinforced by the other, but nevertheless it was clear that the total forces available were far from adequate, even if the stranglehold of fuel shortage had not existed.

17. For the remainder of the year inactivity set in and little change was to follow along the front now running from the Carpathians to East Prussia. In the South, however, Russian pressure was kept up particularly in Hungary. Heavy fighting developed around Kecskemet at the end of October, and all the resources of Fliegerkorps I were thrown into the battle and against Russian armoured forces moving in Budapest. These conditions persisted throughout November, and although the Russians were halted on Lake Balaton, Budapest was becoming increasingly threatened both from North and South. The lull in the North had permitted some reinforcement of Luftflotte 4, whose forces were built up to some 500-600 aircraft (as against some 200 only in July) of which 200 were ground-attack aircraft. Together with a slight easing in the fuel situation, some recovery was therefore possible and by mid-November the effort on this front had already reached up to 400 sorties ; nothing the Luftwaffe could do, however, could stop the Russian advance on Budapest and by December 9th the Danube had been reached North of the city.

18. The six months from June to December, 1944, had thus been a period of unparalleled disaster for German arms both in the East and West. In the East the last of the gains so easily won in 1941 had been wrested from them, nor was there any relief to the gloom such as that temporarily afforded by von Rundstedt's offensive in the West, although plans were already in preparation for a major counter-stroke early in 1945. On all sides, the German forces had been overwhelmed by sheer weight of manpower and material, and the lamentable inadequacy of the Luftwaffe to play a major rôle had been demonstrated to the full. The massive weight of the Soviet Air Force had been such as to outnumber by 5 or 6 to 1 the most powerful forces the German Air Force could put into the air, and it was demonstrably clear now, as in 1943, that the Luftwaffe was no longer a factor to be seriously reckoned with either in the East or West. Once again there had been no margin of reserve, and once again the situation in the West and defence against the bombing offensive over Germany had absorbed the whole of the vast increase of fighter strength during the year. By now the situation was past saving, and although the Germans were to throw all possible resources into the final struggle in the East in 1945, they were powerless to avert the impending catastrophe.

CHAPTER 17

THE GERMAN AIR FORCE IN THE FINAL DEFENCE OF GERMANY

The Allies on the German Frontier

German Recovery After The Arnhem Operation

1. The failure of the Allied attempt at Arnhem[1] to carry the Rhine and break out into the North German plain gave the Luftwaffe the period of rest which was necessary for the completion of its plans for the rebuilding of the fighter force. The month of September, 1944, saw the German aircraft industry at the peak of its effort in the production of single-engined aircraft and, with rapid progress being made in the fighter expansion programme, operational units were able to build up to strengths never before achieved. Experience in France had shown how severe dislocation was immediately caused when the full weight of the Allied close-support force was directed against supply networks and communications of all types. In an effort to avoid a repetition of these conditions, when units found themselves with an ever-dwindling strength and no corresponding supply of replacement aircraft, the policy was adopted of maintaining a substantial reserve of aircraft with the operational units. This was combined with a policy of conservation, in which close support for the armies was cut down to the barest minimum, and which amounted in practice to defensive patrols over the personnel working on the fortifications of the West Wall and to half-hearted defensive activity against Allied fighter-bombers over lines of communication areas well to the rear of the German positions. This period, which included the introduction of jet aircraft, witnessed a final and most remarkable recovery of the Luftwaffe's strength in the face of most adverse circumstances.

Expansion of the Fighter Force[2]

2. Between the beginning of September, 1944, and the middle of November, the German single-engined fighter force expanded from some 1,900 to 3,300 aircraft[3]—an increase in first-line strength of almost 70 per cent. This programme of expansion was of long standing and would certainly have shown solid results by July or August, 1944 had not the heavy wastage incurred, particularly during the early stages of the Allied invasion and on withdrawal into Germany, delayed its full development. The expansion had been in four stages :—

> (a) The programme inaugurated in 1943 for the building up of a single-engined night fighter force to assist the rapidly growing twin-engined force had been completed in the Spring of 1944 by the formation of three new single-engined night fighter Gruppen, bringing the strength of this force up to some 200 aircraft. By June they had been virtually withdrawn from night fighter operations and were converted to day

---

[1] Refer to Chapter 14, paragraph 27.
[2] See also Chapter 12.
[3] See footnote to paragraph 19.

fighting, thus proving a welcome addition to the inadequate day fighter strength ; in this capacity, they were employed particularly for bad weather operations.

(b) From May, 1944, the day single-engined fighter units were expanded from three Staffeln to four Staffeln per Gruppe whilst at the same time the establishment of each Staffel was increased by 50 per cent.

(c) After 6th June, 1944, at least six new single-engined day fighter units were created.

(d) The first rocket-propelled fighter, the Me.163, was introduced into operational units in June, 1944, followed by the jet-propelled Me.262 and Arado 234 in September and October.

The expansion achieved was all the more remarkable in so far as its last phase occurred simultaneously with the major programme of re-equipment of existing units made necessary by the *débâcle* in France. Between mid-August and the end of October, 15 fighter units decimated on the western front were restored, re-equipped and returned to operations. All this was rendered possible by the flood of new aircraft from production.

The Eclipse of the Bomber Force

3. This recovery would not, however, have been possible without a corresponding deterioration, amounting almost to disintegration, in the long-range bomber and reconnaissance forces. During the first nine months of 1944 at least 25 first-line bomber units had been disbanded and the process of dissolution was not yet completed. Of these 25 units 80 per cent. had been disbanded from July onwards. The anti-shipping force now consisted of only some 60 torpedo-carrying Ju.88's and Ju.188's, the FW.200's and He.177's equipped for operations with remotely-controlled bombs having been moved to Norway where they were withdrawn from operations. The torpedo-bombers were based in Germany and Norway, being held in reserve in anticipation of follow-up landings by sea on the Dutch coast. The Ju.88 bomber force in the West had dwindled to a mere token force of some 60 aircraft whose main occupation was the undertaking of desultory minelaying operations, while a further 60 He.111's were being converted for the launching of flying bombs against England.

4. The manpower released by this dissolution of the bomber force was being employed in four different ways, in which the strengthening of the pilot position of the single-engined fighter force was prominent. Some personnel were returning to industry, others were being formed into new units for the Parachute Army or for the Luftwaffe Fortress Battalions. But priority was given, among flying personnel, to the defence of the Reich. The German explanation given at the time for the decline of the bomber force was the decreased necessity for offensive forces in view of the development of new weapons (V1 and V2). In fact, it was the acute manpower shortage throughout the armed forces, the continuous demands of the expanding fighter arm on manpower and production, and the limitations imposed on offensive operations by the shortage of fuel which were the real causes. The success of the fighter arm in building up its aircraft strength was almost paralleled by its success in building up a comparatively healthy pilot position which in July and August had been seriously weak ; from the second half of September onwards until December, 1944, pilots ready for operations with units always outnumbered the total of

serviceable aircraft, thanks to the energetic re-training of personnel from the disbanded bomber crews. This fact, however, should not be allowed to obscure the true state of affairs which was that the quality and operational efficiency of the force as a whole was in inverse ratio to that of its numbers. This state of affairs was due to (1) the fuel situation and urgent need for fighter pilots leading to re-training being reduced to a quite inadequate minimum ; (2) the enforced lowering of standards in the selection of pilots, and (3) the vast expansion of fighter strength which thus caused further dilution of the small number of experienced pilots and formation leaders.

The Decline of the Night Fighter Force[1]

5. The twin-engined night fighter force, which during 1943 and the first half of 1944 had been built up into the most efficient branch of the Luftwaffe was now showing serious signs of deterioration. As late as 31st July, 1944, General Schmid, the A.O.C. of the German Fighter Command, had been able to congratulate the night fighter crews on their success during the night of July 28th-29th when R.A.F. Bomber Command lost 62 aircraft out of a total of 760 attacking Stuttgart and Hamburg. But the same A.O.C. castigated the failure of the night fighter defences on the night of October 6th-7th, when only 10 aircraft of Bomber Command were lost out of a total of 725 attacking Dortmund and Bremen. It was not the crews who were chastised : it was the aircraft reporting services, which were " wholly inadequate for the successful use of our forces ". The air situation had been completely misjudged and " the failure of landline and radio services afforded staggering proof of the incompetence of signals officers of all grades ".

6. These statements by General Schmid contain a large part of the story of the deterioration of the defensive night fighter force brought about by the Allied successes on the Continent. The chief reason for this rapid decline was the occupation of France and the Low Countries by the Allies, thereby depriving the enemy of his early warning system for detecting approaching raids. Supplementing this were the effective R.A.F. countermeasures and intruder operations which had compelled the Germans to restrict the use of airfield lighting and assembly beacons. Owing to fuel stringencies the training of night fighter crews was also not as thorough as formerly, whilst the demands for manpower throughout the whole of the armed forces and industry had brought about a marked decline in the quality of the servicing and ground staff. Further, part of the metropolitan night fighter force had had to be drawn off to the East to counter Russian bombing.

7. The night fighter force was nevertheless continuing to expand as the following figures show :—

	1st July, 1944	1st October, 1944
Total Night Fighters	800	1,020
Engaged against R.A.F. Bomber Command	685	830

Whereas, in July, the line of night fighters extended from Denmark to Paris, in October it ran from Denmark to Switzerland, thus enabling Allied bombers to approach German territory without interception on the way.

---

[1] See also Chapter 12.

367

8. Opposition to night bombing had also been weakened by the diversion of a number of units to other tasks. Regular night reconnaissance patrols had to be flown over the North Sea to pick up early warning of Allied raids. The demands of the Armies for assistance from the Luftwaffe had been answered to some slight extent by the employment of night fighter aircraft on night ground attack missions, but so far this was restricted to crews who were not ranked as " key-crews ".

9. In spite of all these handicaps, the German twin-engined night fighter force, whose numerical strength was now greater than ever, remained sufficiently intact as a fighting arm to constitute a serious threat to R.A.F. Bomber Command, particularly when it was engaged on deep penetration raids. But since the first half of 1944, the outlook for the force had changed from the prospect of increasing efficiency to a probability of declining effectiveness as the cumulative effect of poor training, shortage of fuel, diversion of effort and shortage of manpower became increasingly perceptible.

Improvement of Reconnaissance

10. In the sphere of reconnaissance considerable improvement had been brought about by the bringing into operations of the jet aircraft, the Arado 234. The German failure to produce good reconnaissance aircraft to replace the various versions of the Ju.88, which had been tried but which had all proved inadequate against Allied defence, had resulted in the almost complete cessation of both long-range and tactical reconnaissance on the western front. The disastrous results of this omission had been seen in the defective picture of Allied preparations which the German High Command possessed prior to 6th June, 1944, and more recently the speed and direction of Allied spearheads after the break-out from Normandy.

11. With the bringing into operations of the Arado 234 at the end of September a reconnaissance detachment was equipped with these aircraft and based in North-West Germany. The speed of the aircraft enabled it to carry out tasks which had become almost impossible whilst the Germans were still dependent on the Ju.88 or 188. Immediately, the routine task allotted to the new reconnaissance detachment was the covering of British harbours on the East coast of England between the Thames Estuary and Yarmouth, in addition to airfields in South-East England. This was aimed at disclosing any Allied preparations for further airborne or seaborne landings in Holland. Further, reconnaissance of the Allied forward and rearward areas on the Continent once more became possible and only a comparatively short period of time elapsed before aerial photography of large areas of the Allied front lines was being successfully undertaken as the number of Ar.234's with reconnaissance units increased.

Use of Night Harassing Units

12. Notwithstanding the elimination of the bomber force, the prospect for offensive operations was also brightening. The Germans, having decided to cut their losses as far as the long-range bomber force was concerned, placed reliance for the first time on the western front since 1940 on the obsolescent dive bomber, the Ju.87. This time, however, that aircraft was employed in night ground-attack operations backed by FW.190's, some of which were equipped for carrying a 2,000-lb. bomb. The use of the Ju.87 for night

harassing operations was of long standing on the Russian front, and its effectiveness and comparative invulnerability to Allied defence had been well tried out in Italy. Its lack of speed was of advantage in avoiding attacks' by night fighters, and losses at night to A.A. were inconsiderable. It could only be used with any hope of success during periods of moonlight, however, but during such periods it was used intensively. Double sorties were almost routine and in times of emergency three, four or five sorties were made by some crews.

The Advent of Jet Aircraft[1]

13. The aircraft on which the greatest hope was placed were the jet-propelled Me.262 and Ar.234. With these aircraft the Germans, particularly Hitler, hoped to retrieve the fortunes of the close-support force and to develop a striking arm which could once more play a prominent part in daylight operations. Already at the beginning of October, one unit was almost at full strength with the Me.262, and plans for the retraining and re-equipping of nine former long-range bomber units were under way. Hitler himself had insisted on the development of the jet aircraft for bombing purposes, against the advice of those officers—notably Galland—who were best able to realise its capabilities. This led directly to the failure to build up a sufficiently strong defensive fighter arm equipped with this aircraft to contest Allied air superiority over the Reich later in the year and during the early part of 1945. That such an arm could have been formed, had unnecessary and heavy wastage not been incurred by the use of the aircraft as a bomber, is without question, and, in fact, some fifty Me.262's were at this time being employed in fighter units. That Allied bomber forces never had to encounter strong formations of these aircraft was due entirely to Hitler's obsession for close-support and to Goering's failure to support Galland's claims for the use of the aircraft as a defensive fighter.

14. In outward appearance, therefore, the German Air Force in the Reich and in the West was experiencing a period of revival. The strength of the daylight defensive force was rapidly increasing, the night fighter force was still expanding and a power to be reckoned with, offensive close support was about to be renewed, and the possibility of widespread reconnaissance would give additional confidence to the plans of the Army commanders. Against this, however, were the ever-growing restrictions on fuel and training difficulties which affected operations of the first-line units. The Allied advances on all fronts were depriving the Germans of training ; dispersal areas and airfields inside Germany were rapidly becoming overcrowded, offering very profitable targets for Allied bomber and fighter-bomber attacks. Moreover, use was having to be made of second-rate airfields which in many cases were immediately rendered unserviceable in wet weather. Thus, a situation was already developing in which the Luftwaffe found itself much stronger numerically than at any period since July, 1943, but quite incapable of making any satisfactory use of its strength.

Redisposition of Forces

15. The operational policy which was adopted for the period between the conclusion of the Arnhem undertaking and the launching of the Ardennes offensive was entirely defensive and was dominated by the urgent need to

---

[1] See also Chapter 13.

conserve strength in preparation for the countering of the Allied offensive into Germany both on land and in the air. The defence of the Reich had had to be sacrificed during the campaign in France to the urgent demands of the Armies. From now on the emphasis was laid almost exclusively on defence, and at the end of September and the beginning of October, 1944, sweeping changes were made in the disposition of the close-support units. The total fighter force left to the western front command—Luftwaffe Command West, operating through Jagdkorps II in the North and Jagddivision 5 in the South—was reduced to about 350 aircraft, the remainder—some 500 single-engined fighters—being transferred to Germany either for rest and refit, or for home defence under Jagdkorps I (see Map 26). These aircraft moved mainly to North-East Germany (Jagddivision 1 area) to defend Berlin and the vital oil targets to the East. Thus in spite of the Allied push on Aachen in the first and second weeks of October, culminating in its surrender on the 21st, German Air Force operations by day were almost non-existent. The total force left for operations under Luftwaffe Command West was thus reduced to not more than 640 aircraft in the third week of October, when it consisted of :—

					Aircraft
Jet Bombers (Me.262) ..	..	..	..	..	25
Long Range Bombers ..	..	..	..	..	70
Ground-Attack ..	..	..	..	..	35
Night Harassing Units ..	..	..	..	..	70
Single Engined Fighters	..	..	..	..	350
Reconnaissance ..	..	..	..	..	90
					640

16. In contrast, the forces now subordinated to Luftflotte Reich for home defence comprised :—

					Aircraft
Single Engined Fighters	..	..	..	..	900
Twin Engined Day Fighters ..	..	..	..	—
Jet- and Rocket-propelled Aircraft ..	..	..	90
Night Fighters ..	..	..	..	..	830
					1,820

There were, in addition, no less than 1,000 further single-engined fighters in units resting and non-operational in Germany at the time.

Strategic Defence

17. Of the 350 fighter aircraft left in the West, two-thirds were frequently debarred from operations over the battle area and held in readiness for interception of heavy bombers. From October 8th, Goering had ordered that Jagdkorps II, covering the northern sector, was to function as a defensive command and only on very infrequent occasions was the order relaxed. The need to throw all available fighter forces into defence had been made painfully obvious on October 7th, when some 3,000 Allied heavy bombers together with appropriate escort had attacked targets in Germany. This building-up and strengthening of the defensive units continued during the whole of November and early December, although—as will be shown later—the insistence of the

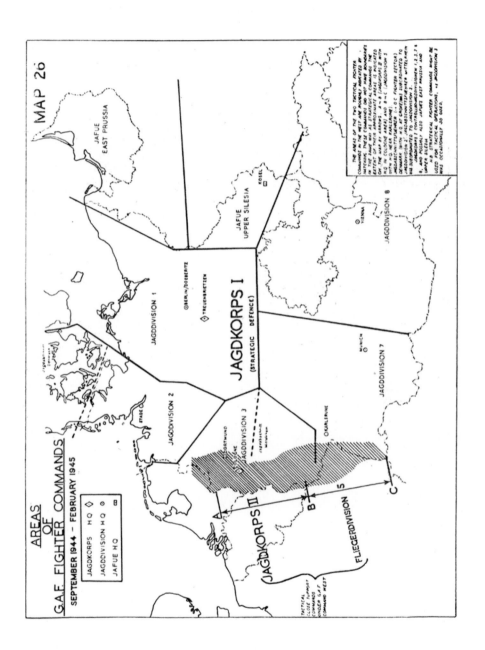

MAP 26

AREAS
OF
G.A.F. FIGHTER COMMANDS
SEPTEMBER 1944 — FEBRUARY 1945

JAGDKORPS HQ ◇
JAGDDIVISION HQ ⊙
JAFUE HQ ⊞

GENERALMAJOR DIETRICH PELTZ

Born 9.6.14. Entered an M./T. Abteilung April, 1934, transferred to the Air Force, October, 1935. At the outbreak of war was a Staffel commander in dive bombers. Transferred to heavy bombers in August, 1940 and in March, 1941, was O.C. of Gruppe. Directed dive bombing courses at Foggia (Italy) between November, 1941 and September, 1942, when he became O.C. I/K.G.60, active in the Mediterranean at the time of the Allied invasion of North Africa. Appointed acting A.O. for Bombers and Inspector for Bomber Aircraft in December, 1942, and O.C. attacks on England from March, 1943, combining it with that of A.O. for Bombers from May, 1943. O.C. Fliegerkorps IX on Western Front in September, 1943. O.C. Jagdkorps II in support of Ardennes Offensive, December, 1944–January, 1945. Then transferred to O.C. Fliegerkorps IX(J) in charge of conversion of long-range bomber units to fighters. Fate unknown; possibly in Russian hands.

Supreme Command, and particularly Hitler, on the need for close-support did not allow it to continue unimpeded. Opposition to Allied daylight attacks on Germany did not become noticeably heavier, owing probably to bad weather, until November, and even at that time the defensive effort never attained a scale commensurate with the number of aircraft available. On November 2nd some 500 fighters opposed the Allied aircraft attacking Merseburg but it was noticeable that the quality of the reaction was low and of the 63 Allied aircraft lost, only 15 were known to have been destroyed by fighters. Many Luftwaffe fighter units were still resting or engaged in training, many others were operating with inadequately trained crews, and the need to distribute fuel on a very strict rationing basis was becoming increasingly felt. However, on November 21st, 650-700 fighters opposed the 8th U.S. Air Force, engaged on yet another attack on Merseberg, and on November 25th, 750-850 aircraft came up against the American formations attacking Misburg and railway communications. But much of the effort, even on these, the peak efforts of the defensive forces, was weak or ineffective. On November 21st, for example, of two formations of 170 and 180 fighters, only 6 and 30 respectively, engaged the American bombers.

18. These operations were the nearest it was possible to approach to the carrying out of a major fighter operation against the 8th Air Force which had been planned by Galland under the code name of " Der Grosse Schlag " (the Big Blow).[1] Careful preparations had been made for this operation, the requirements for which were that a large part of the 8th Air Force should head for Germany on a clear day. The first interception was to be made by no less than eleven battle units comprising up to 1,000 aircraft, 300-400 of which were expected to take off on a second sortie. In addition, from 80-100 night fighters were to intercept crippled bombers attempting to reach Switzerland or Sweden. The absence of suitable weather conditions, a change of Allied bombing policy, and preparation for the Ardennes offensive, however, never afforded a suitable opportunity to carry out this plan, which was intended to impose such heavy losses as to call a halt to the daylight offensive against Germany. Even had the opportunity occurred, however, it is highly doubtful, having regard to the poor quality of the fighter force, whether the success hoped for could at this stage have been attained.

Close Support

19. On the western front, operations were left during this period mainly to those aircraft which operated by night. By day the few Me.262's available carried out attacks, usually by single aircraft. During the Allied push on Aachen in the first part of October, 1944, the small force of some 70 second-line Ju.87's operated intensively against Allied communications and airfields and, in the two weeks prior to the surrender of Aachen on October 21st, maintained a nightly effort of 40-60 sorties ; night fighters, too, were diverted to the same tasks. The Me.262's directed their effort first against Nijmegen and Grave, and later against Allied close-support airfields. At the end of the month and early in November the offensive started by the American 3rd Army and the French Army in the South brought about a redisposition of the few tactical aircraft in the West. The single-engined fighters from the North were switched to the South as were the Ju.87's and the few FW.190 night ground-attack aircraft.

---

[1] See Chapter 15, paragraph 23.

(83331)

But beyond making adequate use of the Ar.234 reconnaissance detachment put at their disposal, the 5th Jagddivision which was in command in the sector made little attempt to carry out full-scale air operations. No attempt was made to reinforce the area from Germany, and the offensive, which culminated in the Allied capture of Belfort, Mulhouse, Metz and Strasbourg by November 24th, was almost completely unimpeded by the Luftwaffe. The Wehrmacht was already intent on its preparations for the Ardennes offensive, the preparations for which were already setting at naught all the plans for the winter employment of the single-engined fighter force in a defensive rôle. As was shown above, the peak defensive efforts occurred on November 21st and 25th, after which the strength of the fighter force began to decline[1] and the dissipation of the single-engined fighters in close-support tasks from that time onwards did not permit this increased defensive effort to be maintained.

Offensive Defence : The German Counter-Attack in the Ardennes

Plans and Preparations

20. Towards the end of October, 1944, the operational commands of the Luftwaffe first received warning of a large-scale project in which they were scheduled to play a prominent part. The real meaning of the project was not disclosed, and orders from the Air Force High Command for preparations for the undertaking implied that its purpose was defensive[2]. On October 21st it was stated that it was obvious that the Allies would attempt to force a decision before the end of 1944, and as a full-scale counter-offensive was not at that moment possible, it was important to dispose Luftwaffe reserves so that the coming defensive battle would lead to a German success. Hitler had therefore decided to collect the operational army reserves becoming available opposite the Allied concentrations and also in the area Traben-Trier-Kaiserlautern. Luftflotte Reich, in charge of the air defence of Germany, was to be prepared to reinforce this area at short notice, and a strong mobile Flak reserve was to be formed.

21. To provide the necessary air support, fighter reinforcements were to total 20-23 Gruppen (a total of at least 1,200 aircraft) all from Germany, whilst Luftflotte 6 on the Russian front was to provide three Gruppen of FW.190 fighter-bombers and one anti-tank Staffel (about 100 aircraft in all). All available jet bombers and fighters were to be disposed in the Vechta-Twente-Wesel area, and airfields west of the Rhine were to be used for elements of these formations.

22. Orders for secrecy were elaborate, and included a detailed cover-plan in which the impression was to be given that the Air Force deployment was to support German counter-attacks from the Eifel area and from North-West

---

[1] The trend of first-line single-engined fighter strength during the last 6 months of 1944 was as follows :—

1st July	..	..	..	1,520
1st October	..	..	..	1,975
20th November	..	..	..	3,200
31st January, 1945	..	..	..	2,275

These figures are extracted from the records of the 6th Abteilung, German Air Force General Staff.

[2] See Appendix , paragraph 10.

of Cologne against the expected large-scale Allied attack on the line of Cologne-Bonn. Army unloadings were to take place partly by day in the North, only by night in the South. Every effort was to be made to maintain the appearance of strength in the North, and movements were to take place only at night. The flying units were to move only on receipt of an order from Luftwaffe High Command, and transfers, when effected, were to take place in low-level flights in complete radio silence. On arrival radio silence was to be maintained by the new units and no change was to be permitted in the normal W/T picture.

23. In spite of the orders that flying units were not to move to the West until the launching of the operation was imminent, the drawing off of the fighter forces from Germany began about the middle of November. By the beginning of December some 650 aircraft had already arrived and were being used in limited numbers in tactical operations over Alsace-Lorraine. At the same time, close-support tasks and defensive patrols over or near the battle area still remained second priority to the defensive tasks. Meantime, Goering had ordered that the conversion of fighters for fighter-bomber operations must be possible within 24 hours, and preparations for the reception of the reinforcing aircraft had been undertaken. These preparations did not proceed smoothly, for many of the airfields scheduled for the reception of these aircraft proved to be unusable owing to the wet ; shortage of fuel and supplies were endangering the state of readiness of many others.

24. On November 14th the true purpose of these preparations was disclosed by Goering in an order to the Air Force, and it seems clear that the offensive was intended to begin considerably earlier than it did. All Air Force preparations were to be completed by November 27th and moving up of all units was to be possible in three days.

Object of the Offensive

25. The aim of the attack was to destroy the Allied forces North of the line Antwerp-Brussels-Luxemburg. C.-in-C. West, with two Panzer armies and supported by two armies to consolidate the ground gained, was to break through the weak front of the American Army between Monschau and Wasserbillig. The attack was to be made in bad weather, thus countering, initially at any rate, the Allied air superiority. The first objectives were the crossings of the Meuse between Liège and Dinant, and from there a thrust was to be made to Antwerp and the West bank of the Scheldt estuary to cut off all the British forces and the northern wing of the 1st American Army from their supply area, and to destroy them. For all practical purposes the British would drop out of the war as military opponents.

26. This ambitious programme was ruled out as impossible by the Army commanders concerned, and it seems clear that in the final execution of the offensive, Manteuffel, G.O.C. 5th Panzer Army, and Von Rundstedt (C.-in-C. West) set themselves the more limited task of reaching the Meuse and wiping out the Aachen salient.

27. The author of the operation was undoubtedly Hitler. Von Rundstedt has denied that either he or Field Marshal Model had anything to do with the conception or even the planning of the offensive. All protests from the Army commanders, based primarily on the insufficiency of forces for such a far-reaching operation, were turned down. The prerequisite for success was

375

undeniably air superiority, and no matter what reinforcements were brought up this could never be achieved, either qualitatively or quantitively. What the planned operation was to effect, as far as the Air Force was concerned, was in the first place a serious interruption in the plans for the consolidation of the defensive force of single-engined fighters (which numerically was to be very strong indeed), and secondly, the dispersal of this force on close-support work in which it was to achieve little at heavy cost in aircraft and pilots, and from which it was destined never to be released. The conception that the Air Force was but an auxiliary of the Army once more won the day, in spite of the disasters which Allied heavy bombing was bringing to German oil, communications and industry—disasters which, if no serious attempt were made to prevent them by strong defensive methods, must inevitably bring the German armies to a standstill.

Employment of the German Air Force

28. The Air Force was to support the offensive by an all-out effort to protect the Army against air attack and to give direct support at decisive points, especially the Meuse crossings. By a single concentrated air attack on all Allied airfields near the front, the Allied close-support forces were to be knocked out. Freedom of movement was to be assured to the troops by fighter protection ; at the same time units in the rear were to protect industry in central Germany. Ground-attack aircraft were to be used at the points of greatest concentration—especially the Meuse crossings—and elements equipped for firing rockets were to be used against tanks. The Me.262 jet bombers were to take part in the concentrated attack on airfields and later be used against airfields and towns. Bomber and night ground-attack aircraft were to be employed against reinforcements and reserves, especially at nodal points of communications. Night fighters were to carry out night strafing as well as to protect the German deployment. Finally, important objectives, such as bridges on the flanks of the operational area, were to be destroyed by Mistel (pick-a-back) aircraft, not used since their unsuccessful employment in the early stages of the invasion.

Opening of the Offensive

29. The offensive opened early in the morning of December 16th after three postponements, the first from early in the month, the others from the 10th and 14th. Artillery preparations and the bringing up of troops and supplies had been considerably hampered by Allied air action. The bulk of the German Air Force units were transferred to the operational area in the last week before the attack began, and some preparatory operations had been carried out in the form of minelaying in the Scheldt estuary with the aim of denying the Allies the use of the port of Antwerp. Single-engined fighter aircraft were all fitted with bomb racks, elements of a second unit of Me.262 bombers had been brought up, and 140 Ju.88 night fighter aircraft had been allotted to each single-engined fighter Geschwader as pilot aircraft for the attack on Allied airfields. The weather prevented such an attack being carried out as the initial operation in the offensive, thick fog covering the battle area during both December 16th and 17th. Thus, the German Army was able to advance unimpeded by Allied air attacks. The Air Force had built up an impressive

force, consisting of over 2,300 aircraft subordinated to Luftwaffe Command West for this operation, the balance of forces as between the western front and the defence of Germany being in consequence changed to the following :—

	Western Front	Defence of Germany
Long Range Bombers	55	—
Jet Bombers	40	—
Ground Attack	155	—
Night Ground Attack	135	—
Single Engined Fighters	1,770	400
Twin Engined Fighters	140	1,100
Reconnaissance	65	—
	2,360	1,500

The single-engined fighter figures of 1,770 on the western front and 400 reserved for strategic defence contrast with the figures of 300 and 1,300 respectively at October 1st, and at the same time reflect the expansion which had taken place in these units. There was little possibility of further strengthening from other fronts, for Italy was already denuded and the forces facing the Russians were even more in need of reinforcement with the enemy on the banks of the Danube North of Budapest and an offensive all along the Russian front apparently imminent. The transfer of General Major Peltz from the command of the now moribund bomber forces of Fliegerkorps IX to that of O.C. Jagdkorps II controlling the close-support forces for the operation was a further token of the determination to exploit to the full the restored vitality and strength of the fighter forces in the West.

30. The air operations began with the dropping by night of some 1,000 parachutists, whose task was to secure important road crossings ahead of the advancing troops. Considerable evidence is available to show how unsuited to their tasks were both the parachutists and the aircrew who transported them. A large proportion of the former had never jumped before and many of the aircrew had had no training in blind flying. Moreover, early preparations had been chaotic : airfields which existed only in plans of 1939 and which had never been developed were allotted for the assembly of the Ju.52's before the operation ; no fuel was available for the aircraft on the airfields where they were perforce based, and the officer commanding the operation could get no satisfactory orders from any of his superiors as to what his task was to be. Diversionary operations which had been planned against England—the revival of night fighter intruder operations[1] over R.A.F. Bomber Command bases and the greatly stepped-up effort of the He.111 flying bomb carriers[2]—did not materialise at this stage owing to the weather, and the attack on Allied close-support airfields which should have heralded the offensive was similarly ruled out.

31. The thick fog, which had aided the beginning of the ground offensive, lifted only slightly during the next week, in consequence of which both Allied and German air operations were very badly hampered. During December 17th

[1] Refer to Chapter 8, paragraphs 17 and 18.
[2] Refer to Chapter 14, paragraph 44.

the German close-support force flew some 600 sorties, mainly on ground strafing missions, whilst during the following night bombers, night ground-attack and night fighter aircraft flew 250-300 sorties directed against the movement of Allied reserves. In the first stages of the operation, the ground forces, some of which had made rapid progress towards Dinant on the Meuse, were most sensitive to the threat of Allied action against their northern flank from Maastricht and Arnhem : consequently, air operations were directed mainly against roads and important communications centres, primarily Liège, in that sector. Fighter aircraft attempted to give continuous cover over the spearheads of the advance, orders for the 18th showing that 150 aircraft every hour were to provide protection. But the overall plans soon began to collapse, although Malmédy was by-passed and Stavelot reached on the 17th, St. Vith taken by the 20th, Bastogne by-passed on the 21st and Stoumont reached in the North.

32. This progress was very far from that projected in the order of December 2nd, in which it was stated that Hitler agreed with C.-in-C West that it should be possible to seize the Meuse crossings on the first day. The American refusal to withdraw or capitulate when by-passed or surrounded was causing great difficulty in the supplying of the forward troops, besides absorbing effort and equipment badly needed to support the most advanced elements ; nor was the German Air Force in any position to help the progress of the spearheads by direct attacks on the Allied positions in their path. The deepest penetration was reached on December 22nd at Laroche, a distance of 40 miles from the starting point, but disasters and defeats began to follow. The fog lifted on December 24th and the Luftwaffe was amongst the first to feel the weight of the Allied air attacks which followed. On that day 11 airfields needed for operations were very badly damaged, and continued Allied attacks on numerous others successfully cut down what effort might have been put up in support of the now harassed ground troops. Moreover, bad servicing of the Luftwaffe's aircraft was becoming more widespread, and pilots were all too ready to seize on the slightest excuse for returning early from their missions. That many pilots, insufficiently trained as they were, had no zest for facing the heavy Allied air onslaught which was carried out during the four days of good weather, December 24th-27th, is clearly demonstrated in one of Goering's typically flamboyant orders at this time : '' No pilot is to turn back except for damage to the undercarriage : flights are to be continued even with misfiring engines. Failure of auxiliary tanks will not be accepted as an excuse for turning back. The shirkers who do not realise the decisiveness of the hour are to be removed from the ranks of fighter pilots ''.

33. During those four days of good weather, the initiative was wrested entirely from the Germans. Already almost at a standstill as the result of American stubbornness in holding out in encircled positions well behind the German spearheads, and because of the speedy redeployment of British and American forces along the line on the Meuse, the offensive now became even more of a precarious enterprise in which the possibility of disaster was very real. Allied fighter-bombers and medium and heavy bombers were all thrown in, and Allied ascendancy was such that German troop movements by day became almost impossible. The bombing of roads and railways in the rear was so successful that the supply situation, already bad, became catastrophic. Yet, so great was the need of the forward troops for protection that the Luftwaffe was compelled to leave the Allied heavy bombers unmolested during

the attacks on rearward supply and communications areas, whilst attempting to provide defence against Allied close-support aircraft for their armoured spearheads. About 600 sorties per day were flown during this critical period, and night fighters, night ground-attack and bombers contributed a further 200–250 sorties per night. One third of the whole German night fighter force was even temporarily diverted to ground-strafing tasks during this period but with little respite for the ground troops. The jet bomber aircraft had not played any effective part owing to their small numbers and their inability to hit pinpoint targets—hit and run raids against Liège being their most important contribution : the Mistel composite aircraft, Ju.88/Me.109, had also proved a dismal failure. Bad weather which set in again on December 28th gave both the Luftwaffe and the German Army a badly needed respite, but the damage was done. Von Rundstedt had already decided that the time to pass over to the defensive had come, although the Supreme Command still insisted on further attempts being made to reach the Meuse. Bastogne was relieved on the 26th and Allied preparations immediately begun for an offensive from that bastion. On December 31st Rochefort was recaptured and the offensive between Bastogne and St. Hubert by U.S. forces began.

The New Year's Day Attack on Allied Airfields (1945)

34. At this stage, belatedly, the Luftwaffe attempted the sudden bold stroke against the Allied Air Forces which should have been the forerunner of the whole offensive and which had been carefully planned by Goering and organised by Peltz. All the single-engined aircraft, fighters and fighter-bombers, were prepared during the final days of the year for the attack on Allied close-support airfields which was carried out on 1st January, 1945. Complete tactical surprise and considerable success was achieved, but at a cost which the Luftwaffe could ill afford. Unusual measures were taken to ensure that the large force of aircraft concerned reached its targets—for taking part in this greatest of all operations since D day were many very inexperienced pilots, who could not be at all certain of reaching even the target area. Each Gruppe of single-engined fighters was allotted two Ju.88 night fighters to act as pilot aircraft : these Ju.88's led the single-engined formations by D.R. navigation and by the use of visual aids on the first part of the course.

35. After assembly, formations flew in low level formations in complete radio silence. The lack of good formation leaders—which had so often in the past rendered ineffective many operational sorties—was modified to some extent by the bringing up of instructors from training units and by the raising of the ban on participation in operations by unit commanders. But in the actual event errors and blunders were numerous : some aircraft were late in starting and never caught up with their formation ; security measures were so strict that pilots and unit commanders were not briefed until the previous evening, and were therefore inadequately prepared, while some pilots had even not attended briefing and were very vague about their targets. It is not surprising therefore that there were errors in navigation, neither were the Ju.88 pilot aircraft a complete success. These Ju.88's did not cross into Allied territory, but turned back on reaching predetermined points, consequently, the onus of reaching the actual target was left to the single-engined fighter formation leaders. Some units did not reach their targets, owing, it was reported, " to the strength of the defences "—an unlikely reason since complete surprise was achieved. There

379

was confusion over the targets and a few collisions occurred. But, in all, 16 Allied airfields were attacked in Holland and Belgium and one in France, and low-level attacks were made on Antwerp docks, probably as a diversion. Between 750 and 800 fighter aircraft were used in the operation, which resulted in the total loss of 134 Allied aircraft with a further 62 damaged beyond unit repair. The cost, according to Galland, was some 220 aircraft and the loss of an almost equal number of pilots. Claims on both sides reached enormous proportions, both the Germans and the Allies claiming over 500 enemy aircraft destroyed. The loss of 220 German aircraft reported by Galland is in keeping with British Intelligence estimates at the time and is probably accurate.

36. The attack on the Allied airfields brought no measure of relief to the German armies : whilst it was successful in destroying a large number of aircraft, it was neither sufficiently widespread nor devastating to affect the Allied striking power in any appreciable degree. Further, it was much too late to be of any assistance in the offensive, which had already become a defensive operation. Losses and a sharp decline in serviceability effectively cut down close-support operations in the Ardennes sector for the ensuing period up to the middle of January, and the secondary German offensive which had been launched in Northern Alsace created a split in the forces available. During the first week of January the German advance North of Strasbourg and in the vicinity of Bitsche was given priority for air support, and between 400 and 500 close-support aircraft, including 20 Me.262's transferred from the North, were diverted to it. But such numbers were quite inadequate ; having shown itself, even when concentrated for the Ardennes offensive, incapable of providing support over the German spearheads, Luftwaffe Command West was now called on to split its forces and to undertake defensive tasks over the Ardennes as well as offensive tasks in Alsace. Poor weather conditions during the first half of January also seriously affected enemy air operations and little more than 250 sorties per day were flown, divided more or less equally over the two battle areas. Operations by Me.262's—of which there were some 45–50 employed as day bombers—and by other categories, were of little account. Whilst weather conditions were doubtless partly responsible for this poor effort, the respite was by no means unwelcome. The effect of the comparatively intensive operations undertaken during the second half of December, culminating in the very costly undertaking of January 1st, was revealed in the urgent attempts made at this time to restore serviceability and to secure formation leaders. Servicing difficulties, too, were numerous.

37. By now, Russian preparations for the offensive into East Prussia and Poland were nearing completion and thus, at a time when Allied forces in the West were beginning their attacks to wipe out the Ardennes Salient, the German Air Force was obliged to begin a large-scale withdrawal of forces to the eastern front. So serious was the threat of the Russian offensive that considerations of the defence of the Reich were cast aside. By January 15th, the western front forces had been weakened by the transfer to the East of 300 aircraft, and by January 22nd, a further 500 had already gone or were about to go. Due to this large-scale withdrawal of aircraft—for 20 Gruppen of fighters and 3 of ground-attack, equivalent to the whole reinforcement for the Ardennes offensive[1]

---

[1] Cf. paragraph 2. The difference in numerical strength (as opposed to units), as compared with the reinforcement of the West in December, is accounted for by losses and the consequent decline in the aircraft strength of units.

were transferred direct from the western front. Units which remained in the West were held at maximum strength, and a rigid policy of conservation was inaugurated. Measures were taken whereby only 50 per cent. of the fighter force still remaining was to be employed on operations, the remainder having to rest. All single-engined fighter-type aircraft were forbidden to operate beyond the front line ; combat, even against heavy bombers, was to be avoided except in the most favourable circumstances ; when operations were carried out, formations were to be used in the maximum possible strength " concentrated in space and time ". Defence of the supply lines was the first consideration.

38. Thus, whilst the heavy withdrawal of aircraft to the East was to some extent offset numerically by this policy, the support which was given to the Army in the closing stages of the Ardennes enterprise was negligible, for units were unable to make use of more than a small proportion of their forces—so severe was the shortage of fuel. That the western front had once again become a secondary theatre, so far as air operations were concerned, was further demonstrated by the appointment of Generalmajor Wilke to succeed Peltz as O.C. Jagdkorps II, the latter returning to his former command, now renamed Fliegerkorps IX (J), to take over the retraining and conversion of former long-range bomber units to the rôle of single-engined fighters.

The German Air Force in the West after the Failure of the Ardennes Offensive

The Western Front

39. The air situation on the West following the failure of the Ardennes offensive could be characterised, so far as the German Air Force was concerned, as one of exhaustion due (a) to the large-scale withdrawal of fighters to the East during January, 1945, and (b) to a recurrence of the fuel crisis. At the beginning of February, 1945, offensive activity had become barely perceptible, while defensive operations against Allied close-support aircraft behind the front line area was also consistently low ; moreover, the total strength of forces engaged in the West did not now exceed 1,000 aircraft, of which 600 were single-engined fighters. The main commitment was now virtually limited to reconnaissance by jet aircraft of Allied movements in Belgium and South Holland, and to such harassing of the Allied supply build-up as was possible, but which in fact, amounted to a negligible effort.

40. The background to this apparent paralysis lay mainly in the fuel situation. The desperate battle now raging in the East in Silesia and along the Oder called for the maximum effort, and consequently Jagdkorps II was constrained on February 5th to issue a general order, on the instructions of the German Air Staff, imposing new restrictions on operations in the West in view of the increased fuel consumption in the East ; the employment of fighters was thereby rigidly limited to those situations which really promised success, while even the jet bombers' activity was, for the first time, curtailed and reserved only for decisive attacks. These conditions persisted for the great part of the month ; they were further emphasised a week later by an order from Jodl (Chief of Staff of the Supreme Command), which stated that all air operations must now be ruthlessly limited owing to the more critical aircraft fuel situation, and all operations which did not directly relieve the fighting troops were to be cancelled ; Army headquarters were moreover, ordered to restrict their demands for air support.

41. The renewal of the British 21st Army Group offensive on the northern sector of the line in mid-February failed for this reason to provoke any serious Luftwaffe reaction during the first 10 days, neither were any air reinforcements forthcoming, for the simple reason that they could not be effectively employed, apart from other considerations imposed by the crisis in the East. A further factor which also defeated such attempts as were made to provide air support was the intensity and success of Allied air patrols over Luftwaffe bases ; these interfered with the taking-off of aircraft and resulted in their interception and engagement before even the front line area could be reached.

42. As the Allied pressure continued to be maintained and progress towards the Rhine accelerated, some relaxation of the fuel restriction was permitted at the end of the month, and a small reinforcement of jet-bombers took place, all of which were now concentrated under a new battle unit commanded by Oberstleutnant Kowalewski. During the first few days of March, there was therefore an appreciable recovery in the scale of effort, which rose to 300–400 sorties per day, when weather permitted, all in defence of lines of communication and airfields used by jet aircraft ; the jet bombers also flew up to 50 missions per 24 hours against Allied river crossings and spearheads. By night, the harassing Ju.87 units, numbering some 140 aircraft, put up a major effort reaching 150 sorties, long-range bombers being now a thing of the past with the Luftwaffe. Nevertheless, the value of all these operations was insignificant and ineffective, and produced no visible effect against the irresistible Allied advance to the Rhine.

Strategic Fighter Defence

43. In defence against the Allied heavy bomber offensive the picture during February was little different ; the fighter forces for strategic defence had been whittled down to the bone to support operations in the East, and a heavy daylight attack on Magdeburg on February 14th could be countered by only a meagre 100–130 sorties, while assaults on Dresden and oil communications on the two following days could be met with only negligible opposition. Deep penetration daylight raids during the remainder of the month continued to be only weakly opposed, despite the growing seriousness of the internal situation with the transport system steadily deteriorating.

44. By night, also, the night-fighter force was showing consistently poor results against R.A.F. Bomber Command ; the heavy raids on Dresden and Chemnitz on February 13th-14th and 14th-15th were countered by a considerable effort of some 200 night-fighter sorties, but barely 1 per cent. losses could be inflicted. The inability of the Germans to overcome the elaborate and successful British countermeasures, so as effectively to oppose deep penetration raids by night, was by now amply proved, while the shortcomings against border targets in western Germany had long been manifest.

Intruder Operations over England

45. A new feature during February in the struggle against R.A.F. Bomber Command was the undertaking of long and carefully planned intruder operations against the home bases of returning aircraft. Although such activity had been a minor feature earlier in the war in the autumn of 1941[1], no attempt had ever been made to develop and exploit such harassing tactics on more than a minor

---

[1] Refer to Chapter 8, paragraphs 17 and 18.

scale ; the reason for this lay in an early intervention by Hitler in Air Force matters, when he asserted, in the face of records and crew reports to the contrary, that such operations could have no success. This ban had been maintained from 1941 up to this time ; now, however, the increasing weight and accuracy of R.A.F. Bomber Command's attacks, coupled with the declining effectiveness of the night-fighter defences, called for a desperate measure in the hope of imposing a serious deterrent to night bombing operations.

46. Accordingly, in suitable conditions of the night March 3rd-4th, 140 night-fighters took off to attack Bomber Command bases ranging from Northumberland to Oxfordshire. Rather less than 100 aircraft succeeded in penetrating overland, assisted by a few pathfinder aircraft, carrying out widespread attacks on airfields and shooting down 22 bombers over their bases ; a small follow-up operation was carried out on the following night, but although some degree of success was attained, over 20 aircraft were lost and no attempt was made to maintain or intensify this activity, which was never again repeated. Among the reasons which caused the breaking off of this activity was the surprising one that Hitler now ordained that such operations were unprofitable from a propaganda point of view and that from the point of view of morale it was preferable that bombers should be shot down over Germany, where the people could see them falling in flames. Thus, together with the increasing fuel shortage, the now limited night fighter resources were henceforth confined to adhering to more normal, if less successful, activity.

Torpedo-bomber Operations

47. It was during this period that virtually the last major torpedo-bomber operations were made by the units withdrawn to Germany and Norway after the débâcle in France in the preceding summer. For the first time for six months, operations were resumed on February 6th against Allied shipping and naval forces off the Norwegian coast ; on this and the following four days no less than 200 torpedo-bomber and reconnaissance sorties were flown, but although many claims of successes were made, the attacks were entirely unsuccessful, and much of the effect was expended in purely abortive sorties. Further operations were undertaken between February 18th-23rd against a convoy returning from Russia, during which some 60 aircraft were engaged and one vessel sunk, but thereafter the torpedo units relapsed into inactivity from which they were for the last time to emerge only in the last days of the war.

Reorganisation of Commands

48. At this time a considerable reshuffle of Commands also took place in Germany. On the western front, Jagdkorps II, the tactical fighter command engaged on the northern sector, was disbanded and its place taken by two Fliegerdivisions, 14 and 15, Generalmajor Wilke formerly A.O.C. Jagdkorps II taking over command of the latter ; at the same time Jagddivision 5, operating on the southern sector, was renamed Fliegerdivision 16, all three being subordinated to Luftwaffe Command West. The strategic air defences of Germany were similarly reorganised, Jagdkorps I being also disbanded, and its functions taken over by Fliegerkorps IX (J), the command engaged in the conversion of former long-range bomber units to fighters.

49. This downgrading of major commands was in itself a portent of the steady decline in the fighting power and effectiveness of the German Air Force ; the whole of this interim period between the end of the Ardennes offensive and

the Allied crossing of the Rhine had, indeed, shown a growing realisation of the need for new departures from normal tactics if anything were to be done to save the situation and, at the same time, the absolute impotence of the Luftwaffe owing to dearth of fuel and lack of resources. The final stages of dissolution and collapse were to be seen once the Rhine and Oder had been crossed.

CHAPTER 18

THE FINAL ALLIED OFFENSIVE FROM EAST, WEST AND SOUTH (January to May 1945)

The Débâcle in Italy[1]

1. Following the German evacuation of Central Italy and the withdrawal to the Gothic Line, the German Air Force in Italy at the end of July, 1944, was reduced to a mere token force of 50 single-engined fighters, 35 miscellaneous reconnaissance aircraft and 40 Ju.87 night harassing bombers. This force was clearly incapable of effective operations, whilst its activities were constantly circumscribed by drastic fuel restrictions, and its only commitment, upon which any value was laid by the Germans, consisted in periodical reconnaissance of the Adriatic and Liguarian Seas and of those Mediterranean ports which lay within range of aircraft based in North Italy. It was, in fact, clearly laid down by the Luftwaffe High Command that, now that air strength in Italy had been reduced to a minimum, its main commitment was to observe Allied shipping movements in the Mediterranean. In addition the night harassing bombers operated weakly and ineffectively against Allied forward lines of communication when moonlight conditions permitted, whilst the small fighter force concentrated on somewhat inadequate attempts to intercept Allied heavy bombers from Foggia en route to or returning from targets in Central Europe.

2. The Allied landings in southern France on August 15th caused a temporary transfer of the single-engined fighters to the Rhône valley, but the aircraft returned to Italy a week later, whilst a projected transfer of the anti-shipping units based in southern France to North Italy never materialised. Strength consequently shows little fluctuation until the third week in September, when the single-engined fighter force was transferred to the western front.

3. During the last quarter of 1944 the Luftwaffe in Italy remained dormant, enlivened only by the arrival of a Staffel of FW.190 fighter-bombers from the western front ; after delivering some sharp attacks on Allied forward headquarters in early December, however, it left again to take part in the Ardennes offensive.

4. The New Year found the German Air Force in Italy, with good reason, somewhat apprehensive of the part it would play in the Allied attack which was clearly to be anticipated as soon as the weather permitted. With this in view preparations were made to refit the night harassing unit with FW.190's, and to base a jet reconnaissance Staffel in the Milan area. Partial re-equipment with FW.190's had in fact taken place, whilst a few jet reconnaissance sorties had been flown by the time that the Allied offensive was opened on April 9th. Luftwaffe operations were hardly perceptible in the ensuing débâcle, and the wholesale destruction of the German forces and their subsequent surrender on April 29th engulfed what little remained of the German Air Forces in Italy.

---

[1] Continued from Chapter 11.

The Final Russian Offensive

The Advance to the Oder and Occupation of the Silesian Industrial Area

5. The attack on Allied airfields in Holland, Belgium and France on 1st January, 1945, was the last concerted effort exerted by the German air forces which had been concentrated in the West prior to the Ardennes offensive. The Russian advance was by now driving into East Prussia and through eastern Poland and Hungary. Budapest had been outflanked early in December and Russian troops stood before Warsaw. Under these circumstances it was clearly illogical to maintain the German Air Force evenly balanced as between the eastern and western fronts. In the West there were on 1st January, 1945, some 1,900 aircraft, of which 1,200 were fighters, and in the eyes of the German Command it was clearly illogical to concentrate these resources against an enemy whose future offensive capabilities had been temporarily limited by the Ardennes offensive. With a further 1,700 twin-engined and single-engined fighter aircraft reserved for defence of the Reich, all that was left to defend the vast eastern battle front stretching from the Baltic to the Adriatic, and on which serious events were clearly impending, was some 1,875 aircraft.

6. This force was divided into three main Commands : Luftflotte 1, now isolated from the rest and fighting a delaying action in Courland and the Gulf of Riga area, Luftflotte 6 defending the main eastern approaches to Germany from East Prussia to the Carpathians, and Luftflotte 4 covering the southern flank in Hungary and Jugoslavia. The forces under these commands on 1st January, 1945, were composed as follows :—

	L.R. Bomber	Ground Attack	Night Harassing Units	S.E. Fighters	T.E. Fighters	L.R. Recce.	Tac. Recce.	Coastal	Total
Luftflotte 1	—	30	100	85	—	—	30	—	245
Luftflotte 6	10	390	40	190	100	120	180	30	1,060
Luftflotte 4	70	200	130	85	—	25	60	—	570
Total ..	80	620	270	360	100	145	270	30	1,875

7. It was not until the second week in January that a transfer of German formations from West to East was set in train. This transfer involved in all a total of 650 single-engined fighters and 100 ground-attack aircraft, comprising 6 single-engined fighter and 1 ground-attack Geschwader. Even then progress was slow. By the third week in January only some 300 aircraft had arrived in the East, whilst some units earmarked for transfer were still located on airfields in western Germany at the end of the month. Meanwhile, wastage had been heavy. The Russian advance was gaining in momentum—Warsaw, Lodz, Cracow, Allenstein and Insterburg had been captured, Russian troops' had entered Pomerania and Brandenburg and taken Gleiwitz in Silesia, whilst German aircraft in ever-increasing numbers were being captured on their own airfields. The reinforcements, in consequence, only brought German air strength in the East up to a total of some 850-900 single-engined fighters and 700 ground-attack aircraft. Of these the bulk—750 single-engined fighters and 450 ground-attack aircraft—covered the northern sector between the Baltic and Carpathians, with the main point of focus in the area East of Berlin.

8. The shortcomings of the Luftwaffe were ill met by the supply of single-engined fighter formations—least of all by those whose past employment had consisted mainly in air-to-air combat against bomber formations. The crying need was for ground-attack aircraft for employment against Russian armoured spearheads and transport columns—and for fuel—and the 450 available in the northern sector proved quite inadequate for the task. It was consequently decided to fill the breach with night fighters. It will be remembered that during the Ardennes offensive in the West each night fighter Gruppe in Germany had provided one Staffel of Ju.88's or Me.110's, equipped with bomb racks and flown by other than " key " interceptor crews, to operate against Allied lines of communication. The total force amounted in all to some 140 aircraft. At the beginning of February these were again withdrawn from their parent units and transferred East for operations in the Stettin-Breslau area.

9. The month of February showed further Russian advances. The Oder was crossed on both sides of Breslau, which was invested by the 15th. Further penetration of the Silesian industrial area continued, and the transfer of some 60 ground-attack and 20 long-range bomber aircraft from Luftflotte 4 in Hungary, bringing total strength between the Baltic and Carpathians under Luftflotte 6 to 1,700 aircraft, did little to bolster up the much reduced German air striking power.

10. In the meantime, the Russian drive into western Poland and Silesia caused a general upheaval among the numerous fighter training units hitherto based in these areas, and the problem of their accommodation elsewhere was to prove exceedingly difficult. The increasing number of aircraft for which room now had to be found on airfields in Germany was reaching huge proportions, and the difficulties of transfer were further accentuated by shortage of fuel both for motor transport and aircraft. In the end the displaced training units settled down at new bases in Denmark and the Leipzig area, but inevitably training was hampered and dislocated, and new stresses and strains were thus set up in the already tottering edifice of the German Air Force.

11. The most serious direct consequence of the Russian advance was the loss of several important aircraft assembly, component and repair factories, aircraft depôts and dumps, in the territory now being overrun. Not only was production capacity appreciably reduced thereby, but also vast quantities of material of all description were captured by the Russians. The important factories lost to Luftwaffe production at this time included the FW.190 assembly plants at Marienburg and Sorau, repair depôts and factories at Rahmel (near Gdynia), Warsaw and Riga, together with important component factories at Breslau, Posen and Kreising ; other major losses, affecting the forwarding of aircraft and supplies to the Russian front, included the aircraft forwarding stations at Insterburg, Bromberg, Kupper-bei-Sagan and Liegnitz.

12. These losses involved assembly plants responsible for about 25 per cent. of FW.190 output, as well as important FW.190 component factories and the principal FW.190 park (at Liegnitz). While, however, the loss of all these seriously upset the production and repair programme, no immediate effects were felt in the strength of FW.190 units in view of the generally strong reserve position, and soon afterwards the strangulation of the German transport system by Allied bombing was to have far wider and more adverse effect on the whole of German war industry.

The German Counter-offensive in Hungary

13. When the military and air concentrations assembled for the Ardennes offensive finally moved to the East, their paths diverged. Whereas the air forces moved to eastern Germany to oppose the Russian threat to the North German plain, the 6th S.S. Panzer Army, which had provided the bulk of the armour in the Ardennes, was transferred via southern Germany to North-western Hungary in the general area of the Bakony forest and Veszprem. The strategic conception underlying this somewhat inexplicable division of forces was as follows : the 6th S.S. Panzer Army was, in the first phase, to undertake an all-out offensive to relieve the German garrison besieged in Budapest. It was then to force bridgeheads across the Danube South of Budapest and, turning North-eastwards, to destroy the remaining Russian forces in northern Hungary. The stage would then be set for a combined attack (a) from North-eastern Hungary, and (b) from East Prussia, to converge in the general area of Warsaw, thereby eliminating the Russian forces in eastern Germany and western Poland.

14. In the initial stages the German counter-offensive in Hungary achieved some success. Starting from the area of Lake Balaton, a wedge was driven which reached the Danube South of Budapest. This, however, was the limit of its progress. The Budapest garrison remained unrelieved, and finally surrendered on February 13th. Meanwhile, the very limited resources of the 6th S.S. Panzer Army had been strained to breaking point. The Russian counter-offensive, when it came, drove the German forces in headlong retreat back to the Austrian frontier, culminating later in the capture of Vienna and Wiener Neustadt.

15. The part played by the German Air Force in these operations remained throughout a minor one. Total strength between the Carpathians and the Adriatic was a mere 500-600 aircraft, including some 100 single-engined fighters, 180 ground-attack, 60 long-range bomber and 80 reconnaissance aircraft. This force was utterly inadequate to support even the original drive by the 6th S.S. Panzer Army to the Danube, let alone an overall strategic plan on such a grandiose scale as was originally envisaged. Its strength was further weakened in the middle of February by the transfer of 20 long-range bombers and 60 ground-attack aircraft to northern battle areas, and petrol shortage resulted in a very considerable proportion of the force being captured intact on its airfields in the course of the final débâcle.

The Battle for Berlin

16. By the end of February, 1945, the Russian forces had reached the general line of the Oder opposite Berlin, where they halted their advance and concentrated on cleaning up the German centres of resistance in their rear. Throughout March and until the final Russian attack in the middle of April no outstanding air operations were carried out. The Germans were planning attacks by pick-a-back aircraft on the Russian power stations, particularly those at Gorki, in the course of this period, but such plans never came to fruition. Instead attacks were made by aircraft-launched flying bombs and by pick-a-back aircraft against Russian bridges over the Vistula and crossing-points linking the Oder bridgeheads with the main Russian positions. Beyond their nuisance value and their novelty, however, such operations had little significance.

17. By the second week in April the Anglo-American advances in western Germany had compressed the Luftwaffe into a relatively small area of Central Germany, and it was no longer possible to differentiate between airfields holding

units engaged on the Russian front and those employed as bases against the Western Allies. A point of particular interest, however, was the fact that, although the Russian forces at this time were still more or less stationary—at all events in the vital area East of Berlin—the Germans made no use of the seasoned ground-attack units from the Russian front against the British and American tank spearheads then ranging more or less at will across western Germany. In this, German air strategy at the time of the Normandy landings was repeated, but by now it is probable that the German High Command had already decided on its policy of sacrificing unlimited areas of western Germany to the Western Allies, rather than permit any further Russian advance into Prussia.

18. It was consequently not surprising that when the final Russian attack was launched across the Oder in the middle of April it aroused the most intensive reaction by the Luftwaffe. The latter was now based mainly on the Berlin airfields and, until these airfields were lost, some 1,000 sorties per day were flown against the advancing Russians, with 100–150 bomber sorties by night and regular attacks by pick-a-back aircraft against the Oder bridges. Hopelessly outnumbered, short of fuel, accommodation and servicing facilities the German Air Force failed, however, to have any influence on the train of events. After the loss of the Berlin airfields, with vast numbers of intact aircraft, to the Russian forces, sorties dropped to about one-half of their previous intensity, and the wholesale disbanding of units became, for the first time, a recognisable feature. Operations were still aggressive on the part of those aircraft which remained, but the piecemeal destruction of the Luftwaffe continued apace, and by the beginning of May, commands from the Russian front, without aircraft, were located as far West as Kiel. Berlin itself surrendered to the Russians on May 2nd.

The Final Anglo-American Breakthrough in the West

19. By the middle of March, extensive withdrawals to the Russian front, and the rising toll of casualties levied on the Luftwaffe as Allied air superiority became more complete, had reduced its strength on the western front to some 1,000–1,100 aircraft of which 80 were in the jet ground-attack category. A further 1,000 aircraft were available for strategic defence of North-western Germany, divided roughly equally between single-engined day fighters and twin-engined night fighters, with some 50 Me.262's operating in an interceptor capacity.

20. The Allied advance to the Rhine, culminating in the establishment of the Remagen bridgehead, and the piecemeal destruction of the Ruhr airfields, had led to some local redisposition of German forces, and night harassing bomber units, amounting to 100 second-line Ju.87's, had been forced back to the area west of Kassel and north of Frankfurt. The seizure by the Americans of the Remagen bridgehead over the Rhine had, however, resulted in a stepping up in the tempo of Luftwaffe operations, which rose to an average of 400 tactical sorties per day. Jet ground-attack units concentrated on the Remagen area, the Ar.234's attacking the bridge with 1,000-kg. bombs, the Me.262's operating with lighter armament against the troops in the bridgehead proper. These operations were supported by FW.190's employed in a fighter-bomber rôle and by the night harassing aircraft, which operated intensively by night and, where cloud cover permitted, by day also.

389

21. Further to the North the Me.109 units based north of the Ruhr were occupied to capacity in attempting to protect the jet ground-attack bases from the Allied fighter screens, which effectively swamped most jet operations almost before the aircraft were airborne. Meanwhile, German apprehensions of the impending large-scale crossing of the Rhine continued, and reconnaissance activity was mainly concerned with the spotting of Allied preparations for an airborne attack across the river. Defensive measures against such an operation, such as the destruction of airfields not required for operations, continued on an ever-increasing scale.

22. Until March 23rd the air situation was dominated by the rising scale of Allied preparations for the crossing of the Rhine, and it is certain that by the 23rd the Germans had appreciated that a large-scale Allied attack across the river supported by airborne forces was imminent in the Wesel area. It is, hence, all the more remarkable that no attempt was made to reinforce the western front at the expense of the 2,200 aircraft then disposed in the East, the only reaction being to prepare for operations by night fighters against ground targets. The prior demands of the Russian front remained unquestioned, however (Kuestrin had been captured on the 12th, and Danzig was to fall in a week's time) and strength in the West remained at 1,050 aircraft.

23. Apart from the German numerical weakness, an important feature in keeping down such Luftwaffe reaction as could be mounted, was the Allied '' blitz '' against enemy airfields[1], which commenced on March 21st and almost immediately rendered all the main jet airfields and many single- and twin-engined fighter bases unserviceable. A further factor was the fresh American 3rd Army drive across the Upper Rhine at Oppenheim on March 23rd. This fresh bridgehead drew the Me.262 ground-attack aircraft from the northern sector to the area East of Darmstadt and Frankfurt, and absorbed a very considerable part of the total German effort both on March 23rd and on the following day. Fifty Ju.87's operated against the Oppenheim area on the night 23rd-24th, but activity on the next night had been reduced by one-half, due to shortage of fuel and lack of airfield accommodation. Day fighter effort on the 23rd against the same target area totalled some 150 sorties, but dropped to 60 on the next day due to the heavy casualties involved. An organised air opposition to this thrust collapsed on March 25th, when the airfields in the Darmstadt and Frankfurt area were overrun by 3rd Army's spearheads.

24. In consequence, the reaction to the British 21st Army Group's attack on March 23rd was mediocre. Day fighters flew some 200 sorties against the Wesel crossings, but all the jet aircraft were grounded owing to the unserviceability of their airfields, and operations on the next day were even lower owing to fuel shortage and low operational strength. By night the Ju.87's remained committed against the Oppenheim area, leaving only the night fighters available for employment at Wesel. Some 30 sorties per night were flown by these aircraft against ground targets for the first three nights of the offensive, whilst the long-range bombers, of which some 60 were available, remained grounded through lack of fuel.

25. In the 10 days following the launching of 21st Army Group's attack across the Rhine, German Air Force strength in the West dropped from 1,050 to 850 aircraft, but the collapse of air resistance as a whole was even more

---

[1] See illustration on page 337.

outstanding, due initially to the attacks on airfields which commenced on March 21st, and thereafter to the constant withdrawals from bases threatened by the advance of the Allied ground forces. The rapid breakthrough of the 12th Army Group to Kassel forced the withdrawal of flying units to behind the Weser, leaving the Germans fully engaged in attempting to extricate their units and to bring them to bear in the Bremen, Brunswick and Erfurt areas.

26. The offensive across the Rhine also now showed the Luftwaffe's utter lack of recuperative power. No reinforcements were brought up from the Russian front, nor were any made available from the 800 or so day fighters engaged in defence against heavy bombers ; few of these fighters were fit to operate and, had they been serviceable, little fuel was available. Overall strength, as stated above, had dropped by 200 aircraft, the jet force by one-third of its previous strength, and the single-engined fighter force by some 100 aircraft, whilst the long-range bomber force could now be discounted. Despite an abnormally low scale of operations due to dislocation and exhaustion, the Luftwaffe's weakness was accentuated by increasing fuel shortage, the disruption of communications and supply routes and the congestion of aircraft on Central German airfields. All operational Me.262's were in southern Germany, as were the only operational night harassing bombers—whose strength had dropped from 100 to 25—due to the untimely shift of these forces to counter the American thrust at Oppenheim. The Ar.234 jet bombers remained in North-western Germany, but had withdrawn to Marx and were incapable of operating. Total tactical effort had dropped to a maximum of 150 sorties per day, and was normally much lower. Night-fighter operations lapsed entirely between March 27th and April 1st, when some 25 night fighters operated in the Nuremburg area. Night ground-attack operations were negligible and the jet fighter bombers virtually non-operational. What air operations there were, were directed mainly against the American spearheads approaching Wuerzburg.

27. The beginning of April showed the first clear signs of the dissolution and disintegration of the German Air Force. The old chain of command had fallen to pieces[1], numerical strength had by now completely lost its meaning, and the wholesale scrapping of units was well under way. The orthodox fighter aircraft, as opposed to the jets, were finished, and their last operation of significance occurred on April 7th, when 120 of them, encouraged by the strains of martial music over the radio, attempted a mass suicide ramming operation at immense expense against U.S. heavy bomber formations. Thereafter, effective operations by them were restricted to the Russian front, and the Luftwaffe in the West could be assessed as a fighting force solely in terms of the 200 jet aircraft still at its disposal. Potential crews for jet aircraft had been called for from all quarters, and at this point the process was speeded up and the entire jet force placed under General Kammler of the S.S. The jet-bomber force had by now been virtually written off, but the Germans still hoped to pull off a miracle. Belatedly, they realised that their jet aircraft had been misemployed, and they now concentrated all their efforts in building up a jet fighter force capable, in some measure, of challenging Allied air superiority. During this period—up to April 10th—the only effective enemy operations consisted of Me.262 reaction, on a scale of some 50 sorties per day, against heavy bomber formations.

---

[1] See Chapter 19, paragraphs 8–10.

28. By the middle of April the plans for the building of a jet force had already been overtaken by events—the jet units were moving back to Prague in considerable confusion due to the threat, both from East and West, to the Berlin airfields, and to the havoc caused by air attacks on jet airfields in the Munich and Berlin areas. Orthodox single-engined fighter strength had dropped by 1,000 aircraft in a fortnight—due in part to bombing, but mainly to the disbanding of units and the overrunning of airfields. Operations remained entirely ineffective, and although sorties theoretically amounted to up to 150 per day, these consisted in little more than take-offs, quickly culminating in disaster or a rapid return to base. After April 10th no attempts were made to intercept day bombers, and even unarmed Allied transport aircraft flew deep penetrations without being in any way molested. Night-fighter effort was down to a maximum of some 25 sorties per night, whilst overall German strength in the West was by now a bare 400 aircraft.

29. The third week in April showed a continuing general reduction in strength, though the scale of operations rose to a token 200 sorties per day against the Allied bridgeheads over the Elbe and the American advance on Nuremburg. Effective opposition had by now ceased. The American and Russian forces linked up at Torgau on the 26th, and the remaining air units North of this line lapsed into chaos. By the end of April all operations against the Western Allies had ceased. The last remnants of the Luftwaffe, a heterogeneous collection of units of all types which had so far escaped destruction, and amounting in all to about 1,500 aircraft, remained in northern Austria and Bohemia, and operated intermittently against the Russian forces until the final surrender on 8th May, 1945.

PART FIVE

Conclusions

CHAPTER 19

THE POSITION OF THE GERMAN AIR FORCE IMMEDIATELY BEFORE CAPITULATION

Air Force Manpower : Release to the Army and S.S.

1. Up to August, 1944, manpower in the Air Force had remained at a high level of around 2,800,000, which showed little diminution compared with the previous 12-18 months. From August onwards, however, a decline set in owing, in the first place, to the contraction of territory over which the Air Force was now deployed and which continued thereafter steadily to shrink, and secondly, to the elimination of the long-range bomber force, which also created a considerable redundancy of personnel. There was, in consequence, an extensive cutting down of commands, staffs and ground organisations at all levels which led to the personnel concerned being drafted in large numbers into ground fighting units, and to an accompanying reduction in the intake of new recruits. The reduction would, in fact, have been greater had not some 200,000 Air Force men been drafted into the parachute troops for ground fighting from the beginning of 1944, and therefore remained within the Luftwaffe organisation. Others with technical knowledge were in many cases returned to industry.

2. The drain of manpower away from the Air Force therefore made itself initially most noticeable in the 1906 and younger classes, which dropped from 1,096,000 on August 1st to 838,000 by October 1st and subsequently shrank further to 675,000 by mid-December. While, during the remainder of the war, all categories subsequently declined, it was in this class that the contraction was most felt, so that by 1st April, 1945, it numbered only 383,500 out of a total personnel strength which had by then fallen to 1,798,000, a decline of 1,000,000 since August, 1944.

3. The nature of the rapid reduction in strength during the concluding four months of the war, as it affected the principal branches of Air Force organisation, may be seen from comparative figures for 15th December, 1944 and 1st April, 1945 :—

	15th December 1944	1st April, 1945
General Duties, Administrative and Ground Organisation	596,250	450,000
Flak (Anti-Aircraft)	816,200	656,000
Signals	305,000	251,000
Supply	109,100	62,000
Medical and Veterinary	42,500	34,000
Works Units	9,100	5,000
Passive Defence (Air Raid)	63,250	48,500
Paratroops	200,100	187,500
Miscellaneous	163,000	104,500
Total	2,304,500	1,798,500

4. It will be seen that big reductions were effected in the General Duties, etc., and Flak branches (20-25 per cent), and particularly in the supply personnel (40 per cent.), the paratroops alone continuing almost to maintain their strength. In the case of the latter, the fall may largely be attributed to their casualties in ground fighting to which they were heavily committed on all fronts, since, as late as the end of March, new parachute divisions (the 10th and 11th) were being set up. It was, however, envisaged that their establishment would drop from 17,500 to 12-13,000 men each, but even so they would have been numerically stronger than ordinary infantry divisions (11,500 men).

5. During April there was an insatiable demand for men to sustain the parachute forces, and the month saw the widespread disbanding of flying training units, ground personnel and even front-line flying units, such as night fighters, where they were incapable of further flying activity. Frequently, however, transport and other difficulties were such that Air Force personnel were increasingly absorbed into Army or S.S. formations, although not welcomed owing to their lack of the necessary training and experience. The cutting down of Air Force strength up to April 1st did not itself contribute in any striking way to the Luftwaffe's growing ineffectiveness, which was primarily due to other and more widespread causes ; nevertheless, all-round efficiency undoubtedly suffered, particularly in technical branches. In the final stages of collapse, the ebb of manpower from the Air Force was supremely significant of the onset of creeping paralysis, which led ultimately to general dissolution and disintegration.

Collapse of the Luftwaffe Chain of Command in the Field

6. The final fall of the Luftwaffe was revealed most clearly in the collapse of its chain of command, precipitated in March and April after the Allied crossings of the Rhine and Oder. Up till then, the Command organisation had remained firmly established on the normal lines in the main operational theatres, although, as has been seen, the two main Fighter Commands (Jagdkorps II, tactical in the West) and Jagdkorps I (strategic in the Centre) had been disbanded during February, their functions continuing to be performed in the one case by two Fliegerdivisionen and on the other by Fliegerkorps IX (J)[1]. At the beginning of March the main structure of the Commands, in its essentials, was as follows :—

Western Front	Centre	Eastern Front
Command WEST	*Luftflotte REICH*	*Command Courland*
(Gen. Leut. Schmid)	(Gen. Oberst Stumpff)	—(Ex-Luftflotte 1,
—Fliegerdivision 14	—Fliegerkorps IX (J)	isolated in Latvia).
—Fliegerdivision 15		
—Fliegerdivision 16	(Gen. Major Peltz).	*Luftflotte 6*
	—Jagddivisions	(Gen. Oberst Ritter von
	1, 2, 3, 7, 8.	Greim).
		—Fliegerkorps II
Air Force Generals in :—		—Fliegerkorps VIII
Norway (Gen. Leut. Roth)		
Denmark (Gen. Leut. Holle)		*Luftlotte 4*
Italy (Gen. Ritter von Pohl)		(Gen. Oberst Dessloch)
		—Fliegerkorps I
		—Fliegerdivision 17

---

[1] See Chapter 17, paragraph 48.

7. The immediate effect of the Allied crossing of the Rhine was to set in train the general retirement of all Air Force Headquarters in the West, a process which had begun already in the middle of March. By April 1st the command had already been split, Command West withdrawing South-westwards into Bavaria with Fliegerdivision 16, and taking over Jagddivision 7 from Luftflotte Reich. Its remaining commands, Fliegerdivisions 14 and 15, simultaneously were made subordinate to Luftflotte Reich, and in the circumstances the long-standing division between tactical and strategical fighter forces went by the board, all units being now liable to be put up for all tasks as and when required. Furthermore, in the welter of competing interests, General Major Peltz, commanding Fliegerkorps IX (J) strove to maintain his position in control of all the Me. 262 jet units for defence against heavy bombers. Still greater confusion was now also being caused in the confined spaces of the Reich by the fact that eastern and western front units found themselves based on the same or on neighbouring airfields.

Germany Divided in Two

8. On April 7th, the Army chain of command in the West was reorganised following the splitting of Germany from East to West, and in conformity with this, Fliegerdivision 14 was allocated to the support of Gen. Feldmarschall Busch (C.-in-C. North-West), and Command West to Gen. Feldmarschall Kesselring (C.-in-C. West) ; a week later, in the centre, Fliegerkorps IX (J) had withdrawn to Prague from Weimar and by the 29th to the Munich area.

9. With Germany now divided completely in two, still further sweeping changes of organisation were put into effect on April 14th by which Luftflotte 6, under General Oberst Ritter von Greim, now took over command in the whole south-eastern and southern area of Germany incorporating in :—

S.W. Germany ..   Command West, with Jagddivision 7 under it.

S.E. Germany ..   Command 4 (ex-Luftflotte 4) with subordinate commands, now including Jagddivision 8 formerly under Luftflotte Reich.

Eastern Germany   Fliegerkorps VIII.

The northern area was similarly placed under the command of General Oberst Stumpff, A.O.C. Luftflotte Reich ; under him remained Fliegerkorps II, upgraded on April 11th to Command North-East and operating against the Russians, the remnants of Jagddivisions 1 and 2, and, in the West, Fliegerdivision 14 (see Table 5).

10. Even so, the process of dissolution was not complete. On April 25th, Admiral Doenitz, C.-in-C. of the German Navy, was entrusted with full powers for the defence of the northern area ; Luftflotte Reich was subordinated to him, together with all Luftwaffe units in the area, including the Air Force Generals in Norway and Denmark and Air Force Command Courland (ex-Luftflotte 1) still holding out in Latvia. In the South, following upon the promotion of Ritter von Greim to take over Goering's post as C.-in-C. of the German Air Force on April 26th, General Oberst Dessloch was appointed to command Luftflotte 6, his place in turn being taken by General Leutnant Deichmann as A.O.C. Command 4 ; at the same time, by reason of his incompetence, General Leutnant Schmid was relieved of Command West and replaced by General Leutnant Harlinghausen. There were also numerous other inexplicable changes in commanding officers in the last feverish days of turmoil and confusion.

11. The rapid sequence and complexity of events are eloquent of the chaos reigning in the final hours of the Luftwaffe, and the ousting of Goering, following upon Hitler's misunderstanding of his telegram of April 23rd from Berchtesgaden requesting permission to take over the affairs of the Reich, set the seal upon the débâcle. It remains to summarise briefly the final break-up of the Oberkommando der Luftwaffe and the German Air Ministry, and therewith the higher direction and organisation of the whole German Air Force.

TABLE 5

SUBORDINATION OF AIR FORCE COMMANDS
14TH APRIL, 1945

AIR FORCE HIGH COMMAND (O.K.L.)

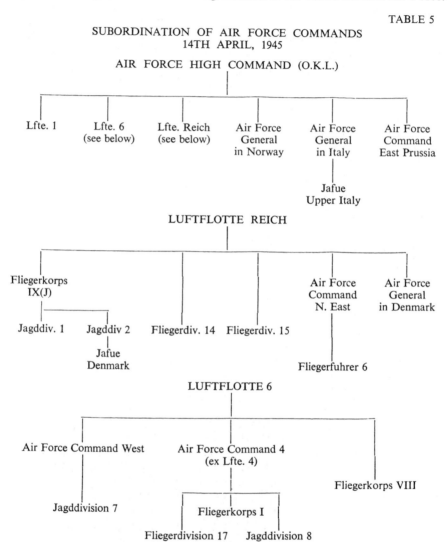

The Collapse of O.K.L. (Luftwaffe High Command)

12. Throughout the war the German Air Staff had been mainly concentrated in and around the Berlin area, with an operational headquarters at Hitler's headquarters in East Prussia. Early in March, 1945, the increasing threat to Germany, and to Berlin in particular, saw the beginning of the move of Air Ministry departments, in the first instance to central and South-western

Germany, and heading for the so-called " Redoubt " in the Bavarian and Austrian Alps. An alternative Battle Headquarters for O.K.L. had already been established by the end of February in a lunatic asylum at Wasserburg, near Munich, and on March 4th the A.O. for Training was moving his department to Weimar as the first stage of evacuation, while the A.O. for Ground Attack was already partly at Ansbach, whither he was soon to be followed by the A.O. for Bombers. By March 21st, the Director-General of Signals had also moved to Weimar, where the Luftwaffe Operations Staff had by now arrived from Berlin ; it was to the Weimar area also that the staff of Army High Command was first evacuated from its headquarters at Zossen, South of Berlin, at the end of February.

13. The assembly of operational staffs in the Weimar area was, however, short lived as more and more of Germany was overrun by the Allied forces ; by the end of March, Air Ministry departments were already by-passing Weimar and proceeding direct to Wasserburg and other destinations in southern Germany which had been fixed as the main alternative area when the scattering of the large staffs of the Supreme Command had been ordered earlier in the year. Here, they remained in improvised quarters until April 28th when General Koller, Chief of Air Staff held a conference at Wasserburg to discuss the situation ; main subjects discussed were supplies, and the division of the Air Staff into those who would transfer to Berchtesgaden when the enemy approached and those who would remain behind in Wasserburg and allow the front to roll over them ; Koller himself left for Berchtesgaden the same day, whither he was followed by the staff chosen to proceed there.

The Fate of the Luftwaffe High Command

14. On May 3rd, Koller decided to transfer his first echelon to Thumersbach, an isolated village on the lake at Zell am See, in Austria, himself remaining with the rest at Berchtesgaden ; by the 6th he had moved on to Thumersbach where, on May 8th, he was joined by Ritter von Greim, completely collapsed, wounded and walking on crutches. Here, in this remote alpine village the curtain finally came down on the last moments of the drama, and the remnants of the German Air Staff, including Goering himself, surrendered to American forces ; in all some 90 officers remained, including the heads of the principal departments and their staffs, amongst which, in addition to the Operational Staff, were the Quartermaster-General, Director-General of Signals, the Personnel Office, etc. Others were scattered around the neighbouring countryside where large quantities of their surviving documents and records were dispersed and concealed ; others still had failed to complete the journey South and had disappeared into oblivion in the final holocaust.

15. At the end, some 2,000 aircraft still remained in the northern area under Stumpff and 1,500 in the south under Dessloch, but the units were broken, scattered and disorganised, without supplies, and incapable of further operations. In any case it is clear that the final collapse of Command during the closing six weeks of the war, with staffs moving and dispersed in widely separate localities, and commanding officers being changed at the shortest notice, had rendered any further coherent direction and organisation of the Luftwaffe utterly impossible ; from then on, it could only be a question of time before the final sorties could be flown.

CHAPTER 20

LESSONS AND CONCLUSIONS

1. The foregoing chapters have described, in some detail, the operational employment of the German Air Force throughout the course of the war ; they have also shown, at the principal turning points, the various factors bearing upon its early and almost unbroken run of success and upon its progressive, but fluctuating, decline and decay as it became increasingly outnumbered and outfought. Viewed objectively and in the light of history, it must be conceded that certainly up to the end of 1943, despite weaknesses already apparent, the Luftwaffe had fought well and was a formidable force to be reckoned with. Its ground organisation, supply and signals elements were highly efficient and well knit over the vast extent of occupied territory in Europe and western Russia ; it was largely this administrative efficiency which formed an important element in the ability of the German Air Staff to make an air force, numerically insufficient to meet its full commitments, go a long way towards doing so. This was achieved by dint of exploiting its remarkable flexibility between different fronts by the rapid moves of units, or even entire operational commands, with the utmost speed. This faculty for quickly developing an effective air striking force at vital points was a characteristic extremely well marked throughout almost every phase of the war, and did much to contribute to the early German successes.

2. Many of the senior German Air Force officers, both in the High Command and in the operational commands, were men of outstanding ability who undoubtedly succeeded in extracting the maximum possible results from the forces at their disposal ; they showed great skill in handling the increasingly difficult problem of their strategic deployment, particularly as the Luftwaffe became steadily inferior in numbers. Among such men may be mentioned Milch, von Richthofen, Kesselring, Korten, Koller, Kammhuber and Student, together with a number of younger officers, some of whom reached exalted heights after having shown outstanding ability as unit commanders in the field ; among these may be counted Galland, Peltz, Hitschold, and Herrmann. The General Staff Officers, particularly the Chiefs of Staffs of commands in the field, were also of a universally high standard of excellence not generally appreciated in view of their tradition of self-effacement.

3. But it would be wrong to infer that the senior staff appointments were consistently good : Jeschonnek, as Chief of Air Staff until 1943, was probably too immature for the tasks entrusted to him, and he undoubtedly showed much short-sightedness in appreciating the problems which the Air Force in due course would inevitably come to face, thereby contributing to the eventual débâcle of 1944. Again, the appointment by Goering of Udet as *General Luftzeugmeister*, responsible for technical development in 1941, appears to have been made on purely personal grounds ; he had neither the experience nor competence to fit him for such a test at a time when plans for future technical development were of paramount importance. It is significant that both these men came to untimely ends by suicide, Jeschonnek because his policy was demonstrably bankrupt, and Udet from a realisation of his inability to fulfil his task. The choice of Schmid as Chief of the Intelligence Branch in the vital years of 1938-42 was also not a happy one ; such appointments as these were made by Goering in order to keep as much power as possible in his own hands by the installing of favourites, thereby avoiding dictatorship by the Air Staff itself.

4. The reasons for the failure of the German Air Force in 1944 must be traced further than the German Air Staff itself. The failure lay far more in the hands of Hitler, as Supreme Commander of the German Armed Forces, and his immediate entourage, and particularly with Goering, who, with a declining prestige after the Battle of Britain, failed to secure adequate appreciation of the needs and shortcomings of the Luftwaffe at Hitler's headquarters. The extraordinary circumstances prevailing in this circle, with its blind optimism and unshakeable belief in victory round the corner, branded as defeatism any endeavour to present a realistic picture of the true state of affairs. Time and again plans and programmes drawn up by the most responsible members of the Air Staff were rejected, and there was frequent intervention from these quarters over the heads of the Air Staff consonant neither with sound policy nor strategy in air matters. It was upon the Air Staff, however, that the inevitable shortcomings, when they materialised, drew down still further reproaches and recriminations, engendering mutual mistrust and lack of confidence. Under such conditions there is little room for surprise that the German Air Force was unable to acquit itself better in the closing stages of the war.

5. The consistent refusal of the short-sighted political leadership in Germany to listen to the advice of the Air Staff was due partly to ignorance of air matters, and lack of a sane appreciation of events. It was also in an important degree accounted for by the narrow-mindedness of the Supreme Command, composed almost exclusively of senior army officers, to which the Air Staff was itself subordinate, and only represented by a small number of junior officers who could not carry sufficient weight and authority. Frequently, therefore, claims for priority for the Air Force for manpower, equipment, etc., would be turned down as a one-sided and prejudiced view of the Air Staff ; never was it possible until the eleventh hour to impress the realisation that, without air supremacy, the ultimate fate of the Armed Forces and therewith Germany was inevitably sealed.

6. Had things been otherwise, and had Hitler been receptive and able to comprehend the real lessons that early German air supremacy had taught, the course, though not necessarily the conclusion, of the war might conceivably have been different. Had the vast fighter production, including the jet programme, been developed in 1943 instead of being stimulated under pressure of events in 1944, there would certainly have existed an extremely formidable force to defend Germany against bombing and to oppose the Allied landings. It was certainly within the power of German industry to have achieved this vast production a year earlier, seeing that German war production as a whole did not reach its peak until the summer of 1944, up to when it had been operating well within its full capacity. When the effort came to be made it was too late.

7. To sum up, the rise and fall of the German Air Force was primarily bound up with the direction of German military and political strategy at the highest level. So long as the tide flowed in Germany's favour, brilliant results were achieved in all fields—so brilliant indeed that they blinded Hitler, Goering and others at the top to realities, and to sober appreciation of where their apparent successes were leading them. With the reckless extension of the war into Russia, and the entry of America, nobody at the top could be brought to

realise that Germany's strength and resources were far from adequate both to hold the territory already gained, and to meet the vast output of war material from the Allied countries. Most notably there was a failure to foresee in time the consequence of the loss of air supremacy to the combined productive, manpower and training resources of Britain, Russia and the United States, notwithstanding the efforts made by the German Air Staff to drive this point home. While this was a definite, and perhaps the most important factor limiting the Air Staff's capabilities, nevertheless, the Air Staff's own short-comings, especially up to 1943, contributed also to this weakness. Most important of these shortcomings were the failure to evolve an adequate training policy, the delay in introducing new and improved aircraft of a quality equal to the equipment of the Allied air forces—thereby 'further emphasising the numerical inferiority of the Luftwaffe, and the lack of resolution displayed in advocating the adoption of a sound air policy, inevitable perhaps in the abnormal conditions of the Nazi regime.

8. So, relentlessly, the inevitable sequence of events moved to its foregone conclusion. The German Air Force no longer had adequate strength to protect industry and communications in Germany against the Allied bombing offensive, and no longer was in a position to afford the indispensable support to the ground forces on the battle fronts. By force of circumstances it had to be frittered away, first on one then on the other of these two inescapable commitments until, finally exhausted and broken in the effort, it fell to pieces and collapsed in the death struggle of Hitler's Third Reich.

Epilogue

GENERAL KARL KOLLER

Born 22.2.98. Entered the Army August, 1914, transferring to the Flying Corps and training as a pilot, May, 1917. Served in the Bavarian Police Force, 1920-1935. Transferred to the Air Force in August, 1935. In April, 1938, he became head of the operations staff of Luftwaffengruppe 3 (later Luftflotte 3), until January, 1941, when he became its Chief of Staff. Koller was appointed head of the Luftwaffe Operations Staff in September, 1943, and Chief of the General Staff in November, 1944, in succession to Kreipe, who had filled the post after Korten's death. Surrendered to the Allies, May, 1945.

EPILOGUE

Extract from the memoirs of General Koller, Chief of the German Air Staff

Why We Lost the War

" We have lost the war. Far-sighted persons had already long seen this coming, but one is always moved by the questions 'Why' and 'Couldn't it have happened differently ? '. There are many reasons why Germany lost the war ; political, economic and military reasons which were our own fault. None of these reasons were decisive in themselves, nor were they together decisive. Had they been avoided, a more favourable development of the situation might indeed have been possible. Quite apart from them, what was decisive in itself was the loss of air supremacy.

" The campaigns in Poland, Holland, Belgium, France and Norway had proved unequivocally how important air supremacy is in a modern war. Instead of radically drawing the proper conclusions, the German High Command strove to forget the historical facts as soon as possible and covered with glory branches of the service which in the opinion of honest leaders had played a less than moderate part in gaining the victories.

" Not Germany, who showed what superior air forces and skill in leading them mean, learned the lesson, but on the contrary the enemy countries, who drew the proper and logical conclusions and with an iron tenacity built up a superior air force which alone could lead to victory. As long as we had air supremacy, nobody interferred with our shipping in the North Sea, along the German coast and from Holland to Brest, Bordeaux and Spain. The British Fleet did not show itself ; no noticeable traffic dared to enter the Channel and they often hardly dared to go into the southern part of the Irish Sea, and everything was forced to the far North.

" As long as we had air supremacy, nobody threatened our industries or the peaceful life of our homeland ; our lines of communication in the Mediterranean were not interfered with. If our air supremacy had been kept up right from the beginning and at the cost of other armament programmes, we would not have been defeated in Africa or in the Mediterranean area. German air supremacy—and we would have been able to maintain a capable industry and intact lines of communication ; German air supremacy—and England's supplies would have been badly damaged before she could have built up her maximum war production. German air supremacy—and this massed concentration of strong air forces in England would not have been as easy as it was. German air supremacy—and there would have been no invasion, or it would have been turned back with the loss of much blood. But the political leadership in Germany, in its short-sightedness and in complete misjudgement of the tenacity and mentality of the Anglo-Saxons and the potential war power of the United States in the background, had believed that the war in the West had already been won in 1940 and started out on the folly of the Russian war. The calls of us outsiders and ' little ' General Staff Officers for aircraft and more aircraft and for new types were either not heard or they were laughed off.

" We remained voices crying in vain in the wilderness. Promises were made to build up the largest air force possible after the close of the Russian war. Millions of soldiers were then to be released from the Army and were to be sent to the aircraft industry and to the German Air Force. Only the Air Force was to be built up. In the meanwhile, however, the air armament was put way down on the list; first were submarines, then came tanks, then assault guns, then howitzers or Lord knows what, and then came the Air Force. Meanwhile, the Russian war was eating away men, material, armament and planes and the only thing that remained for the Air Force was a promise that was never kept. Its task was to make sacrifices.

" Let nobody claim that this complete failure of the Luftwaffe was the fault of the A.O.C.-in-C. alone. The Supreme Command, at its head the Fuehrer, was as much to blame if not much more so. The Fuehrer decided the war aims himself, the distribution of the tasks and the armament. The Supreme Command's duty was to recognise and decide which branch of the service would be most important in future operations in the decisive years and distribute the armament accordingly. The fact that the Luftwaffe claimed priority was considered by the Supreme Command to be a one-sided view of the Luftwaffe; perhaps it was not emphatic enough about its claims. The Supreme Command itself was too short-sighted for such far-reaching conceptions. Its mental horizon was too narrow and how could it be otherwise ? Few men there were able to think in terms other than those of the ground combat troops. The Fuehrer himself had repeatedly asked ' Why should Air Force leaders be required ? ' A general of another branch could lead the Air Force just as well. An infantry general had been in command during the World War. The Fuehrer told me that as late as April, 1945. What a view to take ! It wasn't only that the production figures were not increased ; new types of aircraft were not forthcoming either. At the end of the war we were still flying the same types, though highly developed, as at the beginning of the war. A failure of the air armament industry, although it would have to be determined whether this was due to inherent incapability within our own industry or whether it was a result of the structure and leadership forced on the industry by the State.

" It is true that unheard-off inventions and progress were made in individual fields, far ahead of the rest of the World, but they all came too late and again because of the short-sightedness of the German High Command and of certain ' know-alls ' at the head of the German industry, they came in such small numbers that they could no longer be decisive. We were smothered by the enormous superiority of American and Russian material, because the German High Command undertook too much on the ground in the East and because it did not direct the main weight of armament right from the beginning towards air supremacy and thereby safeguard Germany's vital zones and armament industry and ward off any attack from the West.

Outlook and the Future

" Everything depends on air supremacy, everything else must take second place. The supremacy of the sea is only an appendage of air supremacy. Look at the development in the European war and the developments in the situation in the Pacific area. Even the strongest fleet is of no value if the enemy has air supremacy. It can no longer leave its ports or does so only to be destroyed. The country that has air supremacy and vigorously strengthens its air power over all other forms of armament to maintain its supremacy, will rule the lands and the seas, will rule the world. The proper conclusions with respect to leadership and planning of armament must be drawn from this fact. A strong and independent Air Force command, put far above the others, or an Air Force command on equal footing with the command of the rest of the Armed Forces.

" The requirements for maintaining air supremacy are decisive in all questions of organisation, relative strength, allotment of manpower and supplies. All plans for the defence of a country, a continent or a sphere of interest or for offensive operations must be in the hands of the Air Force command. The Army and Navy commands are subordinate authorities. Although they cannot be done away with entirely, they must adapt themselves to all requirements in the air, which covers the entire world and extends to the high heavens.

" The Air Force must be allowed to move its wings freely and must be relieved of the ballast of ground and naval forces. Future Supreme Commands must have Air Force officers in the decisive positions, men who can think in terms of the world and who have a wide horizon. Every soldier generally thinks only as far as the radius of action of his branch of the service and only as quickly as he can move with his weapons. For this reason, naval officers will rarely, and army officers almost never be able to keep pace with the large-scale thoughts and wide horizon which the men of all air forces in the world have more or less acquired.

" What a giant machine a Corps with a number of divisions is on the ground ; 50,000 men with thousands of vehicles and a great deal of artillery, a large command machinery, and it fights on a front of 15 or 20 kilometres. A monster, and yet it is interested only in its neighbours on the right and on the left ; what happens an army or two further on is hardly noticed by the Corps. But the Air Force officer, sees much, much more and thinks further ; he thinks in entirely different channels. What is the large fighting front of a Corps even to a little Leutnant flying long-range reconnaissance ? The width of a thumb or no more. That is the way it is on the battlefield, how must it be in the High Command ?

" We have been beaten and eliminated, we have nothing more to say. But it will be interesting to watch the development of the Great Powers and the battle of wits. Will it be as it always has been, that they all, every one of them, will not learn from the past and will continue to make the old mistakes again and again ? "

(83331)

P

APPENDIX

THE PART PLAYED BY THE AIR FORCE IN GERMAN COMBINED PLANNING

The Supreme Command of the Armed Forces (O.K.W.)

History and Organisation

1. Before describing the position of the German Air Force in the overall German war organisation, it is necessary to sketch briefly the history and organisation of O.K.W.[1], the Supreme Command of the German Armed Forces. By the Treaty of Versailles, Germany was permitted to retain a Ministry of Defence. With the introduction of conscription in 1934, the title of Defence Minister was changed to War Minister and Commander-in-Chief of the Armed Forces (Reichskriegsminister and Oberbefehlshaber der Wehrmacht), a position held by von Blomberg at that time. By a decree of 4th February, 1938, Hitler, who up to that date had been content to remain in the background in military matters, took over direct control of the 'German Armed Forces, and the " Oberkommando der Wehrmacht ", as such, was born. At the same time von Blomberg was dismissed, his powers as Minister for War being vested in Keitel as Chief of O.K.W. and his position as Commander-in-Chief absorbed by Hitler in his capacity as Supreme Commander.

2. The powers of the O.K.W. did not differ essentially from those of the former War Ministry, except that the Chief of O.K.W. occupied a position in the chain of command only equal in authority to the C.s-in-C. of the three branches of the Armed Forces, while the Minister for War had been their superior, and between these Cs.-in-C. and Hitler. By the change, therefore, the Commanders-in-Chief of the Army, Navy and Air Force gained the right of direct access to Hitler for consultation on all questions which appeared of vital importance to them, while the Chief of O.K.W. had to concern himself with matters of principle concerning the Armed Forces as a whole and issued orders only as Hitler's representative, not in his own name.

In actual practice, however, the change in the chain of command had little, if any, real effect on the position of the German Air Force. Goering had always rejected the conception of an authority interposed between himself and Hitler, and even when, in theory, he was subordinate to von Blomberg, in view of his political standing and his position as Minister for Air with the seat on the Cabinet Council which it entailed, the authority exercised over him in practice was very slight. At that time the conception of the functions of O.K.W. was fairly sound, viz., that it should concentrate on the broad principles of the conduct of the war and that it should plan strategic and economic direction, propaganda and the organisation of the intelligence services. It was to issue

---

[1] Oberkommando der Wehrmacht.

411

general directives to the three services, leaving the details to be worked out by the High Commands of the Army, Navy and Air Force (O.K.H., O.K.M. and O.K.L.).

3. During the course of the war three drastic changes took place which radically effected the position of O.K.W. These were as follows :—

(a) In the winter of 1941-42, the German armies found themselves in great difficulties in Russia and Hitler, considering himself the only man who could save the situation, himself took over command of the Army. The practical result was that O.K.W. ceased to have any responsibilities at all for the eastern front, which was looked after entirely by Hitler as head of O.K.H., with O.K.L. working on Hitler's instructions to Goering for the air war. Although retaining its name and theoretical position, O.K.W. became in most respects only a parallel staff to O.K.H., and was obliged to abandon its main task as the supreme authority for strategical planning for all theatres of war.

(b) In the old Ministry of War there had been a War Economy Staff (*Wehrwirtschaftsstab*) which, on the disappearance of the Ministry, became a department of O.K.W. and was renamed the War Economy and Armaments Department (*Wehrwirtschafts und Ruestungsamt*) under General Thomas. Its chief functions were the formulation of detailed plans for economic mobilisation for war, the co-ordination of the requirements of the three services and the preparation of directives for the armaments industry. The department had a regional organisation of Armaments Head-quarters (*Ruestungskommandos*). In January, 1940, a new Ministry, the Ministry of Arms and Munitions, was created, under Todt. In February, 1942, Todt was killed and Speer took over the Ministry. Then began the process of centralising Germany's armaments production in Speer's hands. In May, 1942, the larger part of the War Economy and Armaments Department, together with its vast regional organisation was transferred to Speer. Thomas still remained for a while as head of the department under Speer. The very small remnant left in the O.K.W. was later renamed the Field Economic Department (*Feldwirtschaftsamt*) and was concerned almost solely with the collation of economic information on occupied and foreign territories. Thus, O.K.W. suffered the loss of one of its most important functions.

(c) The third major change in the organisation of O.K.W. took place in the autumn of 1944, when Hitler ordered the transfer of the Intelligence Branch (*Amt Ausland/Abwehr*) of O.K.W. under Admiral Canaris to the S.S. Main Office for State Security (*Reichssicher-heitshauptamt*) under Himmler.

4. Officers of all three branches of the Armed Forces were employed at O.K.W., but none of the heads of departments was an Air Force officer. There is also no evidence that an Air Force officer of higher rank than Oberst (Group Captain) was ever employed in that organisation, and in this connection the following figures, taken from an establishment table for O.K.W. dated 31st March, 1942, are of interest.

	Army	Navy	Air Force	Total
(a) *Officers—Equivalent rank of—*				
Field Marshal	1	—	—	1
General	2	—	—	2
Lt. General	2	1	—	3
Maj. General	2	1	—	3
Colonel	23	4	4	31
Lt. Colonel	51	12	13	76
Major	135	41	36	212
Captain	20	2	7	29
	236	61	60	357
(b) *Officials*	322	42	49	413
	558	103	109	770

These figures are given merely to illustrated the proportional representation of the three services and give no indication of the total personnel employed at O.K.W. In addition to the above officers and officials, at this date, there were 1,162 employees of lower status at O.K.W. proper and many thousands' of officers, officials and employees at subsidiary headquarters of O.K.W. It will be seen that the Luftwaffe representation at O.K.W. was little better than the much less important Navy. They were dominated numerically by the Army by over 5 to 1 and outranked by the latter to the extent of seven officers of General rank and above. By far the most important section of O.K.W. was the Armed Forces Operations Staff, which performed the functions of a joint General Staff. As Chief of this Staff, Jodl had great responsibilities. It was he rather than Keitel, who was in direct contact with Hitler and was the latter's chief adviser on strategy and planning. Keitel's responsibilities were more those of a Minister for War, while Jodl played the part of Chief of Staff of the Armed Forces, and as such was more influential with Hitler. In spite of the importance of the Armed Forces Operations Staff, the Luftwaffe representative there only held the rank of Major. O.K.W., in common with O.K.H., O.K.M. and O.K.L., was designed to split into two parts at the outbreak of war, an advanced echelon to work in the field near the major theatre of operations and a rear echelon to remain at its peacetime station, normally Berlin. The object of this division was to relieve the advanced echelon of all matters not connected with the immediate prosecution of the war, leaving it free to concentrate on the operational control of forces in the field.

Hitler

5. The advanced echelons of O.K.W. (including the Armed Forces Operations Staff), and the advanced echelons of O.K.H. and O.K.L. (but not O.K.M.) were situated near Hitler's Headquarters (*Fuehrerhauptquartier*) in the field, the latter forming, in fact, the Supreme Military Authority of the Reich. The people who forgathered here every afternoon for the so-called " Situation Discussion " (*Lagebesprechung*) normally included the following:—

    (1) Hitler.
    (2) Personal Adjutant of Hitler.
    (3) Adjutants (Liaison Officers) of the Army, Navy and Air Force with Hitler.

O.K.W.
- (4) Chief of O.K.W.
- (5) Chief of Armed Forces Operations Staff.
- (6) Deputy Chief of Armed Forces Operations Staff.

O.K.H.
- (7) Chief of Staff of the Army.
- (8) Head of Department Ia (Operations).

O.K.M.
- (9) C.-in-C. Navy.
- (10) Permanent Representative of C.-in-C. Navy.
- (11) Naval Representative with Armed Forces Operations Staff.

O.K.L.
- (12) C.-in-C. Air Force.
- (13) Chief of Staff of the Air Force.
- (14) Head of Department In (Operations).

There were also representatives of the Party Chancellery, Foreign Office, Ministry of Armaments and War Production, Reich Press and, on occasion, commanders of lower military echelons such as Luftflotten, Army Groups, etc.

6. In the evening and during the night, Hitler had the habit of calling further and less formal meetings at which some only of the above were present. In actual practice, the Air Force was not so adequately represented at Hitler's Headquarters as would appear from the above list. Hitler was C.-in-C. Army as well as Supreme Commander, and the Chiefs of O.K.W. and the Armed Forces Operations Staff were both Army men. Goering did not always attend the discussions, leaving the Air Force Chief of Staff with little power to oppose decisions, mostly heavily biased in favour of the Army. There was no permanent representative of Goering corresponding to that of the C.-in-C. Navy. Bodenschatz, head of the Ministeramt, had this title, but did not fulfil this function in practice, as he had to represent Goering in the latter's multifarious activities, including the political side of the Four-Year Plan. The adjutants of the three services with Hitler appear to have played a minor part, being chiefly liaison officers for passing information to Hitler's Headquarters and for forwarding orders to the High Commands which they represented. The Luftwaffe Adjutant had the equivalent rank of Group Captain, the last occupant of the post being Oberst von Below. The afternoon meetings at Hitler's Headquarters began with a briefing on the general situation by representatives of the three services and O.K.W. Minor decisions were taken on the spot and verbal instructions given by Hitler. These instructions could be confirmed in writing over the signature of Hitler, Keitel, Jodl or the Chief of Staff of the Army for the Russian front, but this did not necessarily happen. It then became the task of the service concerned to convert the instruction into an order. If more than one service was concerned, they maintained close contact with each other during the process. Major decisions involving, for example, changes of policy, the planning of new operations, or the reaction of new situations, were taken in a rather more formal manner. The initial step again was discussion at Hitler's Headquarters. Suggestions were made in broad outline, principally by the service representatives. These were then incorporated in a so-called " Fuehrer's Directive " (*Fuehrerweisung*) worked out by the O.K.W. Operations Staff. (The services themselves complained that this meant in practice that their own plans came back to them as the

work of O.K.W.) This would include the object of the plan, the broad method of attaining it, an indication of the strength and type of forces to be used, and an indication of timing. This was then worked on by the high commands involved in the operation, maintaining constant liaison with each other in major matters by direct contact between responsible officers. If any disagreement arose at this stage, the matter was referred back to Hitler's Headquarters for a "Fuehrer's Decision" (*Fuehrerentscheidung*). Ultimately, a detailed plan was submitted to Hitler's Headquarters, covering all aspects of the problem and including nomination of units and commanders, time needed for preparations and approximate demands for material in short supply. This could then be approved, amended or rejected. In the last case, an alternative plan became necessary. The definite order was then prepared by the O.K.W. Operations Staff, giving the tasks of the three services covering beginning and timing of the operation, preparation of supply goods, and provision of a signals and reporting organisation. The final stage was the working out by the three services of the detailed order for subordinate commands. The two types of Hitlerian pronouncement mentioned above must not be confused with the "Fuehrer's Order" (*Fuehrerbefehl*), which was a direct order from Hitler to a command at a lower level. Such orders increased in their frequency towards the end of the war and were apt to take such a form as "such and such a position must be held at all costs".

Relationship of the Air Force to O.K.W. and Hitler

7. The Luftwaffe General Staff retained, as long as the Air Force was successful, a large measure of independence in operational matters. It has been seen that there was no Air Force officer of any importance with O.K.W. or at Hitler's headquarters. O.K.L. could, therefore, only receive from O.K.W. or Hitler broad instructions, and it elaborated plans and orders itself. The personality of Goering seems here to have played an important part. In the early years of the war he enjoyed considerable prestige and was able to suppress any attempt on the part of O.K.W. to take charge of the Air Force. He received orders, or rather suggestions, direct from Hitler, and passed them on to O.K.L. In the closing stages of the war, the failure of the Air Force led to Goering's growing unpopularity. He was forced to be present to a greater degree at the discussions at Hitler's Headquarters, and more and more decisions affecting the Air Force were taken over his head. From about 1942 onwards, the Luftwaffe was no longer equal to all the calls made on it. The major controversy was then whether the forces available should be used in a strategic or tactical rôle. The influence of Hitler and the O.K.W. Operations Staff preferred, on the whole, the tactical solution. Jeschonnek, the Chief of Staff of the Air Force up to the end of July, 1943, was at first a supporter of the strategic solution. He continued to advance these views, but his actions went contrary to them, and he allowed almost the whole of the Luftwaffe to become an Army co-operation force. His successor, Korten, on the other hand, believed that the Air Force should concentrate on the defence of Germany and on strategic bomber operations in the East and West. In this, the leading personalities of O.K.L. were in complete agreement with their Chief of Staff. Goering also seems to have supported these views, although without consistency or much enthusiasm. These views prevailed on the whole and were behind the development of the Air Force in the latter part of 1943 and in 1944. This development was, however, hindered and confusion caused by the direct

intervention of Hitler, which became more and more frequent as time went by. The following may be given as examples of direct intervention by Hitler in the sphere of O.K.L. In theory the only action by O.K.L. which required the personal sanction of Hitler was the movement of forces from one front to another, but this in itself meant a considerable influence on O.K.L. plans.

(a) A curious early intervention of Hitler occurred in the autumn of 1941, when he stopped night-fighter intruder operations against England. He asserted they could have no success, although records showed they had been successful and crews were enthusiastic about them. He maintained this ban down to the autumn of 1944 in spite of repeated démarches by the operational commanders to have it removed.

(b) Hitler himself ordered an all-out effort for the air supply of Stalingrad, and he himself followed and guided the operations in detail.

(c) In the summer of 1943 he insisted on delivery of Me.109 aircraft to the Italians for political reasons, although they were then a total loss for the war effort. This was against the views of Goering.

(d) In the months prior to the Allied invasion of the continent he ordered the storing of large quantities of Air Force material at strategic points, for example Norway and Greece, to make possible a rapid reaction to an invasion. The order was unpopular with O.K.L., a great deal of material being thus " frozen " and subsequently wasted.

(e) He refused to sanction the transfer of a He.111 Gruppe from the Russian front to strengthen forces engaged in minelaying in the Channel at the time of the Normandy invasion. He later refused to allow forces to be withdrawn from the German hydrogenation works, but had ultimately to give way.

(f) His insistence on the use of the Me.262 as a fighter-bomber is well known. Only when the series production of the Arado 234 started in the late autumn of 1944 did he permit the setting-up of a fighter Geschwader equipped with Me.262 aircraft. As late as March, 1945, he refused to allow the allocation of Me.262 aircraft to night fighting. He still maintained that fighter-bombing should have first call on them.

(g) To Hitler was also due the move of the large part of the German fighter force to the eastern front after the failure of the Ardennes offensive.

(h) The initiative for the use of composite aircraft in the closing stages of the war came from Speer. Hitler supported this project against the views of the Air Force Operations Staff. Operations were planned against the Russian armaments industry, Antwerp and Scapa Flow, but were never carried out largely owing to fuel shortage.

8. Little better evidence of the intervention of Hitler·in the affairs of the Luftwaffe can be provided than by the words of General Koller, last Chief of Air Staff.

" The Fuehrer was Commander-in-Chief of all the Armed Forces, and as such, could do anything he wished and could intervene to give orders in any matter. A Supreme Commander, as such, should not do this. It is in any case not correct policy, judged by military principles, but unfortunately Hitler adopted this line of action to an increasing extent, and none of his subordinates could prevent it.

That he did so may have been due to his unbounded mistrust of his subordinates, and to the fact that he had not sufficient military training to concern himself with the detail of military affairs. The Fuehrer was a politician and developed gradually the belief that he was a great military commander as well. No operations could be begun without the prior approval of the Fuehrer. A large staff had to be employed preparing daily reports on the situation, so that the most detailed and astonishing questions by Hitler could be answered. A question about the ammunition used by a *Flakkampftrupp* (a very small unit) on the Don or somewhere, covering details of the types used, the number of time-fuzes, percussion fuzes, anti-tank grenades, etc., was for him nothing unusual.

Movements of Luftwaffe squadrons from one front to another could not usually be carried out without the approval of the Fuehrer. He either reserved to himself the right of decision in any case, or else there was a complaint to him from the Commander on some particular front, when he learnt that Air Force units were being withdrawn from his command. Thus, in practice, the decision had always to be made by the Fuehrer.

The Fuehrer failed to gain a broad general view of the military situation, because he concerned himself entirely with detail—numbers of tanks and guns held by individual units in the field, and by depot units in Germany, etc. He had no understanding of the needs of the Air Force, remaining an infantryman in outlook throughout his life.''

Goering

9. The part played by Goering in the military affairs of the Reich during the war is characterised by his insistence on his own pre-eminence. He was a believer in the " Leadership Principle " and insisted that, as Commander-in-Chief of the Air Force, he had full responsibility. This expressed itself in an exaggerated desire to be to the front in everything and to take all decisions himself. Three reasons have been given by O.K.L. officers in accounting for his ineffectiveness : First, he was not an expert in air matters and either lacked interest or self-confidence in putting over his ideas ; second, he would never look unpleasant facts in the face and take the necessary corrective action ; third, he was completely submissive to Hitler and did nothing to counteract the latter's tendency to treat the Air Force as a mere adjunct of the Army. Abundant evidence of this submissiveness has been provided by Generalfeld-marschall Milch's files of the verbatim stenograph records of Goering's conferences. The connecting thread running through these discussions, as regards Goering's relations with Hitler, is that the Fuehrer's reactions to any particular course of action are decisive for Goering. There is an overwhelming desire on Goering's part to justify Air Force policy to Hitler, a consideration of prime importance to him, as a justification of himself. In minor matters, where principle played less part, his decisions were often arbitrary and capricious, and one decision often cancelled another. A minor but revealing example is that of two orders issued almost simultaneously in the spring of 1945. One was that O.K.L. officers should surrender their arms to the fighting troops, the other that the same officers should receive training in defence measures. He was always threatening to have officers shot for minor offences, and seems to have run the Air Force with much the same methods as those used by the Queen of Hearts in " Alice in Wonderland ''—and with much the same effectiveness.

The " Plenipotentiaries "

10. In the last months of the war a somewhat desperate and ill-digested expedient was resorted to in order to solve restricted planning problems. This was the appointment of " plenipotentiaries " (*Bevollmaechtigte*) for special tasks. These derived their power direct from Hitler or Goering. They had the right to prescribe courses of action direct to the commands and to demand supplies, men and material from the competent authorities. The outstanding example is Hitler's general plenipotentiary for aircraft, S.S. General Kammler, who was doubled by Goering's plenipotentiary for the same task, General Kammhuber. Their task was to get as many Me.262's into the air as they possibly could for the defence of Germany, and they had powers of direction to industrial, transport and supply concerns. In theory, once the aircraft were operational, they came under the normal operational commands. In practice, the plenipotentiaries also gave orders to these commands. The following extract from the O.K.L. War Diary for 31st March, 1945, shows the type of difficulty that was apt to arise :—

> "The Fuehrer's General Plenipotentiary for jet aircraft (General der Waffen—S.S. Kammler) has hitherto had no influence on the *operations* of jet aircraft, in accordance with his terms of reference. Yesterday, however, he ordered operational subordination of Fliegerkorps IX to General Kammhuber and subordination of KG.51 to Fliegerkorps IX for operations in the defence of the Reich. Thereupon General Kammhuber ordered that KG.51 should give up two-thirds of its aircraft to JG.7 and one-third to KG(J). 54. On the other hand, the Reichsmarschall has refused to allow the subordination of Fliegerkorps IX to the General Plenipotentiary (General Kammler) and informed the Chief of Staff accordingly. In case the order for the subordination of Fliegerkorps IX to General Kammhuber should be confirmed in a higher place, the Chief of Staff has submitted a draft order to the Reichsmarschall, according to which General Kammhuber is at once to take over control of fighters in the defence of the Reich with complete responsibility ".

11. In the spring of 1945, Hitler foresaw possible salvation in the destruction of the Oder bridges. He appointed as his plenipotentiary for this task Oberstleutnant Baumbach, Kommodore of KG.200. Baumbach could draw as he wished on the Air Force and also had responsibility for directing artillery fire on the bridges and the operation of special naval weapons against them. Baumbach had many other commitments at the time, so O.K.L. substituted for him Oberst Helbig without Hitler's knowledge. The actual work was done by Helbig, but any reporting to Hitler had of course to be done by Baumbach. At the same time, O.K.L. issued a direction to Luftflotte 6 on the scope of its co-operation with Helbig. These arrangements were naturally very unpopular with Luftwaffe officers belonging to the orthodox command staffs. Helbig seems to have co-operated smoothly with Von Greim, A.O.C.-in-C. of Luftflotte 6, but the danger of unclear subordination, parallel orders and general confusion was obviously very great and led to some friction and a great deal of criticism.

Planning at Lower Levels

12. It is difficult to state in general terms where the line was drawn between planning at O.K.L. level and planning at Luftflotte level. The difficulty is due to the fact that no two cases were exactly alike. Depending on circumstances,

O.K.L. could prescribe an operation in detail or issue a directive in the most general of terms. How far detailed planning was done by O.K.L. depended largely on the extent to which other branches of the armed forces were concerned and on the number of Luftflotten taking part. The more people concerned, the greater the detail from O.K.L. O.K.L. would, however, normally prescribe the forces to be used, including both flying units and Flak, the extent of co-operation with the Army and with other major Air Force formations and, in broad outline, would prescribe supply arrangements, especially the amount of aircraft fuel to be made available and, again in broad outline, the signals arrangements. The following account of the part played by all concerned in planning the German counter-attack in the Kursk region in July, 1943, is particularly true to type[1]. The plan, as far as the Air Force was concerned, was worked out at three levels, as follows :—

(a) Hitler, in his capacity as Supreme Commander of the Armed Forces, issued a directive to O.K.L. in the most general of terms. The Air Force was to support with maximum possible forces the attack in the Kursk area, etc.

(b) O.K.L. worked out the plan, and issued it as an order to the commands concerned, Luftflotten 4 and 6. This order covered the forces to be used, co-operation between the Luftflotten and with the Army groups with which they were working, supply and signals in outline and broad instructions for carrying out the plan, e.g., that an all-out effort was to be made on the first day on a narrow front to help the Army achieve a break-through, and that long-range bombers were to concentrate on Russian communications leading to this breakthrough point. At this stage, constant contact was kept with O.K.H., largely by the Air Force Chief of Staff, Jeschonnek, who was constantly at Hitler's Headquarters.

(c) The Luftflotten then established contact with each other and with the Army groups and filled in the details, including disposition of forces, timings, detailed co-operation between Air Force and Army, etc.

Examples of Combined Planning

13. The following examples are intended to give an idea of the extent to which Hitler's Headquarters, the various branches of the armed forces and various levels of the Air Force were concerned in planning operations.

(a) Norway, 1940[2]

The first step in the preparation of this invasion was a study prepared by an *ad hoc* committee of Air Force, Army and Navy officers shortly before the operation was ordered. It appears to have been a genuine staff study, the people concerned not thinking it would be put into effect. Hitler himself then decided he must forestall an Allied intention to occupy Norway, and ordered preparations to be made. The plans were then worked out by the three services in close co-operation, basing themselves on the staff study. The army planning

---

[1] See Chapter 10, paragraph 24.　　　　[2] See Chapter 3.

was entrusted to Gruppe XXI under General Von Falkenhorst, who worked in close contact with O.K.W. ; the responsibility of this formation included co-ordination of the work of the three services and drawing up the time schedule for the whole operation for all three. This time schedule was, however, enforced by its issue as an O.K.W. order. The air plan was worked out by a small *ad hoc* planning staff drawn from O.K.L. This staff was almost immediately attached as a whole to Fliegerkorps X, the command entrusted with the execution of the air side of the operation. The Sea Warfare Directorate of O.K.M. was responsible for naval planning. O.K.W. itself looked after the political side and gave instructions concerning the treatment of the Danish and Norwegian civilian populations. The plans had finally to be approved by Hitler himself before they were put into execution.

(b) Crete, 1941[1]

The decision to invade Crete was taken by Hitler himself. Initial discussion at his Headquarters centred on the problem whether Malta or Crete should be attacked, as forces were insufficient for both. Hitler's decision to choose Crete was based on the fact that German forces were already in South Greece, and the fact that he did not want to have to consider the Italians. The normal directive was issued to O.K.W., but at Goering's suggestion the work of planning was taken over almost entirely by Luftflotte 4, the Air Force authority on the spot. Jeschonnek, then Chief of Staff of the Air Force was, however, present at the Luftflotte headquarters while the plan was being made. The Luftflotte set up its headquarters at Athens in close proximity to the 12th Army and Navy Group South. These last two authorities were instructed to give Luftflotte 4 all necessary support. Fliegerkorps VIII and XI were subordinated to Luftflotte 4 ; the former controlled all combat aircraft, the latter all transport aircraft and airborne forces. Thus, the 5th Mountain Division, an army formation, was under the control of Fliegerkorps XI for the period of the airborne operations. The divisional commander took control for the ground operations once the landing was completed. Student, the Commander of Fliegerkorps XI, had direct contact with Hitler during the planning phase.

(c) The Ardennes Offensive, 1944[2]

This was also a Hitler conception. By a successful blow in the West, he hoped to win forces for use in the East and perhaps reach an understanding with the Western Powers. The fundamental order was worked out by the O.K.W. Operations Staff, based on Hitler's ideas ; he briefed the Chiefs of Staff, Rundstedt (C.-in-C. West), Model (Army Group B) and Goering in person. The army plan was then worked out by C.-in-C. West, the Air Force plan by four officers of O.K.L., this restricted number being due to the desire to preserve secrecy. Plans were approved by Hitler. O.K.L. then issued the order in considerable detail to Luftwaffe Command West ; Luftflotte Reich, nominally the superior authority of Luftwaffe Command West, was also informed. Hitler was worried about the fact of Allied air supremacy, but the plan for the " lightning blow ", leading to the operation of 1st January, 1945 intended to knock out the Allied tactical air forces, seems to have been due to Goering. The detailed plan for this single operation was worked out by General Peltz, who at this time had the confidence of Goering and had taken over the command of Jagdkorps II for the purpose of this undertaking. That

---

[1] See Chapter 5.   [2] See Chapter 17.

such an operation should take place was, however, included in the general O.K.L. order. The most important order, dated 14th November, 1944, was issued over the signature of Goering. Others were signed by the Chief of Staff or by Ia of the Operations Staff.

Conclusions

14. The outstanding feature in the development of the Supreme Command of the German Armed Forces from 1938 onwards is the gradual extension of Hitler's personal power, culminating in the closing stages of the war when he was intervening in matters of detail. The process was, on the whole, a gradual one, but there are two important points of time. First, in February, 1938, when Hitler abolished the office of Commander-in-Chief of the Armed Forces, thereby subordinating the Cs.-in-C. of the three services directly to himself ; second, in the winter of 1941-42, when he himself became Commander-in-Chief of the Army. There are, therefore, three periods :—

(a) In the first period, down to February, 1938, Hitler is largely a figurehead, as far as purely military matters are concerned. Blomberg is the dominating military figure, with Goering subordinate to him in theory.

(b) In the second period, down to the first Russian counter-offensive in the winter of 1941-42, Hitler is the Supreme Commander, in fact as well as in theory. O.K.W., particularly the Armed Forces Operations Staff, has become his personal staff, and he controls the three services through their Commanders-in-Chief.

(c) In the last period, Hitler also has direct control of the Army on the Eastern front and through O.K.W. of the Army on the other fronts. He also allows far less freedom to the Air Force.

From the point of view of the Air Force, this development represented a steady degeneration in the Supreme Command. Senior O.K.L. officers interrogated after the war professed themselves very happy about the arrangement in period (a). In their opinion period (b) represented a wrong development, but the arrangement was still capable of functioning satisfactorily. The organisation of the Supreme Command in period (c) was for the Air Force little short of disastrous. The O.K.L. officers interrogated started out with the assumption that the primary rôle of an air force is strategic, that is, it should be used independently to attack sources of enemy strength. Support for the army on the battlefield is of secondary importance. If an air force is inadequate to fulfil both tasks, then the former must have priority. Co-ordination at the top between the branches of the armed forces is, of course, necessary but it should be kept to an intelligent minimum and the air force given the largest possible degree of independence. Hitler, they said, had no conception of the right use of air power. He was essentially an army man and thought exclusively in terms of ground fighting. The same criticism was levelled against O.K.W. Its defective composition, in that it contained no influential member of the Air Force, has already been mentioned. The army-trained officers who dominated O.K.W. have been described by a member of O.K.L. as " sand-table minded ". Thus, there was an increasing tendency to misuse the Air Force, and to look upon it as an adjunct of the Army. Only Goering was in a position to counteract this. He could have insisted that high-ranking and outstanding Air Force officers, capable of counteracting the Army bias and of influencing Hitler, be given important positions in O.K.W. He not only failed to do this himself, but opposed any attempts by others to bring it about. High-ranking Air Force officers at O.K.W. would have been a threat to his own relations with Hitler, a risk which, with his waning popularity, he could not afford to take. Hitler's ever-increasing intervention in the affairs of the Air Force shows that he had lost faith in Goering. He could have removed him. Whatever else has been said of him, however, it is generally agreed that Hitler was loyal to his early political supporters, as long as they did not threaten his own position ; Goering was clever enough to avoid this until nearly the end. Nobody but Hitler could have removed Goering. In the personal and political relationship of these two men lies, therefore, the crux of the matter. Such a relationship is only possible in a totalitarian state, and more damning evidence of the devastating effects of the '' Leadership Principle '' in action can hardly be provided.

(83331) Wt. 35943/M.1539 3,000 1/49 Hw.

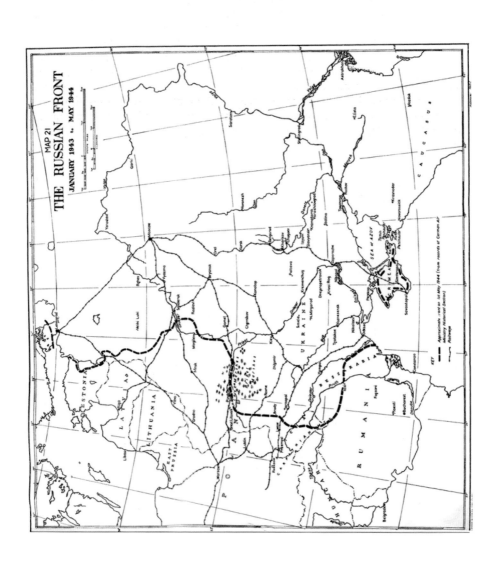

MAP 21
THE RUSSIAN FRONT
JANUARY 1943 to MAY 1944

Index